# POPULATION GROWTH

# AND ECONOMIC DEVELOPMENT IN

# LOW-INCOME COUNTRIES

# Population Growth and Economic Development in Low-Income Countries

*A CASE STUDY OF INDIA'S*

*PROSPECTS*

◇◇◇◇◇◇◇◇◇◇◇◇◇◇◇◇◇◇◇◇◇◇◇◇◇◇

BY ANSLEY J. COALE

AND EDGAR M. HOOVER

◇◇◇◇◇◇◇◇◇◇◇◇◇◇◇◇◇◇◇◇◇◇◇◇◇◇

PRINCETON, NEW JERSEY

PRINCETON UNIVERSITY PRESS

1958

PRINTED IN THE UNITED STATES OF AMERICA

◇◇◇◇◇◇◇◇◇◇◇◇◇◇◇◇◇◇◇◇◇◇◇◇◇◇◇◇◇◇◇◇◇◇◇◇◇◇◇◇◇◇◇◇◇◇◇◇◇◇◇◇

# FOREWORD

◇◇◇◇◇◇◇◇◇◇◇◇◇◇◇◇◇◇◇◇◇◇◇◇◇◇◇◇◇◇◇◇◇◇◇◇◇◇◇◇◇◇◇◇◇◇◇◇◇◇◇◇

THIS is the second of the major studies sponsored by the Office of Population Research to deal primarily with India. Its predecessor, that by Kingsley Davis entitled *The Population of India and Pakistan,* was a general analysis of the demographic position with special emphasis on the sociological aspects of the problem. This work by Coale and Hoover differs from that by Davis in three important particulars. In the first place, it is directed to economic problems. In the second place, it is a sharply focused attempt to give as concrete an answer as possible to a specific question, namely: What difference would it make in economic terms if the birth rate, instead of remaining unchanged, should be cut drastically in this generation? Finally, although the book deals mainly with India, it is directed toward the more general situation of the underdeveloped countries. India is in effect the principal example, but in the latter part of the work the position is reviewed to determine the extent to which the major conclusions drawn for India are valid for other low-income countries, including those with less densely settled populations. Here the major illustration is Mexico, where several aspects of the situation contrast rather sharply with those of India.

Throughout, the authors have endeavored to make their analysis highly specific and to carry it out in quantitative terms as far as possible. Indeed, it is in the exploration of dynamic numerical models for both the economy and the population that this work contrasts most sharply with other attempts to evaluate economic consequences of alternative trends in human fertility.

This work has been made possible by generous financial and technical assistance given by the International Bank for Reconstruction and Development, as well as by the regular financial support contributed to the Office by the Milbank Memorial Fund and the Rockefeller Foundation. However, none of these institutions bears any responsibility for either the form or substance of the work. To the authors alone go both the responsibility and the credit for a highly original demonstration of the way in which careful factual analysis can illuminate the vital interrelations of economic and population change.

FRANK W. NOTESTEIN, *Director*
Office of Population Research
Princeton University

◇◇◇◇◇◇◇◇◇◇◇◇◇◇◇◇◇◇◇◇◇◇◇◇◇◇◇◇◇◇◇◇◇◇◇◇◇◇◇◇◇◇◇◇◇◇◇◇◇

# PREFACE

◇◇◇◇◇◇◇◇◇◇◇◇◇◇◇◇◇◇◇◇◇◇◇◇◇◇◇◇◇◇◇◇◇◇◇◇◇◇◇◇◇◇◇◇◇◇◇◇◇

THIS book is the product of a study of demographic prospects and their implications for economic development in low-income countries. The Office of Population Research at Princeton University has conducted this study for the past three years with substantial support—in financial and other forms—from the International Bank for Reconstruction and Development. The Bank, in addition to a subvention, which by covering extra costs made it financially possible for the Office to carry out the project, has given the authors the invaluable aid of access to its specialists, unclassified materials and research facilities. The Population Council made a grant to the Office of Population Research to defray part of the cost of the authors' visit to India. Neither the Bank nor the Population Council is in any way responsible for the contents of this book; responsibility rests solely with the authors.

The work of the authors has been so fully collaborative that any attempt to decide who was the source of each part of the analysis would be impossible. The study has at all stages developed through conferences, discussions, and arguing-out of disagreements. Much of the material has been proposed by one, written by the other, and revised by both. To the degree that there has been a division of labor within the mutual effort, Hoover has concentrated more on the economic background sections and Coale on the demographic background.

This book would contain more errors and fewer ideas had it not been for the participation of three research assistants. At the Office of Population Research, Mr. Robert Osborn contributed substantially to the conception of the general approach employed, helped especially in developing the methods of population analysis, and supervised the calculation of the preliminary set of projections. Mr. Oswald Honkalehto, who joined the project on Mr. Osborn's departure in September 1955, suggested a number of ideas incorporated in the present manuscript, and prepared the first draft of portions of the economic analysis. He has, through his careful reading and incisive criticism, tightened the analysis at many points.

Mr. Ravi Gulhati served for a time as an exceptionally able research assistant on the economic side of the project in Washington.

A large measure of thanks is owed to the many people who have contributed to the project through discussion; by reading preliminary drafts in whole or in part, offering expert advice; by supplying data and information; by providing introductions to qualified informants; by giving generous hospitality; and by guiding the authors when they were in India and Mexico. First among these we wish to mention our colleagues at the International Bank and at the Office of Population Research.

At the Bank we are particularly indebted to Shri G. R. Kamat, who was Executive Director for India from 1954 to 1956; M. Leonard Rist, Director of the Economic Staff, and many of his staff, in particular his deputy, Mr. Gerald Alter; Mr. Richard Demuth, Director, Technical Assistance and Liaison Staff; Dr. Antonin Basch of the Department of Operations, Asia and Middle East; Mr. Federico Consolo, Assistant Director of Operations, Western Hemisphere; and Dr. John H. Adler, Economic Adviser.

At the Office of Population Research, Professor Frank W. Notestein (the Director) suggested the basic quantitative approach employed in the study, participated in the arrangements that got the project under way, and has given his advice and support at every stage. Professor George Stolnitz has generously permitted the use of his exhaustive collection of mortality data, which were invaluable raw material for parts of the demographic sections. Two Visiting Fellows from India at the Office of Population Research, Mr. V. R. K. Tilak and Dr. S. N. Agarwala, have contributed helpful ideas and information. Mr. Tilak had returned to New Delhi by the time of the authors' visit to India and was extremely helpful and hospitable.

Some 300 mimeographed copies of a preliminary draft of this book were privately circulated in the summer of 1956, and the comments and criticisms returned by readers have been very useful in preparing the present version. Professor Simon Kuznets deserves our special thanks for his exceptionally penetrating and comprehensive comments.

The authors visited India in the fall of 1955 and Mexico in the fall of 1956. We obtained a large volume of data not to be found in the United States, and gained invaluable first-hand knowledge, impressions, and ideas. We wish to thank His Excellency G. L. Mehta, Ambassador to the United States, and Shri G. R. Kamat for providing essential introductions and graciously making our trip easier and more effective. Mr. Federico Consolo's generosity was equally helpful in preparing our way in Mexico.

In India among all of the people who were generous with their time and effort, there are eight who must be given special mention. These were Dr. Tarlok Singh, Joint Secretary of the Planning Commission; Shri Eric P. W. Da Costa, Editor of *The Eastern Economist* and Director of the Indian Institute of Public Opinion; Professor C. Chandrasekharan, Professor of Statistics at the All-India Institute of Hygiene and Public Health; Drs. Marshall C. Balfour and Richmond K. Anderson of the Rockefeller Foundation; Professor Wilfred Malenbaum of the Center for International Studies at Massachusetts Institute of Technology; Dr. John Wyon, Director of the India-Harvard-Ludhiana population study; and Mr. Hyde Buller, Assistant Director of the U.S. Technical Cooperation Mission. In Mexico, Lic. Jorge Espinosa de los Reyes, Comisión de Inversiones; Dr. Javier Márquez, Director, Centro de Estudios Monetarios Latino-Americanos, Banco de México; Dr. D. Alfredo Navarrete, Director de Investigaciones Económicas, Nacional Financiera S.A.; Señorita Ana María Flores, Dirección General de Estadística, and Sr. Victor Urquidi, Naciones Unidas, CEPAL, were exceptionally helpful among a people with notable standards of generosity to visitors.

We wish to express our grateful appreciation also to the following persons in India:

In Delhi: Shri J. J. Anjaria, Economic Adviser to the Ministry of Finance and Chief of The Economic Division of the Planning Commission; Dr. P. V. Benjamin, Adviser on Tuberculosis to the Director General of Health Services; Dr. (Smt.) Bhatia, Adviser to the Minister of Health on Child and Maternal Health; Smt. Kamaladevi Chattopadhyay and Smt. D. Bapat of the All-India Handicrafts Board; Messrs. Douglas Ensminger and Bernard Loshbough of the Ford Foundation; Dr. J. C. Ghosh, Member for Education and Health, Planning Commission; Dr. U. L. Goswami, I.C.S., Deputy Director, Community Projects Administration (now the Ministry for Community Projects); Colonel C. K. Lakshmanan, Director General of Health Services; Dr. T. Laksminarayana, Medical Adviser to the Planning Commission; Shri B. K. Nehru, I.C.S., Joint Secretary, Ministry of Finance; Dr. V. G. Panse, Indian Council of Agricultural Research; Shri I. G. Patel, Deputy Economic Adviser, Ministry of Finance; Dr. R. N. Poduval, Deputy Economic and Statistical Adviser, Ministry of Food and Agriculture; Dr. K. C. K. E. Raja, Officer on Special Duty, Ministry of Health; Dr. B. A. Rao, Deputy Director, Indian Institute of Malariology; Professors V. K. R. V. Rao and K. N. Raj, Delhi University School of Economics; Colonel Jaswant Singh, Director, Indian Institute of Malariology; Dr. Eugene Staley, Consultant, Ministry of Commerce and Industry.

In Bombay: Professor M. L. Dantwala, Bombay University; Sarvashri A. D. Gorwala, B. K. Madan, P. J. J. Pinto, and J. C. Ryan, of the Reserve Bank of India; Shri V. L. Mehta, Chairman, All-India Khadi and Village Industries Board; Dr. K. Paymaster, Association of Trade and Industry; Dr. Sudhir Sen, Great Eastern Shipping Co., Ltd.; Mr. and Mrs. Maurice Zinkin, Lever Brothers, Ltd.

In Poona: Drs. D. R. Gadgil, N. V. Sovani, and N. Dandekar, of the Gokhale Institute; Dr. D. G. Karve; Dr. D. K. Vishwanathan, Director of Public Health, Bombay State.

In Calcutta: Shri S. J. Banerjea, Public Relations Officer, Development Commission, West Bengal State; officials of the Damodar Valley Corporation, and in particular Shri C. Balan, Public Relations Officer; Shri N. Das, Secretary, Department of Industries, West Bengal State; Mr. Jack Gray, Adviser to Development Commission, West Bengal State; Dr. P. C. Mahalanobis, Director, Indian Statistical Institute, and members of his staff; in particular, Dr. Ajit Das Gupta; Dr. P. C. Sen, Officer in Charge, Singur Health Center, and the staff of the Center; Shri Abdus Shokur, Deputy Minister of Agriculture, West Bengal State; Dr. K. S. Vishwanathan, Professor of Public Health Administration, All-India Institute of Hygiene and Public Health.

In Madras: Dr. T. S. Adisubramanian, Director of Public Health, Madras State; Professors R. Balakrishna and P. Zacharias, University of Madras; Dr. Isaac Joseph, Director of the Community Development Public Health Training Center at Poonamallee, and his staff; Shri P. Govinda Menon, Chief, Small Industries Service Institute; Captain R. Narayanan, Health Officer, Poonamallee

Health Unit, and the staff at Poonamallee; Shri A. T. Palaniappan, Director of Industries and Commerce, Madras State; Shri V. K. Parthasarathy, Statistician, Office of the Director of Public Health, Madras State; Shri N. E. S. Raghavacharai, I.C.S., Director of Community Development, Madras State; Shri A. G. Vedasundara Raj, Block Development Officer, Chingleput; Shri S. Venkataswamy, Public Relations Officer, Community Development Department, Madras State.

In Mysore State: Dr. E. Anantha Rao, Deputy Director of Public Health, Mysore State; Dr. S. Krishnaswamy Rao, Health Officer, Ramanagaram Health Training Center, and the staff at Ramanagaram; Dr. Seshagiri Rao, Director of Public Health, Mysore State.

Elsewhere in India: Dr. (Smt.) T. S. Soundram Ramachandran, Treasurer, Gandhigram; Mr. Earl J. Bacon, Extension Adviser, Travancore-Cochin State, Trivandrum; Dr. and Smt. A. N. Verghese, Trichur (Travancore-Cochin).

And in Mexico: Lic. Manuel Bravo J., Ing. Emilio Alanís Patiño, Ing. Fausto Urencio Ramírez, Banco de México, Departamento de Investigaciones Industriales; Ing. F. Carmona, Comisión de Inversiones; Lic. Antonio Carrillo-Flores, Secretaría de Hacienda; Horacio Flores de la Peña, Banco Nacional de Crédito Agrícolo; Ing. Arturo Gonzáles R., Jefe, Servicio de Extensión, Estado de México; Dr. Germán Herrera P. G., Gerente Técnico, Centro Industrial de Productividad; Lic. Gustavo Romero Kolbeck, Comisión de Inversiones; Cristóbal Lara, Celso Furtado, Juan Noyola, Naciones Unidas, CEPAL; Mr. Lotwick, U.S. Agricultural Attaché, American Embassy; Lic. Raúl Ortiz Mena and Lic. Héctor Villa Michel, Dirección de Crédito, Secretaría de Hacienda; Sr. Ernesto Luna Mendoza, Comisión del Papaloapan; Ing. Gonzalo Robles, Departamento de Investigaciones Industriales, Banco de México; Messrs. Vance Rogers and Lester Dame, U.S. Technical Cooperation Mission, American Embassy; Lic. Rosenzweig and Ing. Alvarez, Comisión del Papaloapan; Lic. Octaviano Campos Salas, Director, Departamento de Estudios Económicos, Banco de México; Ing. Raúl Sandoval, Comisión del Papaloapan; Ing. Rudolfo Flores Talavera, Director General de Estadística; Ing. Gilberto Mendoza Vargas, Director de Agricultura y Ganadería del Estado de México; Dr. E. J. Wellhausen and Dr. R. W. Richardson, Rockefeller Foundation Agricultural Program in Mexico.

Finally, there are many persons outside India and Mexico who have notably aided us, including in particular the following: Dr. Wilhelm Anderson, Foreign Agriculture Service, U.S. Department of Agriculture; Mr. Harold Barnett, Resources for the Future, Washington, D.C.; Messrs. David E. Bell and Emile Despres, Harvard-Pakistan Project, Karachi; Professor Harold Belshaw, Victoria University College, Wellington, N.Z.; Hon. Chester Bowles, former U.S. Ambassador to India; Professor L. V. Chandler, Princeton University; Dr. Eli Chernin, Department of Tropical Medicine, Harvard School of Public Health; Dr. Richard H. Daggy, Arabian-American Oil Company; Drs. John Durand, H. W. Singer, Sushil K. Dey, and N. B. Guyol, United Nations, New York; Messrs. John Ferris and John Keen, International Cooperation Administration, Washington, D.C.; Professor John E. Gordon, Chairman, Department of Epidemiology, Harvard School of Public Health; Shri N. D. Gulhati, member of the Indus River Water Commission; Messrs. Horace Holmes and Harrison Parker, Ford Foundation, New York; Mr. Thomas B. Keehn, American International Association for Economic and Social Development, New York; Dean Edward S. Mason, Littauer School of Public Administration, Harvard University; Mr. Albert Mayer, New York City; Professor Arthur T. Mosher, Cornell University; Professor Ragnar Nurkse, Columbia University; Shri P. S. Narayan Prasad and Dr. B. Datta, International Monetary Fund; Professor Robert Reed, Harvard School of Public Health; Professor J. J. Spengler, Duke University; Dr. Carl Taylor, Department of Epidemiology, Harvard School of Public Health.

None of these persons, of course, is in any way accountable for omissions, errors, or other shortcomings of the book.

Edgar M. Hoover
Ansley J. Coale

*November, 1957*

# CONTENTS

xiii

CONTENTS

## TABLES

## APPENDIX TABLES

# CHARTS

## APPENDIX CHARTS

POPULATION GROWTH

AND ECONOMIC DEVELOPMENT IN

LOW-INCOME COUNTRIES

CHAPTER I

◇◇◇◇◇◇◇◇◇◇◇◇◇◇◇◇◇◇◇◇◇◇◇◇◇◇◇◇◇◇◇◇◇◇◇◇◇◇◇◇◇◇◇◇◇◇◇◇◇◇◇◇◇◇

# INTRODUCTION

◇◇◇◇◇◇◇◇◇◇◇◇◇◇◇◇◇◇◇◇◇◇◇◇◇◇◇◇◇◇◇◇◇◇◇◇◇◇◇◇◇◇◇◇◇◇◇◇◇◇◇◇◇◇

THE INFLUENCE of population changes on the economic development of low-income areas has attracted new attention recently, partly because of two prevalent trends. The first of these trends is the rise in aspirations, plans, and programs for expanding national output in countries with very low average incomes. The second trend is the increasingly pervasive pattern of rapid decline in death rates in areas where until recently mortality risks were high. These areas have high birth rates; thus the drop in death rates means that population growth is (or is becoming) very rapid.

Late in 1954 the Office of Population Research began a study of the relations between population growth and economic development. Our research has concentrated on India's prospective demographic and economic changes in the belief that the relationship between population and economic development might be clarified by considering the problem in as specific a context, and in as quantitative terms as possible.

India was selected as our area of study partly because its demographic and economic data are relatively plentiful, and partly because from the analytical point of view the relationship between economic development and population change in India seems comparatively clear. India's population is already very large relative to its resources (particularly agricultural land) and has a large potential for rapid further growth in the near future. Also, because of its size, India must find the solution to its economic and demographic problems mainly within its own borders rather than through international trade and migration. In the light of the current outlook for continued restrictions on international trade and the almost universal desire of countries to industrialize rather than to specialize in agricultural production, it is quite uncertain that a country so large as India could count on obtaining a very large fraction of the food supply for a population substantially larger than the present population by exporting industrial products and importing

3

food. Such a solution might well be defeated by an adverse turn in the terms of trade, or trade restrictions against India's exports, or both. All of this means that analysis of demographic effects in economic terms can appropriately concentrate on internal problems to a greater extent in India's case than in the case of most other countries.

The part of our analysis which is most quantitative and specific is the estimation of the plausible prospective upper and lower limits of population growth over the next twenty-five or thirty years. This specificity is not the result of our ability to foresee accurately the actual course of population events in India, but is rather the result of the specific implications of assumptions about population change. Our principal aim in analyzing the possible changes in the Indian economy is to bring out the important qualitative differences in economic development resulting from a choice of a very rapid population growth or a less rapid population growth. Where possible, the general magnitude as well as the direction of this difference is estimated. In calculating the rough magnitude of the economic effect of differences in population growth, we make extensive reference to official development plans and forecasts. However, our preoccupation with the differential implications of alternative population growth patterns means that we have no wish to suggest or appraise economic policy or to make accurate economic predictions. Our illustrative economic projections should emphatically *not* be considered as an appraisal of Indian plans or as a prediction of the future rate of economic growth.

Since a majority of the world's population has—as does India—low incomes and high fertility, it was natural to see whether our analysis of India's prospects applied elsewhere. The attempt to extend our conclusions took two forms—an exploration of demographic-economic relations in other areas (with frequent use of Mexico as an example), and speculation about relationships more than 30 years ahead.

The book has five major sections. Part One presents a synoptic statement of the relations between population growth and economic development. This statement does little more than list the variables relevant in a consideration of how economic development and population influence one another. The most prominent theory of these relations, evolved on the basis of the economic development

4

of Western Europe, North America, Australasia and Japan, is summarized. The degree to which it applies to the low-income areas of the world embarking today on a course of economic development is explored. Part Two is a description of the Indian population, recent, current, and future—its size, age composition, growth rate, and birth and death rates. The likely upper and lower limits to population growth in India during the next twenty-five or thirty years are described. Part Three outlines the likely changes in the Indian economy in the next two or three decades, emphasizing the determinants of development that are related to changes in population. Part Four shows how economic development would be influenced by which trend of population growth—the upper or the lower—is actually followed. The effects of alternative growth patterns are shown in various ways—in terms of the growth of per capita income, and also in terms of the prospective success of particular development efforts, such as the extension of education or of economic benefits other than rising income (e.g., the widening of employment opportunity). The concluding section, Part Five, examines demographic-economic relations in other low-income, high-fertility areas differing from India in size, current levels of mortality and growth, state of economic advance, and general strategy of development. It also discusses the longer run (beyond thirty years) implications of demographic change.

# PART ONE

◇◇◇◇◇◇◇◇◇◇◇◇◇◇◇

# RELATIONS BETWEEN POPULATION AND ECONOMIC DEVELOPMENT

◇◇◇◇◇◇◇◇◇◇◇◇◇◇◇◇◇◇◇◇◇◇◇◇◇◇◇◇◇◇◇◇◇◇◇◇◇◇◇◇◇◇◇◇◇◇◇◇◇◇◇◇

# CHAPTER II

# THE EFFECTS OF ECONOMIC DEVELOPMENT
# ON POPULATION GROWTH

◇◇◇◇◇◇◇◇◇◇◇◇◇◇◇◇◇◇◇◇◇◇◇◇◇◇◇◇◇◇◇◇◇◇◇◇◇◇◇◇◇◇◇◇◇◇◇◇◇◇◇◇

IN SURVEYING RELATIONS between two complex sets of changes it is natural to begin with the influence of one set on the other, and then to consider influences operating in the opposite direction. Our introductory survey of demographic and economic changes will follow this procedure, beginning in this chapter with a description of how economic development can influence population growth. This influence must operate through one or more of the three determinants of population growth—namely, births, deaths, and migration. Migration as an important cause of economic growth will not be discussed, because in general the substantial international barriers to large-scale migration make it a very uncertain element in the future growth of low-income areas, and in particular international migration seems unlikely to have an important effect on the future growth of the Indian population.

The classical economic theory of population growth (primarily associated with Malthus) held that any rise in incomes (particularly among the poorer classes) tended to increase birth rates and (with more certainty and force) to decrease death rates.

The course of events since Malthus' time, however, has led to the gradual evolution of a theory that postulates a more complicated sequence of birth and death rates as typically associated with economic development. It is sometimes termed the theory of the "demographic transition." According to this theory an agrarian peasant economy (characterized by a high degree of self-sufficiency within each community and even each family, by relatively slow change in technique, and by the relatively unimportant role of market exchange) typically has high average death rates. Moreover, these death rates usually fluctuate in consequence of variations in crops, the varying incidence of epidemics, etc. In such an economy birth rates are nearly stable at a high level. Death rates are high as a consequence of poor diets, primitive sanitation, and the absence of effective

9

preventive and curative medical practices. High birth rates result from social beliefs and customs that necessarily grow up if a high death-rate community is to continue in existence. These beliefs and customs are reinforced by the economic advantages to a peasant family of large numbers of births. The burden of child care rests primarily on the women in a peasant society, and the place of women is typically a subordinate one. The costs of educating children are minimal because of the low level of education given. Children contribute at an early age to agrarian production and are the traditional source of security in the old age of parents. The prevalent high death rates, especially in infancy, imply that such security can be attained only when many children are born.

In other words, an agrarian low-income society, before it undergoes economic development, has a mortality and fertility pattern that fits pretty closely the conditions which Malthus thought, at least in the first edition of his famous essay, to be a universal tendency: high birth and high death rates. Growth of population is usually slow.

Economic development, according to the theory of the demographic transition, has the effect of bringing about a reduction in death rates. Economic development involves evolution from a predominantly agrarian peasant economy to an economy with a greater division of labor, using more elaborate tools and equipment, more urbanized, more oriented to the market sale of its products, and characterized by rapid and pervasive changes in technique. It also involves improvements in transportation, communications, and productivity, and these improvements have had the effect (notably in Europe, the United States, Canada, Australia and New Zealand, and later in Japan) of bringing a striking reduction in death rates. The reduction in death rates may be ascribed partly to greater regularity in food supplies, to the establishment of greater law and order, and to other fairly direct consequences of economic change. Other factors contributing to the decline—improvements in sanitation, the development of vaccines and other means of preventive medicine, and great and rapid strides in the treatment of disease—can themselves be considered as somewhat indirect consequences of economic change. Advances in medical knowledge can occur more readily in a secularized, less tradition-bound society that has resources available to support medical research. The means to build

10

and the will to accept sanitary water supplies, sewage systems, and the like are more likely to exist in an industrial than in an agrarian society. For similar reasons, only in an advanced economy with such characteristics as a high degree of division of labor and high levels of productivity, are there the means to construct large numbers of hospitals, to educate and train large numbers of doctors, and the like. It is often hard to determine in a given historical period whether general economic conditions or specific medical advances had the greater effect. In Europe even before 1800 there had been significant medical discoveries (including vaccination for smallpox with cowpox serum) that must have made *some* contribution to declining mortality. Nevertheless, the Population Division of the United Nations suggests that the reduction of mortality rates in the European cultural sphere in the eighteenth and the first part of the nineteenth centuries was due mostly to more or less direct effects of economic improvement, while in the latter part of the nineteenth and especially in the twentieth centuries the more direct factors at work have been improving medical knowledge and increasingly effective public health methods.[1] This conclusion must be considered highly conjectural.

The theory of the demographic transition asserts that the high birth rates, as well as the death rates, characteristic of an agrarian low-income society are affected by economic development. The changing structure of production, with a declining importance of the family as a production unit, with the growth of impersonal systems for the allocation of jobs, and with the development of economic roles for women outside of the home, tends to increase the possibility of economic mobility that can better be achieved with small families, and tends to decrease the economic advantages of a large family. One of the features of economic development is typically increasing urbanization, and children are usually more of a burden and less of an asset in an urban setting than in a rural. The whole process of economic change, moreover, weakens the force of traditional customs and beliefs. In most countries that have undergone the economic transition from an agrarian to an industrialized, market-oriented economy, the custom of the small family

[1] United Nations, Department of Social Affairs, Population Division, *The Determinants and Consequences of Population Trends*, Population Studies No. 17, New York, United Nations, 1953, pp. 56-61.

11

has started in the urban groups at the higher end of the socio-economic scale and has spread to smaller cities, lower-income groups, and eventually to rural areas.[2]

Just as early decline in the death rate in the European cultural area preceded the development of modern medical innovations, the early decline in fertility preceded the development of modern techniques of birth control. In many areas a marked decline in fertility has depended only on techniques of contraception known in many societies for centuries. However, both the extent and effectiveness of family limitation in industrialized countries have no doubt been facilitated by the development and manufacture of efficient contraceptive devices.

Although the events described by this theory can apparently be traced in every region where the economy has been subject to the evolution from an agrarian to a specialized market-dominated economy, the theory is not sufficiently quantitative and specific to tell how far and how fast the vital rates generally decline. It does, however, contain one further significant generalization, which is that the decline in the birth rates typically occurs after a substantial time lag, in comparison with the decline in mortality rates. The slower response of the birth rate to economic change is attributed to the fact that a fertility decline depends more strongly on the alteration of long-established customs and institutions. Also, there is in almost any society a general consensus in support of the reduction of suffering, illness, and death, while no such consensus supports the desirability of small families and the patterns of sex behavior required to reduce the birth rate. The historical implications of the lag between the decline in the death rate and the decline in the birth rate have been that the countries affected have experienced a substantial growth in population and a rapid one, at least by previous standards. Thus in the period between 1750 and 1950 the "area of European settlement" increased its population sixfold.[3] The population more than doubled in the century from 1750 to 1850 and nearly tripled in the interval 1850 to 1950.

In barest outline the sequence of events, according to the theory

[2] See F. W. Notestein, "Economic Problems of Population Change," in *Proceedings of the Eighth International Conference of Agricultural Economists*, London, Oxford University Press, 1953.
[3] United Nations, Population Division, *op.cit.*, p. 11.

of demographic transition, can be summarized as follows: The agrarian low-income economy is characterized by high birth and death rates—the birth rates relatively stable, and the death rates fluctuating in response to varying fortunes. Then as the economy changes its form to a more interdependent and specialized market-dominated economy, the average death rate declines. It continues to decline under the impact of better organization and improving medical knowledge and care. Somewhat later the birth rate begins to fall. The two rates pursue a more or less parallel downward course with the decline in the birth rate lagging behind. Finally, as further reductions in the death rate become harder to attain, the birth rate again approaches equality with the death rate and a more gradual rate of growth is reestablished, with, however, low risks of mortality and small families as the typical pattern. Mortality rates are now relatively stable from year to year and birth rates—now responsive to voluntary decisions rather than to deeply imbedded customs—may fluctuate from year to year. This short description fits the experience of most countries whose economies have undergone the kind of reorganization we have been calling economic development. The part of the description with the least certain applicability is the characterization of the final stage as a return to a condition of only gradual growth. The populations of Canada, the United States, Australia, and New Zealand are growing at rates that would lead to a doubling approximately twice a century—a rate of growth well above the average rate in the area settled by northern and western Europeans during the period of the demographic transition itself. It remains uncertain how long this rather rapid growth in North America and Oceania will continue.

The theory of the demographic transition has been summarized here because it is the theory which seems to be the best available to describe the expected course of events in the low-income areas of the world today if their economies are developed. Shall we not expect that economic development in the contemporary low-income areas will bring with it a decline in death rates followed by a decline in birth rates, and will produce over an interim period an acceleration of population growth? A superficial survey of the demographic situation and apparent prospects in the low-income portions of the world gives reason for doubting the applicability of the demographic transition as an *exact* description of the likely course of events in

13

these areas. The principal reason for doubting the precise applicability of the theory as to *death* rates is that it appears feasible today to reduce death rates markedly without a major reorganization of a peasant economy. Many low-income areas of the world today—for example, Ceylon, Malaya, some of the Caribbean islands, and much of Latin America—have, without abandoning their present agrarian structure, so reduced their death rates while birth rates have remained essentially unchanged that their rate of natural increase exceeds any recorded in the course of the demographic transition in the areas inhabited by northern and western Europeans and their descendants.

In other words, *substantial economic improvement may be a sufficient condition for a decline in mortality, but it is not today a necessary condition.* The pace of recent improvement in mortality is indicated by the fact that for twenty-one countries where the crude death rate was over 17 during the period 1935 through 1944, the average annual drop in crude death rates from just before World War II until around 1950 was about seven-tenths of a point. (In other words, the death rate was dropping at a pace that would reduce the crude death rate by 7 per thousand population every ten years.)[4] This rate of improvement surpasses anything from the records of areas inhabited by northern and western Europeans. In many instances there is no evidence of major economic changes. The factors primarily responsible for the mortality declines in these areas are innovations in public health. These make possible drastic reductions in mortality at low cost—and in the absence of wholesale social reorganization. A somewhat similar reduction in mortality was achieved prior to World War II in low-income colonial areas where the influence of a more highly developed economy was strong. Colonial administrators frequently succeeded in introducing relatively low-cost programs that had measurable effects on mortality. A notable case is that of Taiwan where, under Japanese administration, the crude death rate declined from an average of 33.4 per thousand in the years 1906-1910 to 18.5 for the years 1941-1943. Mortality declines have recently become widespread

[4] These twenty-one areas were Taiwan, the Federation of Malaya, Malta and Gozo, the Maori population of New Zealand, Egypt, British Guiana, Chile, Costa Rica, El Salvador, Mexico, Puerto Rico, Ceylon, Mauritius, Venezuela, Guatemala, Barbados, Leeward Islands, British Honduras, Ecuador, Hong Kong, and Singapore.

and precipitous, however, through the combined effects of the following factors:

(1) *The development of antibiotics and insecticides.* The incidence of malaria can in most environments be reduced to negligible proportions through the use of residual insecticides, especially DDT, at an annual cost of some 10-15 cents per capita of the population protected. Other serious diseases such as yaws, syphilis, and perhaps eventually tuberculosis, respond to relatively inexpensive treatment with antibiotics.

(2) *The evolution of effective public health organizations in low-income areas.* This development has become possible, in some instances, through the establishment of public health training centers in low-income areas. In other instances, public health workers from the low-income areas have been trained in European or American universities; and in still other instances expert demonstration teams operating under the auspices of the World Health Organization have helped to get programs started.

(3) *The invention of suitable low-cost methods of sanitation* (such as inexpensive hand-flush latrines) and the discovery through public health experiments of effective techniques for introducing the use of such equipment and devices.

Experience in communication, persuasion, and leadership as well as in more directly medical aspects of public health in rural areas is accumulating rapidly. No doubt the lessons learned will make future public health work more effective.

Mortality experience in situations where economic development began in the eighteenth or nineteenth centuries provides a precedent possibly misleading on two scores as a guide to the likely course of death rates in areas with current low incomes. First, the death rate in many low-income areas either is already or may soon be going down more rapidly than it ever did in countries now enjoying high incomes; and second, this rapid drop in death rates can occur with or without pronounced changes in economic structure.

Whether the pattern of fertility decline that has been observed in the industrializing areas of European settlement will be duplicated in the low-income areas of today is very uncertain. No published version of the theory of the demographic transition states precisely what conditions are essential for a fertility decline; much less is it possible to tell whether these conditions will be present in the areas in question during a specific interval. Perhaps the decline in mortality may in itself prove a sufficient cause for a substantial

15

fertility reduction. Since much of the reduction in mortality typically occurs in childhood, it will be apparent that average family size is increasing as mortality rates decline; and the motives of insuring family continuity and of obtaining support for old age can be satisfied with a smaller number of births. However, the record on this score is discouraging. In Taiwan, where the death rate declined substantially under the Japanese colonial administration, birth rates remained essentially unaltered. Similarly, in Ceylon between 1921 and the present, when death rates declined consistently from around 30 per thousand to around 10 per thousand, there has been no important decline in fertility.[5]

The course of the birth rate in Japan shows that the association between declining fertility and the rise of an urbanized industrial economy is not limited to Western European cultures. However, there are countries (notably Egypt and India) where the differential fertility between city and country is slight or even nonexistent.[6] In short, urbanization alone is not always sufficient to cause a reduction in the birth rate. Nor is it certain that small changes in economic organization or slight rises in per capita income will cause a reduction of fertility in low-income areas. It is questionable whether the economic and social change likely in the next two or three decades in many parts of the world will be enough to have an effect on fertility. The level of economic development in European countries (and in Japan) prevailing at the time that fertility began a significant decline might reasonably be regarded as representing the approximate "threshold of decline." It appears unlikely that this threshold will be crossed in the next two or three decades in, for example, Egypt, Pakistan, India, China, Malaya, or Indonesia.[7]

The demographic situation in areas in the incipient stages of economic development seems to differ from the pattern described

[5] The registered birth rate in Ceylon for 1954 was 36.2 per thousand compared to 39.4 for the preceding year. This is the first indication of a marked decline in the Ceylonese birth rate. However, this decline may prove to be temporary or spurious. In the first place, the 1954 monthly figures show an incredibly low birth rate for August. The likelihood that the low figure can be attributed to deficient registration is strengthened by the fact that there were serious civil disturbances in Ceylon during this month. Secondly, the 1955 rate shows a partial recovery to 37.9 per thousand.

[6] cf. M. A. El-Badry, "Some Aspects of Fertility in Egypt," *The Milbank Memorial Fund Quarterly*, Vol. XXXIV, No. 1 (January 1956), pp. 22-43; and pp. 47-48 below.

[7] See below, pp. 57-59.

by the theory of the demographic transition in the following ways: (1) The decline of death rates from the high levels typical of peasant agrarian economies is occurring or is likely to occur more rapidly than it did in regions which industrialized earlier. Moreover, the decline is occurring in advance of (or in the absence of) profound changes in the economy and in per capita incomes. (2) The growth rates established, as mortality declines, are in excess of any observed in the records of areas industrializing earlier. (3) The prospect of rapid growth itself—particularly in areas where the current per capita incomes are very low—contributes to uncertainty about the likely course of fertility. The rapid growth rate may make it difficult to accomplish the economic and social changes that reduce fertility.

Innovations in the field of public health seem to have made it possible for death rates to be substantially reduced in the absence of profound economic changes in low-income areas. However, the classic Malthusian argument makes it all too clear that low death rates cannot be maintained long in the absence of profound changes either in the economy (so as to achieve a rapid rate of growth in output) or in the birth rate (to keep the growth in population at moderate levels). A peasant agrarian economy is not usually characterized by a potential for rapid growth in output. The death rates achievable at low cost by modern public health methods, combined with the birth rate characteristic of such an economy, imply a doubling of the population every twenty to twenty-five years. If economic development does not *precede* the decline in mortality, it must still occur eventually if the decline is to be maintained.

17

◇◇◇◇◇◇◇◇◇◇◇◇◇◇◇◇◇◇◇◇◇◇◇◇◇◇◇◇◇◇◇◇◇◇◇◇◇◇◇◇◇◇◇◇◇◇◇◇◇◇◇◇◇◇

# CHAPTER III

## THE EFFECTS OF POPULATION GROWTH
## ON ECONOMIC DEVELOPMENT

◇◇◇◇◇◇◇◇◇◇◇◇◇◇◇◇◇◇◇◇◇◇◇◇◇◇◇◇◇◇◇◇◇◇◇◇◇◇◇◇◇◇◇◇◇◇◇◇◇◇◇◇◇◇

IN THIS CHAPTER we shall list and briefly analyze the ways in which demographic factors can affect the level of per capita income. There will be no systematic attempt to review the various economic theories from the predecessors of Malthus to the neo-Keynesian stagnation theorists. The emphasis will be on relations relevant to low-income areas today.

There are three aspects of population growth that may be looked at separately in analyzing the effects of population growth on the growth of per capita income. These are (a) the size of a population; (b) its growth rate, and (c) its age distribution.

The relation between population size and per capita income is the subject to which optimum population theory has been addressed. The relationship of size to desired growth rate is straightforward. If optimum population theory indicates that a population is too large, a negative growth or decline is advantageous, and any smaller positive growth rate is to be preferred to a larger. Optimum population theory is in essence an exercise in comparative economic statics. The principal point at issue is that of returns to scale, with two opposing forces at work—economies of scale favoring a rising per capita income, and diminishing returns a falling per capita income, with larger population size. The question is in effect one of the optimum relation of population to the other factors of production.

The question of whether a given population is larger than one yielding maximum per capita output is very difficult to answer in any concrete situation. One of the fundamental difficulties is that the shape of the curve relating output to labor force depends on the available techniques of production, which in turn depends on what skills the population possesses. Thus a population may be in a stage of sharply diminishing returns while it is utterly illiterate, whereas after a generation of education a population of the same size might be of optimum or even sub-optimum size. Moreover, the whole question of increasing and decreasing returns with respect to the size of the labor force depends upon the availability of other factors of production. Indeed, the idea of diminishing returns is simply another way of picturing the consequences of the limited availability of some factor of production. One of the factors most likely to lead to diminishing returns, especially in the low-income areas of the world, is the limited quantity of capital available. With larger quantities of capital, larger-scale techniques at high levels of efficiency might become feasible. Here, again, the locus of the point at which diminishing returns sets in can shift with the passage of time.

The classic example of the factor in fixed supply that causes diminishing returns in other factors is *land* or, more generally, natural resources. When the availability of capital changes, however, the point of diminishing returns to labor with a fixed supply of land may vary. In any event, the effective supply of land or of useful natural resources is in actual fact partly a function of technical knowledge and skills. Hence judgments that a population has too large a size on the criterion of average income should be provisional, and may prove to be obsolete even if originally correct.

The basic defect in analyzing the effects of population growth by considering alternative sizes alone is that such a scheme of analysis ignores the dynamic effect of the *change* in population size or the growth rate of population. The alternative population developments which may in fact be available at any time are usually a range, perhaps a narrow one, of alternative rates of population growth arising through either alternative possible death rates or alternative possible birth rates, or both. It makes a big difference which of these growth rates is selected, quite aside from the question of whether the population with given resources (including the initial stock of capital) and given techniques is too large or too small.

This brings us to the second factor that may be considered in analyzing the effect of population growth on economic development, namely, the rate of growth itself. The significant feature of population *growth* as such is that a *higher rate* of population growth implies a *higher level* of needed investment to achieve a given per capita output, while there is nothing about faster growth that generates a greater *supply* of investible resources. This point may be clarified by a simple example. Assume that technical change is negligible over the short run and that capital and labor force are the only ingredients of output. Then an increase of $x$ per cent per annum in population and of $x$ per cent per annum in accumulated capital will produce an increase of $x$ per cent per annum in output— or an unaltered per capita output. Now consider two populations equal, at a given moment, in size, in accumulated capital, and in output. Assume that population A is growing at a rate of 1 per cent per annum, and population B at 3 per cent. If the ratio of capital stock to current annual output is 3 to 1, population A must invest 3 per cent of current output to maintain its per capita income, while population B must invest 9 per cent of current output. But under ordinary circumstances the supply of new capital will be no greater in B than in A. There is nothing about faster growth *per se* to lower consumption and raise savings—certainly not by such a large margin.

In low-income areas it is especially difficult to attain adequate levels of investment, and there is no visible way in such areas by which more rapid population growth can evoke a significantly greater flow of invested resources. When the supply of capital is inelastic, a higher rate of population growth forces the diversion of investment to duplicate existing facilities, preventing an increase in the capital available for each worker.

Seen from another point of view, the relationship between population growth and investment has served as one of the principal underpinnings for the theory of stagnation that was popular in the nineteen-thirties. Here the point was that economic stagnation is caused by an inadequate level of new investment, and that new investment is sometimes deficient in part because of the slow growth of population. However, this reasoning applies only when the barrier to greater investment is the absence of a motive to invest (low marginal efficiency of capital, in Keynesian terms) rather than a poor supply of investible resources.

In periods of depression in highly industrialized economies, any rise in the prospective profitability of investment should tend to increase the employment of labor and capital that would otherwise be idle, and to raise per capita product. If, in the face of an elastic supply of capital, the greater *need* for capital (to maintain a given level of per capita output) caused by more rapid growth is trans-

20

lated into higher or more certain prospects of profit, population growth serves as an important stimulant to higher investment levels.[1]

We may picture two extreme situations with respect to the effect of population growth rates on the growth of per capita income. One picture is that of a relatively high-income economy where the chronic problem is that of assuring a full utilization of the resources available—to avoid unemployment both of the labor force and of capital goods. Keynesian analysis shows that under these circumstances a rise in the demand for capital goods (a rise in the marginal efficiency of capital) will have a stimulating effect on the whole economy, and will tend toward generally higher incomes. It can well be argued that a possible source of such stimulus to demand is a faster rather than a slower population growth rate. In the other extreme is an economy which suffers from a deficiency not of effective demand primarily but of a supply of capital. In such, an economy, a higher schedule of saving rather than of consumption would help to generate higher incomes in the future by making possible a more rapid rate of investment. Similarly, a reduced need for investment merely to duplicate facilities would permit a greater increase in the amount of capital per worker, higher per capita output, and higher per capita income.

There may be some basis for the belief that in fact deficiencies of effective demand are often a problem in low-income economies as well as in high-income economies. It might sometimes be the case that government deficits or increased spending by upper income groups would serve as a real stimulus to increased output. But even if deficiencies of effective demand as a barrier to economic growth are accepted as a possibility in low-income economies, it does not follow that more rapid population growth will under these circumstances serve as a major stimulus, since there is no apparent way in a low-income economy for greater numbers to be translated into very much higher consumption expenditures or higher prospective returns to capital. Most families will not have the capability for enlarging their consumption, but must spread meager income over a larger number. In other words, faster growth may have little effect in low-income economies on either the consumption function or the "marginal efficiency of capital."

[1] The existence of a greater *need* for investment does not necessarily imply a greater *demand* for investment. Labor force growth could merely add to the unemployed, while profit prospects remained gloomy and investment remained low.

To summarize, if we assume away the problem of effective demand (i.e., assume it either nonexistent or adequately solved through government action in a low-income agrarian economy), rapid growth *does* tend to diminish the amount of capital available for increasing the average productivity of the work force and increasing the average per capita income.

The third factor which enters in an analysis of the effect of population growth on economic development is the distribution of population by age, which turns out to be strongly influenced by the same elements that determine the rate of population growth. We will have to digress before discussing the effect of age distributions on economic growth to discuss briefly the factors determining the shape of an age distribution. If one deals with a closed population (namely, one in which gains or losses by migration are negligible), the principal determinant of the age distribution is the course of fertility. Persistent high levels of fertility give a broad-based distribution that tapers rapidly with age; persistent low levels of fertility give a narrow-based age distribution. If fertility is low enough, the age distribution may be broader in the shoulder than at the base. Even irregularities such as gaps and humps in an age distribution are usually the result of variations in fertility.

Conversely, mortality changes of a sort that usually occur have only a slight effect on the age distribution.[2] The net consequence of these facts is that a change in the growth rate caused by a change in fertility will generally have associated with it a large change in the per cent age distribution. On the other hand, a change in the growth rate brought about by a change in mortality will generally be accompanied by only a slight effect on the per cent age distribution. A further implication is that all low-income agrarian areas, which without exception have relatively high birth rates, have, no matter what their mortality levels, a broadly-based and sharply tapering age distribution, with a large fraction of the population under 15. Of course, low birth rates ultimately lead to higher proportions over age 65, but the decrease in the proportion under 15 outweighs this increase.

The fact is, then, that the burden of dependency, or the ratio of persons who are in a dependent status because of their age (too

---

[2] The chief exception is war casualties, which have their own peculiar incidence by age and sex.

young or too old to work) to persons at ages making them eligible for productive work, is relatively high in areas characterized by persistent high birth rates, and is low in areas with low birth rates.

The reduction of mortality, particularly among children, is an inestimable gain for its own sake. As social goals, reduced pain, suffering and grief rank at least as high as reduced poverty. Moreover, the public health measures that yield lower death rates also raise productivity and morale by reducing absenteeism, weakness, fatigue, lassitude, and disability. But it is *not* true, as is commonly believed, that mortality reduction reduces the so-called "burden of dependency." The argument offered in support of this belief is that when childhood mortality rates are high (and childhood mortality rates are typically high when the general level of mortality is high) the economy must support a large number of children during the part of their lives when they consume only and do not produce; moreover, the economy does not benefit from production by these children during the interval of their working ages, when they might produce more than they would consume. Therefore—so the argument runs—if an improvement in mortality would permit more children to reach adult ages, this waste would be avoided and the burden of dependency would be reduced.

This argument as just summarized makes no explicit assumptions about levels of fertility. If now it is assumed that during the sequence just described levels of fertility are unchanged, the argument proves fallacious. The source of the fallacy is that if more children are enabled to survive to their adult years, there will be not only more workers but also more parents; the larger number of parents, if fertility rates remain unchanged, will produce more children. Analysis shows that the rise in the number of children is indeed somewhat greater than the rise in the number of workers.[3] So while it is true that a decrease in childhood mortality will yield a larger population at the working ages than would otherwise have resulted, it produces an even greater rise in the number of children whom the people of working ages must support.

High childhood mortality rates *do* cause expenditures on children

[3] A. J. Coale, "The Effects of Changes in Mortality and Fertility on Age Composition." *The Milbank Memorial Fund Quarterly*, Vol. XXXIV, No. 1 (January 1956), pp. 79-114; and "The Effect of Declines in Mortality on Age Distribution," *Trends and Differentials in Mortality*, Milbank Memorial Fund (New York 1956), pp. 125-132.

who because they die make no contribution at a later time to the economy. The relevant consideration, however, is the nonproductive expenditures at any moment in support of nonproductive persons. Since the proportion of children *rises* slightly with typical mortality improvements, the economy must "waste" *more* (not less) of its substance on nonproductive persons. A reduction in mortality "saves" more people for the labor force ages, but it also saves them for parenthood, and "wasteful" expenditure is expanded more than the labor force itself. In short, the "waste" of always supporting a much larger next generation (the waste of very rapid growth) replaces the waste of spending on persons who later die. A change in the mortality rate operates primarily on the growth rate of the population—it produces more people in the working age but also produces more people in the dependent ages. On the other hand, a decline in birth rates yields a smaller number of children without immediately affecting numbers at older ages. The effect on the age distribution in the short and long run is a smaller fraction of dependent children.

We shall, in what follows, neglect as relatively minor age-distribution effects of mortality changes, and discuss only the effect of changes of *fertility* on the age distribution. Consider two populations of the same size, one characterized by a history of high birth rates, the other characterized by low birth rates at least over an interval of fifteen to twenty years prior to the date in question. The population with the high birth rates may have some 55-60 per cent of its numbers in the ages from 15-65, whereas the population with the low birth rates may have some 65-70 per cent of its population in the productive ages. With the same resources and capital available, the lower birth-rate population should have higher per capita output and higher per capita income as a direct result of having a higher fraction of its population eligible on account of age for productive work.

Another instructive comparison is between two populations again differing only through the history of their birth rates, which are equal now not in terms of their total size but in terms of the size of their labor force. In this case the labor force in the economy characterized by high birth rates would have to support substantially larger numbers of children. This necessity would have a two-edged effect on the availability of capital for the possible expansion of

24

output. First of all, the supply of capital would tend to be reduced because the larger number of consumers implied by the past history of higher birth rates would exert a depressing force on the level of savings. A family with the same total income but with a larger number of children would surely tend to consume more and save less, other things being equal. Also, an economy that had been characterized by high birth rates would tend to have a more rapidly rising number of children, which in turn would tend to divert some of the capital accumulated each year into expenditures such as for school and child welfare programs. These expenditures would reduce the availability of capital for directly adding to the productivity of the labor force.[4]

The three demographic factors identified as basic in an analysis of the effects of population growth on economic development are population size, rate of population growth, and age-distribution effects. Actually, of course, these three factors are never independent. A continuation of a more rapid population growth inevitably produces, in a closed population, larger numbers. A slower rate of population growth brought about by a reduction in birth rates inevitably has age-distribution effects.

Our study of demographic and economic prospects in India over the next twenty-five or thirty years will take implicit or explicit account of all these factors. All turn out to be important. The device of population projection, through which the likely evolution of death rates and possible variations in birth rates in India can be translated into estimated future populations of India by age and sex, enables us to bracket, we think, the likely variations in potential size, growth rates, and age-distributions for India over the next twenty-five to thirty years. A consideration of the Indian economy at the end of the First Five-Year Plan, plus a consideration of the nature of the next Five-Year Plan, enables us to take account of the actual objectives of Indian economic development and the institutional framework within which that development will likely proceed, and gives us more realistic and detailed ways of appraising the consequences of alternative courses of population growth.

---

[4] In an economy where the level of effective demand is an important barrier to the employment of available resources, there are further important and quite different economic effects of age-distribution differences. If effective demand is deficient, a high burden of dependency—a large number of children as opposed to a small number—should serve as a stimulant to higher consumption and should create a demand for capital investment.

25

CHAPTER IV

◇◇◇◇◇◇◇◇◇◇◇◇◇◇◇◇◇◇◇◇◇◇◇◇◇◇◇◇◇◇◇◇◇◇◇◇◇◇◇◇◇◇◇◇◇◇◇◇◇◇◇◇

# INDIA'S POPULATION—CURRENT
# AND PROSPECTIVE

◇◇◇◇◇◇◇◇◇◇◇◇◇◇◇◇◇◇◇◇◇◇◇◇◇◇◇◇◇◇◇◇◇◇◇◇◇◇◇◇◇◇◇◇◇◇◇◇◇◇◇◇

INDIA RANKS SECOND to China among the countries of the world in total population. The population, according to the 1951 census, was some 357 million.[1] The density of the population, about 300 persons per square mile, is some 40 per cent higher than the density of population in Europe, not including the Soviet Union. (The population of India is about 90 per cent of the population of Europe without Russia, but the area is only about two-thirds as great.) The density in Europe is substantially increased by the large fraction of the population living in cities. Europe's population is more than 53 per cent urban,[2] while India's population in 1951 was only about 17 per cent urban. Thus the density of the rural population in India was about twice that of Europe in 1951. Moreover, at least two-thirds of India's population is dependent on agriculture as the principal means of livelihood compared to less than a third in Europe.[3]

## THE GROWTH OF POPULATION IN INDIA SINCE 1891

The history of population growth in India since 1891 divides itself naturally into two periods, the point of division being 1921. In the three decades 1891-1921, the total growth was little more than 5 per cent, or an average of less than one-sixth of one per cent per annum. In two of those three decades there was no apparent growth. The absence of growth during 1891-1901 can be attributed to the severe famines occurring during that decade. The failure to grow from 1911 to 1921 resulted from the great influenza pandemic of 1918-1919, which was especially severe in India.

[1] Excluding the population of Jammu-Kashmir and the tribal areas of Assam. When estimates for these areas are added the total is about 362 million.

[2] Urban percentage calculated from United Nations, Population Division, *Demographic Yearbook, 1952*, Table 6.

[3] No very meaningful comparison can be made in terms of density per unit of "agricultural land," because the category of meadow or pasture land, substantial in Europe, is of relatively little significance in Indian statistics.

29

In the three decades 1921-1951, the population grew by some 44 per cent or over 1 per cent per annum (Table 1). During these 30 years, there were no extraordinarily severe epidemics or famines.

TABLE 1. POPULATION WITHIN THE PRESENT
BOUNDARIES OF INDIA, 1891–1951

| Census Year | Millions |
|---|---|
| 1891 | 235.9 |
| 1901 | 235.5 |
| 1911 | 249.0 |
| 1921 | 248.1 |
| 1931 | 275.5 |
| 1941 | 312.8 |
| 1951 | 356.9 |

Source: Census of India, 1951, Part I-A, *Report*, p. 122.

BIRTH AND DEATH RATES IN INDIA FROM 1891 TO THE PRESENT

The registration of births and deaths in India is so seriously incomplete that almost no reliance can be placed on the registered figures. The best available evidence concerning the level of deaths for all of India is to be found in the series of decennial censuses. If the Indian censuses gave an accurate count of population by age and sex, it would be possible (since, except for Partition and its aftermath, international migration has been a negligible factor in the growth of Indian population) to make quite accurate estimates of average birth and death rates for each intercensal decade. Unfortunately, the Indian censuses have been subject to extensive misreporting of age, as might be expected when only a small minority of the population is literate. By the use of census data Kingsley Davis has estimated average birth and death rates for the six decades prior to 1941. His estimates for the decades 1891-1941 are reproduced in Table 2. S. P. Jain, the Indian census actuary, computed birth and death rates for post-partition India by means of a comparison of the 1941 and 1951 censuses. His estimate of the birth rate was 39.9 per thousand for this decade, and of the death rate 27.4 per thousand. These rates represent a substantial decline from those estimated by Kingsley Davis for the preceding decades.[4]

[4] Census of India, Paper No. 6, 1954, "Estimation of Birth and Death Rates in India during 1941-1950—1951 Census."

TABLE 2. AVERAGE ANNUAL BIRTH AND DEATH RATES IN
INDIA, BY INTERCENSAL DECADES, 1891-1941

| Decade | Births per 1,000 Population | Deaths per 1,000 Population |
|---|---|---|
| 1881–1891 | 48.9 | 41.3 |
| 1891–1901 | 45.8 | 44.4 |
| 1901–1911 | 49.2 | 42.6 |
| 1911–1921 | 48.1 | 47.2 |
| 1921–1931 | 46.4 | 36.3 |
| 1931–1941 | 45.2 | 31.2 |

Source: Kingsley Davis, *The Population of India and Pakistan*, p. 85.

However, the basis of estimation was not precisely the same, and
much of the apparent decline in the birth rate in the decade 1941-
1951 can be attributed to the use of a different method of computa-
tion. We shall present evidence later strongly supporting the view
that there have been no more than minor declines in India's birth
rate up to 1951. If the view that the declines in the birth rate until
1951 were minor is accepted provisionally, it appears that the course
of the birth and death rates in India between 1891 and 1951 conforms closely to the course that the theory of the demographic
transition ascribes to a country in the incipient stages of economic
development. Between 1891 and 1921 a high and nearly constant
level of fertility was combined with relatively high but fluctuating
death rates,[5] the death rates fluctuating in response to famines induced by crop failures and to the incidence of major epidemics. The
result was a very slight rise in population over the interval 1891
to 1921. After 1921 a relatively high and constant level of fertility
has apparently been associated with a level of mortality which,
while high by Western standards, has not been subject to sudden
and violent rises due to epidemics and famines. The absence of
major calamities of this sort since 1921 has produced a growth rate
that has exceeded 10 per cent in each intercensal decade.

THE INDIAN AGE DISTRIBUTION

Persistent high levels of fertility in India have produced an age
distribution that has remained relatively constant. The details of

[5] "Fertility" is a term relating to the reproductive performance of women of
childbearing ages. Fertility rates are births per 1,000 women of childbearing age;

the age distribution are obscured by gross inaccuracies in age reporting, but the general form is clearly a broad-based pyramid that tapers rapidly with age. According to the census figures the fraction of the population under 15 varied between 38.4 per cent and 39.3 per cent in the interval 1891-1921, and was 38.3 per cent in 1951.[6]

The major reason for the constancy of the age distribution is the stability of the level of fertility. It has been shown elsewhere that variations in mortality conditions tend to have their most pronounced effect on the growth rate of a population and to have only minor effects on the age distribution of the population.[7] The principal determinant of the age distribution of a population is the course of fertility.[8]

To summarize, the following are especially noteworthy characteristics of the Indian population in 1951:

The number of persons (about 357 million in 1951 and about 384 million in 1956) is the second largest among the national populations of the world. The density of the population is very much larger than in any of the other countries with very extensive land areas—Russia, China, the United States, Canada, Australia and Brazil. Indeed, the density is substantially higher than in non-Russian Europe. The density of the population dependent upon agriculture is particularly large by European standards. The growth rate for the thirty years prior to 1951 had averaged about 1¼ per cent per annum in contrast to the three decades preceding 1921, in which famines and epidemics kept the number of persons almost stationary. Birth rates in India have apparently been subject to only

---

birth rates are births per 1,000 total population. The two may change in different degree because of changes in the composition of the population.

[6] The fraction originally reporting an age under 15 in the 1931 and 1941 censuses is not available because the only figures published had been processed to reduce the effects of erroneous age reporting. However, the processed figures for 1931 and 1941 show a proportion under 15 very nearly the same as the proportion under 15 for 1951 when the 1951 census figures are subjected to a similar adjustment. In short, the range 38.3 to 39.3 would include the per cent of the population under age 15 reported in every census from 1891 to 1951 in India if unprocessed data had been published in every case.

[7] A. J. Coale, "The Effects of Changes in Mortality and Fertility on Age Composition." *The Milbank Memorial Fund Quarterly*, Vol. XXXIV, No. 1 (January 1956), pp. 79-114. Earlier work by Lotka, Lorimer, Sauvy, and the Population Division of the United Nations, anticipating many of the conclusions in this article, are cited there.

[8] These statements apply, of course, only to a population not subject to gains or losses by migration nor to the special effects of heavy military casualties.

slight fluctuations and to at most a minor downward trend. According to our estimates, the birth rate just prior to 1951 was about 43 per thousand population. The crude death rate in India since 1921 has averaged in the low 30's. The expectation of life at birth in India has remained very low: about 32 years in the decade 1941-1951.[9] The age distribution of the Indian population has the general form that is the inevitable result of a continuing level of high fertility in a closed population. Something of the order of 40 per cent of the population is under age 15, a little less than 60 per cent is between 15 and 64, and a small fraction—2 per cent to 3 per cent—is 65 and over. Proportions of this general magnitude have characterized the population since 1891. Chart 1 shows our estimate of the 1951 age distribution in India adjusted for misreporting of age.

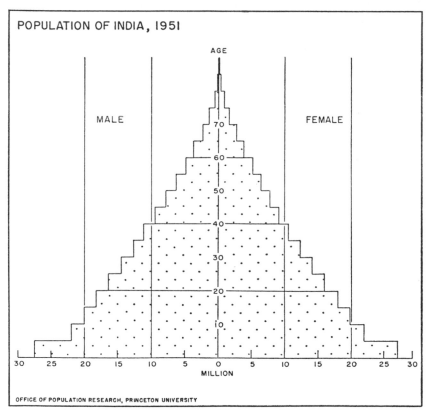

Chart 1. Population Distributed by Age and Sex, India, 1951.

[9] According both to the official Indian life table, and to a life table we constructed by quite different techniques.

33

PROSPECTIVE CHANGES IN INDIAN POPULATION
DURING THE NEXT THIRTY YEARS

We have prepared a set of estimates of the Indian population and its division by age and sex from 1956 through 1986. The results of these projections are shown in Tables 3 through 6 and Charts 2 through 4. The projections are based on our *estimate of the most likely course of mortality* and *alternative assumptions about the course of fertility*.

There is every reason to expect a pronounced and rapid decline in mortality in the next two or three decades. According to our estimates, the crude death rate has already declined from a level of about 31 per thousand in 1951 to about 25½ per thousand in 1956, and will be as low as 21 by 1966 and 15 by about 1975. The evidence behind these estimates will be described in a later chapter. We estimate that the expectation of life at birth, which was about 32 years in 1951, will rise to 52 years or more by 1986.[10]

The alternative assumptions about fertility upon which the projections are based are as follows: First (as an upper limit), that fertility will remain unchanged from 1951 to 1986. Second (as a lower limit), that fertility remains unchanged until 1956, and then begins a linear decline to half its current value by 1981, after which it remains constant. Third, that the decline in fertility is postponed until 1966, at which time a more precipitous linear decline is assumed, again reaching one-half the current level by 1981.

Chart 2 shows our three projected populations in conjunction with the census records of population growth until 1951. Note that the projection based on an assumed unchanging fertility produces an accelerated growth rate and a population rising by 1986 to more than double the 1956 population. On the other hand the assumption of an extensive drop in fertility, beginning in 1956, yields a 1986 population only 53 per cent larger than the 1956 population. Under this latter assumption, the growth in population between 1956 and 1986 is not very much faster than the recorded growth between 1921 and 1951 (53 per cent compared to 44 per cent). The intermediate projection shows that a belated fertility decline, even

10 As Table 6 shows, the crude death rate is different in the later years under different assumptions about fertility, although the expectations of life are the same. The difference in crude death rates arises because the different assumptions about fertility produce different age distributions.

TABLE 3. PROJECTED POPULATION OF INDIA, 1951–1986, BY
FIVE-YEAR AGE GROUPS FOR EACH SEX
(Fertility assumed unchanged)
(thousands)

| ex and Age | 1951 | 1956 | 1961 | 1966 | 1971 | 1976 | 1981 | 1986 |
|---|---|---|---|---|---|---|---|---|
| Males | | | | | | | | |
| 0–4 | 27,500 | 30,200 | 34,500 | 38,900 | 43,700 | 49,900 | 57,700 | 66,300 |
| 5–9 | 22,000 | 23,800 | 27,000 | 31,400 | 35,800 | 40,600 | 46,800 | 54,300 |
| 10–14 | 20,000 | 21,300 | 23,100 | 26,300 | 30,600 | 35,000 | 39,700 | 45,700 |
| 15–19 | 18,200 | 19,400 | 20,800 | 22,600 | 25,800 | 30,100 | 34,400 | 39,000 |
| 20–24 | 16,400 | 17,500 | 18,700 | 20,100 | 22,000 | 25,100 | 29,300 | 33,500 |
| 25–29 | 14,500 | 15,500 | 16,700 | 18,100 | 19,500 | 21,400 | 24,400 | 28,500 |
| 30–34 | 12,800 | 13,700 | 14,800 | 16,100 | 17,500 | 18,900 | 20,700 | 23,700 |
| 35–39 | 11,100 | 11,900 | 12,900 | 14,100 | 15,500 | 16,900 | 18,300 | 20,000 |
| 40–44 | 9,430 | 10,100 | 11,100 | 12,300 | 13,500 | 14,900 | 16,200 | 17,600 |
| 45–49 | 7,870 | 8,470 | 9,330 | 10,400 | 11,600 | 12,900 | 14,200 | 15,500 |
| 50–54 | 6,360 | 6,870 | 7,610 | 8,570 | 9,660 | 10,900 | 12,100 | 13,300 |
| 55–59 | 4,940 | 5,340 | 5,970 | 6,790 | 7,750 | 8,800 | 9,890 | 11,000 |
| 60–64 | 3,610 | 3,920 | 4,440 | 5,110 | 5,900 | 6,790 | 7,710 | 8,670 |
| 65–69 | 2,430 | 2,650 | 3,040 | 3,560 | 4,180 | 4,870 | 5,610 | 6,370 |
| 70–74 | 1,420 | 1,570 | 1,840 | 2,210 | 2,650 | 3,150 | 3,680 | 4,230 |
| 75–79 | 660 | 739 | 901 | 1,130 | 1,390 | 1,690 | 2,010 | 2,350 |
| 80–84 | 207 | 231 | 283 | 361 | 460 | 574 | 699 | 831 |
| 85–89 | 32.6 | 33.5 | 35.2 | 41.2 | 52.4 | 66.6 | 83.0 | 101 |
| Total Males | 179,000 | 193,000 | 213,000 | 238,000 | 268,000 | 303,000 | 343,000 | 391,000 |
| Females | | | | | | | | |
| 0–4 | 27,100 | 29,800 | 33,800 | 38,100 | 42,700 | 48,600 | 56,100 | 64,500 |
| 5–9 | 22,000 | 23,700 | 26,900 | 31,100 | 35,400 | 40,000 | 46,000 | 53,300 |
| 10–14 | 19,900 | 21,200 | 23,100 | 26,200 | 30,400 | 34,700 | 39,200 | 45,000 |
| 15–19 | 18,000 | 19,200 | 20,700 | 22,600 | 25,800 | 29,900 | 34,100 | 38,600 |
| 20–24 | 16,000 | 17,100 | 18,400 | 20,000 | 21,900 | 25,000 | 29,100 | 33,100 |
| 25–29 | 14,100 | 15,000 | 16,200 | 17,700 | 19,200 | 21,100 | 24,200 | 28,100 |
| 30–34 | 12,300 | 13,100 | 14,200 | 15,500 | 17,000 | 18,500 | 20,400 | 23,300 |
| 35–39 | 10,600 | 11,400 | 12,400 | 13,500 | 14,900 | 16,300 | 17,800 | 19,600 |
| 40–44 | 9,140 | 9,810 | 10,700 | 11,800 | 13,000 | 14,300 | 15,700 | 17,100 |
| 45–49 | 7,740 | 8,320 | 9,100 | 10,100 | 11,200 | 12,400 | 13,600 | 14,900 |
| 50–54 | 6,410 | 6,890 | 7,580 | 8,440 | 9,430 | 10,500 | 11,600 | 12,800 |
| 55–59 | 5,100 | 5,500 | 6,100 | 6,850 | 7,720 | 8,680 | 9,680 | 10,700 |
| 60–64 | 3,840 | 4,160 | 4,660 | 5,300 | 6,050 | 6,880 | 7,730 | 8,620 |
| 65–69 | 2,650 | 2,890 | 3,290 | 3,820 | 4,430 | 5,100 | 5,800 | 6,520 |
| 70–74 | 1,580 | 1,750 | 2,050 | 2,450 | 2,920 | 3,420 | 3,940 | 4,480 |
| 75–79 | 736 | 831 | 1,030 | 1,290 | 1,590 | 1,920 | 2,250 | 2,600 |
| 80–84 | 232 | 262 | 325 | 421 | 541 | 674 | 813 | 955 |
| 85–89 | 40.4 | 41.0 | 41.8 | 48.5 | 61.7 | 78.9 | 98.5 | 119 |
| Total Females | 177,000 | 191,000 | 211,000 | 235,000 | 264,000 | 298,000 | 338,000 | 384,000 |
| Grand Total | 357,000 | 384,000 | 424,000 | 473,000 | 532,000 | 601,000 | 682,000 | 775,000 |

TABLE 4. PROJECTED POPULATION OF INDIA, 1961–1986, BY
FIVE-YEAR AGE GROUPS FOR EACH SEX[a]
(Fertility assumed to decline linearly by a total of 50 per cent
between 1956 and 1981)
(thousands)

| Sex and Age | 1961 | 1966 | 1971 | 1976 | 1981 | 1986 |
|---|---|---|---|---|---|---|
| **Males** | | | | | | |
| 0–4 | 32,700 | 33,000 | 32,700 | 32,100 | 30,600 | 30,400 |
| 5–9 | – | 29,700 | 30,400 | 30,400 | 30,100 | 28,800 |
| 10–14 | – | – | 29,000 | 29,700 | 29,700 | 29,400 |
| 15–19 | – | – | – | 28,500 | 29,100 | 29,100 |
| 20–24 | – | – | – | – | 27,800 | 28,400 |
| 25–29 | – | – | – | – | – | 27,000 |
| Total | | | | | | |
| Males | 211,000 | 231,000 | 250,000 | 268,000 | 283,000 | 297,000 |
| **Females** | | | | | | |
| 0–4 | 32,100 | 32,300 | 31,900 | 31,300 | 29,700 | 29,500 |
| 5–9 | – | 29,500 | 30,000 | 29,900 | 29,600 | 28,200 |
| 10–14 | – | – | 28,900 | 29,400 | 29,300 | 29,000 |
| 15–19 | – | – | – | 28,400 | 28,900 | 28,800 |
| 20–24 | – | – | – | – | 27,600 | 28,100 |
| 25–29 | – | – | – | – | – | 26,600 |
| Total | | | | | | |
| Females | 209,000 | 228,000 | 246,000 | 264,000 | 279,000 | 292,000 |
| Grand | | | | | | |
| Total | 420,000 | 458,000 | 496,000 | 531,000 | 562,000 | 589,000 |

[a] Numbers not shown are identical with those in Table 3.

though it is more rapid and "makes up for lost time" in reaching a
low level, produces a much greater population total than does an
earlier and more gradual drop in fertility.

The differences between the populations produced by unchanged
fertility and by declining fertility are greater than a mere examination of the population totals or of the crude birth and death rates
would indicate. A more careful look at the alternative projections
brings out two further differences of the greatest importance.

The first difference is in age distribution. A lower level of fertility
produces fewer children each year, thus having the immediate effect
of reducing the broad base of the age pyramid; i.e., reducing the
fraction of the population at the younger ages. The corollary effect
is, of course, to increase the fraction at the older ages. Declines in

36

## TABLE 5. PROJECTED POPULATION OF INDIA, 1971–1986, BY FIVE-YEAR AGE GROUPS FOR EACH SEX[a]

(Fertility assumed to decline linearly by a total of 50 per cent between 1966 and 1981)

(thousands)

| Sex and Age | 1971 | 1976 | 1981 | 1986 |
|---|---|---|---|---|
| Males | | | | |
| 0–4 | 39,900 | 37,200 | 33,400 | 32,800 |
| 5–9 | – | 37,100 | 34,900 | 31,400 |
| 10–14 | – | – | 36,200 | 34,100 |
| 15–19 | – | – | – | 35,600 |
| Total Males | 264,000 | 286,000 | 304,000 | 319,000 |
| Females | | | | |
| 0–4 | 39,000 | 36,200 | 32,400 | 31,900 |
| 5–9 | – | 36,500 | 34,300 | 30,800 |
| 10–14 | – | – | 35,800 | 33,600 |
| 15–19 | – | – | – | 35,200 |
| Total Females | 260,000 | 282,000 | 299,000 | 314,000 |
| Grand Total | 524,000 | 569,000 | 603,000 | 634,000 |

[a] Numbers not shown are identical with those in Table 3.

mortality alone would tend to raise slightly the fraction in the childhood ages and in the ages over 65, and to lower somewhat the fraction of the population between the ages of 15 and 64. However, the changes in age distribution in the absence of any change in fertility are not very large. The fraction under age 15 could be expected to rise from something like 39 per cent to approximately 42 per cent, and the fraction over 65 to rise from slightly less than 3 per cent to something well under 4 per cent. With respect to dependents at young and old ages which must be supported by a population in the working ages, it can be stated that improvements in mortality with no changes in fertility tend to increase the burden of dependency somewhat, but to a relatively minor degree. On the other hand, if fertility were to decline to half its current values by 1981, the resultant decline in the number of children under 15 would reduce their proportion from about 39 per cent in 1956 to less than

37

TABLE 6. VARIOUS MEASURES OF VITAL RATES FOR PROJECTED
POPULATION OF INDIA, 1951–1986

| | 1951 | 1956 | 1961 | 1966 | 1971 | 1976 | 1981 | 1986 |
|---|---|---|---|---|---|---|---|---|
| Expectation of life (years) | | | | | | | | |
| Males | | | | | | | | |
| At birth | 31.5 | 37.1 | 42.6 | 45.5 | 48.5 | 50.0 | 51.5 | 51.5 |
| At age 10 | 41.4 | 44.9 | 48.4 | 50.3 | 52.2 | 52.2 | 52.2 | 52.2 |
| At age 50 | 15.7 | 17.4 | 19.2 | 20.0 | 20.9 | 20.9 | 20.9 | 20.9 |
| Females | | | | | | | | |
| At birth | 32.8 | 38.5 | 44.2 | 47.3 | 50.3 | 51.7 | 53.1 | 53.1 |
| At age 10 | 41.2 | 44.8 | 48.4 | 50.4 | 52.4 | 52.4 | 52.4 | 52.4 |
| At age 50 | 16.6 | 18.3 | 20.0 | 20.8 | 21.7 | 21.7 | 21.7 | 21.7 |
| Birth Rate (per 1,000 population) | | | | | | | | |
| Fertility un- changed | 43.2 | 42.8 | 41.9 | 40.9 | 40.2 | 40.0 | 40.0 | 40.0 |
| Fertility decl. by 50% from 1966–1981 | 43.2 | 42.8 | 41.9 | 40.9 | 34.0 | 28.2 | 22.6 | 24.0 |
| Fertility decl. by 50% from 1956–1981 | 43.2 | 42.8 | 38.0 | 33.8 | 30.2 | 26.8 | 23.0 | 23.4 |
| Death Rate (per 1,000 population) | | | | | | | | |
| Fertility un- changed | 31.0 | 25.6 | 21.0 | 18.1 | 16.3 | 15.2 | 14.6 | 14.3 |
| Fertility decl. by 50% from 1966–1981 | 31.0 | 25.6 | 21.0 | 18.1 | 15.7 | 14.2 | 11.7 | 13.9 |
| Fertility decl. by 50% from 1956–1981 | 31.0 | 25.6 | 20.4 | 17.1 | 15.4 | 14.4 | 12.8 | 14.3 |

30 in 1986, while the fraction between 15 and 64 would rise from
about 58 to about 65 per cent.

The second major difference between the projections based on
unchanged and on declining fertility that is not immediately apparent is that after thirty years the difference between the high- and
low-fertility populations promises to widen rapidly. In other words,

38

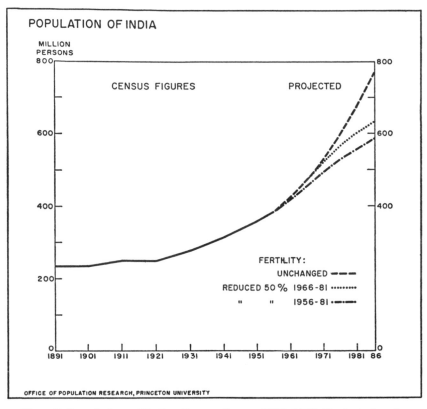

Chart 2. Population of India. Census figures 1891-1951, Projected under Various Assumptions to 1986.

the population in which fertility has not declined would have *built-in prospects for further rapid growth*, while the population which has experienced a declining fertility would look forward to a declining rate of increase even if fertility itself did not decrease further. There are two important reasons why the gap between the high- and low-fertility populations could be expected to widen further after 1986. The first reason is simply the difference in fertility itself. A change in fertility takes time. The assumption of unchanging fertility until 1986 implies that an appreciable interval after 1986 would be needed to bring fertility to low levels. The second built-in difference is the difference in age distribution. The number of parents in the population with fertility reduced prior to 1986 would increase in the years after 1986 slowly (if at all),

39

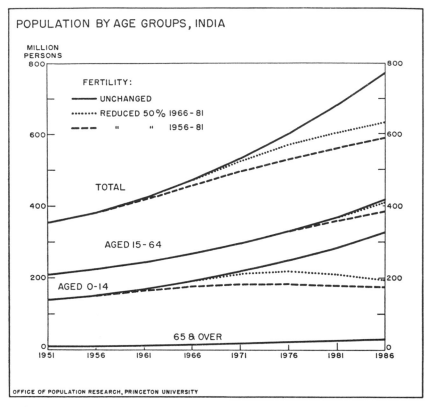

Chart 3. Distribution of Projected Total Population by Broad Age Groups under Various Assumptions, India, 1951-1986.

while the number of parents in the case where fertility had remained constant would continue to swell rapidly for twenty-five or thirty years more.

The growth of population according to our projections is much more rapid than in other estimates of India's future population. As Table 7 shows, the population we project for 1971, 1976, and 1981, even under the assumption of a pronounced decline in fertility, exceeds official population estimates by scores of millions. The reason for this difference is that the estimates published in India assume slight and nearly equal declines in birth and death rates (and hence a continuation of recent growth rates), while our projections are based on a rapid decline in mortality. The drop that we expect in mortality would produce a temporary increase in

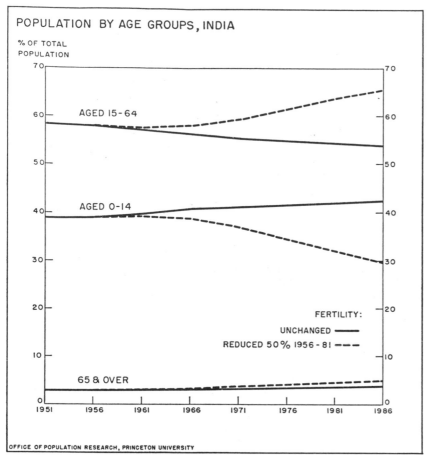

Chart 4. Per Cent Distribution of Population by Broad Age Groups under
Various Assumptions, India, 1951-1986.

growth rate even if fertility declined 2 per cent of its present value
each year from 1956 to 1981. By 1981 the growth rate with reduced fertility would be lower than the present rate, but in the
meantime the growth would have greatly exceeded the mere continuation of the 1941-1951 average annual per cent increase. The
basis for believing that the prospective course of mortality is a
rapid decline is described in Chapter VI. To state the basis most
succinctly: We believe mortality will decline rapidly because where-
ever (in low-income areas within or outside of India) the health
measures of the sort India is undertaking have been applied, death

41

TABLE 7. PROJECTED POPULATION OF INDIA, 1961–1981
ACCORDING TO OFFICIAL INDIAN FIGURES, AND
TO THE OFFICE OF POPULATION RESEARCH
(Estimated population)
(millions)

| Source of Estimates | 1961 | 1971 | 1976 | 1981 |
|---|---|---|---|---|
| Census of India, 1951, Part I-A, *Report*[a] | 407 | 464 | – | 529 |
| Planning Commission, *Second Five-Year Plan*[b] | 401 | 459 | 494 | 529 |
| Office of Population Research Fertility declining by 50%, 1956–1981 | 420 | 496 | 531 | 562 |
| Fertility unchanged | 424 | 532 | 601 | 682 |

[a] These figures are adjusted for a slight difference of coverage in 1951. They are the "upper-limit" estimates based on a continuation of 1941–1951 growth rates.

[b] From a private communication received from the Planning Commission adjusted for difference in coverage. These projections are based on the following assumptions: "the quinary age group survival probabilities for quinquennial intervals were assumed to improve progressively at a uniform rate of about .5 per cent (.489 per cent with minor adjustments) in each quinquennium over the preceding quinquennium. Progressive improvement of about 1 per cent (.958 per cent to be precise) in the probability of surviving the first year of life was assumed in each quinquennium." "The general fertility rate defined as the ratio of total births during a year to the mean female population in childbearing ages 15-44 is assumed to decline from an initial level of .188 (corresponding to a crude birth rate of 41.2 per thousand) in 1951 to .160 in 1976." The crude birth rate in the Planning Commission projection declines from 41.3 to 35.7, while the death rate declines from 30.5 to 21.8 between 1951 and 1981. However, the growth rate in 1951–1961 is assumed to be the same as in 1941–1951.

rates have dropped. Our estimates may understate or overstate the rapidity of declining death rates, but there can be little doubt that a substantial drop below pre-1951 experience is to be expected. It seems clear that Indian expectations and plans for the future are based on unrealistically small estimates of population growth.

42

CHAPTER V

◇◇◇◇◇◇◇◇◇◇◇◇◇◇◇◇◇◇◇◇◇◇◇◇◇◇◇◇◇◇◇◇◇◇◇◇◇◇◇◇◇◇◇◇◇◇◇◇◇◇◇◇◇

# RECENT INDIAN MORTALITY
# AND FERTILITY TRENDS

◇◇◇◇◇◇◇◇◇◇◇◇◇◇◇◇◇◇◇◇◇◇◇◇◇◇◇◇◇◇◇◇◇◇◇◇◇◇◇◇◇◇◇◇◇◇◇◇◇◇◇◇◇

IN THE PRECEDING chapter, the course of population growth and the general trends of its principal determinants (birth and death rates) were briefly summarized. We presented a set of alternative projected population trends in India over the next thirty years. In this chapter the basis for the estimates of birth and death rates in the recent past will be explained in more detail.

Recent mortality and fertility trends must be estimated because the usual direct record (registered births and deaths) is not of a calibre to serve as a reliable indicator of mortality and fertility. Moreover, different interpretations of the decennial censuses and of other evidence with respect to vital rates are possible; and our conclusions are somewhat different from those published by the Census of India. It is our belief, contrary to the most widely published estimates, that the birth and fertility rates in India have *not* declined to any important degree in recent years. We also believe that recent infant mortality rates are very much higher than registered rates, and somewhat above the middle estimates employed in the Indian Life Tables, 1941-1951.

Table 8 shows a comparison of our estimates of various measures of vital rates for the period preceding the 1951 census with official figures for the decade 1941-1950 and average rates for the period 1921-1950. We shall in this chapter give the reasons that led to estimates somewhat at variance with the official ones.

The official estimates of death rates by age and of average intercensal birth rates are derived by means of comparisons of consecutive decennial censuses.[1] The estimation of mortality rates by age (and of the general level of both mortality and fertility) through a comparison of successive censuses depends on a simple

[1] Census of India, Paper No. 6, 1954, "Estimation of Birth and Death Rates in India during 1941-1950—1951 Census," and Paper No. 2, 1954, "Life Tables—1951 Census."

43

## TABLE 8. ESTIMATES OF VARIOUS VITAL MEASURES IN INDIA FOR YEARS PRIOR TO 1951

|  | Office of Population Research estimate, pre-1951 | Indian Census estimate, 1941–1950 | Average for 1921–1950 from official sources and Kingsley Davis |
|---|---|---|---|
| Birth Rate (per 1,000 population) | 43.1 | 39.9 | 43.8 |
| Death Rate (per 1,000 population) | 30.9 | 27.4 | 31.6 |
| Growth Rate (per 1,000 population) | 12.2 | 12.5 | 12.2 |
| Expectation of life at birth (years) | 32.2 | 32.5 | 30.5 |
| Proportion dying in first year of life (per 1,000 live births) | 225 | 183 | 211 |

Sources: Office of Population Research, unpublished material. Census of India, Paper No. 2, 1954, "Life Tables—1951 Census." Census of India, Paper No. 6, 1954, "Estimation of Birth and Death Rates." Kingsley Davis, *The Population of India and Pakistan*, United Nations, *Demographic Yearbook, 1953*, Table 17.

principle: Where migration is negligible, the difference between any age group and the same group ten years older in the census taken ten years later equals the number of deaths experienced during the decade by the original members of the group. Computations based on this fact enable actuaries to estimate the approximate risk of dying at each age according to the average experience during the intercensal period—in other words, to construct a life table. Once mortality risks by age are estimated, the crude death rate for an intercensal decade is readily calculated. Then the fact that the average *birth* rate, less the average *death* rate, equals the average intercensal *growth* rate makes it easy to calculate the birth rate and to derive the average fertility rates of women of childbearing ages.

Unfortunately, the age reporting in Indian censuses is clearly faulty to a degree that precludes precise estimates of death rates by age through differencing consecutive censuses. The census data are always "smoothed" in an attempt to correct for errors in age reporting before two censuses are compared. The defect is particularly serious with respect to estimating death rates among infants and young children—where the problems of estimation are most

44

difficult, where death rates are known to be high, and where enumeration is especially bad. Because of the difficulties inherent in estimating death rates by taking differences between figures from censuses adjusted for faulty age reporting, we have looked for an alternative method. Our estimates of death rates by age and of the general level of fertility have been based on a wholly different technique we have developed for the purpose.

The technique is based on the following four elements: (1) the general similarity of age distribution in Indian censuses since 1891, and the especially closely repeated age pattern in 1931 and in 1951,[2] (2) the relatively constant growth rate of the Indian population from 1921 to 1951, (3) the relationships (formulated mostly by Alfred J. Lotka) among fertility rates, age-specific mortality rates, growth rate, and the age distribution in a stable population, (4) the close relation between the age-pattern of mortality, on the one hand, and the general level of mortality above age 10, on the other—observable in the mortality experience of a large number of different areas with relatively high death rates.

On the basis of these elements it is possible to estimate: (1) a life table (or death rates by age) for a period preceding 1951; (2) a birth rate and the general level of fertility for the same period; (3) a distribution of the population in 1951 by age and sex that is corrected for mistaken age reporting, is consistent with a plausible sex ratio at birth, and is also consistent with the observed stability from census to census in age distribution and growth rate.

The complicated procedure by which these estimates are made is described fully in Appendix A. We have already shown (Table 6) some of the measures of vital statistics that this procedure produces. Life tables for 1951 are reproduced in Appendix A. Chart 5 shows three age distributions in 1951 by five-year age groups of males and females: the unsmoothed figures from the census, the figures as smoothed by the Indian Census Actuary, and the figures as estimated by stable-population techniques.

We turn now to the evidence that leads us to conclusions different from official estimates: namely, our belief that fertility declines have

---

[2] The age distribution for only a few provinces is available from the 1941 census, which, on account of the war, was never fully tabulated. The structure of the age distribution in 1941 is very similar to the 1931 and 1951 censuses in those provinces for which tabulations were made. The principal differences in pattern were apparently a greater misreporting of age in 1941.

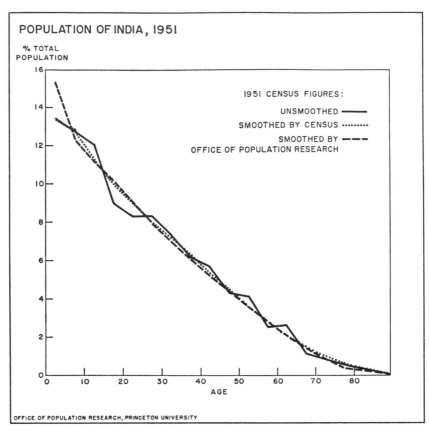

Chart 5. Per Cent Distribution of Population by Five-Year
Age Groups, 1951.

been nonexistent or only moderate, and that infant mortality rates prior to 1951 were above 200.

The ultimate basis of almost all sound estimates of Indian vital rates is the series of decennial censuses. Had there been a substantial decline in fertility in the period preceding 1951 as compared to the period preceding 1931, there should have been a changed relationship between the number of young children on the one hand and the rest of the population (especially women in child-bearing ages) on the other. The fact is that the ratio of the number of children under 4 to the total population rose from 10.6 to 10.9 per cent between the 1931 and the 1951 census, while the ratio of female children under 4 to females 17 to 43 rose from 27 to 28 per cent. This slight rise in the proportion of young children in the population is the sort of change that accompanies a moderate decline in infant mortality. In fact, these ratios are also consistent with a fairly substantial decline in infant mortality offset by a slight drop in fertility rates. Thus one of the possibilities is that the birth rate may have fallen moderately (from 46 to 43, perhaps) while the infant mortality rate fell from (let us say) 275 to 220. These changes happening concurrently would not perceptibly affect either the age distribution or the growth rate. However, a really large drop in fertility must produce a noticeable change in the age distribution, and the indisputable fact is that the age distribution in 1951 (aside from changes in detail apparently due to improvements in age reporting) is very nearly identical with the age distribution of the 1931 census.

There is another set of reasons, rather negative in character, but nevertheless quite compelling, for doubting that fertility levels in India have been subject to any major decline. There is no evidence of changes in Indian customs or social structure in the decade before 1951 that would have led to a major drop in fertility. No competent observer believes, for example, that the rural population (which is still 83 per cent of the total) took up birth control to an appreciable degree during this decade. Moreover, the incipient stages of a decline in fertility almost inevitably involve the development of markedly lower fertility among special large segments of the population. In other words, the low-fertility pattern would naturally appear first among special groups rather than simultaneously throughout the whole society. Indeed, it must be conceded that in India today low fertility has become established among very small groups of urban, highly educated people, constituting, however, a negligible fraction of the population. Most of the available evidence casts doubt on the existence of consequential differentials in the fertility of numerically important groups. According to the 1951 census, in Travancore-Cochin the number of children ever born to women 45 and over who are still married was 6.6 among the rural population and 6.4 among the urban population. In eastern Madhya Pradesh the number of children ever born to still married women over 45 was 6.1 for the rural population and 6.3 for the urban. In other regions of Madhya Pradesh, the corresponding figures were 6.6 for rural and 6.4 for urban, and in another instance 6.2 for rural and 6.7 for urban. According to a survey conducted under the joint auspices of the United Nations and the Government of India in Mysore State, the number of children ever born to still married women over 45 was 5.8 for rural areas and 5.9 for Bangalore city.[3] Studies of differential fertility by caste or by various indices of socio-economic status show only small differences in marital fertility. The National Sample Survey has tabulated the results of a question on fertility from the second and fourth rounds of the Survey. A total of about 34,000 rural couples and 6,000 urban couples throughout India were questioned. The number of children born to couples at various durations of marriage up to 12 years shows no important differentials according to the following classifications: rural-urban, possession of land in rural areas, or caste.[4] The completed size of family for ever-married women will sometimes be higher for groups of higher status. The smaller completed families among the lower status groups can be explained by the higher incidence of widowhood caused by higher death rates. Kingsley Davis found insignificant differentials by caste and occupation in the 1931 census.[5] The 1951 census maternity data on Travancore-Cochin and Madhya Pradesh show no important differences in the completed size of family among agricultural laborers and tenants, agricultural land owners, and nonagricultural families. In Bangalore, Chandrasekharan found completed size of family for unbroken marriages up to the age of 45 to be 6 or higher for illiterate, primary school and middle school women, 5 for women with a high school education, and 2 for women with college or university education. However, the number of women with high school or university education is too small to have any measurable effect on the all-India fertility levels.

A development in India which is often cited as a possible explanation of the alleged decline of fertility is rising age at marriage. Calculations of age at marriage from census figures (derived from data on the percentages of single women) indicate a rise from

[3] See Census of India, Paper No. 5, 1953, "Maternity Data—1951 Census"; and C. Chandrasekharan, "Economic and Social Factors Affecting Fertility in Mysore State," a paper presented to the Annual Meeting of the Population Association of America, May 1954.

[4] The National Sample Survey, No. 7, *Couple Fertility*, Government of India, Ministry of Finance, December 1955.

[5] Kingsley Davis, *The Population of India and Pakistan*, pp. 70-82.

13.6 to 15.4 years in the average age at marriage of Indian women between 1921 and 1951. The National Sample Survey has estimated age at marriage on the basis of questions asked of a national sample of married couples. For rural India their estimates show a rise in average age at marriage for women from 13.6 in 1920-1929 to 14.6 in 1946-1951.[6] Thus the age at marriage will need to rise considerably more than it had by 1951 before fertility rates are appreciably affected.[7]

There are several special rural health units where the vital statistics are much more reliable than in the rest of India; and the birth rates recorded in these units support, in two ways, estimates of the Indian birth rate above 40 per thousand. In the first place, these rates themselves are typically above 40 per thousand. The crude birth rate for the years 1945 through 1950 in the Sirur Health Unit in Bombay State was 44; the crude birth rate in Singur Health Unit outside Calcutta shows an apparent rising trend reaching 41 in the last two recorded years of 1953 and 1954. The apparent rising trend in Singur is almost certainly due to improvements in registration, and it seems more than likely that the registration is still somewhat incomplete.[8] In Ramanagaram District in Mysore State, where there has been a vigorous effort in recent years to improve the

[6] The National Sample Survey, No. 7, *Couple Fertility*, p. 24.

[7] The calculations referred to in the text were made by S. N. Agarwala, while at the Office of Population Research. See: "The Age at Marriage in India," *Population Index*, April 1957, pp. 96-107; and *The Mean Age at Marriage in India as Ascertained from Census Data*, A Dissertation Presented to the Faculty of Princeton University in Candidacy for the Degree of Doctor of Philosophy, September 1957. In Madras State the age at marriage for women has apparently reached about 18 years, which is possibly an advanced enough age to begin to have an effect on fertility. Moreover, not all marriages take place at the mean age, and the rising average age at marriage has meant an increase in the percentage who are single above the mean age at marriage. A rough calculation using Agarwala's estimates of per cent single shows that increases since 1921 in the proportion over 15 unmarried would account for a 4 per cent reduction in the birth rate—say from 45 to 43 per thousand. Some observers believe, on the other hand, that postponing first cohabitation from 15 or 16 to 18 or 19 might have the effect of increasing the ultimate size of completed family because of the possibility that reproductive performance may be impaired by births at too early an age.

[8] The completeness of registration in Singur in 1945 and 1946 was checked by a survey. The estimated true value of the birth rate for the two years was 53 per thousand, while the registered rate was only about 35. Registration was about 67 per cent complete. Even the recently registered rates over 40 may be well short of reality. Chandra Sekar, C., and Deming W. Edwards, "On a Method of Estimating Birth and Death Rates and the Extent of Registration," *Journal of the American Statistical Association*, Vol. 44 (1949), pp. 101-115.

completeness of birth reporting, the recorded birth rate has been at least 40 in every year since 1950 and was 42 or higher in the three years ending in 1954. The second way in which the data from these health units support the view that the all-India birth rate is above 40 is that the birth rate in each health unit is higher than the estimate made by the census for the province where the health unit is located. This fact suggests the possibility of a consistent tendency for the census estimates of the birth rate to be slightly too low for the decade 1941-1951.[9]

Our estimates differ from the official Indian figures with respect to the level of infant mortality rates as well as with respect to recent fertility trends. The registered infant mortality rates for India in the years preceding 1951 were running at a level of about 125 deaths per 1,000 live births. The registered rate is clearly an understatement. S. P. Jain, the Census Actuary, gave lower and upper bounds for the infant mortality rate of about 155 and 240 deaths per 1,000 live births and used a middle value between these bounds of about 185 in the official all-Indian life tables for the decade 1941-1950.[10]

A different estimated range of infant mortality prior to 1951 is incorporated in the life tables, crude death rates, and estimated age

[9] The fact that the Indian birth rate may be *no higher than* in the low 40's is indeed more puzzling and more in need of explanation than the fact that it appears to be above 40. Higher fertility performance is quite common where effective birth control is not practiced. There are nine areas in the world reporting a birth rate above 45 per thousand in 1953 in the United Nations *Demographic Yearbook* for 1954. The average interval between births among Indian married women is substantially longer than among women not using contraceptives in Western countries. (This is pointed out by Robert G. Potter, Jr., of the Office of Population Research, in an analysis of the design of the India-Harvard-Ludhiana Population Study.) Among the factors which keep marital fertility from being still higher, there are the following possibilities. First, poor health, which can reduce the birth rate through increased rates of stillbirths and miscarriages and, in the case of chronic fevers, such as are associated with malaria, can reduce cohabitation rates. Second, Indian family customs and modes of living which reduce cohabitation rates, in some instances enforcing complete separation of husband and wife. One of these customs is that of the return of a pregnant woman to her mother's household for the birth of her children, particularly the first and second children; the young mother typically stays at her parents' home for some time after the birth of the child and not infrequently the grandmother returns with the young mother to help care for the infant and often sleeps beside the mother during this period. Third, a factor reducing the general level of fertility, though not of marital fertility, is the custom of prohibiting the marriage of widows; widowhood is very common because of the high level of mortality rates experienced in India, and thus a rather large class of women is kept infertile.

[10] Census of India, Paper No. 2, 1954, "Life Tables—1951 Census," p. 20.

distributions presented here. The upper estimate of the infant mortality rate is 250 per 1,000 live births and the lower is 200 per 1,000 live births. The tables and figures presented in the preceding chapter were based on an intermediate value of 225. The evidence that leads to an estimate of infant mortality above 200 is of two sorts—scattered direct evidence indicating high levels of infant mortality, and indirect evidence based on observed relations among vital rates. Even the evidence referred to as "direct" does not consist of records of infant mortality rates above 200. The reason why such rates have not been observed is that accurate observations tend to be limited to relatively favored groups with lower mortality rates. For example, a survey conducted in Calcutta among middle-class women, the majority of whom were literate, yielded an infant mortality rate of 194 during the years 1938 through 1949.[11] The infant mortality rate of children born to these women is no doubt much below the average value for women of all classes in Calcutta.

The National Sample Survey tabulated results from its second and fourth rounds that yield estimates of infant mortality rates based on answers to a question about the number of children ever born and the number of these children who died in the first year of life. The apparent infant mortality rate calculated on the basis of the responses of some 35,000 couples shows the highest infant mortality for the most recent marriages. The reported infant mortality rates rise from 102 for marriages occurring before 1910 to 182 for marriages occurring in the interval 1946-1951.[12] It is a reasonable inference that the most recent marriages (and hence the most recent average date of birth) provide the most nearly accurate data. However, mortality rates—particularly infant mortality rates—determined on the basis of household surveys are notably deficient; and one would expect even the infant mortality rate of 180 obtained for the marriages during the five years preceding the survey to be a substantial understatement of the true infant mortality rate.[13]

The other more or less direct evidence in support of the high infant mortality rate is the fact that the rates in the special health units referred to earlier are all well up in the hundreds even though

[11] K. N. Mitra, et al., *Sankhya*, June 1951.
[12] The National Sample Survey, No. 7, *Couple Fertility*, p. 161.
[13] cf. United Nations, Statistical Office, Department of Economic and Social Affairs, *Handbook of Vital Statistics Methods*, Studies in Methods, Series F, No. 7, April 1955, p. 6.

the quality of the medical care available in these units is much better than what is generally available in rural India. The Sirur Health Unit in Bombay State had an infant mortality rate which averaged 190 per 1,000 live births during the interval 1941-1950. Between 1944 and 1953 the infant mortality rate in the Singur District outside of Calcutta declined, according to the recorded figures, from 168 to 104. In Ramanagaram Training Centre in Mysore State the infant mortality rate had declined from 132 in 1950 to 115 in 1954.

The indirect evidence referred to earlier that supports an estimated level of infant mortality above 200 arises from a comparison of the infant mortality rates in these regions (the special health units) with relatively good statistics, and the crude death rate in these same districts. The crude death rate had an average value of about 24 per 1,000 during the interval 1945 to 1950 in the Sirur Health Unit; in Ramanagaram from 1950 to 1954 the crude death rate averaged 14; and in Singur the crude death rate declined from a recorded figure of 21 in 1944 to a recorded figure of 10 in 1954. If a graph is constructed with a crude death rate, year by year, in these special units on one axis, and the infant mortality rate on the other, there is a clear positive relation between the two. We can hardly accept the infant mortality rates for these special health units as typical of Indian experience unless we are prepared to accept the crude death rate as typical. Since there are many convincing indications that the crude birth rate in all India is between 40 and 45 per 1,000, and since the growth rate since 1931 has been relatively constant at a level of approximately 12-13 per 1,000, the conclusion is inescapable that before 1951 the crude death rate for all India was about 30 per 1,000 or slightly higher. In short, the crude death rate for all India was obviously at a significantly higher level than the crude death rates of 12 to 24 observed in the special health units. Finally, if one draws a straight line representing the relationship between the infant mortality rates and the crude death rates in the graph where data from the special health units are plotted, he is led to associate an infant mortality rate of over 200 with a crude death rate of 30 (Chart 6).

Although our survey of all of the evidence with regard to the infant mortality rate leads to a conclusion that the rate is very likely above 200, there is an insufficient basis for arriving at a very precise

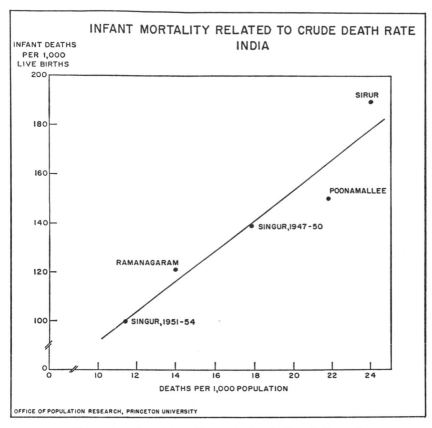

Chart 6. Infant Mortality and Crude Death Rates in
Special Health Units, India.

figure for the actual rate. Since our estimate of the birth rate is
dependent on the estimate of mortality rates, and since an important
part of the overall death rate is the infant death rate, the uncertainty
in the level of the infant mortality rate introduces an element of
uncertainty in our estimates of all vital rates. We have set an upper
and lower bound of 250 and 200 deaths per 1,000 live births,
respectively. In order not to clutter up the tables with alternative
figures, the calculations shown in most of the tables and charts
have been based on an intermediate figure of 225 for the 1951
infant mortality rate. The birth rates, death rates, and expectations
of life associated with an infant mortality rate of 200, 225, and 250
are shown in Table 9. Alternative sets of projections associated

with the limiting estimates of infant mortality are presented in Appendix A.

TABLE 9. VITAL MEASURES ASSOCIATED WITH ALTERNATIVE ASSUMED INFANT MORTALITY RATES, 1951

| Infant Mortality Assumed Rate (per 1,000 live births) | Birth Rate (per 1,000 pop.) | Death Rate (per 1,000 pop.) | Life Expectancy at Birth (years) |
|---|---|---|---|
| 200 | 40.6 | 28.4 | 34.1 |
| 225 | 43.2 | 31.0 | 32.2 |
| 250 | 45.7 | 33.5 | 30.2 |

This chapter has marshaled evidence in support of the position that fertility levels in India have not been subject to major declines in recent years, and indeed that the general level of both fertility and mortality was relatively constant in the twenty or twenty-five years preceding the 1951 census. The principal elements of this evidence are the unchanging age distributions in the decennial censuses, the relatively constant growth rate in the last several intercensal decades, the absence of large groups of the Indian population with greatly reduced fertility, and the levels of birth performance observed in those segments of the Indian population for which reasonably reliable direct observations are available.

These estimates of vital rates pertain to the period before 1951, the date of the last census. There is reason to believe that no substantial changes in fertility have occurred since then. However, on many grounds it appears likely that mortality rates have begun a fairly precipitous drop. Discussion of these recent declines in death rates is deferred to the next chapter, where prospective changes in vital rates are analyzed.

◇◇◇◇◇◇◇◇◇◇◇◇◇◇◇◇◇◇◇◇◇◇◇◇◇◇◇◇◇◇◇◇◇◇◇◇◇◇◇◇◇◇◇◇◇

# CHAPTER VI

# PROSPECTIVE CHANGES IN INDIAN MORTALITY AND FERTILITY

◇◇◇◇◇◇◇◇◇◇◇◇◇◇◇◇◇◇◇◇◇◇◇◇◇◇◇◇◇◇◇◇◇◇◇◇◇◇◇◇◇◇◇◇◇

THE PROJECTIONS summarized in Chapter IV (Tables 3 to 6 and Charts 1 to 3) depend on estimates of the course of Indian fertility and mortality after 1951. In this chapter the basis of these estimates is described.

The course of Indian fertility during the next thirty years is quite uncertain. The closest precedents in other countries indicate the probability of essentially constant or even rising fertility. However, the existence of unprecedented elements—particularly the intention on the part of the Government to include family limitation in the program for Indian development—makes the experience of other areas an unreliable guide. Therefore, the range of possibilities extends from constant (or slightly rising) fertility to a major decline. There are separate projections for these contrasting possibilities. The discussion of fertility in this chapter supplies more detailed reasons why either a constant high level of fertility or a major decline could occur.

There is less uncertainty about the probable course of mortality. India is well launched on large-scale attacks on some of the most common causes of death. The most spectacular program—the one that is no doubt having the most immediate impact on mortality rates—is the nationwide anti-malarial campaign. There is a substantial body of experience—from other low-income areas and for special sections of India—to show how fast and how far mortality can be reduced by the measures India is taking or doubtless will take during the next twenty-five years.

Our population projections are predicated on a single estimate of the probable course of mortality. The section of this chapter devoted to mortality changes describes the way in which the experience of other areas is used as a guide in estimating the likely extent of mortality declines.

THE RANGE OF PLAUSIBLE CHANGES IN FERTILITY

The fundamental reason why there is a wide range of uncertainty as to the future course of fertility rates in India is that any major downward trend is likely to depend on the effectiveness of nation-wide programs designed to reduce the level of birth performance. At present writing there are no sure indications of the magnitude of the resources the Government plans to devote to such programs, and only scanty evidence with respect to the influence any program can have on fertility rates, and to the pace with which any program can be extended through the nation. It is because of these uncertainties that we have resorted to simple contrasting patterns of future fertility trends. The three trends upon which projections have been based include an upper-limit assumption of unchanging fertility and a lower-limit assumption of a linear decline in fertility beginning in 1956 and ending in 1981 at a level of half the estimated current rate. A third projection, which yields a population intermediate between the first two, is based on an assumed trend of fertility with no change until 1966, followed by a precipitous linear decline that in the next fifteen years (i.e., by 1981) reduces fertility by half.

The purpose underlying this section is to justify the assumption that with a minimal program of family limitation, or with an ineffectual program, fertility might remain unchanged for the next twenty-five or thirty years. A second purpose is to justify the contrasting assumption that a well-designed and well-executed program of introducing family limitation could reduce fertility by about half in twenty-five or thirty years.

To justify an assumption that fertility might remain unchanged, it is necessary to examine one by one the arguments usually cited in support of the belief that fertility will more or less inevitably decline. The most important of these arguments are:

(1) The level of fertility in India has already declined, and the decline now underway will continue.

(2) Fertility is already low among upper socio-economic groups, and the low-fertility pattern will spread to the rest of the population.

(3) A continuation of the upward trend in age at marriage will reduce fertility.

(4) India is now launched on a series of Five-Year Plans for economic development. Economic development always brings a

56

decline in fertility as the population becomes urbanized and as per capita incomes rise.

(5) The decreases in infant and child mortality rates may themselves cause fertility declines, since the motives for having large families would be satisfied at lower levels of fertility as mortality rates decrease. If 75 or 80 per cent of those born alive were to survive to adulthood rather than some 50 per cent, a smaller number of births would provide an adequate supply of child labor during seasons of peak requirements for agricultural labor; and where each child is much more likely to survive, a smaller number is needed to insure support for the parents in their old age.

The available empirical information that we have on these points in no case provides a valid basis for expecting much decline in fertility during the next twenty-five years. The evidence with respect to the first three points was reviewed in the preceding chapter. In a few words it comes to this: There has probably been in fact no significant downward trend in fertility in India. Moreover, the groups in the population which to date have markedly below average fertility are so small as to have no noticeable effect on the all-India fertility levels. Age at marriage has increased slowly, and not yet to an extent that would decrease completed size of family. Unless the trend is greatly accelerated, the effect on fertility in the next few decades will be minor, especially since postponements of marriage from the middle to the late teens may actually raise completed family size.[1]

The fourth factor commonly cited in support of the view that fertility will be greatly reduced even without a massive program requires a more extended examination. It must be conceded that in every country for which records exist that has been transformed from a largely agrarian to a primarily industrial country, there has been a really consequential decline in fertility rates. However, if we are going to argue from these precedents, it is important to raise the question of how far the transformation from agrarian to industrial organization, and the rise in per capita income, must proceed before fertility patterns are importantly influenced. When this further question is posed, the experience in other areas can no longer be taken as indicating that fertility in India is likely to decline

---

[1] Any postponement of first births, however, whether or not the completed size of family is affected, would cause a *temporary* decline in the birth rate.

significantly in the next twenty-five or thirty years as a consequence of its economic development.

In Japan the incompleteness of population data prior to 1920 makes it difficult to establish with any degree of certainty the course of fertility until then, but there is almost no doubt that the greater part of the decline of fertility in Japan occurred after 1920. Thus the estimated gross reproduction rate in Japan was 2.5 or higher in every year from 1920 to 1928—a level of reproduction not much lower than what we estimate as prevailing in India. The major decline came after 1930. By 1954 the gross reproduction rate had fallen to 1.2.[2] Not even the most optimistic view of India's possible economic development during the next thirty years would entail the achievement of a degree of industrialization or the achievement of levels of income like those prevailing in Japan in the 1920's. By 1930, nearly 80 per cent of Japan's net output (and 50 per cent of its labor force) could be credited to nonagricultural sectors of the economy.[3] With the exception of France and Ireland, it appears that the substantial declines in fertility in the countries of Northwestern Europe came in the last half of the nineteenth century or later. Here again, the level of economic development exceeds what is likely to be reached in the next thirty years in India. There are few if any examples of a fertility decline occurring at a stage of economic development within India's reach during the next twenty-five or thirty years. There are, to be sure, indications that fertility in Puerto Rico has declined somewhat since 1950. However, in Puerto Rico special circumstances, including access to American markets, access on favorable terms to American funds, and the possibility of offsetting natural increase by large-scale emigration to the United States, have been unusually favorable to rapid growth of income; and estimated real per capita income in Puerto Rico rose by two-thirds in the decade 1939-1949, from a starting level well above that of India. Thus Puerto Rico is probably not a valid exception to our proposition that the stage of economic development India will reach does not bring an automatic drop in fertility. Puerto Rico perhaps represents a stage of development that is close to the

[2] Japanese fertility data from Irene B. Taeuber, *The Population of Japan,* Princeton, 1958.

[3] William W. Lockwood, *The Economic Development of Japan,* Princeton, 1954, p. 103.

upper limit of what India might attain in the next twenty-five or thirty years.[4]

The fifth factor commonly cited in support of the position that Indian fertility will decline without intervention is the prospective improvement in mortality, especially infant and child mortality. It does seem plausible that the basis for high fertility would be weakened by a greatly increased probability of surviving the child-hood years. However, the record of fertility in areas that have achieved at most a moderate evolution from a low-income agrarian status, but have reduced their mortality to relatively low levels, does not support the belief that reduced mortality automatically brings with it reduced fertility. Ceylon reduced its death rate from levels in the early 1920's comparable to India's estimated levels (a crude death rate of approximately 30) to a level by 1953-1955 lower than we assume will prevail in India in the next twenty-five or thirty years. Meanwhile, fertility remained at a sustained high level. The Japanese colonial administration in Taiwan succeeded in reducing the crude death rate from over 33 deaths per 1,000 persons to less than 19 between 1908 and 1942, while the crude birth rate remained at a level of approximately 42.[5] It also appears that in Jamaica, Trinidad and Tobago, and other Caribbean areas declines in mortality have been accompanied by essentially un-changing fertility. The available evidence indicates similar develop-ments in Malaya. In short, the statistics that can be uncovered contradict the plausible-sounding hypothesis that when death rates decline radically a pattern of small families tends to develop. In at least two areas where the mortality decline has been pronounced over a period of thirty years, there has been no observable effect on fertility.

On balance, then, there is little justification for a belief that fertility in India is in the incipient stages of a more or less inevitable decline. There are even forces at work in India that tend to raise fertility rates. Improving health conditions will tend to raise the

[4] Another example of fertility declines at low levels of economic development is Eastern Europe between the two World Wars. In Bulgaria the birth rate fell from 39 in 1921-1925 to 21.4 in 1939, while the population remained predomi-nantly rural. However, in other ways (including contact with the rest of Europe) Bulgaria was more advanced. For example, by 1934 more than 80 per cent of males over 10 were literate.

[5] George W. Barclay, *Colonial Development and Population in Taiwan*, Prince-ton, 1954, p. 147.

number of live births in two ways. In the first place, the kinds of poor health prevalent in India probably depress marital fertility rates by increasing the incidence of stillbirths, miscarriages, and spontaneous abortions; and also poor health (particularly chronic fevers such as malaria) may reduce cohabitation rates. Secondly, lower mortality rates among males will reduce the incidence of widowhood. If widows in India had fertility rates as high as married women of the same age, the number of births in India would be nearly 10 per cent higher than it is.[6] In other words, if marital fertility rates were to remain unchanged and mortality rates among married men were to be greatly reduced, a rise in fertility of perhaps 5 per cent or somewhat more might be expected. In addition (and more conjecturally), it may be noted that the loosening of bonds of tradition—generally expected to permit the acceptance of birth-control practices—can also lead to the abandonment of practices that have kept Indian fertility rates from being even higher.

Since the factors that might lead to a decline in fertility seem weak in force or in some instances quite probably altogether absent in India, and since there are factors tending to raise the level of fertility, an assumed upper limit of a constant level of fertility during the next two or three decades is conservative. If fertility has long been nearly constant in India, if the segments of the population that have reduced their fertility are very small, if the expected magnitude of economic change in India in the next two or three decades seems insufficient according to historical precedent to affect fertility substantially, and if health improvements alone do not bring about fertility reductions, it is the alternative extreme assumption of a fertility decline of 50 per cent in twenty-five years that seems the more difficult to justify.

The basis for this assumption is indeed somewhat conjectural. A major decline may be assumed only if the government undertakes an unprecedented, nationwide program designed to introduce family limitation into every Indian village. There are many formidable problems: of finding the best methods of communicating widely

[6] The number of widows in 1951 between the ages of 15 and 44 was about 11 per cent of the number of married women. In the extremely fertile age span from 25 to 34, the widows were 9 per cent as numerous as the married women. (Census of India, Paper No. 3, 1953, "Summary of Demographic and Economic Data, 1951 Census," Table VI.)

both the advantages of family limitation and elementary facts about the physiology of reproduction; of discovering means of birth control that are at once acceptable to the Indian population, simple to use, effective, low in cost, and easy to store; and of ascertaining a feasible way of incorporating family planning with other elements of the program for Indian development.

Even if some solution to these problems is found and an effective government program is designed and put into operation, no one knows how long it would take to extend the program to all of India or how rapid and how large the response to the program would be. Justification for assuming that there can be major progress in fertility control is based on fragmentary evidence in various parts of India (including the rural areas) indicating a widespread interest on the part of married couples (both men and women) in the possibilities of birth control and family limitation. A study under the auspices of the World Health Organization showed that in two areas, one primarily rural in Mysore State, and the other a housing unit near New Delhi, more than 75 per cent of the couples expressed a desire to learn a method of family planning.[7] A survey of districts in Bombay State near Poona found nearly 50 per cent of the population interested in obtaining information about contraception.[8] The pilot phases of a study designed to test the possibility of introducing fertility controls through public health techniques in rural Punjab areas has shown between 30 and 40 per cent of married couples willing to accept some form of birth control.[9] Another indication that Indian couples might prove receptive to an effort to introduce family planning is the experience of a few doctors in different regions of India. They found, without an organized campaign, Indian parents—especially fathers—who voluntarily submit to sterilization to prevent further increases in the size of their families. These scattered indications can be taken to show, not that significant reductions in fertility will occur spontaneously, but that there might be popular acceptance of effective birth control if the

[7] World Health Organization, *Final Report on Pilot Studies in Family Planning*, New Delhi, September 1954.

[8] Sovani and Dandekar, "Fertility Survey of Nasik, Kolaba and Satara (North) Districts," Gokhale Institute of Politics and Economics, Publication No. 31, 1955.

[9] From unpublished data concerning a project sponsored jointly by the Ludhiana School of Medicine, the Harvard School of Public Health, and the Government of India.

61

right methods of education, manufacture, distribution, etc., are discovered.

Since there is no precedent that we can use in estimating the extent to which a government program can affect fertility, there is little more than guesswork behind the assumption that the fertility decline could be as much as 50 per cent in twenty-five years. This assumption was made as a lower limit in part to create a large contrast with the assumption of unchanging fertility. A clear contrast in the course of fertility makes it easier to bring out the nature of the economic effect of alternative population courses. Moreover, there *are* precedents for national fertility declines of this order. To be sure, these precedents are instances where fertility declined in response to forces other than a government program. Japanese fertility was just about exactly halved between 1930 and 1954.[10] In the experience of Hungary, Germany, Norway, and Sweden there has been a decline of at least 50 per cent in fertility in no more than twenty-five years.

THE EXPECTED COURSE OF MORTALITY

The projections of the future population of India presented in Chapter IV are calculated on the basis of what we believe to be the most likely course of mortality rates. This involves a rather sharp decline in death rates beginning in 1951 and reducing the crude death rate 5 points by 1956. The estimated course of mortality to 1986 is shown in Chart 7.

Two general guides were employed in estimating the extent and rate of mortality improvement in India. The first guide was the experience in Ceylon in implementing an anti-malarial campaign (Chart 8). We drew on this experience in attempting to estimate the effect of the anti-malarial campaign in India, which we assume will achieve full national coverage by 1961. The second general guide was the improvement in mortality rates in the recent experience of other low-income areas where public health campaigns other than anti-malarial have been applied. This experience was taken as an indication of how rapidly Indian mortality rates might be expected to fall as a result of a gradual introduction of latrines, better sources of drinking water, the use of antibiotics, the campaign against tuberculosis, etc.

[10] Irene B. Taeuber, *op.cit.*

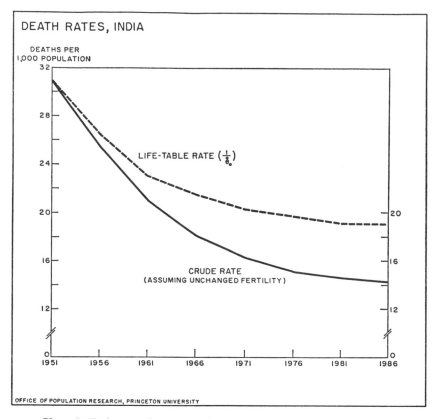

DEATH RATES, INDIA

DEATHS PER
1,000 POPULATION

LIFE-TABLE RATE $(\frac{1}{\overset{\circ}{e}_0})$

CRUDE RATE
(ASSUMING UNCHANGED FERTILITY)

Chart 7. Estimated Crude Death Rate and Life-Table Death Rate,
India, 1951-1986.

The basic rationale underlying the estimates of the probable
course of mortality in India is that in 1951 India was an area of
very high death rates which resulted from a combination of primitive
environmental sanitation, the widespread endemicity of a whole
family of infectious diseases, and the absence of facilities for any
kind of adequate curative medicine—and all of these causes of
death are under attack. In recent years other areas (including iso-
lated sections of India itself), initially faced with similar health
hazards, have been able, through public health programs recently
developed, to bring about prompt and drastic reductions in mortality
rates. India has undertaken several of the programs which have
proven so effective in other areas. The estimates presented in Table
6 show what would happen to Indian mortality if the average pace

63

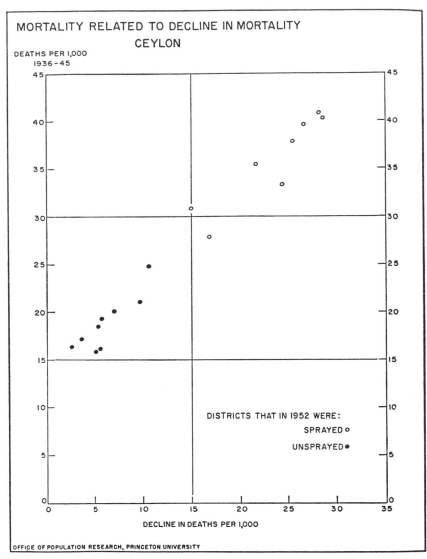

MORTALITY RELATED TO DECLINE IN MORTALITY
CEYLON

DEATHS PER 1,000
1936-45

DISTRICTS THAT IN 1952 WERE:

SPRAYED o

UNSPRAYED ●

DECLINE IN DEATHS PER 1,000

OFFICE OF POPULATION RESEARCH, PRINCETON UNIVERSITY

Chart 8. Relation of Drop in Mortality between 1936-1945 and 1950-1952 to Mortality of 1936-1945, by Districts, Ceylon.

of improvement in a set of other low-income areas were to be duplicated by Indian experience.[11]

[11] The projections of Indian population to 1986 required estimates of death rates by age. The techniques by which age-specific death rates were estimated and the technical demographic details underlying the projection of mortality are described in Appendix A.

64

Malaria was analyzed separately for two reasons: the importance of malaria as a cause of death in India and the fact that a campaign that will probably reduce it to secondary importance as a cause of death should have complete coverage by 1961.

No adequate basis in Indian data exists for estimating the number of deaths caused by malaria. But if the death rate in the malarious regions of India was as much affected by malaria as was the death rate in the malarious regions of Ceylon prior to Ceylon's anti-malarial campaign, there must have been about 2 million deaths caused by malaria per year in India prior to 1951 of an annual total of some 10 to 11 million deaths.

A word about the epidemiology of malaria may make it easier to understand why, under favorable circumstances, the disease can be so readily eliminated as a prominent cause of death. Malaria can be transmitted from one person to another only when a mosquito—of certain species within the genus anopheles—ingests the malarial parasite in taking a blood meal from an infected person, survives for the 11-14 days required for incubation of the parasite in the mosquito's body, and thereafter infects another person in another feeding. When the mortality rate of anophelene mosquitos (indeed, only the mortality rate of mosquitos who have bitten a malarious person needs to be affected) is raised so that the probability of the mosquito's surviving for something like 12 days is greatly reduced, the disease will begin to disappear.[12] The transmission of malaria by many species of anophelene mosquitoes can be effectively ended merely by spraying the interior walls of dwelling units with DDT or some other residual insecticide once or twice a year. It is not necessary to eradicate the mosquito population by killing the larvae or by swamp drainage, or the like, since the effective carriers will be exposed to a high risk of death in the dwelling units themselves. The cost of spraying with DDT varies from 10 to about 25 cents per capita per annum. Residual spraying of this sort has had a high degree of success in reducing the incidence of malaria in a variety of regions throughout the world. In a number of areas malaria has been essentially eradicated. A striking example is in Sardinia, where 75 thousand new cases of malaria were recorded

[12] Note that if the mortality rate of insect vectors is high enough to reduce the probable number of persons infected by mosquitos biting a given malarious victim to less than one, malaria will be on the wane.

65

in 1946; after three years of intensive DDT spraying the number of reported new cases was 40; and after four years the number of new cases was 9. The success of some DDT programs has been threatened by the development of resistance to DDT among anophelene mosquitoes. DDT resistance on a wide scale has not been reported in India, however; and measures to cope with resistance (such as the use of non-related but equally effective residual insecticides) are being developed.

An analysis of the mortality data from different districts in Ceylon during the period in which an island-wide DDT campaign against malaria was instituted has made it possible to estimate the excess mortality prevalent in the malarious regions prior to spraying. We have assumed that a similar excess mortality characterized the malarious regions of India prior to the beginning of the Indian National Malaria Control Programme.

In Ceylon the anti-malarial campaign got under way in 1946. Within three years all of the regions where malaria had been endemic were being covered by a DDT spraying program. Annual mortality rates are published for the different districts of Ceylon; and it is possible to compare the course of mortality in those districts of Ceylon that were classified as nonmalarious and were not sprayed with the mortality rates in the malarious regions that were involved in the DDT campaign. Figure 8 shows the "pre-campaign" death rate for each district on the vertical axis and the decline in the death rate from before until after the campaign on the horizontal axis. The "pre-campaign" death rate is actually the average for the years 1936 through 1945, and the "post-campaign" death rate is the average for the years 1950 through 1952. The observations fall in a striking fashion along a straight line in such a way that the higher the mortality before the anti-malarial campaign, the greater was the reduction during the period the campaign was getting under way. Moreover, the degree to which the drop in mortality for a district with a high initial death rate exceeded the drop in mortality for a district with a low initial death rate was just about equal to the mortality disadvantage prior to spraying. In other words, the differential mortality between malarious and non-malarious districts disappeared during the introduction of DDT.[13]

[13] One of the surprising conclusions suggested by Chart 8 and data for all Ceylon is that the decline in mortality in the regions that were *not* sprayed was more than half of the overall decline in mortality for Ceylon. To put this conclusion in other terms, the DDT campaign apparently accounted for something

It seems a reasonable inference that the use of insecticides was responsible for the elimination of the difference in death rates between the malarious and nonmalarious districts. The crude death rate in the malarious districts declined by about 16 per 1,000, while the death rate in the nonmalarious regions declined by about some 5 per 1,000. The pre-campaign difference between the regions was about 11 per 1,000 and the difference after the campaign was negligible. It may be inferred that DDT rid the malarious portions of Ceylon of excess mortality of about 11 per 1,000 during a period in which malarious and nonmalarious districts alike shared an improvement of about 5 per 1,000 on account of a vigorous island-wide public health program, the introduction of antibiotics, and the like. We have assumed that the virtual elimination of malaria in India through the use of insecticide would lower the death rate in malarious regions of India by 11 per 1,000.[14] The official estimate of the population in 1951 residing in malarious areas in India is 200 million.[15] This is approximately five-ninths of the Indian population. Our projections are based on the assumption that five-ninths of the Indian population will experience a decrease in mortality of 11 points by 1961 as a consequence of the anti-malarial campaign. A National Malaria Control Programme got under way in 1953 in India. There had been earlier experience with the use of insecticides as a means of malaria control on a considerable scale in Bombay State, in Delhi, and in other scattered parts of India. The National Programme called for the establishment of malaria control units, each to be responsible for spraying an area containing approximately a million inhabitants with residual insecticides. By late 1955 the administration of the program estimated that the populations living in areas protected from malaria by insecticide spraying had surpassed 100 million. Thus our assumption that the coverage of

---

less than half of the total mortality decline in Ceylon between the period 1936 through 1945 on the one hand, and 1950 through 1952 on the other.

[14] Dr. Viswanathan, Public Health Officer for Bombay State and an eminent malariologist, believes, contrary to this assumption, that the decline in mortality in malarious regions in India will be much less than in Ceylon because of the more highly seasonal character of malaria in many of the malarious parts of India. (See D. J. Viswanathan, "Public Health and Population Pressure in India," a paper presented at the United Nations Seminar on Population in Asia and the Far East, Bandung, Indonesia, 21 November–3 December, 1955.)

[15] Information provided by the Government of India to the World Health Organization Conference on Malaria in Bangkok in 1953.

the spraying program will be virtually complete by 1961 is reasonably conservative.[16]

There are other elements than the anti-malarial campaign that promise to contribute to a large reduction in mortality rates in India. Poor sanitation is a major contributor to high mortality rates in India, both because of cholera, enteritis, and dysentery and other diseases caused by inadequate sanitation and because of intestinal parasites whose life cycle depends on human contact with night soil. Improved sanitation is an important part of the Community Development Programme. Improvements include both the provision of a better supply of drinking water and the introduction of sanitary latrines. There is a growing body of experience in community development work itself and in the demonstration health units with regard to the design of low-cost sanitary facilities and with respect to effective ways of getting rural villages to accept the idea of improved sanitation, to do the necessary work in installing better facilities, and to put them into actual use. Improvements in sanitation, however, cannot be introduced with the speed and at the low cost that are possible in the Malaria Control Programme.

Other mortality-reducing factors may be expected to develop, some beginning immediately, some at later dates. There is, for example, a large-scale campaign under way for inoculation with BCG as an anti-tubercular measure. The Ministry of Health hopes to inoculate the great majority of tuberculin negatives under 20 years of age by 1961. The biggest impact of such mass inoculations would occur after 1966, when those who had been inoculated would be concentrated in the age span 15-30, which is the span at which tuberculosis causes the highest mortality rates.[17] The increasing use of antibiotics should have an increasing effect in reducing deaths due to infectious diseases, quite probably including tuberculosis.

The rate at which these other factors will affect the risks of dying in India has been estimated by calculating the average annual de-

[16] The statistics with respect to the population living in malarious regions and with respect to the population covered by the Control Programme are crude estimates. The crudity is suggested by the assumption that each control unit covers a population of a million persons. The estimate of 200 million people living in malarious areas was by no means based on a medical survey of the incidence of malaria in all India, but is rather the sum of the estimates by the health officers of each state of the number of persons living in malarious areas.

[17] From an interview with Dr. P. V. Benjamin, Adviser in Tuberculosis to the Director-General of Health Services.

crease in the probability of dying in a group of low-income countries that have had relatively good mortality records, and have enjoyed the benefits of modern public health programs. None of the countries experienced spectacular gains in per capita income, and none benefited in a major way during the interval covered from a modern anti-malarial campaign.[18] The average rate of improvement in mortality above age 5 for these countries was calculated.[19]

The estimates of mortality changes in India were based on the assumption that the mortality risks in India began to decline in 1951 at an average rate paralleling the experience of these other areas. This average rate of improvement was considered to be shared by the population at large and was considered as additional to the improvement in mortality experienced by the population living in malarious districts on account of the anti-malarial program. It is assumed, in constructing the mortality estimates, that the improvement in mortality above age 5 will continue until 1971, at which time further improvements are assumed to cease. This assumption of an arrested decline in mortality is based on an impression that once the relatively easy public health measures have been exploited, further improvements in mortality will be more difficult to gain. The estimates of mortality rates below age 5 are based on the guess that the infant mortality rate by 1981—after twenty-five or thirty years of mortality reduction—will have been reduced to levels between those recorded for special health units in India today and those recorded for Ceylon.

A few comments on the plausibility of the estimated vital rates and of the projections which depend upon them may be in order. In the first place it should be made clear that the specificity of number that results from population projection techniques should not be interpreted as implying that future developments can be precisely calculated. On the fertility side, it would be quite surprising if actual developments were to fall very far outside the upper and lower limits which we have assumed. Whether the difference between these limits exaggerates the potential effects of a state-sponsored

[18] The countries and intervals were: Formosa, 1906-1938; Jamaica, 1921-1946; Ceylon, 1921-1946; Trinidad and Tobago, 1921-1946; British Guiana, 1921-1946; Chile, 1920-1940; Costa Rica, 1927-1950; and Portugal, 1941-1951.

[19] As is explained in Appendix A, the procedure was to calculate the average rate of increase in the expectation of life at age 10 and, ultimately through the use of regression lines, to convert the improvement in expectation of life at age 10 into estimated improvements in age-specific mortality rates.

69

program of family limitation cannot be judged on the basis of information currently available. With respect to the mortality estimates, they may be expected to err in detail. For example, the estimated effect of the anti-malarial campaign may prove to be exaggerated on either of two scores. First, malaria may turn out to be a lesser cause of death in India than it apparently was in Ceylon. And, second, there may have been fewer than 200 million people living in malarious regions in 1951. However, the overall estimated improvement in mortality by 1971 fits in quite well with what is known on other grounds about the potentialities of public health work in India. It is reassuring to find that the assumption that Indian mortality can be expected to follow the experience of other low-income areas that have applied modern public health techniques to problems similar to those of India yields a level of mortality risks in India in 1971 that closely resembles the recorded mortality risks in 1951 in the Ramanagaram Health District. The expectation of life at age 10 for all India, according to the estimates presented here, in 1971 is 52.3 years; the corresponding figure for Ramanagaram in 1951 is 52.5 years. The crude death rate, under the assumption of unchanged fertility, is estimated at 16.3 for 1971, compared to 16 in Ramanagaram in 1951. This similarity is reassuring because it shows that in rural Indian areas the use of low-cost public health techniques is sufficient to yield mortality rates as low as those we assume can be achieved in all India after fifteen or twenty years more of developmental work.

The highest annual per capita expenditures in Ramanagaram through 1954 were less than two rupees. Even after allowance is made for additional public health expenditures by Mysore State within the district, the total was well under three rupees per capita. If it is assumed that in 15 or 20 years the level of skills and techniques applied in Ramanagaram is available throughout rural India, a mortality level of the sort estimated would be attainable.

Two features of the projected mortality experience require further comment: the absence of any mention of India's economic prospects in connection with the estimates of future mortality rates, and the assumption that mortality improvements will level off after 1971.

The neglect of India's economic prospects is provisional. Experience in other low-income areas shows that pronounced improvements in mortality can occur without important changes in per capita income; but it is very doubtful that mortality declines in India could be achieved and maintained if per capita consumption—particularly of food—fell off markedly from current levels. The projected mortality rates cannot be accepted as compatible with unchanged fertility unless the national supply of essential consumer goods can be expected to at least double in the next 30 years. This question will be considered in the chapters that follow.

The assumption that no further mortality improvements above age 5 will occur after 1971 and in childhood after 1981 is a crude approximation of the general tendency for mortality reduction to become less steep as rates are reduced. However, the flattening off is assumed to take place at a level where in other countries mortality reduction has recently been precipitous. In this respect our estimates of future mortality improvements are conservative. Since the projection of mortality on the basis of recent experience in other low-income areas leads to a decline much more rapid than in other estimates of the future population of India, a conservative bias in part of the mortality estimates may be in order. In any event, improvements in mortality after 1971 would have only minor effects by 1986 on the size and age composition of the Indian population. The growth rate in 1986 might (with unchanged fertility) rise to 30 per thousand instead of the estimated 26, but the cumulative effects of faster growth would become large only in years past 1986.

❖❖❖❖❖❖❖❖❖❖❖❖❖

# PART THREE

# FACTORS IN INDIAN ECONOMIC
# DEVELOPMENT

CHAPTER VII

◇◇◇◇◇◇◇◇◇◇◇◇◇◇◇◇◇◇◇◇◇◇◇◇◇◇◇◇◇◇◇◇◇◇◇◇◇◇◇◇◇◇◇◇◇◇◇◇

# GUIDING PRINCIPLES IN INDIAN ECONOMIC DEVELOPMENT

◇◇◇◇◇◇◇◇◇◇◇◇◇◇◇◇◇◇◇◇◇◇◇◇◇◇◇◇◇◇◇◇◇◇◇◇◇◇◇◇◇◇◇◇◇◇◇◇

HAVING DEVELOPED our views on the range of possibilities for India's population growth in the next three decades in the previous chapters, we turn in Part III (Chapters VII–XIII) to the other basis on which our principal argument will rest—the factors determining economic growth. When these factors have been described, we shall be in a position to assess (in Chapters XIV–XVIII) the differential economic significance of sustained as opposed to reduced fertility: in other words, to see how different population trends affect the probable trend of economic growth.

We shall find it useful to examine the determinants of economic growth at some length in Chapters VIII–XIII. However, these chapters constitute something of a digression from our main theme. The principal conclusions of this survey on the determinants of growth are summarized at the end of this chapter, so that the reader who wishes to follow the thread of the argument without delay may skip from Chapter VII to Chapter XIV.

The economic growth of India will be shaped in part by the ideological framework of the Indian economy—for example, by the goals that will dominate economic planning, and by the nature and extent of government action in the economy. Before we summarize the principal determinants of economic growth, some fundamental aspects of India's probable development policy will be stated, with a liberal use of apposite quotations from recent Indian planning documents.

## A. Prominent Objectives in India's Economic Development

### 1. AID TO AGRICULTURE AND THE RURAL ECONOMY

India has always been a predominantly agricultural country, and agriculture will be fostered in the process of development, and not neglected in favor of industrialization. Although the proportion of

75

output and employment accounted for by agriculture (at present about one-half and seven-tenths, respectively) will decline during the period under review, the raising of agricultural output will continue to be an important objective of national policy.[1]

There are several reasons underlying these assertions:

a. The present relative importance of agriculture. A development plan that did not provide for substantial gains in agriculture would for this reason alone be incapable of effecting any sizeable early improvement in overall output or national well-being.

b. The fact that India is a huge country and at present is roughly self-sufficient in agriculture, with imports and exports amounting to only a very small proportion of output. Any course of development along the lines of increasing nonagricultural production rapidly and exporting large quantities of nonfarm products to pay for import of a large part of the agricultural products needed would encounter great difficulties (including adverse effects on the terms of trade) because the quantities involved would be large in relation to available outside markets and sources.

c. The fact that the leaders of India are firmly committed to a policy of development that does not ignore the welfare of any economic or social group, but attempts to raise levels all round and to reduce present intergroup differentials in level of living. (See also Section 2 below.) For this reason, active aid to agriculture (and more generally the rural sector of the economy) is a foregone conclusion.

d. Devotion of a sizeable proportion of planning effort and investment to improving agriculture is clearly indicated on technical and economic grounds—present yields and productivity levels in Indian agriculture are so low, and the ways of raising them are so many and well-tested, that these great opportunities can hardly fail to be exploited to a major extent.

e. Any program which did not attempt to provide additional rural jobs for the expanding rural population would aggravate the

[1] "Agriculture will for long remain the most important economic activity of our people; and without an adequate supply of food and raw materials, there can be no economic development. . . . The Second Plan . . . is designed further to strengthen the agricultural base of the economy . . . The economy needs both an agricultural base and an industrial base; these are not in conflict but are really complementary, and beyond a certain initial stage of development, the growth of one conditions and facilitates the growth of the other. Hence the greater priority assigned to agriculture in the First Plan and that proposed to be assigned to industry in the Second Plan. All the same, we would underline the importance of maintaining and expanding agricultural production in the Second Plan period." ("The Second Five-Year Plan, Basic Considerations Relating to the Plan Frame," p. 7; in Planning Commission, *Papers Relating to the Formulation of the Second Five-Year Plan*, New Delhi, 1955.)

already formidable problems of rural-urban differentials and migration, housing, community facilities, and social readjustment in the towns and cities. The accepted policy is to try to provide jobs in the countryside for as large a part as possible of the natural increase in rural population, though a part of the increase will in any event flow off to the larger towns and cities so that India will gradually become more urbanized.

"Much as we hope for from a more secure, balanced and progressive agriculture there is no doubt that not only the proportion to the total population but also the absolute numbers of those dependent on agriculture have to be lowered. The most natural way of bringing this about is to provide as near to the village as possible means of non-agricultural productive employment . . . A realisation of the essential superiority of the small and medium-sized town as a centre of socio-economic life in an egalitarian democracy would emphasize the need of a re-orientation of our attitude towards the further growth of some of our large cities like Bombay and Calcutta . . . The pattern of industrial activity that should gradually emerge is that of a group of villages having its natural industrial and urban centre."[2]

## 2. CURBS ON CONSUMPTION, ETC.

Although a large amount of consumer choice will be preserved, the development program will be austere and egalitarian, in the sense that necessities will be stressed at the expense of luxuries, thrift and hard work encouraged, and a strong effort made to reduce economic disparities among the population and to have all groups share in improvement.

"A measure of privation to start with and austerity for a fairly long period are thus unavoidable under conditions of rapid development, even in countries with vast unutilized resources."[3]

"Additional taxation of a wide range of luxury or semi-luxury products, at fairly substantial rates, accompanied by broad-based taxation of articles of mass consumption at comparatively low rates, is . . . indicated . . . For any substantial receipts from commodity taxation and appreciable restraint on consumption in the economy as a whole, it will be necessary to extend excise and sales taxation to the consumption of lower-income groups and of goods which are commonly classed as necessaries . . . An extension of the taxation of necessaries

[2] Planning Commission, Report of the Villages and Small-Scale Industries Committee, October 1955, pp. 21-22.
[3] *First Five-Year Plan*, p. 15.

appears unavoidable, if significant results by way of diversion of resources for financing public investment are to be secured."[4]

"The need for utmost restraints on the growth of non-development expenditure, whether at the Centre or in the States, can hardly be over-emphasized."[5]

". . . the attainment of a wider measure of equality in incomes, wealth, and opportunities must form an integral part of economic development and social advance currently. The principle of a limit on income disparities and on private accumulation beyond a point is part of accepted thinking on these problems . . . The Taxation Enquiry Commission suggested thirty times the prevailing per family incomes as a reasonable 'ceiling' on net personal incomes after tax, and it is necessary to advance towards this objective by stages . . . Fiscal measures can assist in this process; but more important than these are positive measures to increase incomes at lower levels, to expand training facilities all round and to eliminate exploitative credit and marketing arrangements. The problem, briefly, is not merely one of reducing existing inequalities, it is the positive one of creating conditions in which great disparities in income will not develop. From this point of view organisational changes, such as reform of land tenures, reorganisation of land management, the encouragement of decentralised modes of production and the increasing role of the public sector are of vital importance."[6]

## 3. PROVISION OF FULLER EMPLOYMENT

Underemployment and unemployment present a problem of such magnitude now that it is unlikely it will be completely solved during the period under review. This fact, in combination with the broad social concerns and orientation of the leaders and their political support, will tend to ensure that the provision of fuller employment will continue to be regarded as a primary criterion of economic progress.[7] To a large extent the promotion of employment even in relatively unproductive jobs will represent an effort to utilize labor potential that would otherwise go to waste, and reflects a realization that a small output per man is better than none at all—but employ-

[4] Taxation Enquiry Commission, *Report*, Vol. I, p. 149.
[5] *ibid.*, p. 210.
[6] *Second Five-Year Plan, Draft Outline*, February 1956, p. 19.
[7] Official statements of India's development policy generally state as the basic objectives the increase of output, the provision of fuller employment, and the ultimate "achievement of a socialist pattern of society." Cf. for example *Second Five-Year Plan, Draft Outline*, February 1956, pp. 6-10. (This source will henceforth be cited as "*Second Plan Outline*.")

ment-creating and employment-spreading policies can of course be pushed beyond that point, to the extent where they actually diminish total output.[8] This can be justified, within limits, on broad welfare grounds reflecting the realization that to provide two jobs for two people is often better than leaving one of them idle, even if the other might be able to produce a little more by himself than the two together. The importance of situations involving conflict between maximum output and maximum employment under current Indian conditions, however, is often exaggerated, and we think it unlikely that any really serious conflict will arise between these aims when both are viewed in fairly long-range terms.

## 4. SOCIALISM AND POPULAR WELFARE

The concept of a "welfare state" with broad public responsibility will continue to prevail, and it is probable that the fraction of the economy under public ownership and control will expand somewhat during the period under consideration. Despite state ownership of railways, airlines, and telecommunications, aggregate public expenditure in India still accounts for a smaller portion of the national product than in the United States. However, public responsibility for the development of some key industries (such as steel, electric power, chemical fertilizers, and petroleum) will undoubtedly continue, and there will be a readiness to extend public control and investment into new areas to the extent that voluntary private investment is deemed inadequate.[9]

[8] "Reliance on relatively labour-intensive modes of production might mean a smaller increase in the supply of consumer goods than might be possible otherwise. But . . . the sacrifice diminishes as more power, more transport, and better tools, machinery and equipment become available for increasing the productivity of consumer goods industries, and in the long run the community gets increasingly large returns. Meanwhile, the stress on utilisation of unutilised or under-utilised labour-power alleviates the immediate problem of unemployment." *Second Plan Outline*, p. 8.

[9] "The achievement of a socialist pattern of society has been accepted as the objective of economic policy. This means that the basic criterion for determining the lines of advance is not private profit but social gain. Major decisions regarding production, distribution, consumption and investment—and in fact the entire pattern of socio-economic relationships—must be made by agencies informed by social purpose. The benefits of economic development must accrue more and more to the relatively less privileged classes of society, and there should be a progressive reduction of the concentration of incomes, wealth, and economic power . . . the State has to take on heavy responsibilities as the principal agency speaking for and acting in behalf of the community as a whole. The public sector has to expand rapidly and the private sector has to play its part within the framework of the comprehensive plan accepted by the community." *Second Plan Outline*, p. 9.

"A total investment of Rs. 3500 crores was envisaged in the First Plan; of this about a half was in the public sector. For the Second Plan, the total investment envisaged is some 75 per cent larger than in the First Plan, and the ratio of public to private investment works out at 62:38."[10]

## 5. SELF-SUFFICIENCY

India will continue to strive to maintain approximate overall self-sufficiency in food and to acquire approximate self-sufficiency as soon as possible in the principal basic industries.[11]

## B. Summary of the Determinants of Economic Growth

The details of this economic analysis will be found in Chapters VIII–XIII. In order that the reader may, if he wishes, proceed as directly as possible to our main remaining problem, the differential effects of fertility on economic development, we shall present in the next few pages a summary of the material in those chapters.

## 1. AGRICULTURAL DEVELOPMENT

Agriculture at present is the way of life of 70 per cent of India's population and accounts for half the national output. Substantial progress in that most backward part of the economy is a prerequisite to successful development of the Indian economy as a whole.

Our examination of the prospects of Indian agriculture leads, by and large, to quite hopeful findings. On the basis of programs now in operation or envisaged, and the resources available, we find it not unreasonable to look for an approximate doubling of total crop output within the next twenty-five years, along with substantial progress toward modification of the crop pattern in the directions agreed to be desirable. This rate of development exceeds the most

---

[10] ibid., p. 24.

[11] "It is only by developing basic industries that a secure foundation for capital formation can be laid and the country made more and more independent of imports of vitally needed plant and equipment . . . A country which seeks rapid development cannot rely on the export of food and raw materials for satisfying the major part of its increasing requirements of capital goods. Nor can a comparative late comer in the field of industrialisation hope for a sizeable expansion in the exports of manufactured consumer goods." "A Tentative Framework," p. 76, in Planning Commission, *Papers Relating to the Formulation of the Second Five-Year Plan*, New Delhi, 1955. (This volume will henceforth be cited as "*Second Plan Papers*.")

rapid population growth rate we envisage, and is unlikely to be limited by manpower availability.

However, such rapid growth will not be automatic or easy. Major factors now limiting Indian agricultural efficiency are obvious: the badly depleted fertility of the soil and the lack of dependable water supply in a major part of the total area; the lack of capital evidenced by use of primitive equipment and inability to afford even small outlays promising a high rate of return; the prevalent illiteracy and ignorance; and the excessively small scale of farm operations, made still more of a handicap by fragmentation of holdings and by the lack of adequate organization for securing supplies, financing, and marketing. Under any foreseeable population growth trend, it appears likely that any substantial rate of overall economic development would entail demands for agricultural output that could not economically be met in full by increased domestic production. Accordingly some development of a nonagricultural export surplus is likely to be necessary within the next two or three decades.

## 2. LIMITING FACTORS ON OVERALL ECONOMIC GROWTH

The distribution of manpower between farms and other sectors is not likely to be a factor limiting overall economic development, in view of the present general redundancy of manpower and the numerous ways in which adjustment is feasible if relative shortages in any important sector should arise. The policy of promoting rural small-scale industry provides, incidentally, an important vehicle for adjustment.

Assuming farm output can be doubled within about twenty-five years, the supply of farm products from domestic sources is likely to prove adequate to support overall output expansion up to somewhat more than double the present level, without any great departure from the present state and objective of approximate agricultural self-sufficiency. For any still more rapid expansion of total output, however, the question of balance with the agricultural sector might well arise in the form of an urgent need to secure more farm products from abroad as a precondition for further progress in the nonfarm sector and the economy as a whole. In that event it appears likely that some adjustment will be set in motion involving a rise in farm prices relative to other prices.

It seems unlikely that lacks of any basic materials or energy

81

resources will constitute primary limitations on this growth. India is much more favorably situated in these respects than many countries which have developed rapidly and attained a far higher level of productivity. No drastic disruption of the pattern of external trade, nor any extensive recourse to high-cost domestic substitutes, seems indicated in the light of mineral and energy resources and requirements in the period under consideration.

*The crucial deficiencies are in capital, labor and management skills, and organization.* These are the main factors accounting for the present extremely low levels of productivity in India. The adoption of already-known improvements in technology, and the evolution of further improvements adapted to Indian conditions, require not merely increased capital investment in capital goods, but also extensive outlays devoted to improving the quality of the human factor and the stock of applicable and tested technology.

### 3. THE SUPPLY OF DEVELOPMENT FUNDS

The proportion of national income available for development is determined by two factors: the willingness and capacity of households and the private industrial sector to save, and the government's capacity and disposition to obtain revenue through taxation and other devices. The two factors are not wholly separate. The government is assuming a primary role in the effort to increase *total* saving and investment. Both private saving and the payment of taxes by the individual are at the expense of his immediate consumption, and for this reason encounter a common limit or resistance.

The domestic supply of funds for development purposes will depend on a number of important changes which can be foreseen in direction though not with quantitative precision. These are:

1. The growth of total and per capita incomes, primarily as a result of the development outlays themselves.
2. Changes in the distribution of income.
   a) Changes in the relative importance of different productive sectors of the economy. The industrial sector, the larger private enterprises, the cooperative sector, and the public sector are all likely to grow faster than total national output does.
   b) Effects of public policies designed to lessen disparities of income among individuals, economic groups, and regions.
3. Increasing monetization of the economy, with the role of the non-monetized "subsistence" sector eventually becoming very small.

4. Effects of public policies designed to discourage nonproductive consumption and investment and to mobilize saving.

Taking all of the above factors into account so far as possible, we see the possibility of a quite substantial growth in domestic savings. But the savings forthcoming *from any given level of total national income* will be quite different according to whether the increase in total income reflects primarily an improvement in welfare or merely an increase in numbers.

In addition to domestic savings, there is likely to be a certain amount of public and private aid and investment forthcoming from outside India.

We cannot attempt to evaluate all the factors which may determine the availability of foreign public or private funds in the next few decades. The major economic limiting factor seems likely to be the judgment of governments and private investors in lending countries, and of international lending institutions, regarding India's creditworthiness. That in turn will depend partly on the treatment given to outside investments and firms, but perhaps even more basically on the success with which the internal resources of the Indian economy are mobilized. The rate of increase in per capita income, and the proportion of national income devoted to development, will be the crucial indicators.

## 4. PRODUCTIVITY OF DEVELOPMENT OUTLAYS

A crucial factor in determining the pace of economic growth is the quantitative effectiveness of given developmental outlays. There are some reasons for expecting a favorable (i.e., rather low) overall investment-output ratio in India in the near future, as compared with experience in the more advanced industrial countries.

However, many of the most important considerations making for a low ratio will have a diminished effect in that direction as development proceeds. The backlog of unutilized trained manpower and equipment in some of the small industries will be progressively absorbed or will deteriorate; the demand for housing and welfare services will become more insistent; further urbanization will contribute to this last effect and also add to the costs of satisfying even minimum standards; the effort to increase agricultural output will almost certainly eventually run into increasing capital costs; and as India's level of technology rises, probably a larger relative outlay

83

will be called for in order to maintain an adequate position in research and development.

A major factor determining the extent to which available funds can be used to enhance productivity is the requirement for providing housing, education, health and other "welfare" or consumer-type facilities and services.

CHAPTER  VIII

◇◇◇◇◇◇◇◇◇◇◇◇◇◇◇◇◇◇◇◇◇◇◇◇◇◇◇◇◇◇◇◇◇◇◇◇◇◇◇◇◇◇◇◇◇◇

# POTENTIAL  DEVELOPMENT
# IN  AGRICULTURE

◇◇◇◇◇◇◇◇◇◇◇◇◇◇◇◇◇◇◇◇◇◇◇◇◇◇◇◇◇◇◇◇◇◇◇◇◇◇◇◇◇◇◇◇◇◇

## A. Scope and Importance of the Agricultural Sector

THE AGRICULTURAL sector, as defined in Indian official statistics, includes the raising of crops, animal husbandry, fisheries, and forestry. The last two are both of relatively slight importance, accounting together for about 1 per cent of net national output. Agriculture accounts at present for roughly half the net national product and is the principal means of support for roughly 70 per cent of the population. The crop area is allocated as shown in Table 10.

### TABLE 10. PERCENTAGE DISTRIBUTION OF CROP ACREAGE IN INDIA, 1954–1955

| Crop | Percentage of Total Gross Sown Area |
|---|---|
| Foodgrains (cereals, millets, pulses) | 75 |
| Other food crops | 4 |
| Oil seeds | 9 |
| Cotton, jute, and other fibers | 6 |
| Other non-food crops | 6 |
| Total | 100 |

Source: *The Agricultural Situation in India*, July, 1956, Table 23.1, p. 292. Figures are provisional and subject to revision.

Average income in agriculture is well below both the nonagricultural and urban averages. The per capita income of landowning cultivators is roughly half the urban average, but landless agricultural laborers earn on the average less than half the income of the landed cultivators.[1]

[1] These comparisons take approximate account of income received in kind from retained production or barter. Cf. Table 21 on p. 133.

## B. Past Trends of Agricultural Development

For some decades prior to 1950, Indian agriculture had shown signs of failure to keep pace with the growth of population. The land under cultivation had slowly increased (as had the irrigated area), but not at as fast a rate as either the farm population or the total population. The proportion of people engaged in farming had been slowly rising rather than falling as it normally does in an advancing economy. A century ago only about half the people were devoted primarily to agriculture; by 1950 this proportion had risen to 70 per cent. Per capita food supply diminished substantially between the years just prior to World War II and the end of the 1940's. Average yields per acre had failed to increase significantly, and in the case of some crops seemed even to be trending slightly downward. The cattle population remained practically constant. Farming procedures had changed very little.

Under the First Five-Year Plan, programs for agricultural development were given first place; outlays for agriculture and community development, along with irrigation and power, accounted for about 45 per cent of the total outlay under the Plan.[2] The immediate objective was that of the Grow More Food Campaign which antedated the Plan—to increase the output of basic foodstuffs (primarily foodgrains) and remove India's dependence upon food imports while raising somewhat the level of consumption. In addition, a groundwork was to be laid for continuing expansion and reorganization of the farm economy through the community development and rural extension programs.

During the First Plan period, the area under irrigation was expanded from 50 million to about 67 million acres, or by about one-third. The consumption of ammonium sulphate, the chief commercial nitrogenous fertilizer, was more than doubled. Several million acres of land were reclaimed or improved, and the gross cropped area (i.e., counting double-cropped land twice) increased by 7 to 8 per cent.[3] Development or extension service blocks were set up in nearly a quarter of the rural area, and some progress was made in the promotion of use of improved seeds, better farming practices and better livestock management.

[2] Second Plan Outline, p. 89.
[3] ibid., pp. 37, 90.

As a result of this intensified activity and also more favorable weather conditions, a substantial increase in crop output occurred during the First Plan, exceeding the targets in the case of most of the major crops. Table 11 summarizes these results. The overall

TABLE 11. OUTPUT OF PRINCIPAL CROPS IN INDIA,
1949–1956

| Crop | Unit | Production in Base Years[a] | Estimated Production 1955–1956 | Percentage Increase in Production | |
|---|---|---|---|---|---|
| | | | | *(target)* | *(actual)* |
| Total foodgrains | million tons | 54.0 | 63.5 | 14 | 18 |
| Cereals | " " | 46.0 | 53.3 | 14 | 16 |
| Pulses | " " | 8.0 | 10.2 | 12 | 28 |
| Major oilseeds | " " | 5.1 | 5.6 | 8 | 10 |
| Sugar cane (in terms of gur equivalent) | " " | 5.6 | 5.9 | 12 | 5 |
| Cotton | million bales | 2.9 | 4.0 | 45 | 38 |
| Jute | " " | 3.3 | 4.1 | 64 | 24 |

[a] Base year for foodgrains is 1949-1950; for other crops, 1950-1951.
Source: *Second Five Year Plan*, p. 255, and final 1955-1956 estimates from *The Agricultural Situation in India*, September 1956, Table 2, pp. 394-395.

official index of agricultural production stood at 100 in 1949-1950, 96 in 1950-1951, and an estimated 114 in 1954-1955 and 115 in 1955-1956.[4]

Imports of foodgrains have consequently been reduced from about 5 million tons a year at the outset of the First Plan to well under 1 million at present, and this small importation is designed primarily to build up stocks against the contingency of an unfavorable monsoon. The easing of the foodgrains supply position has led to a shift in emphasis in the Second Five-Year Plan. Agriculture as a whole will receive a reduced share of the total development outlays (though in absolute terms an increased allocation); and within the general area of agricultural programs there will be much more emphasis on diversifying production, improving the land and putting it to the most efficient use, improving farming practices, and boosting the production of fruits and vegetables, fodder, dairy products and wood for fuel.[5]

[4] *Second Five Year Plan*, p. 255.
[5] *ibid.*, p. 90.

## C. Requirements and Objectives

### 1. FOODSTUFFS

Food supplies in India have long been inadequate by almost any accepted standard of nutritional needs. Prior to 1951 the situation was evidently getting worse, though the risk of actual famine on a large scale had been reduced by improvements in transport, better control over crop distribution, and easier availability of emergency supplies from abroad.

As a measuring rod let us look at the dietary standard set up as an objective several years ago by the Nutrition Advisory Committee (NAC) of the Indian Council of Medical Research:[6]

| | Ounces per day per "equivalent adult" | Annual requirement in millions of long tons gross weight, for 1956 population of 317 million equivalent adults |
| --- | --- | --- |
| Cereals | 14 | 50 |
| Pulses | 3 | 10 |
| Vegetables and fruits | 13 | 45 |
| Milk and milk products | 10 | 33 |
| Sugar (raw sugar basis) | 2 | 7 |
| Vegetable oil and ghee | 2 | 7 |
| Fish and meat | 3 | 9 |
| Eggs | 1 egg | 115 billion eggs |

[6] Indian Council of Agricultural Research, *Human Nutrition vis-à-vis Animal Nutrition in India*, New Delhi, 1954, p. 11. In calculating the population in terms of "equivalent adults," children under 10 are counted as 0.5 each, and women of 10 and over as 0.9 each. In the second column of the table, the gross crop weights are calculated from the net weights given in the report cited, for cereals, pulses, fruits and vegetables, sugar, and oils, by adding 10 per cent to the net figures given in the table cited, to make allowance for losses in handling, storage, etc. This is suggested as a conservative allowance in the report cited, p. 27, Note 2.

This dietary standard has been characterized as follows: "The [Nutrition Advisory] Committee had taken into consideration the current dietary practices and had aimed at formulating a diet which would provide the essential nutrients in adequate measure to ensure maintenance of good health. . . . The net calories available from this diet would be . . . about 2,700 calories. This net calorie intake has been considered to be adequate for an average Indian adult of moderate activity. . . . In determining the calorie requirements, the basis has been the work done in India on energy requirements which has given values more or less similar to those recommended by the Health Organisation of the League of Nations. Although there is need for further work to test the validity of the above assumption, for all practical purposes, the above figures could be considered as applicable to India as a whole. In the formulation of the present diet, the whole of the

The present position with regard to adequacy of Indian food crops to meet the nutritional requirements of the population may be summarized as follows:[7]

*Foodgrains*: In the recent good crop years (since 1953) net availability of foodgrains has been (for the first time since the war) slightly higher than requirements according to the NAC standard. The present consumption level is estimated at 17.2 ounces per equivalent adult per day.[8] The situation has greatly improved since the beginning of the First Five-Year Plan, when India had to import substantial quantities of foodgrains to achieve even a somewhat lower level of per capita supply. It should be noted, however, that until a more satisfactory position is attained in the "protective" foods, additional cereals are needed as a partial substitute. It cannot yet be said, then, that there is really a surplus of cereals, and small imports are continuing even in good years to build up reserve stocks.

*Vegetables and fruits*: This is one of the most serious deficiencies. In 1949-1950 and 1950-1951, supply was estimated to cover only about a third of the NAC requirements. In Extension and Community Development areas emphasis has been put upon expanding the growing of fruits and vegetables. Though there are no adequate recent figures on either acreage or production, the progress reports on activities in these blocks suggest that in the average block there has been an expansion of acreage in fruits and vegetables of the order of 300 to 500 acres, which would mean an average of the order of 1,000 square feet per farm holding in these blocks. It may be presumed that the deficiency is still great in most parts of India.

*Milk and milk products*: This is another major deficiency. In 1949-1950 the supply was estimated at less than half of NAC require-

---

population has been considered to be mixed eaters. There is an appreciable but as yet unestimated proportion of the Indian population who conscientiously object to any type of flesh food. In the absence of reliable data on the relative distribution of non-vegetarians and vegetarians, it will not, however, serve any useful purpose in recommending an alternative diet for the latter group." (*ibid.*, pp. 11-12.)

The report cited uses an estimated 1956 equivalent adult population of 313 million. Our estimate is 317 million, and the figures shown in the last column of the table have been adjusted to the latter figure.

[7] The 1955-1956 final official crop estimates of The Ministry of Food and Agriculture are shown in Table 11. For other figures (except as noted), see Planning Commission, "Level of Living," in *Second Plan Papers*, pp. 636-650.

[8] *Second Plan Outline*, p. 92.

89

ments, and the subsequent increases have barely kept pace with increasing population. The current consumption per equivalent adult is estimated at a little over 5 ounces a day as against the 10 ounces required under NAC standards.[9]

*Sugar*: The present consumption level (in terms of gur or raw sugar) is estimated at 1.4 ounces per equivalent adult per day, which is a little less than that of five years ago, and substantially below the 2 ounce NAC standard.[10]

*Vegetable oils and ghee*: As recently as 1952-1953 the daily supply per equivalent adult was only .29 ounces per day, compared with .36 ounces in 1950-1951 and 2 ounces by the NAC standard.[11] This remains a major deficiency category.

*Fish, meat, eggs*: The *potential* meat supply from existing stock, including poultry, is only about 1.25 million tons (even disregarding the limitations upon utilization imposed by the predominance of vegetarian taboos);[12] and fish production alone could not go far to make up the difference between that and even the present fish-cum-meat requirements of 9.3 million tons. The indicated egg requirement, estimated at 115 billion, is even more academic. Present laying capacity is only a little over 2 billion eggs a year.

It is obvious from the above survey that a satisfactory solution of India's food problem within the foreseeable future will call for two things: (a) an increase in the overall food supply at a rate considerably in excess of the prospective rate of increase in the consuming population, in order to overtake the NAC standard or at least make progress toward that end; and (b) a drastic change in the pattern of food production and/or resort to international trade in foodstuffs on a greatly expanded scale, in order to balance up the severe shortage in such protective foods as milk, meat, fish, eggs, fruits and vegetables, and fats.

It is expected that such food imports as may occur will be primarily in cereals (particularly rice), and that production of cash crops for export will be stimulated as one means for paying for such imports.

[9] *ibid.*, p. 95.    [10] *ibid.*, p. 92.
[11] Planning Commission, "Level of Living," in *Second Plan Papers*, Table V, p. 640.
[12] There is vigorous agitation for universal proscription of the slaughter of cattle.

2. THE LIVESTOCK ECONOMY

So far, we have considered primarily that part of agriculture which produces foodstuffs for human consumption. Animal husbandry fits into the picture both as the source of additional food and non-food products and as imposing an additional claim on crop output for feed.

The major questions relating to animal husbandry concern bovine livestock, which will therefore receive primary attention here. Bovines in India number roughly 200 million, divided as shown in Table 12.

TABLE 12. BOVINE LIVESTOCK IN INDIA, 1951
(millions of head)

|  | Total | Cattle | Buffaloes |
|---|---|---|---|
| All classes | 198.4 | 155.1 | 43.3 |
| Adult work stock | 67.2 | 60.7 | 6.5 |
| Males | 64.4 | 58.4 | 6.0 |
| Females | 2.8 | 2.3 | .5 |
| Breeding stock | 68.2 | 46.9 | 21.3 |
| Males | .9 | .6 | .3 |
| Females | 67.3 | 46.3 | 21.0 |
| Young stock, etc. | 62.9 | 47.4 | 15.5 |

Source: *Second Five Year Plan*, pp. 281-282; based on Livestock Census of 1951.

Among both cattle and buffaloes the proportion of breeding bulls is of the order of 1/2 per cent, and the proportion of working females of the order of 1 1/2 per cent. Adult bovines classed by the Census as "useless" include about 4.7 million, though some estimates run much higher.

Among the dairy animals the female buffalo is regarded as the more efficient milk producer (the average buffalo in India produces about 2 1/2 times as much milk as the average cow, and of a richer quality). However, the male buffalo is much less esteemed than the bullock for draft purposes. Consequently both species continue to be bred and used for both purposes, though preferential care and feeding produces strikingly different adult sex ratios in the two species. It has not so far appeared that there will be any clear advantage from a change either way in the cattle/buffalo ratio.

91

The bovine livestock of India are now providing:

1. *Dairy products*, amounting as noted earlier to no more than half of current requirements according to the NAC standard. Milk yields are among the lowest in the world.
2. *Draft power*, barely sufficient for farming on the present scale by present methods. In some regions there is said to be a surplus of draft power, but elsewhere crop yields are known to suffer frequently from insufficient animal power for thorough and timely working of the fields at times of seasonal peak activity.
3. *A major proportion of the rural fuel supply* in the form of dung, and a highly inadequate contribution in manure. At least half the dung supply is estimated to be used as fuel.
4. *Useful by-products* in the form of hides, bones, and meat. As noted earlier, the potential meat supply from existing stock would meet only a fraction of NAC requirements even if utilized; and utilization is effectively limited in nearly all areas by adverse prejudice.

The present livestock population does not make as large a claim on agricultural output as is sometimes assumed. In the main, the livestock subsist on straw and other crop wastes, waste-land grazing, and (primarily in the case of working draft animals and a few of the dairy animals) oil cakes which are a by-product of the vegetable oil industry. The crop acreage devoted to special fodder crops amounts to only about 3 to 4 per cent of the total. A full reckoning of the burden imposed by livestock upon the Indian economy, however, should also take account of the long-run injurious effects of over-grazing.

Inadequate feeding is the most important cause of the very poor performance of cattle and buffaloes in both dairy output and work;[13] less important but still significant factors are disease, poor care and management, and indiscriminate breeding.

In order to provide a larger overall agricultural output, additional

[13] "Studies of animal nutrition indicate that the available supplies of cattle feeds, whether by way of dry fodder or green fodder or concentrate, fall considerably short of requirements. In relation to the supplies available, it is commonly considered that one-third of the cattle population could be regarded as being surplus. Large numbers lead to poor feeding, and poor feeding comes in the way of attempts to raise productivity. . . . Improved methods of cattle management would have an important bearing on increase in the efficiency of bullocks. Studies have shown that for the country as a whole the efficiency of bullocks could be raised by one-half. . . . With increased efficiency agricultural operations are likely to require one-fourth to one-fifth fewer draught animals than at present, thus reducing the pressure on land." *Second Plan Outline*, pp. 94-96.

draft power on the farms will be needed. In general this could most economically be provided simply by feeding no more than the existing number of draft animals more adequately and thus increasing their performance. Over the long run, additional improvements in power can come from selective breeding; and in the still more distant future, it might become economical to use tractors on a substantial scale. The additional draft power is required for tilling additional acres of land, for additional operations (multiple cropping, more intensive cropping, etc.) on existing cultivated land, and in utilizing more effective types of implements such as moldboard plows.

It is considered urgently necessary to try to raise the milk supply, though full attainment of the NAC standard may take decades. The Indian Council of Agricultural Research (ICAR) based its proposals for agriculture on the interim objective of providing only three-quarters of the NAC standard.

As in the case of animals for draft power, it is proposed that the increased production of milk can most economically be secured by increasing the productivity rather than the number of animals; and that this increase of productivity requires primarily more adequate feeding and secondarily, in the longer run, better breeding and care.

The ICAR study of the livestock economy points to the conclusion that a program of improving the quality of present herds so as to keep pace with the needs for animal draft power and to make substantial progress toward human nutritional goals would require very large increases in feed supply; notably an expansion of the acreage in special fodder crops by about five-fold (to 63 million acres, or about 15 per cent of the total crop acreage as against 3 to 4 per cent now) and nearly a tripling of the output of edible oilseeds. In addition, there is presupposed an effective campaign to make more efficient use of natural grasses.

The above is based on a program merely designed to meet more adequately the needs of a population of the *present* size, and makes no explicit allowance for any future increase. Actually, however, the outlook is not so bleak as that might suggest. There are several reasons for hoping that if something of the order of the ICAR program of improved feeding could be accomplished any time within the next decade or two, additional gains might be realized thereafter.

93

For one thing, the ICAR calculation makes no explicit allowance for livestock improvement arising from factors other than better feeding, and it is probable that the factors of improved breeding and management will before long have a substantial additional impact. Again, a further reduction in the draft-animal requirements, and hence in the overall feed requirements, is not unlikely to occur by, say, 1980 as a result of the larger-scale organization of agriculture, permitting more efficient use of draft animals and to some extent making economic a substitution of mechanical for animal power. Another helpful factor likely to be of gradually increasing importance, and not mentioned in the ICAR study, may be the growing acceptance of the idea of using cows for work.[14] Experimental studies indicate that there is a considerable resource of untapped energy there, merely awaiting a change in owners' attitudes.

At best, however, the diversion of anything like an additional 50 million acres to fodder crops at any time in the foreseeable future obviously imposes a formidable pressure on land resources for other crops, and it seems dubious that such a program could be fully accomplished in less than two decades at best. To the extent that it falls short, the result will apparently be continued dietary shortage in the important categories of dairy products and animal proteins. Since even the ICAR program was geared to meeting only part of the deficiency below NAC standards, for the present population, it seems (regrettably) fairly safe to predict that dietary deficiencies in these foods will persist through at least the major part of the period of our study.[15]

[14] According to the 1951 Livestock Census, fewer than 5 per cent of the cows were worked.

[15] The Ministry of Food and Agriculture has stated, "It is expected that during the Third and Fourth Five-Year Plans the production of productive and supplementary food as well as pulses will be increased to such an extent that it will be possible to provide a balanced diet by 1971, and make necessary (sic) downward adjustment in the per adult consumption of cereals." (Ministry of Food and Agriculture, *Proposals for Second Five-Year Plan, Agricultural Sector*, May 1955, p. 2.) We must, however, regard this as optimistic in view of the still unsolved problems which seem especially refractory in the animal husbandry sector. The Ministry's underlying assumptions about population growth in the next 15 years are not stated; we believe the increase will range from 29 to 38 per cent (or 1.7 to 2.2 per cent per annum as against only about 1.3 per cent in the decade 1941-1951 and the 1.2 per cent average implicitly assumed by the Planning Commission for the next five years). A more rapid population growth would (as discussed more specifically in later chapters) seriously aggravate the difficulties of overcoming food deficiencies.

## 3. OTHER CROPS

The remainder of agriculture comprises primarily industrial and export crops, occupying less than one-tenth of the cultivated land at present. In 1951-1952, the percentages of total acreage devoted to crops within this category were:

| Crop | Percentage of total gross sown acreage |
|---|---|
| Cotton | 5.2 |
| Inedible oilseeds (chiefly castor and linseed) | 1.6 |
| Condiments and spices | .72 |
| Jute | .62 |
| Fiber crops other than cotton and jute | .33 |
| Tobacco | .25 |
| Tea | .25 |
| Coffee | .07 |
| Rubber | .05 |

For the crops on this list, it is inappropriate to speak in terms of output "requirements," since (with the principal exception of coffee) these are crops in which net exports or imports bulk fairly large in relation to domestic production and consumption. In two of the most important crops—cotton and jute—India is an important supplier of world markets for the manufactured product and a net importer of the agricultural raw material. This is likely to remain true in view of the advantageous cost position of nearby countries in producing the raw fiber. The extent to which India attempts or is able to cover a larger part of her requirements for these fibers, then, can be considered only in the context of the foreign trade situation and is not necessarily directly related to the growth of India's domestic consumption needs. It is certain, however, that India's domestic textile requirements will increase considerably faster than in proportion to population, as consumer standards are raised and industrial uses gain in importance; and in both cotton and jute, India will doubtless strive to increase the exports of the manufactured products, to provide exchange to pay for necessary imports.

On the whole, it seems hardly possible to say more at this point than that the total output of the nonfood crops may be expected, in line with considerations of balanced development, to increase substantially more than in proportion to population growth and perhaps roughly in proportion to the increased output of food crops.

## D. Potentialities for Increased Output in Agriculture

The foregoing discussion of the chief sectors of agriculture has shown that policy considerations will call for a strong and sustained effort to increase agricultural production as a whole at a rate considerably in excess of population growth. The most acute shortages are in products such as milk, fruits and vegetables, meat, fish, eggs, vegetable oils, and fodder, which are all unlikely to be met from imports in any event. The Indian Government will not, we believe, readily relinquish the ideal of approximate overall self-sufficiency in foodstuffs, which account for the bulk of agricultural output today and will probably long continue to do so.

The Indian Government is setting its sights quite high on long-range agricultural development. It has been stated that the aim is to double overall farm output in less than twenty years (which implies an average annual growth of about 3.8 per cent),[16] and at the same time accomplish far-reaching changes in the pattern on crops and land utilization along lines already indicated.

This is an ambitious goal, for which it would be difficult indeed to find any historical precedent of accomplishment anywhere on a not easily extensible area of cultivation.[17] Many experts doubt that it can be achieved. This objective appears to have been formulated on the basis of expectations of a continued moderate growth of population, and thus reflects a judgment that, even without any

[16] ". . . the index number of our agricultural production will have to be raised . . . to at least 200 by 1971." (Ministry of Food and Agriculture, *Proposals for the Second Five-Year Plan, Agricultural Sector*, May 1955, p. 1). This index (on a base 1949-1950 = 100) stood at 96 in 1950-1951 and at about 115 in 1955-1956. Thus the proposed increase for the next 15 years would be 74 per cent (200% ÷ 115% = 174%); the same rate of increase extended beyond 1971 would bring the index to 230 (or double the 1955-1956 level) by 1975.

[17] Japan's impressive accomplishment between 1885 and 1915 is sometimes cited as an example of what can be done. But in Japan's case farm output increased only 77 per cent in 30 years, with acreage increasing 21 per cent: *i.e.*, output increased 1.9 per cent per annum and output per acre only 1.3 per cent per annum. B. F. Johnson, "Agricultural Productivity and Economic Development in Japan," *Journal of Political Economy*, December 1951, pp. 498-513.

acceleration of population growth, maximum progress in agriculture would be sought.

We shall proceed therefore on the assumption that public policy objectives in agriculture will *not* depend on the rate of population growth but will in any event seek maximum expansion. (Whether the attainable maximum rate will itself depend on how fast population grows is another question, which will receive due attention later.) First of all, we must inquire by what means agricultural output can be increased.

## 1. EXTENSION OF THE AREA UNDER CULTIVATION

The cultivated area expanded very slowly before 1951, falling well behind the growth of population. During the First Five-Year Plan period, however, partly because of favorable moisture conditions, the area under cultivation increased more than had been expected and roughly in proportion to total population growth. Between 1950-1951 and 1954-1955 the net area sown rose by 7 per cent (from 293 to 315 million acres) and the gross area (i.e., counting double-cropped land twice) rose by 8 per cent (from 326 to 352 million acres).[18]

The present programs and long-range planning do not seem to contemplate any large or rapid increase in the cultivated area. Thus, the Planning Commission states,

"The scope for increasing the area under cultivation is extremely limited. Such increase as may take place . . . is likely to increase the production mainly of the coarser grains. As national income increases, there may be a general tendency for demand to shift from the coarser to the superior grains, especially to rice, wheat and maize. In the circumstances, the main source of increase in agricultural production must be increase in yields from more intensive, more efficient and more profitable agricultural production."[19]

Only if the amount of land reclaimed is quite small relative to the area of "marginal" land does it seem likely that abruptly rising cost of reclamation can be avoided in the next few decades.[20]

[18] *The Agricultural Situation in India*, July 1956, Table 23.1, p. 292. The 1954-1955 figures are provisional, and figures for both dates are subject to substantial error.

[19] *Second Five-Year Plan*, p. 260.

[20] About 28 million acres are now classed as "current fallows," another 29 million as "fallow lands other than current fallows," and 57 million as "culturable waste." (*The Agricultural Situation in India*, July 1956, Table 23.1, p. 292.)

Based on the experience of the First Five-Year Plan and certain programs for the Second Plan, it would seem that something on the order of a million acres a year might be reclaimed for addition to the cultivated area on a fully economic basis, with the aid of some power equipment supplied roughly at cost by the state. The ICAR program, with its allocation of 63 million acres (gross) to fodder crops, called for a total net sown acreage of 328 million, compared with the 1954-1955 estimate of 315 million. It would seem that an increase of that order (13 million acres) would not pose too serious problems—the main question is perhaps whether the same increases in output might not be more economically achieved by raising yields.

## 2. EXTENSION OF IRRIGATION

In 1950-1951 at the outset of the First Five-Year Plan about 51.5 million acres (rather more than one-sixth of the net sown acreage) were under irrigation. The accelerated expansion of irrigation has proceeded nearly according to schedule under the Plan, with an increase of about 15 million acres in five years. The objective for the Second Plan, 1956-1961, is a further increase of 21 million acres.[21]

It is not possible to say how long such rates of extension can or will be continued, in view of the fact that the ground water

---

Although this land is all statistically classed as cultivable, it is by no means likely that a major proportion of it will be found economically usable. Thus J. G. Anand ("Reclamation and Settlement of New Lands in India," *Agricultural Situation in India*, Sept. 1954, p. 348) reports as follows: "It is now known for certain that only a very small proportion of this residual area [the 123 million acres of 'other uncultivated lands excluding current fallows'] can be brought under the plough at costs which the expected revenue from their cultivation would justify. . . . The maximum rate of reclamation of new land which might possibly be maintained for a few years would be about 1.5 million acres." According to the same source a nine-State survey in 1949-1950 showed that only 11 million out of 47 million acres were really culturable. Anand considers this indeed over-optimistic and "at best . . . an almost absolute upper limit" for the next three or four decades. More recent surveys have likewise not been encouraging. For example, in four districts of the Madras State, only about 130,000 out of 3,230,000 acres of this category (i.e., about 4 per cent) were found fit for cultivation.

[21] *Second Five-Year Plan*, pp. 322-326. The irrigation program involves important qualitative improvement as well. Thus, in describing the 1950-1951 position the Planning Commission says, "The area that received *secure* irrigation from large and medium-sized irrigation works was only about 25 million acres. The doubling of this area by irrigation works *which would remain effective in years of low rainfall* was adopted as a target to be achieved over a period of about 15 years." (*Second Plan Outline*, p. 102; italics supplied.)

resources are largely unsurveyed and that increasing costs may well be encountered. It has been suggested with some confidence, however, that 100 million acres could be under irrigation by 1971. In the light of recent and current progress, this seems perhaps conservative, and in any event it is not to be viewed as an ultimate limit.[22] Allowing for some slackening-off after 1961 on the assumption that further irrigation developments might by then encounter substantially increasing costs, we may expect that by 1971 there would be, say, 105 million irrigated acres and by 1981 perhaps 120 million.

It may be worthwhile to attempt a rough appraisal of the significance of this expansion in terms of crop output. In gauging the effect of irrigation *per se* on crop yields, the Ministry of Food and Agriculture customarily calculates the incremental yield, in terms of foodgrains, at 0.2 ton per irrigated acre. Since the output of foodgrains in 1955-1956 was about 63.5 million tons (Table 11), we may say that each additional million acres of irrigation would provide an increment equal to 0.315 per cent of the 1955-1956 crop (i.e., 0.2 divided by 63.5).

We shall use this figure of 0.315 per cent per million acres as applied to crops in general, assuming that the effect for agriculture as a whole would not be markedly different from that in terms of foodgrains, which account for some three-quarters of the total acreage.

On this basis, the extension of the irrigated area from 67 million acres in 1956 to, say, 88 million in 1961, 105 million in 1971, and 120 million in 1981 would give increments (measured as percentages of 1955-1956 output) of about 7 per cent by 1961, 12 per cent by 1971, and 17 per cent by 1981. It should be emphasized that these figures do not by any means reflect the probable additional production from irrigation in combination with the more liberal use of fertilizer and other improved practices which irrigation makes possible; they represent merely a theoretical isolation of the effect of irrigation *per se* with other yield-determining factors imagined unchanged.

---

[22] "It has . . . been roughly estimated that about 75 million acres may eventually be irrigated by multi-purpose, large and medium irrigation works. An equal area could be irrigated under other categories of irrigation sources thus making a total of about 150 million acres under irrigation from all sources." *Second Five-Year Plan,* p. 324.

3. FERTILIZER

Indian soil is almost universally short of nitrogen and phosphorus, particularly the former; and very large gains have been regularly achieved where chemical fertilizers have been properly used. The use of commercial fertilizer in India, though it has increased several-fold since Partition, is still extremely low (Table 13). At present,

TABLE 13. COMPARATIVE CONSUMPTION OF COMMERCIAL NITROGEN AND PHOSPHATE FERTILIZERS IN SELECTED COUNTRIES

(Average consumption in metric tons of N or $P_2O_5$ per 1,000 hectares of arable land and land under tree crops, 1953–1954)

|  | (N) | $(P_2O_5)$ |
| --- | --- | --- |
| India | 0.61 | 0.13 |
| Japan | 89.30 | 61.43 |
| Western Europe | 30.43 | 37.64 |
| Northern Europe | 23.11 | 31.15 |
| Southern Europe | 8.09 | 13.29 |
| Egypt | 45.33 | 5.06 |
| United States | 8.99 | 10.77 |
| World, excl. USSR and China | 5.12 | 6.53 |

Source: United Nations Food and Agriculture Organization, *Monthly Bulletin of Agricultural Economics and Statistics*, III:11, November, 1954, Table 1, p. 20.

demand exceeds supply, since the farmers in more and more areas have been awakened in the past few years to the advantages of fertilizer use. Chemical fertilizers are generally applicable on almost all land which has either irrigation or adequate rainfall, which may mean by 1971 some 160 million acres, or about half the total. This is a conservative estimate, since experimental work is now under way to determine the extent to which (and the conditions under which) fertilizer can also be used on poorly-watered land. As a rough calculation, the eventual annual application of 1 1/2 maunds (124 lbs.) of ammonium sulphate fertilizer per acre on, say, 180 million acres of land would call for 10 million tons of sulphate. According to the generally-accepted rule of thumb for yield effects, this would produce increased foodgrains crops in the ratio of 2 to 1, or about 20 million tons. This would be equivalent to 31 per cent of present foodgrains output. Foodgrains account for about three-quarters of the crop acreage, and ammonium sulphate accounts for a similarly preponderant part of the total present and planned output of commercial fertilizers, the most important other type being superphosphate.

A strong effort is also being made to encourage better use of available supplies of natural manures by use of green manure crops, conservation of cattle manure, and better composting practices. The Second Five-Year Plan and longer-range plans include provision for village wood lots in order to make it possible to use a larger proportion of the cattle manure as fertilizer rather than as fuel.

It is probably not too wide of the mark to say that, taking into account presently envisaged limitations on use imposed by water availability, the potential contribution of expanded fertilizer programs to overall farm output in the next 15 to 20 years is of the order of 30 per cent, with a somewhat slower further possible contribution thereafter as the irrigated area continues to expand.

It is not yet possible to foresee how rapidly these programs can go forward. During the Second Five-Year Plan, the goal is to increase ammonium sulphate output from about 400,000 to 1,600,-000 tons per annum and superphosphate output from 100,000 to 600,000 tons per annum. The consumption of nitrogenous fertilizers is expected to rise during the Second Plan period from 610,-000 tons to over 1,800,000 tons per annum in terms of ammonium sulphate equivalent. The crop increment attributed to fertilizers and manures per se during the Second Plan period is estimated as 2.5 million tons per annum in terms of foodgrains; i.e. nearly 4 per cent of present output.[23]

### 4. IMPROVED SEEDS

The distribution of improved seeds is going ahead rapidly, and it is expected that this program will be in virtually full operation by the end of the Third (1961-1966) Plan.[24] Each Development or

[23] *Second Five-Year Plan*, pp. 268, 270; Indian Embassy in Washington, *Indiagram*, June 4, 1956.

[24] This information is drawn from Ministry of Food and Agriculture, *Proposals for Second Five-Year Plan—Agricultural Sector*, May 1955, pp. 89-93. The grand total expenditure by Central and State Government on this scheme would be Rs. 2.3 billion, of which Rs. 1.7 represents the nonrecurring capital cost of getting it started. Recurring outlay, for operating the seed farms, is estimated at Rs. 0.6 billion a year, to be borne by the State Governments. It is not yet clear, however,

National Extension Service block of 100 villages is to be provided by 1961 with a 25 acre seed farm, which would distribute seed through five stores conveniently placed in the area of the block. The scheme as presented covers wheat, gram, paddy, cotton, sugar cane, pulses, jowar, and bajra, which account in all for roughly 70 per cent of the total crop acreage in India. It is estimated that within any one block, requirements for seed could be met in full by the fourth year of operation of the scheme (i.e., for all India by the end of the Third Plan period) and that the resultant increase in crop yields would be of the order of 10 to 15 per cent. Since this is on crops which cover about 70 per cent of the area, the percentage increase in the overall output of Indian crops to be expected from improved seed alone is presumably somewhat smaller—perhaps no more than 10 per cent. During the Second Plan period only, it is expected that the use of improved seeds will contribute about 1 million tons (or 1.5 per cent) to the annual output of food crops alone.[25]

## 5. IMPROVED METHODS OF CULTIVATION

This category covers a wide variety of improved practices, some of them showing rather spectacular effects upon yields. Perhaps the most important category of improvement is the sowing or transplanting of various crops (e.g., paddy, jute) in rows to conserve seed and permit more effective cultivation with row cultivators.[26]

---

whether the necessary funds will actually be forthcoming to meet the proposed schedule. If not, completion of the scheme would presumably be achieved during the Fourth Plan period (1966-1971).

[25] *Second Five-Year Plan*, p. 268.

[26] A fairly detailed account of early experience with the Japanese method of paddy cultivation in India is given in H. G. Patil, "The Japanese Method of Rice Cultivation in Bombay," *The Eastern Economist*, June 4, 1954. Yields in various districts of Bombay State under traditional methods ranged from 441 to 3,667 lbs. per acre, with a State average of 2,205 lbs. (gross weights, in the husk). Under the Japanese method, yields in the same districts ranged from 2,021 to 4,453 lbs. per acre with a State average of 3,477 lbs. The apparent difference was thus nearly 60 per cent on the average. The Japanese method also offers some saving in seed requirement, but this is significant only in certain areas. There were evidences that with further experience in the new method, a still larger increase in yield might be expected, and experimentation to adapt the improved methods to different local conditions is still under way. Labor inputs per unit of output apparently often run a little higher under the Japanese than under traditional methods, but the increase in per-acre yields is such as to give a considerably higher net return per acre under the Japanese method. At present, the Japanese method is used on roughly 2 million acres out of about 70 million in paddy; during the Second Plan it is hoped to extend it to an additional 2 million. See also M. B. Desai, "Technical

Other improvements include better use of cover crops and green manures, contour bunding (embankment), better irrigation practice, planting of vegetable gardens and fruit trees, use of pesticides, and development of poultry and beekeeping. By 1961, it is hoped to secure an additional annual output, by virtue of "general improvements in agricultural practices," amounting to about 2.4 per cent of 1956 output when reckoned in terms of foodgrains alone.[27]

## 6. OVERALL EVALUATION OF AGRICULTURAL POTENTIALITIES

Many of the factors that may contribute importantly to increased farm output are impossible to evaluate quantitatively, particularly in the context of a radically changing pattern of production.

Some suggestion of the importance of factors other than irrigation and fertilizer in the improvement of crop yields may be gained from a pioneer sampling investigation conducted by the National Sample Survey in the 1954-1955 rabi harvest season and covering three principal rabi crops (wheat, barley, and gram).[28] Measurements of yield were made by harvesting of sample plots in community development and National Extension Service blocks, and the resulting average yields were compared with those reported as averages for all areas in the respective districts in the regular sample crop-cutting surveys. The results indicated that in the development and extension blocks the yields ran, with fair consistency, about 25 per cent higher than in the whole districts in which the blocks were located. Since the standard of comparison includes the development and extension blocks too, and at the time of the survey these covered something like 15 per cent of rural India, appropriate arithmetical adjustment would indicate that a ratio of block to *non-block* yields would be of the order of 1.3 rather than 1.25.

It is also suggestive that in the case of wheat and barley, the advantage in yield seemed to be less in Extension Service blocks than in the more intensively developed blocks—though the sample was not

Change in Indian Agriculture—Problems and Possibilities," *Indian Economic Journal*, III:3, January 1956, pp. 278-286.

[27] *Second Five-Year Plan*, p. 268.

[28] "There are two well defined crop seasons: *kharif* and *rabi*. The major kharif crops are rice, jowar, bajra, maize, cotton, sugarcane, sesamum and groundnut; the major rabi crops are wheat, barley, gram, linseed, rape, and mustard." *India, a Reference Annual, 1955*, p. 164. In general, kharif crops arrive at market about the beginning of November, and rabi crops about the beginning of May (*ibid.*, p. 184).

large enough to support any quantitative conclusion on this point. The Extension Service blocks in the survey had been allotted in the previous year, 1953-1954; the other blocks had been allotted partly in that year and partly in 1952-1953.

Despite the great deficiencies and uncertainties of this investigation, which make any reliance on its quantitative results dubious, it seems to be adequate evidence of a substantial differential in yields. This must be ascribed primarily to factors which have operated selectively or exclusively within block areas, including primarily improved methods of cultivation.

On the whole, our cursory review of the factors likely to contribute to increased agricultural output does not lead us to quite so sanguine a view as that involved in expectations for a doubling of output in 19 years. But we do find it not unreasonable to foresee something like a doubling of aggregate farm output within the next 25 years, along with substantial progress toward modification of the crop pattern in the directions indicated as desirable.

## E. Necessary Conditions for a Realization of Potentialities

It should be emphasized that the indicated potential growth of Indian agriculture will not come about automatically, nor is it contingent merely on supplying certain amounts of effort and capital and generalizing the application of presently known techniques. It is a far more complicated undertaking than that, which will require the finding of altogether new solutions to some perplexing problems of production and organization.

Certain factors now limiting Indian agricultural efficiency are relatively simple and obvious. There is the badly depleted fertility of the soil, and the lack of dependable water supply in a large part of the total area. There is the lack of capital evidenced by use of primitive equipment and the inability to afford even small outlays promising a high rate of return (e.g., for better seed or fertilizers). There is the prevalent illiteracy and ignorance. The excessively small scale of holdings is made still more of a handicap by fragmentation and by the lack of adequate organization for securing of farm supplies (seed, etc.), for financing planting and farm improvements, and for marketing.

Realization of the potential growth of Indian agriculture will require building a comprehensive organization for disseminating technical information, for providing seeds, fertilizers, pesticides, and other materials and services to the farmer, for financing outlays on improvements, organizing community works of common benefit, and marketing the products of agriculture. The Indian Government is committed to a policy of fostering the development of a hierarchy of producer cooperatives as the basic machinery for these tasks, with a comprehensive rural extension service supplying technical assistance. A considerable amount of preliminary spadework has been done during the First Plan in creating the organizations, which are now in process of building staff and getting started. During the Second Plan period the organizational structure is to be extended over the entire country—i.e., by the early 1960's there is to be an operative National Extension Service covering virtually the whole countryside, and progress toward a national network of village cooperatives.

Another essential is substantial progress in coping with the problem of cumulative waste of resources through progressive land fragmentation. In accepting an optimistic view of agricultural growth during the next few decades, we assume that land consolidation will be substantially accomplished within the period; though not very much may have happened in the way of actual pooling of land for cooperative or collective cultivation. The probability is, however, that there will in any event be a gradual trend over the long run toward larger-scale operating units, beginning with the pooled use of some large implements and livestock. Eventually this may pave the way for substantial mechanization of farming, but that seems unlikely to get very far within the next twenty-five years, or until the value of human labor has risen to perhaps several times what it now is in India.

Agricultural improvement will call for continued monetized and non-monetized investment and other developmental outlay on a large scale, both private and public. Under the Second Five-Year Plan, the proposed level of public outlay for agriculture, community development, irrigation, and flood control averages Rs. 2.0 billion a year. This compares with about Rs. 1.5 billion a year allotted during the First Plan, not all of which was actually utilized.[29] In addition, private investment in this sector during the Second Plan

[29] *Second Plan Outline*, p. 35.

should be of about the same order, though only a minor part of it will be in monetized form. Even if we ignore the non-monetized investment, it would appear that during the next few years something like 2 per cent of the national income will be devoted to development of the agricultural sector.

The level of outlays for improvement of agriculture will certainly rise further as development proceeds. Although some programs such as irrigation, seed distribution, and land reclamation may now be nearing maximum levels, many other important programs have hardly got under way for the country as a whole. For example, the programs of National Extension and Community Development, begun in late 1952, have so far reached fewer than a quarter of the villages.[30] It is proposed that the Extension Service should cover virtually the entire countryside by 1961 and that the more intensive and costly community development block program, lasting three years in any given block of villages, should be rapidly extended as well.[31]

Each block is estimated to entail public outlays totaling about Rs. 1.6 million during the period of roughly five years from establishment of the Extension block to completion of the standard three-year intensive development phase that follows the preparatory extension work.[32] Subsequent continuing extension expenditures are

[30] "According to the latest statistics prepared by the Community Projects Administration, 1,140 Community Projects and National Extension Service Blocks were allotted throughout India up to February 20, 1956. These covered 124,957 villages and a total population of 81.1 million." Information Service of India, Washington, D.C., *Indiagram*, No. 41, March 1, 1956. About 500 of the blocks are of the extension-service type at present. There is of course a substantial time lag between establishment of a block and any pervasive impact or even contact at the individual village level.

[31] ". . . the National Development Council approved in September 1955 that during the Second Five-Year Plan the entire country should be served by the National Extension Service and that not less than 40 per cent of the national extension blocks should be converted into community development blocks for intensive development. . . . This means undertaking of work in about 3,800 additional national extension blocks, of which at least 1,120 are to be converted into community development blocks during the period of the Second Plan.

"The programme of development envisaged above is estimated to cost about Rs. 263 crores. As against this, a sum of Rs. 200 crores has been allocated. It is proposed that . . . the question whether the budget for community development and national extension blocks should be adjusted, or the programme staggered, or additional resources found, would be considered by the National Development Council at a later date. . . ." *Second Plan Outline*, p. 86.

[32] *Second Five-Year Plan*, p. 242. For breakdowns of these costs, see *ibid.*, and also Ministry of Information and Broadcasting, *India, a Reference Annual*, 1955, pp. 207-208.

at a reduced level which may be taken as Rs. 200,000 or so per annum.[33]

These figures are rough, somewhat ambiguous, and subject to change. With those qualifications, they suggest that if all rural India is covered by about 5,000 blocks by the early 1960's and if by 1971 every block has passed through three years of intensive community-development effort, the total outlays during the period 1956-1971 might range between Rs. 15 and 20 billion, or an annual average of Rs. 1.0 to 1.3 billion. This is double or triple the rate of outlays budgeted under this head in the Second Five-Year Plan.[34]

Thus the cost of pursuing the rural development program will increase fairly rapidly and will make a significantly large demand on national resources both in financial terms and in terms of the requirements for trained personnel.

In terms of visible results, it seems probable that a relatively greater acceleration is in store. Experience to date has shown that a period of at least a few years is generally required in any given development area to overcome the strong initial resistance and factors of inertia. The rural development programs have not yet been in operation long enough to make it possible to judge the range of potential improvement, but by analysis of the results of even the first two years of experience in various categories of blocks, it is possible to get some idea of the pattern of acceleration as local interest is aroused and initial organizational difficulties overcome. Table 14 presents the results of such an analysis. For the four categories of blocks therein distinguished and arranged in progressive order of length of development experience and intensity of development treatment, the reported accomplishments in various lines of activity were reduced to a uniform per-block-per-annum basis. Reading across the table in virtually any row, one may see an encouragingly strong and consistent pattern of acceleration of the tempo.

Table 15 gives some idea of the extent of acceptance and participation achieved in National Extension Service blocks within the first two years of activity.

[33] There has been little experience yet with the post-intensive stage, since the whole scheme dates only from 1952 and the intensive development phase of the earliest blocks was extended to a fourth year in view of their slow start.

[34] *Second Five-Year Plan*, p. 242.

## TABLE 14. PATTERN OF ACCELERATION OF RURAL DEVELOPMENT ACTIVITIES

| Activity and Unit of Measurement | Annual rates per block per annum, based on: | | | |
|---|---|---|---|---|
| | 259 1953–1954 NES blocks, first year | 53 1953–1954 intensive blocks, first year | 167 1952–1953 intensive blocks, first 1½ years | 167 1952–1953 intensive blocks, fourth half-year |
| Compost pits dug (000) | .55 | .76 | .97 | 1.25 |
| Fertilizers distributed (000 long tons) | .08 | .11 | .15 | .40 |
| Seed distributed (000 maunds) | .71 | 1.80 | 1.53 | 2.05 |
| Implements distributed (000) | .04 | .11 | .10 | .33 |
| Demonstrations held (000) | .03 | .70 | .67 | 1.88 |
| Area brought under fruits and vegetables (000 acres) | .15 | .18 | .18 | .38 |
| Bulls castrated (000) | .30 | .52 | .47 | 1.01 |
| Cattle inoculated and vaccinated (000) | n.a. | 28.7 | 8.85 | 20.8 |
| Fingerlings supplied (000) | 3.1 | 6.0 | 10.0 | 27.6 |
| Area reclaimed (000 acres) | .24 | .49 | .42 | .93 |
| Area brought under irrigation (000 acres) | .39 | .72 | 1.24 | 1.96 |
| Miles pucca roads built | 1.11 | 3.17 | 1.21 | 3.06 |
| Miles kacha roads built | 9.6 | 26.0 | 23.3 | 23.5 |
| "People's Voluntary Contribution" (total, Rs. 000) | 44.0 | 100.3 | 105.0 | 142.2 |
| Labor (Rs. 000) | n.a. | 59.3 | n.a. | n.a. |
| Other (Rs. 000) | n.a. | 41.0 | n.a. | n.a. |
| Total government expenditure (Rs. 000) | 37.8 | 151.0 | 238.0 | 331.0 |
| People's Contribution plus government expenditure (Rs. 000) | 81.8 | 251.3 | 343.0 | 473.2 |

Source: *First Five Year Plan, Progress Reports,* 1953-1954 and April-September 1954.

Certain underlying attitudes are crucial in determining the success with which the obstacles to agricultural growth can be overcome. Technical skill, earnest effort by public officials, and the most ample public expenditures are wasted unless there is a successful resolution of these attitudes. The Indian rural development effort has to face, first of all, a massive inertia based partly on ignorance, partly on hopelessness and fatalism, and partly on a not entirely unjustified traditional suspicion of outsiders and "Government people" as

## TABLE 15. COVERAGE OF AGRICULTURAL IMPROVEMENTS IN NATIONAL EXTENSION BLOCKS, 1954

| | Percentage of Households Participating to Total Households in Project Areas |
|---|---|
| **Improvements in Cultivation** | |
| Using improved seeds | 44 |
| Using chemical fertilizers | 23 |
| Using both improved seeds and chemical fertilizers | 15 |
| Using improved implements | 18 |
| Employing other improved methods in agriculture, such as Japanese method of rice cultivation, line sowing, rogueing, bund forming and land reclamation | 22 |
| **Livestock Improvement** | |
| Improvements such as castration of scrub bulls, inoculation, vaccination and artificial insemination | 15 |

Source: M. B. Desai, "Technical Change in Indian Agriculture: Problems and Possibilities," *Indian Economic Journal*, January 1956, p. 285.

oppressors and tax collectors. A second major obstacle is suspicion and antagonism among economic, caste and other groups within the rural community, making harmonious cooperation extremely difficult. Finally (and perhaps most difficult of all to change) there is lack of initiative and unwillingness to accept responsibility. Too often, when other obstacles have been overcome, the villagers simply acquiesce in accepting assistance and instructions for what they regard as a program imposed from outside. It is recognized that programs on that basis are not viable. Sometimes, it is reported, development officials have let zeal betray them into pushing the villagers ahead at the expense of developing a feeling of real participation. It is encouraging that the seriousness of this problem is generally recognized at the top and that steps are being taken to meet it.[35]

## F. Demographic Implications

One purpose of our scrutiny of India's agricultural development prospects was to check certain hypotheses essential to our demo-

[35] See, for example, the Planning Commission's *Evaluation Report on Second Year's Working of Community Projects*, 1955.

graphic analysis. Mortality and fertility rates were projected, as set forth in Chapter VI and Appendix A, on the assumption that changes in the economic level of living in India during the next thirty years would be confined within certain wide limits. Specifically, our demographic projections excluded the possibility of either (1) substantial economic regression with resultant more acute malnutrition or large-scale starvation, or (2) a skyrocketing of Indian per capita income in this period to levels comparable with those of the advanced industrial economies.

On the first of these points and to some extent on the second, we are now in a position to validate our provisional assumptions. With a liberal margin for the uncertainties of estimate and the vicissitudes of Nature, it appears reasonably safe to say that India's output of food and other agricultural products can, for the next two or three decades, increase at least as fast as the maximum rate of growth of the consuming population (78 per cent in 25 years). This validates our dismissal of the increased-malnutrition factor in projecting vital rates. At the same time, our examination of the prospects in agriculture does not suggest that India can soon become a land of plenty. We see no likelihood that agricultural output per capita can increase spectacularly. A view on the possible overall rate of growth of the Indian economy, however, must await the discussion in later chapters.

◇◇◇◇◇◇◇◇◇◇◇◇◇◇◇◇◇◇◇◇◇◇◇◇◇◇◇◇◇◇◇◇◇◇◇◇◇◇◇◇◇◇◇◇◇◇◇◇◇◇◇

# CHAPTER IX

# AGRICULTURAL MANPOWER

◇◇◇◇◇◇◇◇◇◇◇◇◇◇◇◇◇◇◇◇◇◇◇◇◇◇◇◇◇◇◇◇◇◇◇◇◇◇◇◇◇◇◇◇◇◇◇◇◇◇◇

". . . in a closed economy it would be one of the conditions for economic growth that agricultural productivity should be rising rapidly. For if productivity were not increasing faster than demand, agriculture would not be releasing the labour which was needed for expanding other industries, and the expansion of those industries would also be held up by the steady movement of the terms of trade against them (*i.e.*, food prices would be rising relatively to all others.) Even in an open economy it is very convenient to have agricultural productivity increasing, for without this, economic growth raises food imports, and since this upsets the balance of payments unless other imports can be cut or unless exports are growing *pari passu*, economic growth then becomes dependent upon the rate at which exports can be expanded. In addition, if agricultural productivity is rising fast enough, the savings of the farmers, forced or voluntary, may become available to finance investment in other sectors of the economy. This is why the proportion of the population engaged in agriculture and the rate of growth of agricultural productivity are two of the best indices of the extent and rate of economic growth."

W. Arthur Lewis
*The Theory of Economic Growth*
London, 1955, p. 334.

## A. The Present Pattern of Manpower Utilization in Agriculture

According to the 1951 Census, the "agricultural classes" (i.e., persons deriving their support primarily from agriculture, animal husbandry, etc.) comprised 249 million persons, or about 70 per cent of the Indian population. They were divided into the categories shown in Table 16.

There is not as much combining of agricultural and nonagricultural work as is sometimes thought. Only about 4 per cent of the "nonagricultural classes" reported agriculture as a secondary occupation, and a similar proportion of the agriculturalists reported nonagricultural secondary occupations. This does not, of course, take into account the practicing of agricultural and nonagricultural occupations by different members of a household.

TABLE 16. WORK AND OWNERSHIP STATUS OF THE
AGRICULTURAL POPULATION, 1951
(numbers in millions)

|  | Self-supporting | Earning Dependents | Non-earning Dependents | Total |
|---|---|---|---|---|
| Peasant proprietors (cultivators of land wholly or mainly owned) | 45.8 | 21.4 | 100.1 | 167.3 |
| Tenants (cultivators of land wholly or mainly unowned) | 8.8 | 3.9 | 18.9 | 31.6 |
| Landless laborers | 14.9 | 5.3 | 24.6 | 44.8 |
| Landlords or rentiers (cultivating owners of land and agricultural rent receivers) | 1.6 | 0.4 | 3.3 | 5.3 |
| Total | 71.1 | 31.0 | 146.9 | 249.0 |

Source: Census of 1951, Paper No. 3, Table IV.

The total cultivated land of India is a little more than 300 million acres (counting multiple-cropped land only once).[1] The average amount of cultivated land is therefore about 1.2 acres per capita in the agricultural classes, or about 4.2 acres per self-supporting person. The average size of holdings has been shrinking gradually for some decades, as land reclamation has not kept pace with the increase of the farm population. There are no comprehensive data on the size of holdings, but the average holding is about 5 acres, characteristically scattered in a number of plots as the result of division among heirs. The great majority of holdings are smaller than the average 5 acres in nearly every State; and in some areas in the States of Madras, Bihar, and West Bengal it was found in 1949-1950 that most of the holdings were smaller than 2 acres.[2]

The annual net income produced in agriculture is estimated for

[1] It is not possible to set a precise figure, since the last survey of land use (1951-1952) covers only about 7/8 of the total land area of India. The figure reported in that survey was 296 million acres. Ministry of Information and Broadcasting, *India, a Reference Annual*, 1955, Table LX, p. 160.

[2] 1951 Census, *Agricultural Labour* (New Delhi, 1954); Reserve Bank of India, *Consolidation of Holdings*; S. Thirumalai, *Post-War Agricultural Problems and Policies in India*, 1954, pp. 150; *India, a Reference Annual*, 1955, p. 163.

1955-1956 at Rs. 52.3 billion, or nearly half the national income.[3] Since about 70 per cent of the population lives by agriculture, this means that the per capita income of the agricultural classes is roughly 3/7 of that of the nonagricultural classes. The income level of the landless laborers is much lower than that of the peasant proprietors and tenants.

The typical small farm operates with very little capital of any kind, the biggest item apart from the land itself being the livestock. If we take the number of farms as approximately 60 million, there is on the average for each farm about 3.3 bovines, including 1 draft animal and 1 female for milk and breeding. As Table 17 shows, the extent of modernization and mechanization of implements is still insignificant.

TABLE 17. SELECTED AGRICULTURAL IMPLEMENTS AND MACHINES ON FARMS IN INDIA

|  | Total Number on Indian Farms (thousands) | | Farm Population per Unit of Equipment, 1951 (persons) |
|---|---|---|---|
|  | 1945 | 1951 | |
| Wooden plows | 27,306 | 31,780 | 8 |
| Iron plows | 481 | 931 | 267 |
| Carts | 8,483 | 9,863 | 25 |
| Oil engines | 12 | 95 | 2,620 |
| Electric pumps | 9 | 30 | 8,350 |
| Farm tractors | 5 | 8 | 29,800 |

Source: Livestock Census, 1951, Vol. II. See also V. M. Jakhade, "Effects of Technical Changes in Employment in Agriculture in India," *Reserve Bank of India Bulletin*, November 1955, p. 1192.

## B. Prospective Farm Manpower Needs

In Chapter VIII, we discussed the possibilities for extracting from Indian agriculture a greatly increased output in the next two or three decades—something of the order of double the present output. We indicated also some of the things that would probably have to be done in order to realize this potential: e.g., the expansion of acreage by about 10 per cent; the expansion of the irrigated area by, say, 75 to 100 per cent; the general use of more intensive and careful methods of cultivation; better care and feeding of livestock;

[3] *Second Plan Outline*, p. 26.

vastly increased use of chemical fertilizers and pesticides; improved conservation of soil and organic materials for soil improvement and maintenance; consolidation of fragmented land holdings and more efficient land management; expanded and improved organization for finance, procurement of supplies, product-grading, marketing, and dissemination of technical knowledge; large-scale monetized investment and also non-monetized capital formation by the agriculturalists themselves; and development of general and genuine local participation, with adequate incentive and enterprise for the exploitation of opportunities for advancement. We now inquire into the employment implications of these developments.

Some of the changes enumerated above evidently call for additional hours of farm work, in the absence of any major mechanization. In particular, it requires considerable additional labor to irrigate a previously unirrigated field,[4] over and above that involved in constructing the irrigation facilities. To a lesser extent, additional work is also involved in applying fertilizer in larger quantity and more carefully; in sowing or transplanting crops in rows rather than at random; in cultivating and weeding more thoroughly; in handling larger amounts of livestock feed and products and taking better care of the stock.

The "Japanese method" of paddy cultivation in rows appears, on the basis of sample reports, to involve an increase in man-hour input per acre on the order of 40 to 50 per cent.[5] The expected

[4] "Irrigation . . . roughly doubles the amount of work to be done on each acre getting water. . . . The Indian irrigation schemes under the [First] Five-Year Plan should give new employment to 2.25 million people; and fuller employment, perhaps an extra three months a year, to another 3 million." Maurice Zinkin, "Problems of Economic Development in Asia," 12th Conference, Institute of Pacific Relations, Kyoto, September-October, 1954 (Secretariat Paper No. 1).

The Planning Commission has the following to say regarding prospects for additional farm employment under the Second Five-Year Plan: ". . . the quantum of additional work has to be measured not in terms of jobs, but in the form of additional income accruing to them (farmers). For instance, on account of irrigation provided during the plan period, it may be reasonable to assume that of the additional acreage irrigated, about 30 per cent will provide, to the new entrants to the labour force, opportunities of work on a full-time basis according to rural standards. On this assumption about 1.6 million new entrants to the labour force in rural areas may be regarded as securing employment in agriculture. The balance of the irrigation facilities provided will account for relieving underemployment in agricultural pursuits." *Second Plan Outline*, p. 44.

[5] Based on information supplied by the Ministry of Food and Agriculture. For a discussion of the economics of the "Japanese method," see H. G. Patil, "The Japanese Method of Rice Cultivation in Bombay," *The Eastern Economist*, June 4, 1954, pp. 910-911.

extension of this type of cultivation to an additional 2 million acres during the period of the Second Five-Year Plan might be regarded as increasing farm labor input by something like 1/3 to 1/2 of 1 per cent.[6] This is in itself hardly significant, but there seems to be no reason why this technique (with appropriate variations to suit local conditions) cannot eventually be applied to advantage over most of the area devoted to paddy (at present it is used on only 2 out of about 70 million acres), and analogous methods to certain other crops.

Another factor is the prospective increase in farm acreage. Much of this consists of large blocks of land opened up by public reclamation schemes, rather than minor extensions of existing individual holdings. The reclamation project lands are in general being allotted to landless laborers, displaced persons, and certain other special categories of eligibles on the basis of somewhat larger holdings than the average in lands already under cultivation.[7] If we are to think in terms of say 30 million acres of such lands being added in the next 20 to 30 years, and settled on the basis of family holdings averaging 10 acres for 5 people, then these lands might be carrying a farm population of about 15 million by about 1980. This would mean the equivalent of about 6 million "new jobs."

However, there are also some prospective changes which tend to *diminish* the work to be done per acre: some water-lifting devices and improved implements, for example, and particularly the consolidation of holdings, which can save a great deal of time in nearly all farm operations. Improved grazing control, better pest control, and consolidation of holdings all operate to reduce the sizeable amount of time now spent in simply guarding the fields against destructive intruders.

On balance, we may conclude that the man-hours of work required in Indian agriculture will increase slowly for some time to

[6] This is based on a very crude and sketchy calculation. Rice-growing appears to produce something like $\frac{1}{4}$ of the value product of Indian agriculture, on a somewhat smaller fraction of the cultivated acreage. We might then attribute to it roughly $\frac{1}{4}$ of the labor-input requirement. Shifting 2 million of the 70 million paddy acres to a form of cultivation requiring half again as many man-hours per acre would then be equivalent to adding about $\frac{1}{70}$ to the total man-hour requirements in paddy culture, or say $\frac{1}{280}$ to the total manpower requirements in agriculture as a whole.

[7] One reason for this is that the full productivity of the new land (even with traditional techniques) can generally not be realized immediately.

come; at least so long as mechanization is not undertaken on any substantial scale, which probably means for most, if not all, of the next two or three decades.[8]

But apart from the settlement of new lands, it seems more reasonable to think of the employment effect of the prospective development primarily in terms of additional man-hours rather than additional men required. Experts conversant with Indian agriculture are unanimous in finding a redundancy of manpower even under existing farming techniques, and differ only in their estimates of the size of the surplus. On the average, the Indian agriculturalist is occupied for only about three months in the year, and many of the landless laborers even less than that. The following quotations are illustrative of expert appraisal of the situation:

"In India it is thought that, with the bullocks and plows in common use, 100 acres in grain can provide employment for perhaps 15 persons 'gainfully employed' in agriculture; whereas the average number 'gainfully employed' in India per 100 acres is about 30. Allowing for the fact that some of India's agriculture is more intensive than grain, Indian economists estimate conservatively that a quarter of the rural population is surplus, in the sense that its removal from the land would make no difference to agricultural output. This is equivalent to having some 20 million people permanently unemployed."[9]

"The existence of farm units so small in size as to keep idle a large part of the labour available within the owning family, large numbers of casual agricultural labourers . . . and of 'working dependents' . . . support the conclusion that even under present technique there would not be any decline in agricultural output if the number of workers

[8] "Improvement in agricultural productivity will in the long-run mean employment for fewer farmers—but not necessarily immediately. Apart from the problem of getting adequate quantities of mechanical appliances for bringing about an effective transformation and the problems of training and organisation, the first stages of capital-intensification in agriculture are likely to be of the collective variety—river-valley schemes, road development, erosion control, etc.—which would be labour-absorbing rather than labour-saving. For some time at least, capitalisation of agriculture can proceed by way of creating a large set of external economies—offering prospects for an increase in food supply, improvement in incentives, increase in agricultural income and also an increased scope for employment in agriculture." Bhabatosh Datta, *The Economics of Industrialisation*, p. 121.
"If a capital intensity of £8 per acre can make possible a man-land ratio of 1 to 98, the extent of unemployment that mechanisation can create in a country like India is easily conceivable. If the whole of Indian agriculture could be reorganised on this basis the total number of agricultural workers required in India and Pakistan together will be not more than 4 million." *ibid.*, p. 123. (The 1:98 ratio is derived from the East African Groundnut Scheme.)
[9] William Arthur Lewis, *Aspects of Industrialisation*, Cairo, 1953, p. 8.

diverted from agriculture is not very large and if the withdrawal is thinly spread over the entire agricultural area. The fact that the war-time increase in non-agricultural occupation caused labour-scarcity only in the Punjab, where diversion was substantial, and in the military construction zones in Bengal and Assam, where diversion was narrowly localised, confirms a conclusion of this nature."[10]

Much of the additional work involved in any feasible expansion of agricultural production could be done at off-peak times or by persons now partly or wholly unemployed. This applies not merely to current farm activities but also to the capital improvement activities (largely non-monetized investment) which will play an important part in rural development.

India's farm population has so long been redundant that the whole organization and customary technique of agricultural production is built around work-spreading rather than economy in the use of labor. By and large there has been no pressure to reduce labor requirements per unit of output, but rather the reverse. There is thus an enormous potential for labor saving if and when the surplus of labor begins to be absorbed.[11]

We conclude that manpower supply will not be the limiting factor on Indian agricultural progress under any conceivable trend of population growth or economic development. It is probable that a farm labor force of about the present size could proceed just as rapidly with the realization of the potentialities for agricultural growth as could a larger labor force. It may be regarded as certain that even the smallest natural increase in the farm labor force that could occur in the next few decades would be more than adequate to take care of any overall shortages that may arise.[12] And at any later time when the level of productivity in the Indian economy as a whole may have risen enough to justify farm mechanization on a

[10] Datta, op.cit., p. 55.

[11] "Mixed cropping is a rule in Indian agriculture, entailing adoption of a set of cultural practices which help to prolong sowing and harvesting and inter-cultural practices, which in turn provide more work and reduce underemployment. This is a desirable arrangement in a less developed rural economy suffering from chronic underemployment and unemployment, but severely limits, at the same time, technical advance." M. B. Desai, "Technical Change in Indian Agriculture: Problems and Possibilities," Indian Economic Journal, III:3, January 1956, p. 279.

[12] We have projected an increase of 60 to 66 per cent in the population of labor-force age (15-64) in India by 1981, regardless of what happens to fertility. As applied to the present farm labor force of about 100 million (self-supporting persons plus earning dependents) this would mean an increase of 60 to 66 million.

considerable scale, the manpower needs of Indian agriculture could be rapidly reduced to a fairly small fraction of the present labor force.[13]

The statement that the farm labor force is likely to grow faster than is needed does not necessarily imply, however, an aggravation of agricultural underemployment or poverty. As already noted, various improvements will markedly improve the seasonal utilization of farm manpower in any event—the annual *man-hours* of work to be done on farms will probably increase substantially. Even in the highly unlikely event that agriculture should retain all of the natural increase of its labor force during, say, the next 25 years, a doubling of farm output in that period would mean an improvement of some 20 to 25 per cent in the output of the average agriculturalist, and a similar improvement in his real income in the absence of a marked change in the farm/nonfarm terms of trade. This could mean either an advance or a retrogression in welfare, depending on the change during this period in the number of dependents per earner. (See Table 32.)

[13] For a discussion of this question, with a similar conclusion, see V. M. Jakhade, "Effects of Technical Changes on Employment in Agriculture in India," in *Reserve Bank of India Bulletin*, November 1955, pp. 1191-1197.

CHAPTER X

◇◇◇◇◇◇◇◇◇◇◇◇◇◇◇◇◇◇◇◇◇◇◇◇◇◇◇◇◇◇◇◇◇◇◇◇◇◇◇◇◇◇◇◇◇◇◇◇◇◇◇◇◇◇

# AGRICULTURAL AND OVERALL ECONOMIC DEVELOPMENT

◇◇◇◇◇◇◇◇◇◇◇◇◇◇◇◇◇◇◇◇◇◇◇◇◇◇◇◇◇◇◇◇◇◇◇◇◇◇◇◇◇◇◇◇◇◇◇◇◇◇◇◇◇◇

IN OUR EXAMINATION of the potentialities and limiting factors in Indian economic development, we began with the largest sector, agriculture, and have thus far confined our attention to it. We must now broaden the scope of the inquiry to embrace other parts of the economy.

The general factors limiting India's ability to exploit and develop its resources and increase output include the supply of capital, the skills and incentives of the labor force, and the effectiveness of private and public organization. These factors will be appraised more specifically in later chapters, and we shall ultimately try to evaluate the significance of alternative population growth trends in terms of these factors and of possible rates of economic progress. First, however, in the present chapter, it seems helpful to consider in a rather general way the question of "balance" or properly related development of the major sectors of the economy. Having gained some insight into growth possibilities and limitations in the agricultural sector, we shall seek to explore in particular the relations between agricultural and overall development, and to form an opinion on the extent to which one may set the pace for, or limit, the other.

A great deal has been written about the importance of "balance" between economic sectors in a development process, though in much of this discussion the concept itself remains unclear. In essence, however, "balance" appears to mean the minimizing of the waste of productive resources that results when one sector of the economy acts for an unnecessarily long time as the effective limiting factor (bottleneck) on the growth of other sectors. One sector of the economy can hold back another in either of two ways:

(1) By failing to provide it with essential materials or services.
(2) By failing to provide a market for its products or services.

Naturally, at any given time there is always some category of development activity which is effectively limiting the pace: a successful pursuit of balance implies simply that when such bottlenecks appear, they are promptly given sufficient priority in attention (including investment as necessary) so that they do not long continue to limit output.

At the outset, let it be said that the disposition and capacity of the Indian Government to pursue a policy of balanced development appears relatively strong. To the extent that increased effort and outlay can alleviate obstacles to growth, such obstacles are likely to be attacked in most cases with reasonable promptness and efficacy. We should not expect, then, that any specific and remediable bottleneck like, say, a shortage of steel or chemical fertilizers or railway capacity, would be allowed to curb national economic growth over any very long period; though in any given year or Five-Year Plan, any one of these things (or a hundred others) is quite likely to put limits on other aspects of development. All three of those mentioned as illustrations, for example, are currently considered in the bottleneck category and are accordingly being given priority.

Balancing adjustments between agriculture and the rest of the Indian economy, however, are not so quickly or easily brought about. This is true in part because of the size of the agricultural sector, constituting as it does the support of 70 per cent of the population. The importance attached to balance with agriculture also reflects the great differences and barriers between the farm and nonfarm sectors in respect to production techniques, human skills, values, customs and motivations, and development requirements. It was for reasons of this character that we began our analysis of the Indian economy and its prospects with the agricultural sector, in the two preceding chapters. Implicit in this approach was the idea that very substantial progress in that most backward part of the economy was a prerequisite to successful development of the Indian economy as a whole, and that if agriculture was not to be a drag upon overall progress some quite serious obstacles (including among others the small area of land per capita and the initial lack of interest in improved techniques) would have to be overcome or circumvented.

Our examination of the prospects of agriculture, considering that sector by itself, led on the whole to hopeful findings. Subject to some important contingencies mentioned in previous chapters, we feel justified in proceeding to an examination of the rest of the economy on the assumption that the overall output of agriculture can be approximately doubled in the course of the next two or three decades, and that manpower availability (in a quantitative sense) will not limit agriculture's growth even if the bulk of the increment in the labor force seeks nonfarm employment.

Our task in this chapter is to see whether the course of development we have envisaged in the agricultural sector is likely to exercise any important constraints upon development in the rest of the economy, or vice versa, in the course of the next two or three decades.

## A. Characteristic Developmental Behavior: Agricultural and Overall Growth

The process of economic development characteristically involves an increase in the proportion of the total national product originating outside agriculture. As per capita output rises, the output of agriculture rises less than in proportion to total national output; while the output of industry, and the nonagricultural part of the economy generally, rises faster than overall output.

This tendency has been considered sufficiently consistent to permit statement as a quantitative empirical "rule." For example, Egbert DeVries has derived from the data on 34 countries the generalization that for every 10 per cent increase in per capita real income, the fraction of national income arising from agriculture drops by 1 1/2 percentage points.[1]

The characteristic tendency of nonagricultural production to outstrip agricultural in a progressive economy stems partly from the fact that food occupies a less dominant place in the consumer budget, and partly from the fact that in such an economy there is a shift toward varieties of goods (e.g., more elaborate clothing and utensils) which incorporate a larger element of processing cost in their value, even though the basic materials may still be largely of agricultural origin.

[1] *The Balance Between Agriculture and Industry in Economic Development*, a paper for the 4th Meeting of Technicians of the Central Bank of the American Continent, May 1954 (mimeographed). A similar generalization, elaborated in particular by Colin Clark, is that economic development involves faster growth in the secondary and tertiary sectors of the economy than in the primary (extractive) sector. Either generalization is equally applicable to India, since agriculture accounts for nearly all of the primary production in that country.

Some of the characteristically observed decline in agriculture's relative importance in a progressive economy originates in statistical classification. With increasing specialization of tasks many of the functions originally performed by the farmer himself as part of his work or way of life tend to be taken over by specialists and no longer included in "agricultural" activity.

Finally, in countries in which external trade is important, the tendency to a more rapid growth of nonagricultural production may also reflect a shift toward import of farm products in exchange for exports of other products or services.

We find no reason to suppose that India's experience will run counter to the virtually universal rule. The principal factors cited above as basic to the relationship are all applicable (though we have not yet examined the likelihood of an increase in agricultural imports).

Before 1951 India had been economically stagnant for a long time, with per capita income not rising; and the proportion of income and of population in agriculture had remained roughly constant or slightly increasing. In a new phase of development, it is to be expected that output will grow faster outside agriculture than in agriculture. A very slight shift in this direction is even visible in the experience of the First Five-Year Plan,[2] despite the facts that the First Plan was basically only a laying of groundwork, that it gave top priority to the easing of a critical food shortage, and that India's planners have not displayed the uncritical passion for all-out industrialization that has characterized the development planning of some other low-income countries.

The shift is naturally much more in evidence in longer-range plans. As we noted in Chapter VIII, the most optimistic targets of the Indian planners do not provide for a faster growth of farm output than is implied by a doubling in a little less than 20 years. This is considerably slower than the planners' long-range projection of growth of total national income, which calls for a doubling in 15 years (e.g., from 1956 to 1971).[3] If national income were to grow at that projected rate it would have increased by 152 per cent, in an interval (1956-1976) in which even the most optimistic target

[2] The percentage of national income (at 1952-1953 prices) produced in agriculture was 48.8 in 1950-1951, and has been estimated at 48.5 in 1955-1956 and projected to 45.8 in 1960-1961. *Second Five-Year Plan*, p. 73.

[3] *Second Five-Year Plan*, p. 11.

for agriculture is only about a doubling. This would imply that nonfarm output in the same interval would have to expand by at least 185 per cent.

## B. Agricultural Self-Sufficiency

One problem that India must face in the course of development, in view of her limited land resources and large population, is that the demand for food and other agricultural products may outstrip the domestic supply, so that a serious drag on further overall development may be avoided only by turning to some other source.

We have referred in Chapter VII to certain kinds of basic economic self-sufficiency as an important objective of development policy in India. It is appropriate, then, to begin here by examining some of the implications of overall self-sufficiency in agricultural products.

At present, India is quite close to that position, as Table 18

TABLE 18. INDIA'S IMPORTS AND EXPORTS, 1953
(all figures in billions of rupees)

|  | Imports | Exports | Excess of Imports over Exports |
|---|---|---|---|
| All commodities | 5.66 | 5.23 | 0.43 |
| Products of agriculture (incl. animal husbandry and forestry) | 1.93 | 1.77 | 0.16 |
| Food, drink, tobacco | 1.15 | 1.47 | −0.32 |
| Other | 0.78 | 0.30 | 0.48 |
| Manufactured goods and minerals | 3.73 | 3.46 | 0.27 |

Source: Ministry of Information and Broadcasting, *India, a Reference Annual*, 1955, Tables CXXIX-CXXX, pp. 284-286.

shows. These figures may be viewed in rough perspective to the national economy by noting that India's net national product in 1953 was nearly Rs. 100 billion. Thus imports and exports each represented only 5 to 6 per cent of net national product.[4] It is signifi-

[4] Strictly speaking, the proper base to which imports and exports should be compared is *national income plus imports* (Simon Kuznets, *Towards a Theory of Economic Growth*, Columbia Bicentennial volume [processed] 1953, p. 160). This refinement would, however, not significantly affect the point made here.

cant, moreover, that the pattern of foreign trade did not represent a one-sided exchange of agricultural for nonagricultural products. Both imports and exports were 66 per cent agricultural and 34 per cent nonagricultural.

This does not mean, of course, that foreign trade is or will be of little importance to the Indian economy. Many specific types of imports will remain essential to development, and there must of course be exports to pay for them. The picture does suggest, however (in view of the preference for self-sufficiency in food and basic industries expressed by the Indian planners) that in thinking in general terms about the future interrelations between major productive sectors within India, we may take as a reasonable initial *policy assumption* the attempt to equate domestic production with domestic consumption, for agriculture as a whole and for the non-agricultural sector as a whole.

Our examination of the possibilities for Indian agricultural expansion suggested that something like a doubling of overall output in the next 25 years could be achieved, and that this could be done with no more difficulty under our minimum population-growth assumption than under our maximum population-growth assumption. An extrapolation of that rate of growth (averaging 2.8 per cent per annum) for an additional five years would lead to a 1986 agricultural output about 2.3 times that of 1956. The consuming population (as measured by the projected number of "equivalent adult consumers")[5] would increase 60 to 98 per cent in the same 30-year interval, depending on what happens to fertility. We may now ask how adequate this projected domestic agricultural output would be for the demands of this projected population. More specifically, let us ask *what degree of rise in overall living standards* would absorb the projected increase in farm output.

The answer depends upon the extent to which demand shifts away from farm products as living standards improve: or, technically, the "income-elasticity of demand" for agricultural products.[6]

[5] Calculated from the projected populations by age groups, by weighting children under 10 years of age as 0.5 each and women of 10 and over as 0.9.

[6] This income-elasticity represents the ratio of small percentage changes in per capita consumption of agricultural products to the percentage changes in per capita income which are assumed to produce them. An elasticity of unity would imply that consumers spent the same fraction of their incomes on agricultural products regardless of the level of their incomes. An elasticity of less than unity

Investigations of income-elasticity for food and other agricultural products give results always substantially less than unity, but varying considerably according to the type of community. Professor C. M. Palvia, after surveying the available comparative material, favors the use of an elasticity of 0.8 for India for the period up to 1971.[7] Table 19 presents some relevant estimates of the rural and urban income-elasticities of expenditure on food, drink and tobacco, derived from a comprehensive and fairly recent national sample survey of expenditures.[8] It will be observed that (as would be

TABLE 19. INCOME-ELASTICITIES AND DISTRIBUTION OF URBAN AND RURAL EXPENDITURE ON FOOD, DRINK, AND TOBACCO IN INDIA, 1952

| Item | Income-Elasticity of Expenditure | | Percentage of Total Expenditures | |
|---|---|---|---|---|
| | Urban | Rural | Urban | Rural |
| Foodgrains | .52 | .75 | 21.3 | 41.2 |
| Pulses | .75 | .76 | 2.6 | 3.9 |
| Spices, salt, sugar[a] | .64 | .77 | 4.4 | 4.2 |
| Tobacco | .77 | .88 | 2.0 | 1.9 |
| Pan (betel) | .70 | .89 | 1.2 | 0.7 |
| Meat, eggs, fish | 1.03 | .90 | 3.3 | 2.0 |
| Vegetables | .75 | .90 | 3.0 | 2.1 |
| Edible oils | .85 | .90 | 2.9 | 2.1 |
| Refreshments | .88 | .91 | 3.6 | 1.0 |
| Fruits and nuts | 1.49 | .97 | 1.9 | 1.1 |
| Intoxicants | 1.18 | 1.12 | 0.4 | 0.6 |
| Milk and milk products | 1.35 | 1.37 | 8.6 | 6.4 |
| All Items | .81[b] | .85[b] | 55.1 | 67.3 |

[a] Unweighted average of elasticities of the three items.
[b] Weighted average, with weights based on percentages shown in last two columns (urban and rural respectively).
Source: Based on data collected by the National Sample Survey for the Taxation Enquiry Committee. We have computed the average elasticities shown. Elasticities for specific foods published in *Quarterly Economic Report* of the Indian Institute of Public Opinion, Vol. II No. 1, April 1955, p. 36.

implies that as levels of living rise, the expenditure on agricultural products rises by a smaller percentage.
[7] C. M. Palvia, *An Econometric Model for Development Planning (With Special Reference to India)*, dissertation, Rotterdam School of Economics, The Hague, 1953, pp. 31-32.
[8] Fourth Round of the National Sample Survey (April–September 1952). For a description of the methods and some of the results of the survey, see Taxation Enquiry Commission, *Report*, Vol. I, pp. 45-84.

expected) the elasticities are lowest for the cheap staples (food-grains and pulses) and highest for the luxuries and so-called protective foods such as fruits, vegetables, and dairy products. The variation is particularly marked in the case of the urban consumers with their considerably higher incomes and wider choice of diets.

The overall weighted average is 0.81 for the urban consumers and 0.85 for the rural. In view of the prospect of a gradually rising standard of living and a much faster increase in the urban than in the rural population, 0.8 seems reasonable as a projection of the future income elasticity of demand for food as a whole for the entire Indian population.

If we now assume agricultural production increasing at 2.8 per cent per annum (100 per cent in 25 years or 130 per cent in 30 years), and take our two extreme population projections and a range of assumed values for the income-elasticity of demand for agricultural products, we find that the assumed increase of agricultural products would just meet the demands occasioned by growth of *per-consumer income* at the rates shown below:

| *Elasticity* | *Annual percentage increase in income per consumer*[9] | |
|---|---|---|
| | (Under high-fertility population growth) | (Under low-fertility population growth) |
| 0.9 | .6 | 1.3 |
| **0.8** | **.6** | **1.5** |
| 0.7 | .7 | 1.7 |
| 0.6 | .8 | 2.0 |

For comparison with these figures, we may note that the Planning Commission envisages per capita income rising at an average rate of 3.4 per cent per annum during the next two decades.[10]

The results of this calculation suggest the following tentative conclusions:

[9] The formula for this calculation is as follows, with $c$ representing the annual ratio of growth of consumer population, $e$ the income-elasticity of demand, and $r$ the figures shown as percentages in the table (annual increase in per-consumer income):

$$r = 100 \left[ \sqrt[e]{\frac{1.028}{c}} - 1 \right]$$

[10] *Second Five-Year Plan,* p. 11.

1. Even the rather rapid increase of agricultural production we have posited as feasible (2.8 per cent per annum) would not leave much margin for meeting increased domestic demand over the next 30 years if living standards are to rise even moderately. A per-consumer income growth rate even remotely approaching that sought by the planners might be expected to out run, some time before 1986, the ability of domestic agriculture to supply domestic demand. Recourse to imports, or some other adjustment, is thus probably a necessary condition for continued successful development in India, if we look beyond the near-term future of the next Plan period or two.

2. The more rapid course of population growth under high fertility considerably increases the pressure on agricultural resources and the need to seek other sources or make adjustments, for any given degree of economic growth. It is of course obvious that the total demand for agricultural products would be greater in the high-fertility case than in the low-fertility case at assumed equal levels of *per-consumer* income. Not so obvious is the fact that the total demand under high fertility would be the greater even at assumed equal levels of *total* income—since at lower per-consumer income levels, a larger proportion of income is spent on agricultural products.

Actually, as will be shown in later chapters, we believe that the low-fertility case would show the faster growth in terms of *both* total and per-consumer income (cf. Table 38, p. 273). Rough calculations based on our economic projections suggest, however, that total demand for agricultural products is unlikely to rise significantly faster under low fertility than under high fertility despite the far more rapid economic progress achieved.

## C. Price and Trade Adjustments

There are two principal types of flexibility that could come into play in order to permit overall output growth to proceed faster than would be implied by any rigid quantitative relation to farm output. One is a rise in the terms of trade (price ratio) between farm products and other products in India, which would accelerate the shift of demand, in real terms, toward nonfarm goods and services. The other adjustment is a change in India's external trade pattern, in the direction of a net import balance of agricultural products paid for by a net export balance of other goods and services.

These two adjustments are of course interrelated; either, or more likely both, might be expected as a natural response to the strain upon domestic farm production capacity which seems likely to develop within the period under study.

If at any juncture the output of Indian agriculture should fail to keep pace with the output of other goods and the resulting internal demand, the terms of trade would presumably change to the advantage of the farmer. This would in turn have several effects. First, it might provide some additional stimulus to increased farm output— though we do not believe this effect would be large, and shall therefore retain the assumption of a 100 per cent increase in farm output in the next 25 years. Secondly, the shift in relative prices would encourage a shift in external trade in the direction of importing more agricultural products and exporting manufactures (the stimulus to exports representing the sum of several indirect effects). Some informed observers believe that this will happen in any event, and that the objective of overall agricultural self-sufficiency will be abandoned within the next decade or two.[11]

Finally, the structure of consumer demand itself is responsive to such price changes. A rise in the ratio of farm prices to nonfarm prices would tend to make the volume of consumption of farm products somewhat less, and the volume of consumption of nonfarm products somewhat greater, than would be the case in the absence of a change in the terms of trade. This factor is examined by Professor Palvia in his monograph on Indian development prospects, and he uses two alternative numerical values, $-0.3$ and $-0.625$, for the price-elasticity of demand for farm products (i.e., the ratio between small percentage changes in the quantity of farm products bought per capita and the associated percentage change in the ratio of farm prices to other prices). On the basis of considerations advanced by Professor Palvia himself, we shall use the smaller of these elasticities, namely $-0.3$.[12]

[11] See for example W. Arthur Lewis, "India's Economic Prospects for 1980— The Need to Develop Export of Manufactures," *Capital*, Supplement, December 16, 1954, pp. 7ff. Professor Lewis believes that food output can be raised by only about 45 per cent from 1955 to 1980, while population will increase 45 per cent, national income 118 per cent, and food demand 90 per cent. To meet this situation, he sees India by 1980 importing about Rs. 21.5 billion worth of food per annum, and paying for it by exports of manufactured goods.

[12] C. M. Palvia, *op.cit.*, pp. 32-33. The author comments, "But the writer is inclined to take as an alternative [to various higher figures], another figure, namely

Table 20 presents the results of an illustrative calculation designed to give a rough idea of the degree of adjustment required and the alternative forms it might take. All the figures refer to the year 1986. For each of our two extreme projections of the consumer population (629 million under "high" fertility and 507 million under "low" fertility) we have taken four levels of 1986 per-consumer income, corresponding to upward trends from 1956 to 1986 at 1, 2, 3, and 4 per cent per annum. This gives the eight different cases shown in the eight rows of the table.

For each of these cases, the demand for agricultural products in

TABLE 20. RESULTS OF FORMULA RELATING 1956–1986 CHANGES IN NATIONAL INCOME, NET AGRICULTURAL IMPORTS, AND RISE IN FARM PRICES RELATIVE TO NONFARM PRICES

| Assumed Fertility Trend and Average Annual Rise in Income per Consumer 1956–1986 | National Income, 1986 as Percentage of 1956 | Net Agricultural Imports as Percentage of Total Consumption of Farm Products, 1986 (assumed increase in farm/nonfarm price ratio, 1956 to 1986, shown in parentheses) | | | |
|---|---|---|---|---|---|
| High Fertility | | (nil) | (25%) | (50%) | (100%) |
| 1% | 266 | 8 | 2 | neg. | neg. |
| 2% | 359 | 28 | 23 | 18 | 11 |
| 3% | 479 | 43 | 39 | 35 | 29 |
| 4% | 641 | 55 | 51 | 49 | 44 |
| Low Fertility | | | | | |
| 1% | 215 | neg. | neg. | neg. | neg. |
| 2% | 290 | 10 | 5 | neg. | neg. |
| 3% | 387 | 29 | 24 | 20 | 12 |
| 4% | 518 | 44 | 40 | 36 | 31 |

Note: The notation "neg." indicates that in these cases the assumed 1986 domestic agricultural production (2.3 times that of 1956) would exceed domestic demand.

Assumptions: Domestic agricultural output in 1986 is assumed 2.3 times as great as that of 1956, which is in turn assumed equal to 1956 domestic demand. The income-elasticity of demand for agricultural products is assumed to be 0.8 and the price-elasticity −0.3.

—0.3. He does so because he believes that during the development period, when income would rise, a rise in prices is not going to affect the demand much, as a large mass of people are already living on the subsistence level. . . . Hence, a lower price-elasticity may be more realistic."

1986 was calculated on the assumptions of an income-elasticity of demand of 0.8, a price-elasticity of demand of —0.3, and four different amounts of increase in the ratio of agricultural to non-agricultural prices: zero, 25, 50, and 100 per cent.

The demands for agricultural products as thus calculated were compared with a projected domestic agricultural output 2.3 times as great as in 1956. Any deficiency was assumed to be made up by net imports, and in Table 20 these required imports are expressed as percentages of the total projected consumption of agricultural products in India.[13]

Table 20 underlines the impression previously noted: that anything more than a quite modest rate of progress in per-consumer income (say ½ to 1 per cent per annum under high fertility or 1½ per cent per annum under low fertility) calls for a substantial degree of adjustment of price ratios, imports, or (more realistically, perhaps) both. It is also clear that higher fertility greatly increases the amount of this type of adjustment entailed in any given rate of economic improvement. Finally, the table illustrates the way in which movement of relative prices serves to reduce the required dependence on imports; though with the price-elasticity of —0.3 here assumed, the effect is not very large.

The formula does not purport to yield anything in the nature of a real forecast. It does indicate the considerable degree of flexibility introduced into the relation between agricultural and nonagricultural growth when we allow for the effects of changes in the terms of trade and for net agricultural imports.

It would appear, for example, that something like the Planning Commission's implied pattern (a 3.4 per cent average annual rise in per capita income, concomitant with a 3.7 per cent average annual increase in farm output) would require price and/or trade adjustments if consumer population grew appreciably. At the consumer-population growth rate implied by our lowest projection, these average income and agricultural production trends envisaged

[13] The formula used in calculations for Table 20 is as follows:

$$a = c(y/c)^{.8} p^{-.3}$$

where $y$ is national income, $c$ the consumer population, $p$ the ratio of agricultural to nonagricultural prices, and $a$ the domestic demand for agricultural products, with all four variables expressed as 1986/1956 ratios. The figures in the last four columns are then equal to $(100 — 230/a)$.

by the planners would imply the importation of 36 per cent of the domestic consumption of agricultural products by 1986, in the absence of any price-change effect, and 28 per cent if the terms of trade shifted by 50 per cent. The same conditions applied to our highest population-growth projection would imply resorting to imports for 48 per cent of the supply of farm products in the absence of a price effect, 41 per cent if the ratio of farm to nonfarm prices should rise fifty per cent, and 36 per cent if the price ratio should double.

Realistically, of course, a relative rise in farm prices and a trend toward importation of farm products could be expected to go hand in hand.

Professor W. Arthur Lewis has expressed the judgment that by 1980 India might be able to develop exports (mainly of manufactures) sufficient to pay for net food imports at a rate in excess of Rs. 20 billion per annum,[14] equivalent to 15 to 20 per cent of the probable total requirement at that time. This may be somewhat optimistic, in view of the fact that India's non-food exports now run less than Rs. 4 billion a year,[15] and that her needs for *imports* in that category (now between Rs. 4 and 5 billion) might well increase at least in proportion to the growth of nonfarm output, or perhaps by 200 per cent or more in the next few decades. Under those circumstances the development of an annual *net* exports of non-food items of the order of Rs. 20 billion within 25 years is not likely to be easy.

It is interesting, however, to note that this rate of external trade adjustment (involving the importation by 1986 of, say, 20 to 25 per cent of the agricultural products consumed) corresponds to what is shown in Table 20 as the adjustment needed for (1) a 2 per cent annual rise in per-consumer income under high fertility, or (2) a 3 per cent annual rise in per-consumer income under low fertility (in each case, with a substantial shift [25 to 50 per cent] in the terms of trade).

## C. *"Income Parity" and the Distribution of Population*

A further consideration of "balance" between agriculture and the rest of the economy involves the relative levels of productivity

---

[14] Lewis, *loc.cit.*    [15] Table 18.

and per capita income in the respective sectors. Development experience in various countries indicates the virtually universal persistence of a per capita income differential between agriculture and the nonagricultural sector. Such differentials show some tendency to be larger when industrialization and urbanization are proceeding rapidly, and it is believed that they are required to produce a redistribution of the labor force away from agriculture and other "primary" occupations. For example, Colin Clark remarks that, "From the study of other countries [than the U.S.A. and Japan, where the ratio is somewhat lower], it may be deduced that the situation is fairly stable when the agricultural worker is receiving something between a third and a half of the average income of secondary and tertiary producers."[16]

It may be noted that in India, as recently as 1951, per capita farm income was about half of per capita nonfarm income (Table 21).[17] A differential of this order seems to have been associated with a roughly constant ratio of agricultural to total population, but with a steady increase in the ratio of *urban* to total population. The fact that the rural nonfarm sector has been declining in relative importance, while its per capita income is roughly equal to that of cultivators, suggests that if the rural nonfarm sector is to be reinvigorated, it is likely to require a more favorable income differential with relation to agriculture, though probably not nearly so large a differential as that between urban and rural per capita incomes.

[16] *The Economics of 1960*, London, 1944, pp. 37-38. For a table showing this ratio in 20 countries, see DeVries, *op.cit.*, p. 8.

[17] This is a rough estimate of the ratio. According to the 1951 census, nearly 70 per cent of the population was supported by agriculture and ancillary occupations, and that sector accounted for nearly half the total national income. Both of these proportions have probably declined somewhat in subsequent years. If half the total income is produced by the agricultural 70 per cent of the population, then per capita income in agriculture must be 3/7, or about 43 per cent, of per capita income in the rest of the economy. However, sample surveys of expenditures, conducted by the National Sample Survey, appear to indicate a much smaller differential between *urban* and *rural* per capita *expenditure*: the rural is more than 2/3 of the urban. Even the most liberal allowances for (1) the presumably higher ratio of expenditure to income in the rural sector, and (2) the presumably higher level of per capita earnings in the rural nonfarm population as compared to the rural farm population, are not sufficient to reconcile these National Sample Survey findings with the farm/nonfarm income ratio derived from the 1951 census and the national income estimates. The ratio we shall use here (1 to 2) is on middle ground, but has little else to be said for it.

TABLE 21. RELATIVE SIZE AND PER CAPITA INCOME
LEVELS OF URBAN AND RURAL GROUPS IN
INDIA, 1950–1951

| | Percentage of All-India Population | Per Capita Income of Group, as Percentage of All-India Per Capita Income |
|---|---|---|
| Urban | 17 | 209 |
| Rural | 83 | 77 |
|    Nonfarm rural | 16 | 93 |
|    Farm rural | 67 | 74 |
|      Cultivators | 44 | 93 |
|      Laborers | 23 | 38 |
| Urban combined with nonfarm rural | 33 | 153 |

Source: Based on reports of the Census of 1951, National Income
Committee, and All-India Agricultural Labour Enquiry. Per capita
income of the rural nonfarm population has been set equal to that
of cultivators, on the basis of findings by the Gokhale Institute,
Poona, in connection with the Poona Schedules of the National
Sample Survey.

The situation in India is modified by the fact that for at least
a part of the period under consideration it is likely that rural incomes will be supplemented by subsidy to some extent, so that
differentials in terms of per capita income *received* will be somewhat smaller than differentials reckoned in terms of income *produced* in the respective sectors.

Experience would suggest that the movement of manpower from
farm to nonfarm occupations, and from country to city, is quite
responsive to income and employment differentials over any extended period of years, and this would be increasingly the case if
more manpower should really be needed outside of agriculture. But
since the farms appear to have retained an approximately constant
or slightly increasing proportion of the population for some decades
before 1950, despite increasingly severe overcrowding on the land
and the existence of something like a 2-to-1 superiority of nonfarm
over farm per capita incomes, it might appear necessary for this
differential to widen still further in order to entice any appreciable
portion of the natural increase of farm population into nonfarm

work.[18] This in turn would seem to go counter to the Government's policy of seeking to reduce economic inequalities between groups, and seeking in particular to raise the relative well-being of the smaller farmers and the farm laborers.

There are several considerations, however, which make it appear probable that a rapidly increased labor supply for nonfarm work would be available (at the expense of some of the growth of the farm labor force) even if the per capita income differential is kept from widening.

One important factor is that the development objectives include an arresting and a reversal of the decline of the small industry sector, which accounts for a good part of nonfarm rural employment and also for much of the lower ranges of earning in the towns and cities. It is believed that the level of income in that sector is not much different from that of the landowning cultivators as a class. So far as manpower supply is concerned, it can certainly be recruited to the full extent of the requirements of this part of the nonfarm economy without an earnings premium (over agricultural earnings) of anything like 100 per cent. A quite considerable shift from farm to nonfarm employment, then, might be quite consistent with a simultaneous narrowing of the farm-nonfarm differential and a substantial growth in earnings for the individuals involved, in both categories.

Another factor to be taken into account is the probable trend in relative living costs on and off farms. In a poorly organized economy where distribution is inefficient and in which a large proportion of consumer expenditure is devoted to farm products, nonfarm living costs (particularly in cities) are quite high relative to living costs on farms. Not all of this difference can be measured statistically. It seems probable, though, that improved distribution facilities and rising consumer standards will act to reduce the great difference between urban and rural living costs, which would pro-

---

[18] It may be argued with some justice that in view of the prevalent Indian practice of sharing income and housing with relatives in extended family groups, particularly in rural areas, some kind of average income per head is really a significant factor determining occupational choice, rather than it being primarily a question of actual additional jobs or labor requirements as would be the case in some other types of society. Actual *un*employment in the sense in which it appears in an industrialized economy is of minor importance compared to pervasive *under*employment in India (especially rural India); and this may long continue to hold true.

vide the urban nonfarm worker with a supplementary economic advantage over the farmer over and above any change in relative money incomes.

Finally, it is by no means certain that the Government would be disposed or able to insist on a narrowing of the per capita income differential between farmers and nonfarmers as groups, if such a policy were seen to be impeding overall economic development because of the high costs imposed upon industry to produce subsidies for the farmer. It is more likely in such event that the policy of reducing economic inequalities might take either the form of trying to assist low-income individuals within whatever occupational group they happened to be (e.g., through highly progressive taxation or social welfare measures), or of seeking to improve the opportunities and welfare of farmers by encouraging and assisting their transfer to better-paying nonfarm jobs.

In the light of the foregoing discussion it does not appear that concern for the farmer's relative well-being is likely to impose any substantial obstacle to the growth of nonfarm and total output. However, it may be worthwhile to see what any projection of overall growth implies about the shifting of population from the farms. If, for example, a given projected development would require, in view of the policy objectives in regard to parity of farm incomes, a massive shift off the farms, that would raise economic and social problems of the first magnitude. Is such a situation likely?

The projected size of the labor force in 1981 is about 241 millions under our low-fertility projection and about 249 millions under high fertility—a relatively insignificant differential. A simple illustrative calculation will show some of the implications of the following assumptions:

1. A doubling of agricultural output by 1981: i.e., agricultural output in 1981 roughly equals total national output in 1956.
2. Maintenance of at least the 1956 ratio (about 1:2) between average income in the agricultural sector and in the rest of the economy.

Under these assumptions, it can be shown that the maximum fraction of the total labor force that can be on farms in 1981 will be equal to the ratio

$$\frac{216}{108 + \text{national income in 1981 (Rs. billions)}}$$

135

Table 22 shows some of the results that follow therefrom, for three different assumed levels of 1981 national income. Since we have posited the amount of growth in the agricultural sector (100 per cent), a higher assumed 1981 level of total national income re-

TABLE 22. RESULTS OF ILLUSTRATIVE CALCULATIONS ON SOME IMPLICATIONS OF FARM AND NONFARM INCOME PARITY, 1956–1981

| National Income | | Necessary Conditions for Maintenance of Farm/Nonfarm Income Parity | |
|---|---|---|---|
| Average Annual Percentage Increase, 1956–1981 | 1981 as Percentage of 1956 | Maximum Size of Farm Labor Force in 1981 (millions) | Minimum Required Net Shift of Workers from Farms, 1956–1981 (millions) |
| 3 | 209 | 155–161[a] | 5–6[a] |
| 4 | 267 | 131–136[a] | 30 |
| 5 | 339 | 110–113[a] | 51–53[a] |

[a] Ranges shown reflect the difference between low-fertility and high-fertility population growth projections.

quires much higher growth rates in the nonfarm sector, and a larger shift of population from the farms if the 1:2 productivity ratio is to be maintained. Raising the ratio would of course call for still larger shifts.

The table shows the maximum farm labor force in 1981 that would be consistent with the income-parity stipulation. These figures are then subtracted from what the 1981 farm labor force would be without migration (i.e., if it grew *pari passu* with the total labor force and thus numbered 160-165 millions by 1981 as compared with about 100 millions in 1956).

In this calculation no allowance is made for any change in the farm/nonfarm terms of trade. Previous discussion in this chapter suggested that such a change, in favor of the farmer's purchasing power, might well occur in situations of rapid growth of nonfarm output. Allowance for such a change would tend to raise the figures in the third column and lower those in the last column.

These figures are all in terms of labor-force members. If we ignore possible farm/nonfarm differentials in the ratio of population to labor force, but allow for the effects of changing age distribution, the figures in the last column of Table 22 might imply net "migration" of population of the order of 13-14 million, 73-79 million, and 123-139 million over the twenty-five-year period, in the respective hypothetical cases.[19] These ranges reflect the differential effect of higher as compared to lower fertility, via age distribution and the size of workers' families.

We have referred to these figures as "migration"; but they substantially overstate the number of people who would actually have to migrate in order to accomplish the indicated redistribution of population. They really comprise all the *1981 survivors of 1956-1981 migrants and their progeny.*

Despite the rather large relocation shifts of population implied by these calculations, we do not feel that this represents a major threat to successful development. At worst, the implication might be drawn that the voluntary shift of population could turn out less than the figures shown, and that in the effort to prevent widening of the farm-nonfarm per capita income gap the Government might feel impelled to subsidize farmers more heavily at the expense of the development of nonfarm production. This seems hardly likely. It is rather to be expected that in the course of development the surplus farm population will become increasingly responsive to the income differential; and that, if it is clear that a faster movement away from farms would be in the interest of both the national economy and the individuals concerned, the Government's policy would be along lines of assisting transfer to nonfarm jobs.

It is appropriate to note here that there has been a steady trend toward *urbanization* of the Indian population even prior to the development effort of the Five-Year Plans. Data for recent decades suggest that the urban population has tended to grow somewhat more than twice as fast as the total population.[20] If a 2-to-1 relation

[19] Since this "migration" may be imagined as occurring on an increasing scale throughout the period 1956-1981, the applicable ratios of population to labor force have been chosen as weighted averages for the period with higher weights for the later years. The ratios by five-year intervals are shown in Table 36 below.

[20] ". . . it has been assumed that in the decade 1951-61 the urban population will increase by 33%. This rate of urbanization is somewhat higher than that of the decade 1931-41 (31%), but is lower than the rate for the decade 1941-51 (40%). The rate of urbanization during the decade 1941-51 was unusually high because of war and Partition. It is reasonable to assume that a smaller rate will prevail during 1951-61 in view of improvements in rural conditions and the emphasis given to the development of a decentralized sector in the economy." *Second Plan Outline*, p. 41. The percentage increase of total population was 14

137

between urban and total percentage annual rates of growth should prevail during the next 25 years, for which we have projected overall population increases in the range of 46 to 75 per cent, then the urban population in 1981 might range from 151 to 217 millions. That would represent an excess of *52 to 93 millions* over what the 1981 urban population would be on the basis of natural increase alone without rural-urban migration.

This reasoning suggests that under almost any conceivable circumstances there is likely to be in the course of the next few decades a draining-off to the cities of much of the rural population increase, involving tens of millions of people.

We may conclude that the distribution of manpower between farms and other sectors is not likely to be a factor limiting overall economic development, in view of the present general redundance of manpower and the numerous ways in which adjustment is feasible if relative shortages in any important sector should arise. The policy of promoting of rural small-scale industry supplies, incidentally, an important vehicle for adjustment. The mobility of labor from farms to rural industry is often likely to be greater than from farm to city, and the problems of community facilities and social adjustment are certainly less. It should be possible to vary the emphasis placed on rural as against urban industrial development to some extent in response to the relative availability of surplus labor in rural and urban areas. Finally there is the general point that a shortage of labor in any sector can be overcome by even a modest resort to labor-saving methods along well-trodden paths of experience, sometimes requiring little or no substitution of additional capital. It seems certain, in fact, that the real problem in getting effective manpower use in India will be posed by the need for devising more efficient *labor-intensive, capital-saving* methods. This is a kind of production research and development to which very little systematic effort has ever been devoted, since it has not been in demand in the development of the advanced industrial countries where funds were available for technical research.[21]

---

per cent in 1931-1941 and also in 1941-1951, and the Planning Commission assumes the same rate for the decade 1951-1961 (*ibid.*, p. 26). A rate of 14 per cent per decade is 1.3 per cent per annum; 33 per cent per decade is equivalent to 2.9 per cent per annum.

[21] "In the United States, research and development is a large and well-established

## D. Conclusions

The discussion in this chapter has been built mainly around a few highly simplified formal relationships of "balance," and by no means exhausts the question of the interrelationships between the agricultural and nonagricultural sectors in Indian economic development. However, this is about as far as it seems profitable to go without introducing such relevant considerations as the supply and requirements for savings and development funds and the role of small-scale industry. Those topics will occupy us in later chapters. Meanwhile, some of the leading points suggested by the present chapter are:

1. Structural interrelations between agriculture and the rest of the Indian economy are likely to be such that if one sector limits the growth of the other, it is more likely to be a case of agricultural growth limiting nonagricultural than vice versa. The relationship between these rates of growth is, however, a flexible one.

2. It seems likely that in order to achieve even moderate progress in raising living levels, India will need, within the next three decades, to develop nonagricultural exports on a considerable scale in order to pay for importation of a fairly substantial part of the requirements for agricultural products.

3. For any specified trend of improvement in levels of living, the above adjustment will need to be considerably greater and come earlier if population grows more rapidly.

4. Manpower supply (in quantitative terms) is unlikely to limit growth significantly either in agriculture or the nonagricultural part of the economy, and it is unlikely that concern for the relative in-

---

industry. Every year this industry turns out with approximately the same regularity that the cotton textile industry produces cloth a flow of innovations—new products and improved ways of producing existing products. . . . The countries of Southern Asia have no such research and development industry. Production techniques tend to be either century-old traditional methods or the most modern techniques prevailing in the West. Western methods of production are, however, designed to fit a situation in which labor is relatively scarce and high-priced and capital relatively plentiful. The situation in Southern Asia, of course, is the exact reverse. . . . The primitive techniques offer many obvious opportunities for improvement; at the same time the shortage of capital would suggest that improvement fall short of an adoption of the extremely capital-using techniques of the West. But devising methods and designing equipment adapted to eastern conditions presuppose the existing of research and development facilities and a tinkering propensity on the part of workers that the East simply does not have." Edward S. Mason, *Promoting Economic Development*, Claremont, California, 1955, pp. 36-37.

come level of farmers will result in policies which significantly limit development.

5. For any specified trend of improvement in levels of living, a faster growth of population greatly increases the amount of farm/non-farm relocation of population which would be necessary to prevent a widening of the present ratio between nonfarm and farm levels of per capita income.

◇◇◇◇◇◇◇◇◇◇◇◇◇◇◇◇◇◇◇◇◇◇◇◇◇◇◇◇◇◇◇◇◇◇◇◇◇◇◇◇◇◇◇◇◇◇◇◇◇◇

# NONAGRICULTURAL AND TOTAL OUTPUT— LIMITING FACTORS AND DEVELOPMENT POLICIES

◇◇◇◇◇◇◇◇◇◇◇◇◇◇◇◇◇◇◇◇◇◇◇◇◇◇◇◇◇◇◇◇◇◇◇◇◇◇◇◇◇◇◇◇◇◇◇◇◇◇

WE HAVE SEEN in the preceding chapter that the progress of agriculture is not likely to set any rigid limits on the expansion of the rest of the economy. There are many factors of long-run flexibility in the role of farm output in the economy, including the price-elasticity of demand, the amount of shift of manpower from farm to nonfarm work, the extent to which nonfarm work is rural, and the extent to which manufactures are exported in payment for agricultural imports.

We must now inquire what other limitations (i.e., other than those inherent in a balanced relation with agricultural development) will affect the potential growth of nonfarm output.

It seems highly unlikely that lacks of any basic materials or energy resources will constitute primary limitations on this growth. India is much more favorably situated in these respects than many countries which have developed rapidly and attained a far higher level of productivity. A recent temporary limiting factor has been the scarcity of steel and the high cost of imported steel; but the expansion of steelmaking capacity is being given high priority with the prospect of substantial self-sufficiency within another decade or so. Ore and coking coal reserves are adequate for the needs of the period under consideration. Though India has as yet found little oil and no natural gas, her solid fuel and hydro resources are adequate for any foreseeable growth. Some minerals (notably petroleum, sulphur, copper, lead, zinc, and tin) will have to be imported on an increasing scale unless important new sources are discovered in India; but iron ore, mica, manganese, and some other minerals can continue as exports indefinitely in raw or processed forms, and bauxite is in ample supply for foreseeable domestic needs and even for some export. In short, no drastic disruption of the pattern of external trade, nor any extensive recourse to high-cost domestic substitutes, seems indicated in the light of mineral and energy resources and requirements in the period under consideration. Looking beyond the 1980's, one can envisage shortage problems (e.g., of coking coal); but if one is to look that far ahead, a multitude of presently unknown developments (e.g., in nuclear and solar energy and food synthesis) might also have to be considered. We shall not attempt to extend our speculations that far into the future.

The obvious crucial deficiencies are in capital, labor and management skills, and productive and distributive organization. These are the main factors accounting for the present extremely low levels of productivity in India. The adoption of already-known improvements in technology, and the evolution of further improvements adapted to Indian conditions, require not merely increased capital investment in capital goods, but also extensive outlays devoted to "investment" in a broader sense—improving the quality of the human factor and of the stock of applicable and tested technology.

Under these circumstances, which are well recognized in India, the appropriate strategy for promotion of development must continue, probably for some decades, to follow certain general principles already accepted: which amount in essence to economizing in the use of the scarce factors of capital, public outlays, and skilled manpower and at the same time seeking to ease these scarcities. More specifically, the policy will be:

1. To make the available supply of new capital go as far as possible; i.e., to seek an allocation which will yield maximum output and/or maximum employment per unit of investment.

2. To make maximum use of the surplus unemployed and underemployed labor in labor-intensive production. This in turn calls for an emphasis on decentralized rural and small-scale production to the extent possible, and on the devising of new production techniques which economize on capital.

3. To economize on labor and management skills and to increase their supply. This also goes with some emphasis on decentralization and small-scale production.

4. To increase the supply of new capital, both from domestic savings and from abroad.

It is a foregone conclusion that the Government will take a large and perhaps increasing role in coping with these tasks. It will seek

142

to increase the amount and mobility of domestic savings and foreign capital, and to allocate the available capital to best advantage; and it will devote considerable outlay and effort to the improvement of productivity through research, training, and allied programs.

The Indian economy stands to benefit to a great extent from the availability of advanced technology and specialized equipment and personnel from the more advanced countries. This type of assistance played an important part in the rapid industrialization of Japan and Russia, to cite only two examples. There are, however, important limitations upon this way of acquiring improved techniques. Generally speaking, an industrial technique cannot be successfully transplanted without numerous adaptations to the new environment; and when the environment is as radically different (in both developed resources and outlook) as India is from the advanced "lending" countries, the problems of adaptation assume primary importance. Foremost among such differences is the relative dearth of capital and redundancy of unskilled manpower in India, especially in the light of the Government's commitment to minimize technological unemployment. This means that a large proportion of the equipment and methods which have been expensively evolved in Western countries in the effort to economize on labor-time are simply not economically applicable in India.[1] In order to establish the most efficient technologies for Indian conditions and to institutionalize further improvement by assuring a future flow of appropriate new techniques, there can be no substitute for indigenous research, development, and training. The Indian Government is already budgeting substantial sums under these heads.

The problem of financing development involves both an overall shortage of investment funds and some special problems in particular sectors, especially in view of the character and objectives of Indian development policy. In Western "Industrial Revolutions," high rates of investment were obtained mainly by a tremendous

[1] Cf. footnote 21 on page 138 above. On the other hand, many "imported" improvements offer such economies in the use of capital, highly-skilled labor, or materials that they are very much worthwhile in India. This is particularly true of processes (e.g., in chemical industry, metallurgy, and heavy engineering) in which economies of scale are pre-eminent. There is not much scope for substitution of cheap labor for capital equipment in a steel works, oil refinery, or electric generating station; and in such cases the cost of on-site labor has already been reduced in Western countries so far that a large share of the more recent improvements have been primarily capital-saving or material-saving.

growth in business profits which were then reinvested.[2] In Japan's case, the State actively aided in the accumulation of productive capital by high agricultural land taxes and other measures designed to prevent the low-income, "low-saving" groups from getting much of the increase in per capita income; and in Communist countries the State has of course engineered and carried out virtually the whole process of capital formation.

It is clear that none of these precedents would quite meet India's policy stipulations, even if administratively feasible. The State will not use its influence to promote the inequality of income, but will remain actively concerned with the mitigation of inequalities and the spreading of employment and opportunity as broadly as possible. It will indeed use taxes and other measures to impose a considerable measure of enforced saving on groups well down on the income scale, including the peasants. But in any event it would not be able to nurture industry at agriculture's expense to the extent that Japan did, because it is unlikely that world market and supply conditions would permit a similarly radical shift in the proportions of agriculture and industry, with the accompanying development of large agricultural imports and industrial exports. India's size alone poses a limit on the extent to which it can rely to any very large extent on outside agricultural suppliers and industrial customers.

In India, then, the State will have an important role in generating increased savings, and will limit the liberty of private individuals and firms to acquire or dispose freely of large incomes. It will (in line with the development strategy outlined earlier) allocate a substantial part of the funds in its control to the financing and fostering of decentralized rural and small-scale industry. Partly because of the crucial role of the Government in the prospective development effort, and partly because of the fact that successful development

---

[2] ". . . the essential change is rather the emergence of a new class in society—the profit-making entrepreneurs—which is more thrifty than all the other classes (the landlords, the wage-earners, the peasants, the salaried middle-classes), and whose share of the national income increases relatively to that of all others. In private capitalism these entrepreneurs have made private profits, and have reinvested on private account; whereas in the U.S.S.R., the great increase in profits has been concealed as a 'turnover tax,' which the planners have reinvested on public account. But, in either case, the essential feature of the conversion from 5 to 12% saving is an enormous increase in the share of profits in the national income." W. Arthur Lewis, *The Theory of Economic Growth*, London, 1955, p. 226.

will require "investment" not merely in the narrow sense of additional capital goods but also in improvement of the human and technological resources, it is inappropriate to consider the problem of financing development simply in terms of net investment rates. "Developmental outlays" outside the ordinary definition of investment (for example, outlays for the current expenses of research, education, training, and extension work)[3] will be as necessary as ordinary investment. And the rate at which both types of outlay can be made in India will depend to a large extent (as will be examined more fully later) on how successful the Government is in getting control of a larger proportion of the national income.

The utilization of surplus unemployed and underemployed labor is an effort in which the Government will play a large role, for several reasons. In part this concern is based on immediate welfare considerations. In addition it is important as a part of the effort to instill a pervasive sense of participation and opportunity, without which the exertions and sacrifices required for the success of development plans will scarcely be forthcoming. Its immediate "good will" or political importance is fairly evident. A still further consideration, at least for some categories of employment, is the long-run improvement of the quality of the labor force through experience and training. Last but not least is the idea that making work for people who now add little or nothing to the national output will result in the production of more than enough additional goods or services to cover the costs involved.

Since unemployment and underemployment imply that the manpower in question is at present not contributing to output, it might

[3] The importance of this category of outlays in the process of "institutionalizing" economic growth seems to be manifest in the observed tendency for the ratio of net investment (in the narrow sense) to income to stop rising, and eventually even decline, in highly advanced countries where productivity and per capita income are both continuing to increase rapidly (e.g., the United States). Once a certain quantum of capital per worker is built up, and the development of new technology put on an established basis, it seems that much of the further improvement of physical capital can take the form of rapid *replacement* by continually better capital goods, involving in some cases little or no net addition to the stock of capital. The real "net investment" in such a situation may to a large extent take the form of outlays for research, training, or forms of "consumption" which maintain the flow of innovations and innovators and the supporting flow of competent technicians. This point is developed in Simon Kuznets, *Toward a Theory of Economic Growth*, Columbia Bicentennial Paper, 1953 (processed). Kuznets' paper also appears in Robert Lekachman, ed., *National Policy for Economic Welfare at Home and Abroad*, Garden City, N.Y., 1955.

145

appear that such labor should, from the standpoint of public policy, be regarded as a "free good" costing nothing to employ. Actually this is never strictly the case: there are always some costs involved, and the output must exceed them if providing the jobs is to be justified on economic (as against say purely morale) grounds.

There are fixed capital costs unless the worker can do the job with his bare hands or with equipment he already has or can make (again, with his bare hands). Many types of rural construction work in India, however, using local materials, do involve a fixed-capital outlay approaching zero.

Administrative costs may be a more important item. Someone has to organize and supervise the job. Here is a draft upon resources which are not super-abundant in India; namely administrative personnel and facilities and the public funds to pay for them. A very considerable share of the outlays for Community Development and National Extension Service programs, for example, which may be running at a rate approaching 1 per cent of the national income in India during the next twenty-five years, is involved in the training, pay, and administration of an army of public servants endeavoring to promote more effective use of India's surplus rural manpower.

Finally, there is the working-capital requirement. At least a subsistence wage must be paid, in some combination of cash and kind. In a few cases, where the output of the employment project consists of something for the direct use of those who produced it (like a village road, school, reservoir, or dike, for example), pure persuasion may be enough to get the labor "invested" without any wage payment at all. A part, though by no means all, of the labor reported under "People's Voluntary Contribution" in the community development program represents this type of effort.[4] But for any really large or sustained addition to employment, and certainly in any case where the product has to be sold after completion, wages have to be paid in advance of realization of the proceeds. This then involves a drain on another very scarce factor in the Indian economy—monetary savings. Where materials (other than free goods) are involved, a further working-capital requirement arises.

[4] See Planning Commission, Programme Evaluation Organization, *Evaluation Report on Second Year's Working of Community Projects*, April 1955, Vol. I, pp. 37-42. To date, local contributions to community development and extension projects have amounted to about 60 per cent as much as the Government outlays. (*Second Plan Outline*, p. 85.)

In estimating costs on labor-intensive public-works projects in rural areas in India, the accepted rule of thumb is to assume that two-thirds of the entire cost of the project is labor cost. It has also been suggested that, on the average, the wage rate necessary to "attract labor from the lowest income groups" will be about Rs. 1 1/2 per day; and that the average worker hired on such jobs already has, and will retain, some work during agricultural peak seasons yielding an income of Rs. 150 per annum, so that what the works project provides is about 200 additional days of work and Rs. 300 of additional income. For each man thus brought to full employment, the annual cost is Rs. 300 in wages and Rs. 150 in nonlabor cost, or Rs. 450 in all.[5]

It thus appears that there is no significant case in which the making of jobs can be soundly regarded as quite "costless," in terms of savings or Government funds or scarce personnel. It is still true, however, that in well-conceived programs the cost may be very low in relation to the additional output forthcoming; and also that some of the considerations other than immediate output might justify some allocation of resources for a later or less tangible return.

Finally, it is essential to take into account that wages paid (in cash or kind) on this type of program do constitute additional income for the recipient and may be in part "recaptured," insofar as they add to the aggregate capacity of the people to pay taxes or make voluntary savings. This last factor is responsible in large part for justifying employment projects on national economic grounds which would not be remunerative for any private entrepreneur since he would not benefit from recapture.

In the light of the above discussion it seems most appropriate to appraise India's development potential in terms of two major controlling factors: (1) the proportion of national income which can be devoted to investment and public developmental outlays, and (2) the effectiveness of such outlays in terms of increased productivity. These will be examined in the next two chapters.

[5] Based on an analysis by V. M. Dandekar, as presented by Dr. K. N. Raj in "The Second Five-Year Plan: Investment Magnitudes and their Implications," in *Second Plan Papers*, p. 120. Dr. Raj estimated that the rate of outlay on such projects might reach Rs. 1.5 billion per annum by 1955-1956 and that it should be stepped up to about Rs. 4.2 billion per annum by 1960-1961. The implied employment rates are 3.3 million in 1955-1956 and 9.3 million in 1960-1961.

◇◇◇◇◇◇◇◇◇◇◇◇◇◇◇◇◇◇◇◇◇◇◇◇◇◇◇◇◇◇◇◇◇◇◇◇◇◇◇◇◇◇◇◇◇◇◇◇◇◇◇

# CHAPTER XII

# THE FINANCING OF DEVELOPMENT

◇◇◇◇◇◇◇◇◇◇◇◇◇◇◇◇◇◇◇◇◇◇◇◇◇◇◇◇◇◇◇◇◇◇◇◇◇◇◇◇◇◇◇◇◇◇◇◇◇◇◇

". . . communities in which the national income per head is not increasing invest 4 or 5 percent of their national incomes per annum or less, whilst progressive economies invest 12% per annum or more. The central problem in the theory of economic growth is to understand the process by which a community is converted from being a 5% to a 12% saver—with all the changes in attitudes, in institutions, and in techniques which accompany this conversion."

> W. Arthur Lewis
> *The Theory of Economic Growth*
> London, 1955, pp. 225-226.

## A. Developmental Outlays

To accomplish economic development in India it is necessary to have an increased proportion of the national income spent in ways which contribute to economic growth (i.e., "invested," in the broadest sense of the term). These expenditures are often styled "developmental outlays."

Developmental outlays clearly include all capital investment in productive facilities and additions to working capital. They also include both investment and current outlays on programs for education, research, training, extension work, and the like; though in some of these cases (e.g., primary education and basic research) there may be a wait of a decade or more before any returns begin to appear. In the case of housing and social services, any developmental element may be still more remote; and other outlays (including consumer expenditures and the outlays of governments for purposes of defense and "general government") are generally regarded as not developmental at all.

In this chapter we shall attempt to examine the prospects for increased availability of funds for developmental use. First we may get a rough idea of the main categories of outlay involved, and their present relative importance, by considering Tables 23 and 24 below. Unfortunately, both tables involve some very rough estimates, and the figures presented are not strictly comparable. They will suffice, however, for the present purpose.

Table 23 shows that in a recent year nearly 7 per cent of the Indian national income was going into net capital formation, about 3/8 of which was public investment. The bulk of the rural investment in construction and land improvement, and a substantial part of the investment shown under "agricultural and other implements and small enterprises," (i.e., something like 1 1/2 per cent of national income in all) was in non-monetized form. This table does not take account of additions to inventory, which of course vary widely from year to year and are not known. With some allowance for that item (during the next five years, the Planning Commission estimates the requirement at Rs. 800 million per annum or .65 per cent of national income) and for growth since 1953-1954, it is safe to say that the net investment rate is now running above 8 per cent of national income if non-monetized investment is included.[1]

The percentage ratios of net fixed investment to national income (comparable to the 6.8 per cent shown in Table 23) were as follows in earlier years:[2]

| | |
|---|---|
| 1948-1949 | 5.2 |
| 1949-1950 | 5.8 |
| 1950-1951 | 6.2 |
| 1951-1952 | 6.7 |
| 1952-1953 | 6.7 |

Table 24, based on an earlier and different set of estimates, shows the relation of public investment to other public outlays. The Central and State Governments combined spent Rs. 11.7 billion in 1953-1954, of which a quarter represented net capital formation, mainly under Five-Year Plan programs. Social services (primarily education and health programs) accounted for another sixth of the

[1] *Second Plan Outline*, pp. 24-25. The inventory-accumulation allowance of Rs. 800 million a year, it should be noted, is for a period in which the Planning Commission envisages a considerably faster growth of national output than has prevailed in recent years. The Planning Commission describes the current (1955-1956) "rate of investment in the economy" as "about 7 percent of national income," without indicating what is included in "investment." The context (*loc.cit.*) suggests that this figure refers to monetized investment only. In that case the total for monetized and non-monetized investment would be between 8 and 9 per cent of national income.

[2] From same source as Table 23.

outlay, and about one-tenth consisted of developmental outlays not involving net capital formation (e.g., the operation of the community development and rural extension program). Nearly half of public outlays were clearly non-developmental, being devoted to defense and the routine operations of government.

TABLE 23. ESTIMATES OF NET DOMESTIC FIXED CAPITAL
FORMATION, 1953–1954
(including non-monetized investment)

| | Billions of Rupees | Percentage of Total | Percentage of National Income |
|---|---|---|---|
| Total | 7.2 | 100.0 | 6.8 |
| Government | 2.8 | 38.5 | 2.6 |
| Private | 4.4 | 61.5 | 4.2 |
| Construction | 2.0 | 28.4 | 1.9 |
| Urban | 1.2 | 17.1 | 1.1 |
| Rural | .8 | 11.3 | .8 |
| Land improvement and irrigation works | .8 | 11.5 | .8 |
| Agricultural and other implements and small enterprises | .6 | 9.0 | .6 |
| Mining and manufacturing (excl. small enterprises) | .6 | 8.5 | .6 |
| Transport | .3 | 4.0 | .3 |

Source: Central Statistical Organization and Economic Division of the Ministry of Finance, "Capital Formation in the Indian Union," in *Second Plan Papers*, Table 1, p. 157.

Although the proportion of income made available for investment and other developmental outlays has considerably increased since the beginning of the First Five-Year Plan, it seems clear that the steps thus far taken do not insure a high enough proportion to maintain a satisfactory rate of development. There are several reasons for this assertion.

In the first place, the rate of investment and other developmental outlay at the outset of the First Five-Year Plan (net domestic monetized saving is estimated to have been about 5 per cent of national income) was apparently barely enough to maintain per capita output under conditions of relatively slow population growth. This

TABLE 24. DOMESTIC INVESTMENT AND OTHER OUTLAYS OF
CENTRAL AND STATE GOVERNMENTS, 1953–1954

|  | Billions of Rupees | Percentage of Total Outlays | Percentage of National Income |
|---|---|---|---|
| Total | 11.7 | 100 | 11.1 |
| Net investment | 3.0 | 26 | 2.9 |
| Under Five-Year Plan | 2.8 | 24 | 2.7 |
| Outside the Plan | .2 | 2 | .2 |
| Development outlays on current account | 1.3 | 11 | 1.2 |
| Under Five-Year Plan (maintenance and depreciation) | .7 | 6 | .7 |
| Outside the Plan | .6 | 5 | .6 |
| Social services | 1.8 | 16 | 1.7 |
| Other current outlays | 5.5 | 47 | 5.3 |
| Defense | 2.0 | 17 | 1.9 |
| General government, etc. | 3.5 | 30 | 3.4 |

Source: Derived from Taxation Enquiry Commission, *Report*, Vol. 1, pp. 136, 244, 260. These estimates were based on revised budget estimates in advance of the final account figures for the year 1953–1954. Adjustment has been made to remove duplication that would otherwise result from double counting of sums transferred from Central to State Governments.

Note: In the first column of figures above, the figures 2.8, .2 and .7 are estimates of the Taxation Enquiry Commission (*op.cit.*, p. 136). The grand total of 11.7 is the sum of the reported central and State outlays on revenue account (p. 244) and on capital account (p. 260). The figures for social services (1.8) and other current outlays (5.5) are revenue-account outlays under the indicated heads (p. 244). Apparently .6 billion of net investment outlays were charged to revenue account (this being the excess of the investment according to the T.E.C.'s estimates over the total capital-account outlays). We have assumed that this entire .6 billion fell in the "development outlays" category of revenue-account expenditure and have derived the figure for "development outlays on current account outside the Plan" on that basis as a residual. It is thus possible that the .6 and the 1.3 figures should be higher and the 5.5 lower.

situation of stagnation was similar to that prevailing in many other low-income countries.[3]

Since the outset of the First Plan, real national income per capita is estimated to have increased by about 10 per cent[4] and the propor-

[3] Professor W. Arthur Lewis, in *The Theory of Economic Growth*, London, 1955, p. 208, concurs in the judgment that the Indian pre-Plan investment rate was "at best . . . only enough to keep up with population growth" at 1 1/4 per cent per annum. Some evidence suggests that per capita real income in India was in fact gradually declining.

[4] *Second Plan Outline*, p. 26. The figures (at 1952-1953 prices) are Rs. 255 per capita in 1950-1951 and Rs. 280 per capita in 1955-1956.

tion of income invested and devoted to developmental outlays has also increased (as noted in connection with Table 23 above). It is generally agreed, however, that both the increase in savings and the accompanying growth in national income were aided by certain fortunate circumstances which cannot be relied on to continue to such an extent in future. These fortunate circumstances included better weather conditions for agriculture, with resulting improvement in crops and an indirect stimulus to the whole economy, and also the existence of substantial excess industrial capacity, which made it possible to expand output with relatively little new fixed investment.

Finally, even the 3 1/2 per cent per annum increase in national income obtained during the First Plan would hardly be satisfactory under a markedly faster rate of population increase. The Indian planners have set the sights of the Second Plan on an increase at about 4 1/2 per cent per annum and hope to continue with such a rate in subsequent Plan periods.

Table 25 shows the proposed pattern of outlays under the Second Five-Year Plan (1956-1961) on an annual average basis. The categories shown are not entirely comparable with those in the previous tables, so we shall not attempt to draw conclusions from the apparent differences. It should be noted that these figures *do* include investment in increased inventories, but do *not* include non-monetized investment.

The total (monetized) investment envisaged under the Plan averages about Rs. 12 billion a year, or nearly 10 per cent of average national income during the Second Plan period as projected by the planners. With an allowance for non-monetized investment, the ratio would presumably be between 11 and 12 per cent, as compared with 8 to 9 per cent now. Of the total monetized investment under the Plan, about 5/8, or 7.6 billion is public; and this public investment is complemented by nearly Rs. 4.9 billion of further public developmental expenditure. Of the total public outlay of Rs. 18.7 billion per annum, about 2/3, or Rs. 12.5 billion is developmental.

## B. Factors Determining Availability of Resources for Development

What are the prospects of diverting an increased proportion of the national income into development expenditure?

152

TABLE 25. PROPOSED MONETIZED PRIVATE INVESTMENT AND
PUBLIC OUTLAYS DURING SECOND FIVE-YEAR PLAN,
1956–1961

(Plain figures are annual averages in billions of rupees; percentages of national income
are shown in parentheses)

| | Public Investment and Other Outlays | | Monetized Private Investment | |
|---|---|---|---|---|
| Organized industry and mining | 1.4 | (1.1) | 1.0 | ( .8) |
| Agriculture, irrigation, flood control, community development and rural extension | 2.0 | (1.7) ⎫ | | |
| | | ⎬ | .6 | ( .5) |
| Village and small-scale industries | .4 | ( .3) ⎭ | | |
| Transport and communications | 2.8 | (2.2) ⎫ | | |
| Electric power | .9 | ( .7) ⎬ | .2 | ( .2) |
| Plantations | — | ⎭ | | |
| Construction not shown under other heads | — | | 2.0 | (1.6) |
| Social services, housing, and rehabilitation | 1.9 | (1.5) | — | |
| Additions to inventory | — | | .8 | ( .6) |
| Miscellaneous Plan outlays | .2 | ( .2) | — | |
| Totals | 9.6 | (7.8) | 4.6 | (3.7) |
| *Of which, investment accounts for:* | *7.6* | *(6.1)* | *4.6* | *(3.7)* |
| Public development outlays outside the Five-Year Plan | 2.9 | (2.3) | | |
| Total public development outlays | 12.5 | (10.1) | | |
| Public nondevelopment outlays | 6.2 | (5.0) | | |
| Grand total public outlays | 18.7 | (15.1) | | |

Source: *Second Plan Outline*, pp. 24, 35; "India's Development Plans and Progress," January 1956 (processed). Percentage ratios to national income (in parentheses) have been calculated on the basis of a projected national income totalling Rs. 618.1 billion and averaging Rs. 123.6 billion during the Plan period. This figure is derived by taking the Planning Commission's national income figures for 1955–1956 and 1960–1961 (Rs. 108.0 and 134.8 billion respectively, 1952–1953 prices), interpolating for the intervening years by assuming a constant percentage rate of growth, and then adding up the figures for the last five of the six years (i.e., for the five years contained in the Second Plan period).

It is well known that, among the individuals or households in an economic group, the percentage of income saved varies positively with the level of per capita income. But statistical coefficients describing this relationship (even if they were available for India) could not be used to predict what will happen when the level of the whole economy rises. We cannot assume that if the Indian peasant of 1970 has an income equal to that of the urban Indian of 1956, he will save the same percentage of it then as the latter does now. Observation of historical series for advancing countries has shown, indeed, that the ratio of saving to income does not necessarily respond to a rising trend in per capita income. For example, in the United States since 1870, the proportion of national income saved has not shown a rising trend, despite the fact that per capita real income has grown rapidly.

One reason for this is that over any extended period of time people's consumption standards are flexible and tend to respond to changes in income. These consumption standards are more powerfully influenced by forces of social imitation of other consumers (the so-called "demonstration effect") than they are by persistence of past absolute levels of consumption.

The chances of raising the proportion of national income invested in any country depend not simply on rise in per capita income, but to an important extent on increases *in the proportion of income going to those who have a high propensity to save and invest.* In the words of Professor W. Arthur Lewis:

". . . the correct explanation of why poor countries save so little is not because they are poor, but because their capitalistic sectors are so small. No nation is so poor that it could not save 12 percent of its national income if it wanted to; poverty has never prevented nations from launching upon wars, or from wasting their substance in other ways. Least of all can those nations plead poverty as an excuse for not saving, in which 40 percent or so of the national income is squandered by the top 10 percent of income receivers, living luxuriously on rents. In such countries productive investment is not small because there is no surplus; it is small because the surplus is used to maintain unproductive hordes of retainers, and to build pyramids, temples and other durable consumer goods, instead of to create productive capital. If this surplus were going instead as profits to capitalists, or as taxes to productivity-inclined governments, much higher levels of investment would be possible without inflation. It should also be noted that when we say that saving is low because the capitalist sector is small, we do not refer only to private capitalists, but use the term also to refer to state capitalism, or to any other form of economic organisation where capital is used to employ people, and where, after payment of wages and salaries, a substantial surplus remains of which a large part is reinvested productively. In practice, judging by the U.S.S.R., the state capitalist can accumulate capital even faster than the private capitalist since he can use for the purpose not only the profits of the capitalist sector (disguised as taxation) but also what he can force or tax out

154

of the peasants, or squeeze out of the economy as a whole by inflation."[5]

The factors particularly conducive to attainment of a higher ratio of investment (in addition, that is, to an increasing level of per capita income) appear to include:

1. Concentration of a large part of total private output in large business units (factories, mines, plantations, etc.) rather than in small subsistence-type units.
2. A large ratio of foreign trade to national income (since foreign trade is easily subject to State control for revenue and other purposes).
3. A high ratio of profits to rent in the incomes of the wealthier classes.
4. A relatively large "public sector" in the economy.

Factors 1 and 3 are directly conducive to higher ratios of private investment, while factors 1, 2 and 4 are conducive to a high rate of public saving out of State revenues (assuming of course a development-minded government).

How does India stand in regard to these criteria? Certain initial handicaps are fairly evident. Commenting on this point, Professor Lewis concludes:

". . . one of the [countries] worst off is India, with a large part of its output produced by subsistence producers and small scale units, hard to reach, and with less than 10 percent of national income passing in foreign trade."[6]

The factors just mentioned probably played, indeed, a large part in keeping the Indian savings ratio down to a point scarcely sufficient to support a slowly increasing population with no improvement in average output. But important structural changes now in process may greatly alter this situation. Most of these changes appear likely to increase savings capacity.

Basic public policy in regard to stimulation of savings and investment is outlined in the following statement:[7]

[5] Lewis, op.cit., p. 236.

[6] W. Arthur Lewis, "Economic Development with Unlimited Supplies of Labour," The Manchester School, May 1954, p. 168. Ceylon is an example of a country in which a high ratio of tax revenues to national income is relatively easy to attain because of the far greater relative importance of foreign trade there than in India.

[7] Department of Monetary Research and Statistics, Reserve Bank of India, "Estimates of Savings and Investment and an Appraisal of the Problems of Resource Mobilization," in Second Plan Papers, p. 395.

"The principal considerations to be borne in mind in framing policy are the following:

(a) All savings out of current income should be mobilized for financing the Plan;

(b) As income increases, an increasing proportion of it should be diverted to investment;

(c) This diversion should, as far as practicable, be through voluntary rather than 'forced' savings;

(d) Simultaneously, there should be a reduction in income-inequalities; and

(e) In the aggregate, consumption expenditure should keep a step ahead of the increase in population, so that per capita consumption is not reduced."

## 1. PRINCIPAL SOURCES OF SAVING

Estimates of saving in India are highly approximate and incomplete, but some idea of the present principal sources is given by Table 26.

TABLE 26. SOURCES OF DOMESTIC SAVING, 1954–1955

|  | Billions of Rupees | Percentage of Total Saving |
|---|---|---|
| Total public and private saving | 7.50 | 100 |
| Public saving from current revenue | .70 | 9 |
| Private saving channeled to the public sector | 1.70 | 23 |
| Other private saving | 5.10 | 68 |
| New subscriptions to capital of companies | .25 | 3 |
| Corporate savings | .70 | 9 |
| Increase in deposits of scheduled banks | .40 | 5 |
| Insurance companies[a] | .18 | 2 |
| Cooperatives[b] | .12 | 2 |
| Rural savings (largely non-monetized) | 1.70 | 23 |
| Other | 1.75 | 23 |

[a] Net increase in assets, less increase in holdings of Government securities.

[b] "Estimated increase under Share Capital and Deposits of Cooperatives."

Source: Reserve Bank of India, "Estimates of Savings and Investment and an Appraisal of the Problems of Resource Mobilization," in *Second Plan Papers*, pp. 399-400. Cf. also corresponding estimates for 1950–1951 and 1953–1954, with explanations of methods and assumptions, in Taxation Enquiry Commission, *Report*, Vol. 1, pp. 136-139.

This breakdown gives only the roughest idea of where savings originate, since the estimates had to be built up in terms of the channels by which funds seek investment,[8] and there is a large residual category. Governments supplied apparently only about 9 per cent of domestic savings from their surpluses of current revenues over current outlays, but borrowed much larger sums from private savers for public investment purposes and acquired command over a substantial proportion of the community's savings through deficit financing. A very sizeable part of the total saving (perhaps as much as 15 to 20 per cent) occurred in the non-monetized rural sector, much of it in housing.

In the discussion of specific categories of savers which is to follow, we shall give special attention to certain categories which seem likely (1) to increase in relative importance, and (2) to save a high proportion of their incomes. These include in particular the organized private business enterprises, governments, and cooperatives. Some attention will also be paid to the possibilities of greater mobilization of the savings potential of the households and small business units which account for the bulk of total output and income in India but may be presumed to save only a very small proportion of it (particularly in monetized form).

## 2. SAVING BY ORGANIZED PRIVATE ENTERPRISES

An important source of increased saving capacity is in the prospective rapid growth of the organized private business sector, which characteristically saves and invests a high proportion of its own earnings in addition to investing sums borrowed from other savers and furnishing the Government with a substantial share of its tax revenue.

(a) *Large enterprises.* About 8 1/2 per cent of the national income is now produced by relatively large-scale organized mining and factory enterprises, and it may be estimated that about another 2 1/2 per cent is produced by the larger private enterprises in other fields (including plantations, banking and insurance, and forestry).[9]

In the "corporate" sector (companies and other concerns assessa-

[8] Taxation Enquiry Commission, *Report*, Vol. 1, p. 137.
[9] The 8 1/2 per cent figure is shown as an estimate for 1955-1956 in the *Second Plan Outline*, p. 26. The *Final Report of the National Income Committee*, p. 107, indicates that in 1950-1951 the net output of all "large enterprises" other than railways and communications (which are mainly in government hands) was 1.29 times that of mining and factory establishments alone. If this proportion still holds, about 11 per cent of national product arises in the field of organized large and medium-scale enterprises.

ble at company income tax rates) the concerns with incomes over Rs. 100,000 reported in 1953-1954 total profits of Rs. 2.0 billion, and it has been estimated that this figure understated actual profits by at least Rs. 0.7 billion.[10] Corporate profits, then, may run at present from 2 1/2 to 3 per cent of national income. After deduction of income taxes the ratio is roughly 2 to 2 1/4 per cent.

As a concomitant to the process of industrialization, the large-enterprise sector seems almost certain to increase in importance relative to the national income. According to the *Draft Outline* of the Second Five-Year Plan, for example, the proportion of national income accounted for by organized mining and factory enterprises alone is expected to rise from 7.4 per cent in 1950-1951 and 8.6 per cent in 1955-1956 to 11.4 per cent in 1960-1961. Such an increase in the relative importance of larger-scale "secondary production" is quite characteristic in any industrialization process, in the phase in which India will be for many decades.[11]

If we take the large-enterprise sphere as a whole as now accounting for some 11 per cent of national output, then, it would seem reasonable to expect this percentage to rise to something approaching 20 per cent in the mid-1960's and perhaps 25 to 30 per cent in the mid-1970's. If corporate profits after taxes show a similar trend, their ratio to national income would rise from about 2 per cent at present to roughly 4 per cent in the 1960's and 5 or 6 per cent in the 1970's.

The essential point for present purposes is that larger business

[10] Gokhale Institute of Politics and Economics, "Income-Tax Evasion," in *Second Plan Papers*, pp. 504-506. Data are not at hand to determine to what extent the private corporate sector is coterminous with the category described as "large private enterprises." For the purposes of this discussion, which deals only in terms of rough magnitudes, we are treating them as equivalent.

[11] For example, in Japan the proportion of the labor force engaged in mining, manufacturing and construction rose from 9 per cent in 1887 to 13 per cent in 1897 and 18 per cent in 1910. In Sweden the same ratio rose from 12 per cent in 1880 to 21 per cent in 1900 and 35 per cent in 1920. These figures considerably understate the rise in the relative importance of *larger-scale* industrial production, since increase in size of units regularly accompanies industrialization. A further understatement is involved by the use of percentages of labor force rather than net output. After a rather high level of productivity is reached in an economy, the industrial or "secondary" sector characteristically ceases to expand its share of national output, and the fastest increase is in the tertiary sector. The figures cited here are from Simon Kuznets, *Towards a Theory of Economic Growth*, Columbia Bicentennial Paper (processed), 1955, Appendix Table 8, pp. 145-148, and are based largely on Colin Clark, *Conditions of Economic Progress*, 2nd ed., 1951, Ch. IX.

158

enterprises characteristically save and reinvest a much higher proportion of their earnings than do smaller enterprises or individuals (in addition, of course, to investing considerable sums borrowed). Data collected by the Taxation Enquiry Commission for a sample of several hundred manufacturing corporations, covering the years 1946 through 1952, indicate that the proportion of profits (after taxes) retained varied in individual years from 22 to 50 per cent.[12] In view of the fact that this period covers the highly unsettled period of postwar adjustment and Partition, before the impact of the First Five-Year Plan was felt, and a period in which investment was somewhat retarded also by equipment and materials shortages and widespread excess capacity, it would seem in order to take the upper end of this range (i.e., 50 per cent) for projection purposes. A relevant fact is that recommendations of the Taxation Enquiry Commission, now in process of implementation, were designed to encourage reinvestment of earnings in industries where expansion is important in the interests of overall national economic development.[13]

This would suggest that net saving by large business enterprises (primarily corporations) might be expected to increase from probably no more than 1 per cent of national income at present to something like 2 per cent in the 1960's and 2 to 3 per cent in the 1970's. (b) *Cooperatives.*[14] Cooperative organization has grown considerably in India since the early 1940's. Membership and outstanding loans of primary societies increased 10 per cent and 40 per cent, respectively, in the three-year interval from 1950-1951 to 1953-1954. In 1954 there were about 190,000 cooperative societies of all types in India, with total working capital of about Rs. 3.5 billion. Agricultural credit societies are the most important type, with nearly 6 million members.

In most parts of the country, however, cooperation still plays only a minor role in the overall financial and organizational scheme. The cooperatives' current rate of contribution to total saving is apparently quite small (Table 26).

[12] *Report*, Vol. 1, pp. 309-319.
[13] *Report*, Vol. 2, Chapter VII.
[14] Reserve Bank of India, *Rural Credit Survey* 1954; Reserve Bank of India, *Statistical Statements Relating to the Cooperative Movement in India for the Year 1953-54*; D. G. Karve, "Place of Cooperatives in the Second Five Year Plan," in *Second Plan Papers*, pp. 583-590; *Second Plan Outline*, Ch. V.

A potentially significant factor in increased national saving capacity is the prospective growth of cooperatives, especially in agriculture and small-scale industry, which is expected to begin to accelerate rapidly during the Second Five-Year Plan. Recommendations for a reorganized and revitalized national cooperative system, with State partnership participation on various levels and State financial support from the top through the Reserve Bank of India, were prepared during the First Plan period after a thorough-going study of rural credit problems, and are now in process of implementation as one of the major aspects of the development program.[15] During the Second Five-Year Plan, it is hoped to quintuple the total outstanding loans of cooperatives: from Rs. 430 million to Rs. 2,250 million. It was proposed in 1955 by a conference of State Ministers in charge of cooperation that by 1971, cooperatives should be extended so as to embrace as much as half of all rural credit, marketing, processing and other business operations.

With respect to the promotion of business investment and also the increased opportunities for effective taxation, cooperatives in India would seem to offer some of the same increased-saving effect as has been secured in other countries through the expansion of the spheres of large-scale private and state enterprise. In general, the legislation governing cooperatives strongly favors retention and reinvestment of earnings.[16] It seems reasonable to expect that the cooperative sector will be both a "high-saving" sector and a rapidly expanding one.

[15] ". . . the fields which mark themselves out as being specially appropriate for the co-operative method of organization are agricultural credit, marketing and processing, all aspects of production in rural areas, consumers' co-operative stores, co-operatives of artisans and construction co-operatives. *In these fields the objective is to enable co-operation increasingly to become the principal basis for the organisation of economic activity.* This implies that new activities should be co-operatively organised and also that by stages existing activities should be taken over by co-operatives." *Second Plan Outline*, p. 65. (Italics supplied.)

[16] "A satisfactory capital accumulation and the consolidation of co-operative society's activity is a concern of the greatest importance equally for the society's members, its creditors and the public at large. The Indian Acts invariably provide for a carry over of a certain percentage of net profit to a Reserve Fund. Majority of the Acts require at least 25 percent of the net profits to be carried to the Reserve . . . Ordinarily, societies with unlimited liability are barred from paying any dividends on the share capital." C. S. Puri, "Cooperative Legislation in India," *Agricultural Situation in India*, X:11, February 1956, p. 833. Unlimited liability is in general required in the case of primary agricultural credit societies, the most important type. (*ibid.*, pp. 831-832.)

## 3. GOVERNMENTS

The various levels of government in India have in recent years collected 8 to 9 per cent of the national income through ordinary revenue sources and the profits of the public enterprises like the railways.[17]

TABLE 27. COMBINED CURRENT REVENUES OF CENTRAL, STATE AND LOCAL GOVERNMENTS, 1953–1954

|  | Billions of Rupees | Percentage of Total |
|---|---|---|
| Total current revenues | 8.70 | 100.0 |
| Tax revenues | 7.12 | 81.8 |
| Taxes on income | 1.69 | 19.5 |
| Corporation | .38 | 4.4 |
| Other | 1.31 | 15.1 |
| Property taxes | .25 | 2.8 |
| Customs and excise | 3.04 | 34.9 |
| Other taxes and duties | 1.43 | 16.6 |
| Land revenue | .70 | 8.0 |
| Revenues from public utilities and State undertakings | .38 | 4.3 |
| All other revenues (mainly civil administration receipts) | 1.21 | 13.9 |

Source: Taxation Enquiry Commission, 1953-1954, *Report*, Vol. I, Table 3, pp. 16-17. Figures shown here are "revised estimates," not final accounts. Revenue receipts of local governments (exclusive of Central Government grants) are not precisely known, but are believed to amount to substantially less than 10 per cent of the total for all levels of Government combined (*ibid.*, p. 30).

It seems safe to say that the share of the economy under direct Government operation will at least be maintained during this period. Railways and postal and telecommunication services will be expanded at a rate in excess of the growth of national income for some time to come.

Moreover, the Central Government specifically assumed responsibility as long ago as 1948 for assuring the proper development of a considerable list of key industries, and in several of these is an important or even the sole direct producer. The basic industrial policy established in 1948 was extended and somewhat modified in

[17] See Table 27 for a breakdown of these revenues by source.

a policy declaration by Prime Minister Nehru on April 30, 1956.[18] According to the terms of this declaration, the state assumes exclusive responsibility for future development in armaments, atomic energy, iron and steel, and the mining of coal, iron ore, gold, diamonds and copper. A second category of industries is characterized as "progressively state-owned." Government will here take the initiative in establishing new undertakings, but private enterprises may also be required to supplement the Government's efforts. This category includes aluminum and other nonferrous metals, machine tools, antibiotics and other essential drugs, commercial fertilizers, synthetic rubber, and road and sea transport.

The Industries (Development and Regulation) Act of 1951 established wide powers of Government management and control over more than forty industries, including the licensing of all substantial additions to productive capacity. The public sector has been assigned an increasingly important role in the first two Five-Year Plans,[19] and there seems little doubt of a readiness to expand this sector, even in unforeseen directions, rather than to let shortfalls in the private sector threaten the fulfillment of overall plans.

It is, of course, assumed that public policy will continue to aim at a higher investment rate, and that taxes and other revenue devices will be adjusted in the effort to capture a larger share of national income without impinging so seriously on private saving as to offset increased public saving.[20]

The figures in Table 28 have been pieced together as a rough indication of recent responsible Indian views on the fiscal outlook for the Second Five-Year Plan period. Total public expenditures contemplated average 15.1 per cent of national income. Through

[18] The *New York Times*, May 1, 1956, p. 10.

[19] In the First Plan, about half the total development outlay was allotted to the public sector; in the Second Plan, about five-eighths. *Second Plan Outline*, p. 24.

[20] ". . . taxation may be a most effective means of increasing the total volume of savings and investment in any economy where the propensity to consume is normally high. . . . On the whole, the kind of tax system which would be best adapted to meet the requirements of the Indian economy, having regard to the development programme and the resources required for it, appears to be one which would increase the resources for investment available to the public sector with as small a diminution as practicable of investment in the private sector and which, therefore, is accompanied by the largest practicable restraint on consumption by all classes. Restraint on the consumption of higher income groups must, of course, be greater than in respect of low income groups." Taxation Enquiry Commission, 1953-1954, *Report*, p. 149.

## TABLE 28. ESTIMATES OF SOURCES AND USES OF PUBLIC FUNDS DURING SECOND FIVE-YEAR PLAN

| | Billions of Rupees (annual average, 1956–1961) | Percentage of National Income |
|---|---|---|
| Ordinary internal sources of funds | 13.9 | 11.2 |
| Revenue account receipts (a) | 10.7 | 8.7 |
| Railway contribution | .3 | .2 |
| Capital account receipts | | |
| Loans from public | 1.4 | 1.1 |
| Small savings and unfunded debt | 1.0 | .8 |
| Other | .5 | .4 |
| External and supplementary sources | 4.0 | 3.2 |
| External assistance | 1.6 | 1.3 |
| Deficit financing | 2.4 | 1.9 |
| Total visible resources | 17.9 | 14.5 |
| Expenditures on revenue account for nondevelopmental purposes (b) | 6.2 | 5.0 |
| Proposed developmental outlays | 12.5 | 10.1 |
| Under Second Five-Year Plan | 9.6 | 7.8 |
| Outside the Plan (c) | 2.9 | 2.3 |
| Total expenditures contemplated (d) | 18.7 | 15.1 |
| Uncovered gap (total expenditures minus total visible resources) | .8 | .6 |

Source: All items above (*except* those marked with letters, and the subtotals and totals including such items) are taken from *Second Plan Outline*, p. 27. Items (b), (c) and (d) are taken from an unofficial mimeographed paper, "India's Development Plans and Progress," January 1956, which is believed to represent the views of informed specialists. Item (a) has been derived as a residual from the other data. In calculating the percentage ratios to national income, an average national income of Rs. 123.6 billion per annum has been assumed, in line with Planning Commission projections of national income through the Second Plan period. (cf. Source note to Table 25 above).

important changes in taxation, along lines recommended by the Taxation Enquiry Commission, it is hoped to maintain revenue-account and railway receipts at 8.9 per cent of national income, a little above the ratio prevailing in recent years. In the absence of such changes, this ratio might well decline.[21] Internal borrowing in the orthodox sense is looked to for additional funds equivalent to 2.3 per cent of national income; deficit financing, 1.9 per cent; and assistance from abroad, 1.3 per cent. This brings the total inflow of

[21] "The Second Five-Year Plan: An Appraisal of the Financial Resources Likely to be Available in the Public Sector," in *Second Plan Papers*, pp. 337-352.

funds from specified sources to 14.5 per cent of national income, leaving a gap of 0.6 per cent for which no provision is yet in sight. This or any larger shortfall in funds may of course be resolved by a reduction in the rate of expenditures below contemplated levels— for example, the Plan might be spread over a period longer than five years.

It is reasonable to assume that an attempt will be made during the Third and subsequent Plans to maintain, and if possible to increase further, the proportion of income passing into public hands. Professor K. N. Raj (speculating on possibilities through 1960-1961) estimated that complete implementation of all the recommendations of the Taxation Enquiry Commission might raise "the current income of government taxes, fees and profits of State enterprises" from 8 1/2 per cent to something between 9 1/4 and 10 per cent even without any stimulus from "a marked change in the distribution of income in favour of profits . . . or a relative increase in the supply of heavily-taxed commodities, or an increase in the profits of state enterprises."[22] Looking forward into the 1960's and 1970's, it would appear reasonable to expect some further increase, though nothing spectacular. The expansion of the organized industrial sector and of cooperatives at rates much faster than the growth of national income, the progressive monetization of the economy,[23] and the rise in per capita incomes, should all work toward making a somewhat higher proportion of national income available for public use, assuming that the necessary further tax adjustments can be worked out. It does not seem possible to foresee the trend of profits of State enterprises, particularly since no decision appears to have been reached on proposals for extensive resort to State trading and fiscal monopolies. We may hazard as a guess that governments might collect (as revenues and as net earnings of State enterprises) 9 to 10 per cent of the national income during the 1960's and 10 to 12 per cent in the 1970's. The ratio attainable by any given date would depend, primarily, however, on how rapidly per capita incomes rise.[24]

[22] "Investment Magnitudes and their Implications," in *Second Plan Papers*, pp. 127-128.
[23] "The existence, on a large scale, of a non-monetized sector in the economy also makes it difficult to increase tax receipts through the usual forms of taxation." Taxation Enquiry Commission, 1953-1954, *Report*, p. 151.
[24] "A basic explanation for the very low ratio of total taxation to national income is, of course, to be found in the meagre living standards of the people

In addition to the rather sure prospect of an increase in the proportion of national income appearing in public revenues, there is also at least a fair possibility that an increased proportion of public funds might be made available for development. At present, something like 5 per cent of national income goes for public nondevelopment outlays such as the upkeep of the military establishment and the cost of "general government" operations.[25] One proposal for the Second Five-Year Plan, stressing the desirability of economy in nondevelopment expenditure, even urged that:

> ". . . it should be the endeavour to ensure that no part of the additional budgetary resources raised hereafter would be utilised for non-development purposes."[26]

This is almost certainly unrealistic. The same source in fact states:

> ". . . in a period when development expenditure itself is growing, there would be a certain necessary increase in recurring charges, including the costs of administration. With increasing urbanisation, there will be a rise in expenditure on law and order and ordinary government services. As large capital projects are undertaken, until they become remunerative, there is a net addition to interest charges. As for defence, while increases under certain heads may be met by reductions in others on revenue account, the provision for capital expenditure may have to be larger in the immediate years ahead. This has also been generally the experience of governments since 1950. In fact, between 1950-51 and 1953-54, there was a larger increase in non-development expenditure (Rs. 85 crores) than in development expenditure (Rs. 80 crores) charged to revenue account . . ."[27]

However, even if public nondevelopmental expenditures must go on increasing as seems likely, it may well be feasible to keep them from increasing any faster than national income does. The figures shown in earlier tables suggest, in fact, that nondevelopmental public outlays during the Second Plan period will represent a lower proportion of national income than was the case in 1953-1954. This cannot be regarded as conclusive, however, in view of the

---

reflected in low per capita income levels. This sets rigorous limits to taxation for most people in the community, if the existing frugal consumption levels are not to be lowered" (*ibid.*).

[25] Cf. Tables 24, 25, and 28 above, pp. 151, 153, 163.

[26] Reserve Bank of India, "Estimates of Savings and Investment and an Appraisal of the Problems of Resource Mobilisation; Balance of Payments and Planned Development," in *Second Plan Papers*, p. 409.

[27] *op.cit.*, p. 408.

inadequate basis of comparison, the rough and tentative nature of the estimates involved, and the wide latitude for discretion in designating outlays as "developmental" or "nondevelopmental."

The ratio of the Central Government's nondevelopmental expenditures to its current revenues has shown some tendency to decline in recent years.[28]

If, as suggested earlier, government revenues can be increased somewhat faster than national income in the next two decades, and if nondevelopmental public outlays can be kept at a roughly constant ratio to national income, the public revenue available for development might increase quite rapidly, as illustrated below.

|  | Percentage of national income | | |
|---|---|---|---|
|  | Late 1950's | 1960's | 1970's |
| Public revenues (including earnings of State enterprises) | 9 | 9–10 | 10–12 |
| Public nondevelopmental outlays | 5 | 5 | 5 |
| Revenues available for developmental use | 4 | 4–5 | 5–7 |

## 4. MONETIZED VOLUNTARY SAVING BY SMALLER ENTERPRISES AND BY INDIVIDUALS

A substantial part of the net domestic monetized saving comes from smaller enterprises and individuals, who either use it directly in capital formation or, by withholding income from current expenditure, make an additional share of resources available for investment by larger enterprises or governments.

As indicated earlier, governments in India now collect in revenues 8 1/2 to 9 per cent of the national income, while larger enterprises now collect in net profits after taxes about 2 per cent, of which they retain for reinvestment close to half. Disposable incomes of individuals and unincorporated smaller businesses amount, then, to at least 90 per cent of national income.

But total domestic monetized saving is only about 7 per cent of national income, and of this the government and corporate saving out of revenue accounts in all for some 4 to 4 1/2 per cent. It would appear, then, that the individual and small business sector as

[28] "Revenue Surpluses and the Plan," *The Eastern Economist*, March 16, 1956, p. 447.

a whole saves (in monetized form) only about 3 per cent of national income out of the 90 per cent it receives. These figures are, of course, highly approximate—the essential point is merely the relatively low saving ratio of the individual and small business sector.

It is evident that even if the saving behavior of that sector did not change, the prospective shift of income in favor of government and larger organized enterprises would quite substantially improve the *overall* rate of domestic savings relative to national income, simply because both are characteristically high savers, saving something like 40 to 50 per cent of their current incomes.[29]

Actually, there is no reason to suppose that small businesses and individuals will not voluntarily save a substantially *increased* proportion of their disposable incomes during the period under consideration, though the increase is not likely to be spectacular. The incomes of most people will remain so low as to provide little margin for saving, particularly in view of the prospect of increased taxation. The effort to mitigate economic inequalities is likely in and of itself to handicap voluntary saving,[30] in view of the fact that well-to-do individuals ordinarily save a much higher proportion of their incomes than poorer individuals.

However, improved financial organization and certain controls on expenditure and investment are likely to bring substantial improvement.

The present situation has been described by one observer as follows:

"Savings among large sections of the people are not primarily determined by the investment motive, in the sense of a desire for more

[29] As a concrete numerical illustration, let us say that the present savings of 7 per cent of national income are supplied by the saving of 43 per cent of one-tenth of the total income and 3 per cent of the remaining nine-tenths. If at some future time the "43 per cent savers" command 15 per cent of the total income and the "3 per cent savers" only 85 per cent, total savings will have risen to 9 per cent of national income as the result of this shift.

[30] The Planning Commission, in the preliminary draft of the Second Five-Year Plan, recommended a number of measures to reduce inequality of incomes, including an increase in progressive income tax and estate tax rates, a tax on wealth, and an eventual ceiling on personal incomes. The Taxation Enquiry Commission had suggested (*Report*, Vol. 1, p. 154) a ceiling set at about 30 times the average income per individual or family. One of the proposals advanced by the Planning Commission (the taxing of upper-bracket taxpayers on the basis of expenditure rather than income) seems designed to mitigate adverse effects upon individual saving.

167

current income from the investment, but express themselves a great deal in bunched ceremonial expenditure which is high in relation to income, in hoarding as a security reserve, and in land which is the main economic foundation for the perpetuation of the family. As a corollary, investment is not so markedly affected by judgments on the financial rate of return. Much of the additional income of wealthier groups escapes through high ostentatious consumption, or is invested in buildings or land, or in foreign currencies. In using funds to earn more income, there is a preference for trade or finance rather than investment in concrete capital for industrial or agricultural production . . . The problem is both to increase the means to save and change the cultural environment, and improve the institutional arrangements so that the aggregate of savings is increased and investment has a better balance . . . An important aspect in any approach is to demonstrate the possibility of income-earning investment for purposes in which the people are interested . . . Another thing is to bring home the possibility of achieving something worthwhile by aggregating the small units of savings of individuals into larger sums which can be applied effectively. . . ."[31]

All of the hindrances to productive investment cited in the passage quoted are being attacked by various measures, most of which are not sufficiently advanced as yet to permit a judgment of their eventual impact. Land reforms, increased progressive income and estate taxation,[32] luxury excises and curbs on consumer-goods imports, and some discouragement of lavish ceremonial expenditure are already in evidence. A comprehensive system of cooperatives and of banks to finance them is being developed as a principal

[31] Horace Belshaw, *Population Growth and Levels of Consumption*, Institute of Pacific Relations, 1956, pp. 116-117.

[32] It is consistently observed that a wealthy class drawing its income largely from profits is far more likely to save and reinvest a high proportion of income than is the case when landed property is the main basis of large fortunes. The conspicuous consumption of wealthy absentee landholders in India in the past followed a pattern quite characteristic elsewhere under comparable circumstances. At present, however, the category of large incomes from land appears to be rapidly dwindling as the results of land reform and taxation measures. For some time to come, at least, the States will be receiving, as rent or purchase installments, a large part of the income once going to wealthy landlords or intermediaries. Reimbursement has been both partial and deferred (largely in the form of bonds), particularly to the largest former landholders who have been deprived of the bulk of their holdings or rights. There is a potential gain in (public) saving capacity here, though the short-run effect may be in the opposite direction. A strong effort will be made to extract larger revenues from agricultural land, pursuant to the recommendations of the Taxation Enquiry Commission. The task is greatly aggravated by the fact that taxes on real property and on agricultural income are constitutionally reserved to the States. (Taxation Enquiry Commission, *Report*, Vol. 1, p. 8.)

means of "aggregating the small savings of individuals into larger sums which can be applied effectively." Insurance has been nationalized and is likely to be sold aggressively, and there will probably be a certain amount of expansion during the period under consideration in social insurance schemes, which in their build-up stages offer considerable possibilities for accumulation of individual savings. Small savings have increased from Rs. 0.4 billion to 0.6 billion between 1953-1954 and 1955-1956, and it is proposed to improve the existing small savings system to encourage a continued growth.[33]

As to the overall possibilities of increasing voluntary individual saving, it seems safe to say they will be relatively small in the next decade or two at least, and will depend primarily on the rate at which per capita incomes rise but also on changes in the distribution of income.[34]

During the Second Five-Year Plan, aggressive efforts will be made to elicit greater savings from the general public, for both Government and private investment. For Government borrowings, the objective is to raise the net proceeds of "market loans" from its present level of about 1 per cent of national income to an average of 1.2 per cent; for "small savings," now running at about .55 per cent of national income, the target average for the next five years is about .81 per cent. In both cases the recent trend, in percentage as well as absolute terms, has been upward.[35]

5. THE ROLE OF GOVERNMENT DEFICITS
AND PRIVATE CREDIT EXPANSION

In recent years a considerable part of the Indian Government's outlays have been covered by drawing upon Government balances

[33] The proposals are described in Reserve Bank of India, "Estimates of Savings and Investment and an Appraisal of the Problems of Resource Mobilisation," in *Second Plan Papers*, pp. 416-421.

[34] "There are . . . other considerations pressing against the possibility of increasing the proportion of small savings to national income. Firstly, in accordance with the recommendations of the Taxation Enquiry Commission, there are likely to be, in the next few years, all-round increases in taxation on all groups including the lower and middle income groups. This increased taxation will reduce the margin between personal incomes and personal consumption, with consequent reduction in savings. A redistribution of incomes in favour of the lower income groups will undoubtedly result in a tendency to increase consumption expenditure. Consumption expenditure should also increase with the increasing availability of consumer goods. . . ." (*op.cit.*, pp. 418-420.)

[35] *Second Plan Outline*, pp. 27, 28.

and borrowing at the Reserve Bank of India, which is what is called "deficit financing" in Indian usage; and a further part by borrowing from the public and from commercial banks. In the proposed financing of the Second Five-Year Plan, very heavy reliance is placed on continuance of these procedures.[36]

These proposals for public deficits and borrowing are generally regarded, even by their proponents, as precariously high, involving calculated risks of harmful inflation and interference with needed private investment. It appears that they are likely to be curtailed substantially if indications of their effects seem to warrant it.

For our purposes in this study, which concern basically the long-run outlook over the next few decades in relation to possible trends of population growth, we see no need to enter into the current controversy about the appropriate role of deficit financing and credit expansion in the next few years. It is appropriate merely to indicate briefly the relation of these devices to the growth process in the Indian context.

We may first note that in a growing economy, an increasing supply of the means of payment (money) is required in order to finance the growing volume of transactions, if the well-known inhibiting effects of deflationary price decline are to be avoided. The following comments from a report by a mission of the International Monetary Fund are apposite:[37]

"As the economy of India develops, a gradual increase in the money supply will be needed. The increase in the money supply that will be necessary is likely to be not less than in proportion to the increase in production, and it may have to be somewhat more, if industry, commerce, and even agricultural production for the market gain in importance relative to agricultural production for the village com-

[36] "Deficit financing" (in the restricted Indian sense noted above) is set at Rs. 12 billion for the five years of the Plan period, representing about 1/4 of total public outlays under the Plan or roughly 2 per cent of expected national income. Borrowing from other sources is set at a like additional amount (cf. Table 28.) Thus the total of "deficit financing" in the Indian sense plus Government borrowing from the public and from commercial banks amounts, as proposed, to half the public Plan outlays, nearly 4 per cent of national income, or about 9/10 of the expected *increase* in national income over the five years.

[37] International Monetary Fund, *Economic Development with Stability: A Report to the Government of India*, Washington, 1953, pp. 39, 40. It follows of course that in a period in which foreign exchange assets are being reduced, a compensating additional expansion of internal credit is required in order to maintain an adequate money supply. This is relevant to the Second Plan period, in which India expects to draw upon its sterling balances.

munity. Such an increase in the money supply is not inflationary; and a smaller increase may prove to be inadequate for the needs of a stable economy."

"There are only two ways in which the money supply can be increased: by the acquisition of foreign exchange assets and by the creation of credit. That part of the growth in the money supply which is not matched by the accumulation of foreign exchange assets must arise from the creation of credit."

The "money supply with the public" (i.e., excluding Government cash balances) is currently about Rs. 21 billion, about 2/3 in currency and 1/3 in bank deposits.[38] It thus represents very nearly 1/5 of the annual national income. If over the long run this proportion were to be maintained, net additions to the money supply would amount to 1/5 of increments to national income—and if the national income were growing at a rate of, say, 4 per cent per annum, the annual additions to the money supply would have to be .8 per cent of national income. This is of course only a roughly indicative figure. It makes no allowance for the prospective growth in the monetized sector of the economy compared to the total, and on the other hand makes no allowance for the possibility of more rapid circulation of the means of payment (and consequently reduced needs for new money) as the financial system develops further in India. We feel that the former factor is likely to outweigh the latter for a considerable period. Thus, it seems justifiable to surmise that over the long run the annual rate of net additions to the money supply (consistent with price stability) may be of the order of 1/2 per cent to 1 per cent of national income. As will be noted later, accumulation or depletion of foreign exchange assets is unlikely to be a major long-run factor in this connection, so the same rough range of magnitudes is applicable to internal credit expansion.

Let us now quote again from the Fund mission report:[39]

"The increase in the amount of money held by the public represents savings matched by real resources that go into investment. Where growth in the money supply is the result of the accumulation of foreign exchange, the investment is represented by the foreign exchange. Where growth in the money supply is the result of the creation of bank credit, the investment is represented by the projects financed by bank credit. The creation of bank credit within the limits of an

[38] *Reserve Bank of India Bulletin,* current issues.
[39] *op.cit.,* pp. 41, 43.

appropriate money supply makes it possible for the public to hold enough of its savings in the form of money to assure price stability in a growing economy. The allocation of the Bank credit among different borrowers affects the direction of investment arising from these savings."

". . . To the extent that the expansion of the money supply takes place through deficit financing and by Government borrowing from the commercial banks, it makes available to the Government the resources represented by such saving. To the extent that the expansion of the money supply takes place through business borrowing from the commercial banks, it makes available to the private sector the resources represented by such saving."

It is clear, then, that expansion of the money supply (by deficit financing, government borrowing from commercial banks, or private borrowing from commercial banks) is not to be regarded as a source of investment funds additional to those examined in earlier sections of this chapter, but merely as one device for (1) determining whether the public sector or the private sector disposes of a certain fraction of the community's savings, and (2) maintaining monetary income and spending at such a level that the supply of cash equals the community's desire to hold cash at the existing price level, and thus maintaining price stability and avoiding the drag on development which a declining price level would exert.

It should be noted that there are also other important devices (e.g., in the tax field) serving each of these objectives; and that in our examination of the prospects for mobilization of funds for public use and for private investment, we have already assumed accomplishment of the above objectives in line with a reasonable development policy.

Any single increase in the money supply (whether by government deficit financing or borrowing from banks, or by private borrowing from banks) tends to generate a multiple increase in money incomes, according to the well known Keynesian "multiplier" principle. When the original borrower spends the funds, they are income for the various recipients (e.g., employees and material suppliers for a construction project). These recipients in turn will spend the greater part of this added income, thus increasing the money incomes of still others. The effects of the initial money-creation are exhausted only when the total additions to holdings of

172

cash balances match the amount of the original creation of new money; and since the average recipient of added income will choose to put only a small part of it into idle cash, the increase in money income will be several times as great as the addition to the money supply. So long as the increase in money spending is matched by an increase in the real output of goods and services (which it may help to stimulate) there will be no inflationary rise in prices.[40]

In a situation where there are generally available throughout the economy combinations of productive factors (e.g., unused industrial capacity which can be reactivated as soon as additional sales demand appears), such an increase in money incomes can help to speed the increase of production. Under these circumstances a rapid increase in the money supply can be justified as non-inflationary. This is the situation characteristic of an industrial economy in a depression phase.

It applies in India only to the very limited extent that idle productive facilities are at hand throughout the economy which require *only* the stimulus of additional demand to bring them into use. As we have seen already, this is not generally the case. The really effective limiting factors in Indian economic growth are rather different: shortage of actual physical capital (including land), deficiencies in organization and technical know-how, and shortages of trained manpower are the principal ones. Though there appears to have been, and perhaps still to be, some margin of unutilized plant capacity in some industries, we find nothing to suggest that over the long run the rate of growth of real output in India is likely to be effectively limited by the money supply.

Arguments have indeed been made for a policy of deliberate inflation, on the grounds that it might help to accelerate growth by producing a shift in real incomes to sectors of the population having high savings and investment propensities (e.g., corporate enterprises). Even if such effects might occur in the short run (which seems not at all certain in the light of such factors as wage determination in the organized and public sectors), it seems that any lasting gains would be unlikely, and that the deliberately inflationary approach will continue to be regarded as incompatible with broader

[40] We are of course not concerned here with the increased productive potentialities which an investment outlay in a given period may provide in some later period when the additional productive facilities get into operation.

173

public policy objectives including those involving the distribution of income. The following comments from the International Monetary Fund mission report are indicative and are believed to be in line with responsible Indian views:[41]

"Inflation is a socially costly and economically wasteful means of increasing investment. It encourages excessive investment in inventories, real estate, and foreign balances; and it discourages investment in agriculture and certain fields of industry, particularly if controls hold down prices while costs rise. Thus, inflation diverts the limited resources available for development to sectors where their effect on production is negligible. This is not to deny that there may be a temporary increase in investment as a consequence of inflation; but the experience of many underdeveloped countries is that after an initial increase which may continue for perhaps two or three years, socially productive investment may revert to an even lower level than prevailed prior to the inflation."

"The problem for India is not to secure a short spurt of a relatively large amount of investment. That has been the problem for certain industrial countries at a time when a once-for-all rapid expansion in particular types of production was necessary. For India, however, as for other underdeveloped countries, the basic problem is to secure a steady rise in investment in many sectors of the economy and over a long period—in fact, until the momentum of the economy and the growth in its capacity to save will make such a level of investment normal. It would be shortsighted to jeopardize the structure of the economy and its growth in the directions suited to the needs of the people for the sake of a temporary spurt in investment induced by inflationary means."

"Even in the short run, the problems confronting the Government of India would be greatly intensified by inflation. Inevitably, inflation would impair the international payments position of the country. Exports would become less profitable; foreign exchange receipts would decline. The lack of foreign exchange would make it difficult to acquire the imported equipment and materials required for the Five Year Plan. If the payments problem should become very acute, even the ability to maintain adequate imports of food grains and other essential goods, not directly related to the development program, might be threatened. Moreover, it would not be possible to attract foreign capital to supplement domestic resources for development if payments difficulties should emerge and persist."

From what has been said earlier, it is clear that only a part of any warranted expansion in the money supply can take the form

[41] *op.cit.*, pp. 4-5.

of public deficit financing or borrowing from banks. This follows in part simply from the fact that the private sector is expected to share in the growth of the Indian economy, and consequently there must be a continued expansion in private credit. Moreover, any short-run public deficit spending designed to improve the utilization of resources and maintain an adequate money supply could be expected to induce some additional private borrowing, unless this were deliberately to be prevented. Over the long run, the relative roles of the public and private sectors in obtaining funds from additions to the money supply will depend upon (1) the extent to which public outlays generally account for an increasing share of the total spending in the economy, and (2) the extent to which the public sector relies on alternative means (e.g., taxes and the proceeds of public enterprises, and borrowing from individuals) for securing funds.

Finally, there is a point that may be significantly related to the question of alternative rates of population growth and their implications. The crucial factor determining how far public and private borrowers may safely go in using new money is the disposition of the community at large to *hold* additional cash. This in turn will depend very largely on the rate at which per capita incomes rise. A slower population growth and a more rapid growth of per capita income mean a higher marginal propensity to save, for the community as a whole even if not for each individual. Some of these additional savings are directly invested by the savers or lent to private or public investors. What is retained as additional cash balances can be matched by the creation of new money for the Government or for private investors.

Thus the scope for safe and useful monetary expansion will depend on the growth of per capita as well as total national income. As we have seen above, it is unlikely over the long run to involve more than a small fraction of the total mobilization of savings, and only a part, perhaps a minor part, of the total new money can be made directly available to the public sector.

## 6. NON-MONETIZED SAVING AND INVESTMENT

As already noted, something of the order of 1 to 1 1/2 per cent of the net national product represents capital formation outside the money economy. Most of this investment is in rural construction, performed by unpaid family or community labor with free local materials like mud, thatch, and bamboo. Some non-monetized investment also takes the form of local road building and improvement of farms.

In many other countries, this type of investment might be expected to decline not merely relatively but absolutely as well, with high output levels and the development of a monetized exchange system. Ultimately this will happen in India too. But for a considerable time, quite possibly through most of the period under study, it is more likely to increase in absolute amount. The reasons for this lie in the extreme poverty of the Indian peasant; the great scarcity of capital; the fact that the climate makes rather primitive housing adequate for protection from the elements; the availability, over most of the year, of a huge surplus of idle labor-time; and last, but not least, the fact that the Government's rural development plan strongly stresses (for both economic and ideological reasons) an increased utilization of the potentialities of non-monetized investment. This is seen dramatically in the community development program. Not only are peasants encouraged, instructed, and aided in improving their houses and farms by their own efforts, but there has also developed an important amount of voluntary unpaid work on village projects such as the building of wells, schoolhouses, community centers, access roads, and the like. It is perhaps to be expected that in any one village, the voluntary individual contribution of labor for community works may fairly quickly be routinized into an organized village effort, with pay to the individual perhaps first in goods and eventually in cash secured by a local tax or assessment.

At least three-fourths of rural India still awaits the impact of community development and national extension programs. The spread of these programs over the remainder of the countryside could bring about a continued increase for many years to come in the aggregate non-monetized investment of surplus rural labor-time, even if the increase in any particular area turns out to be short-lived. It is even possible that for some years the non-monetized component of investment may increase a little faster than national income. Its effects will be felt primarily in rural housing, to some extent in agricultural land improvement and to a smaller extent in small-scale industry.

## C. Summary on Prospects for Increased Domestic Supply of Funds for Development

The domestic supply of funds for development purposes will, as the foregoing discussion has noted, depend on a number of important changes which can be foreseen in direction though not with quantitative precision. These are:

1. The growth of total and per capita incomes, primarily as a result of the development outlays themselves.
2. Changes in the distribution of income.
   a) Changes in the relative importance of different productive sectors of the economy. The industrial sector, the larger private enterprises, the cooperative sector, and the public sector are all likely to grow faster than total national output does.
   b) Effects of public policies, designed to lessen disparities of income between individuals, economic groups, and regions.[42]
3. Increasing monetization of the economy, with the role of the non-monetized "subsistence" sector eventually becoming very small.
4. Effects of public policies designed to discourage nonproductive consumption and investment and to mobilize savings.

Taking all of the above factors into account so far as possible, we have concluded that:

*Retained corporate earnings* will increase faster than national income, and may be expected to reach 2 per cent of national income by some time during the 1960's and to average between 2 and 3 per cent during the 1970's. This growth will depend to some extent on government policies regarding taxation, business investment, and extension of the public sector, but will also depend markedly on how fast both total and per capita income rises in the economy as a whole.

*Governments* will be able to increase their current revenues a little faster than national income—perhaps to 9 to 10 per cent of national income in the 1960's and 10 to 12 per cent in the 1970's. Over the long run the chief limitation on the rise of the revenue "take" will be the necessity of leaving the individual at least a minimum acceptable rise in his income after taxes. The growth of *per capita* income

---

[42] ". . . a certain measure of territorial or regional redress of inequalities is a conspicuous feature of Indian public expenditure as also of the entire system of public finance. This redistributive progress takes place both directly through the redistribution of Central expenditure regionally or indirectly through the division of shared taxes on the basis of population and by way of larger grants-in-aid to the more backward or financially weaker States. . . . There are, of course, limits to this process of regional equalisation, but there is no doubt that it forms a significant feature of the system of public expenditure in this country." Taxation Enquiry Commission, *Report*, Vol. 1, pp. 42-43.

is thus crucial. If public nondevelopmental outlays are kept at a roughly constant proportion of national income, say 5 per cent, governments should thus be able to save from current revenue for development at the rate of 4 to 5 per cent of national income in the 1960's and 5 to 7 per cent in the 1970's. In addition, governments will devote to development comparably large sums secured from private savers.

*Smaller enterprises and individuals* will continue to save only a small proportion of their incomes, and will be receiving a somewhat diminishing proportion of total national income. The percentage of national income represented by monetized savings of this group is now about 3 but might rise to 4 or 5 during the next two or three decades.

*Cooperatives* will assume a major role in rural and small-scale production by some time in the 1970's and may serve as a vehicle for a considerably increased generation of savings and investment in that sector during the latter part of the period under study. If so, the previously indicated increase in total savings by "individuals and small enterprises" would be reduced but this would be more than offset by the growth in cooperative savings.

*Non-monetized saving and investment*, occurring primarily in rural housing and agriculture, may remain between 1 and 2 per cent of national income for many years, but is likely to diminish markedly in relative importance by the 1970's.

What emerges from these outlooks for various sectors is the overall prospect for a substantial growth in domestic savings. Total monetized domestic savings, probably no more than 7 per cent of national income at present, might be say 9 to 12 per cent by some time in the 1960's, and say 12 to 16 per cent by some time in the 1970's. Non-monetized savings would range between 1 and 2 per cent, probably declining considerably in percentage terms at least before 1980.

These ranges of uncertainty are wide. They would still be wide even if we had far more detailed information than is at hand for analyzing present savings behavior and predicting the progress of the various relevant institutional changes. Wide latitude in projecting savings growth would still remain because a major factor determining the potential growth of nearly all types of savings is the degree to which the growth of total output keeps ahead of the growth of population. From each of the sources of savings examined, with the possible exceptions of non-monetized saving, reinvestment of corporate profits and monetary expansion, the savings forthcoming at any given future date *from any given level of total national income* will be vastly different according to whether the increase in total income reflects primarily an improvement in welfare or merely an increase in numbers. In later chapters we shall be introducing our alternative projections of population growth and assessing their effect in terms of saving, investment, and other determinants of output growth. The present discussion has aimed merely at identifying the determinants and the general range of possibilities.

## D. *Funds from Abroad*

All of the foregoing discussion has dealt with domestic sources of funds for investment and other development purposes, and with ways of mobilizing these funds. In addition, there is likely to be a certain amount of public and private aid and investment forthcoming from outside India, and India has external assets which can be used to pay for net imports.

External assistance to India during the First Five-Year Plan was mainly in the form of loans. The net inflow of private investment capital averaged about Rs. 0.25 billion a year, largely in the form of oil refinery construction by foreign interests. There was some drawing upon India's sizeable accumulation of sterling balances in 1951-1952, but subsequently those balances were maintained and even slightly increased.[43]

The proposed financing for the Second Five-Year Plan includes an allowance for foreign assistance averaging about Rs. 1.6 billion per annum, or about four times the rate at which such assistance was available and utilized during the First Plan period. But this figure is not a forecast even in the qualified sense that most of the other Plan figures are. The Planning Commission says of it:

> "In the nature of things, external resources that may become available to supplement domestic savings cannot be estimated in advance. . . . Rs. 800 crores (for the period 1956-1961) represent the order of *requirements.* . . . External assistance of the order of Rs. 800 crores is *not beyond the range of practical possibilities in terms of the surpluses available in more developed countries for investment abroad.*"[44]

[43] Reserve Bank of India, "Balance of Payments and Planned Development," in *Second Plan Papers*, pp. 429-430.
[44] *Second Plan Outline*, p. 29 (italics supplied); cf. also, *ibid.*, pp. 27-34.

The figure was derived on the following basis:

|  | *Average per annum in Rs. billions* |
|---|---|
| Balance of payments deficit on current account, derived from projections of trade and other requirements and prospects implied in the Plan objectives | 2.2 |
| *Less:* | |
| Reduction in sterling balances | — .4 |
| Estimated net private capital inflow | — .2 |
| Remaining deficit for which external assistance would be required | 1.6 |

Our concern is of course with longer-range potentialities. Over any long period it does not appear safe to count on a continued drawing-down of foreign balances; in fact eventually, with a growing balance of international payments to be stabilized, some net acquisition of gold or exchange reserve would have to be provided for, representing a minor drain on the resources available for investment in the usual sense.[45]

We cannot attempt to evaluate all the factors which may determine the availability of external public or private funds in the next few decades. We shall, however, suggest that the major economic limiting factor may not be "the surpluses available in more developed countries for investment abroad," so much as the judgment of governments and private investors in those countries, and of international lending institutions, regarding India's credit-worthiness. That in turn will depend partly on the treatment given to outside investments and firms, but perhaps even more basically on the success with which the internal resources of the Indian economy are mobilized and put to productive use. The rate of increase in per capita income, and the proportion of national income devoted to development, will be the crucial indicators. The first of these of course depends largely on the second. Accordingly, we shall not attempt to improve upon the very simple and convenient hypothesis that the availability of external funds will vary proportionately with the mobilization of internal funds for development.

[45] "If these balances are drawn down to the extent of Rs. 200 crores over the next Plan period, they would fall to approximately Rs. 500 crores at the end of the Plan. Reserves of this order would then correspond to about 7 months' imports and should be regarded as essential for enabling the country to tide over temporary balance of payments difficulties." (*ibid.*, p. 33.)

◇◇◇◇◇◇◇◇◇◇◇◇◇◇◇◇◇◇◇◇◇◇◇◇◇◇◇◇◇◇◇◇◇◇◇◇◇◇◇◇◇◇◇◇◇◇◇◇◇◇◇

# CHAPTER XIII

# THE PRODUCTIVITY OF DEVELOPMENTAL OUTLAYS

◇◇◇◇◇◇◇◇◇◇◇◇◇◇◇◇◇◇◇◇◇◇◇◇◇◇◇◇◇◇◇◇◇◇◇◇◇◇◇◇◇◇◇◇◇◇◇◇◇◇◇

AT THE END of Chapter XI it was proposed that the economic development potentialities of India during the next two or three decades could best be assessed in terms of (1) the rate at which resources could be allocated to investment and other developmental purposes, and (2) the efficacy of such outlays in raising productivity. Chapter XII examined the prospects for mobilizing funds for development. It remains to consider the relation between development outlays and the resulting improvements in productivity.

In the formulation of the First Plan, considerable attention was given to the question of the prospective ratio between investment outlays and growth of total national output. Historical experience in other countries was consulted for guidance, and some attempt was made to allow for different conditions in India. The upshot was as follows:

". . . one can assume a capital-output ratio only in relation to the pattern of development visualised for a particular country, the capital stock already at its command, and the extent to which the available capital resources are being utilised. In some of the relatively more developed countries of the world, *a unit increase in national income has apparently required, in the last few decades, something between 3 and 3 1/2 times as much in terms of additions to capital stock*; in limited periods and in particular instances the ratio has of course varied. These relationships are subject to the various qualifications mentioned, but they indicate the range within which the capital-output ratio may fluctuate. In making any assumption about India for the future, we have to take into account several diverse factors, *e.g.*, the possibility of raising yields in agriculture with relatively small additions to capital equipment, the need for expanding basic industries and services like irrigation and power which are highly capital-intensive, the lack of technical skill which is likely to be reflected in lower productivity of labour in the initial stages, the scope for intensive use of equipment in at least some industries through full utilisation of capacity, shortage of housing in urban areas needing early attention, the 'external' economies likely to follow development of transport, power, marketing, and credit, etc.

"For the purposes of our calculations regarding possible rates of development in India in the next few decades, we have made by way of first approximation the following assumptions . . . : *a unit increase in national output and income will require about three times as much by way of additions to capital stock, and the increased output will materialise in the third year from the date of the investment . . .*"[1]

The ratio finally selected for planning purposes (3 to 1, with a lag) was apparently in keeping with the fragmentary historical evidence available for other countries; although that for India itself might have suggested a higher ratio. The Indian national output had apparently been scarcely keeping up with a population increase of 1 1/4 per cent per annum, with net investment then estimated at about 5 per cent of national income, or four times as much.

Experience with the First Five-Year Plan was such as to engender considerable optimism about the capital-product ratio, and it has been quite generally argued in India that the original ratio was too conservative. The statistics of investment and growth during the Plan may seem to give some support to this contention, but such a short period hardly provides adequate basis for any definitive revision. It now appears that during the five years of the First Plan (1951-1952 through 1955-1956) an average of about 7 1/2 per cent of national income went into net domestic capital formation (including very rough allowances for non-monetized investment and for increase in inventories).[2] The national income (at 1952-

---

[1] Planning Commission, *The First Five-Year Plan*, New Delhi, 1952, pp. 19-20. (Italics supplied.) With a growth of national income at 3.9 per cent per annum (which is what the formulators of the Plan projected as an average over the next 27 years), a 3-to-1 ratio with the lag described would require that about one-eighth of current national income be invested.

Professor W. Arthur Lewis, drawing primarily on the work of Simon Kuznets and Colin Clark in this field, says: "The estimates of the growth of capital and of income, for what they are worth, show remarkable agreement on two propositions; first, that in the industrial countries the ratio of the value of capital to the value of output seems to be pretty constant at the margin, when capital-intensive and capital-sparse industries are taken together; and secondly, that this marginal ratio lies between 3 to 1 and 4 to 1, when the value of land and other natural resources is excluded from capital and the value of external assets from both capital and income." *The Theory of Economic Growth*, London, 1955, p. 201.

[2] This statement is based on annual estimates, 1951-1952 through 1953-1954, for total monetized and non-monetized fixed capital formation, from "Capital Formation in the Indian Union," in *Second Plan Papers*, p. 158; on a comparable 1954-1955 estimate in the same volume, p. 399; and, for 1955-1956, on the state-

1953 prices) rose from Rs. 91.1 billion in 1950-1951 to an estimated Rs. 108.0 billion in 1955-1956: i.e., at an average annual rate of nearly 3 1/2 per cent. On this basis, the ratio between net investment and increase in national income would work out to only 2.14 on a synchronous basis. If the lag were allowed for (i.e., if the investment were measured for an earlier period or the income rise for a later period) the ratio would presumably be a little smaller still. Inclusion of non-investment developmental expenditure would raise the ratio; exclusion of inventory accumulation and/or non-monetized investment would lower it.

Reference has already been made to some factors that may have made a rather low ratio possible during the First Plan period. One is the great improvement in weather conditions for crops after 1950-1951, which produced a direct stimulus to agricultural output and an indirect stimulus to the growth of the rest of the economy. The increase in nonagricultural production in turn was facilitated by the large margins of idle capacity in many industries at the beginning of the Plan period, which made it possible to expand output with relatively little new investment.[3] Another factor

ment that in 1955-1956 total "investment" (contextually interpreted as monetized fixed investment and inventory accumulation) was 7 per cent of national income (*Second Plan Outline*, p. 25). In combining these estimates, we have assumed inventory accumulation to be 15 per cent of the current *increment* in national income (in line with the rough allowance made for the *Second Plan Outline*, p. 24) and have taken non-monetized investment at 1 to 1.5 per cent of national income. On this basis one arrives at the following average 1951-1956 percentages of national income: monetized fixed investment, 5.6 to 6.0; total monetized investment including inventories, 6.1 to 6.5; total fixed investment (including non-monetized), 7.0 to 7.1; grand total including both inventories and non-monetized investment, 7.5 to 7.6. The ranges here indicated result from alternative assumptions (1.0 and 1.5 per cent) for the share of non-monetized investment.

[3] "The First Five-Year Plan laid considerable stress on fuller utilisation of idle capacity. The increase in the supply of consumer goods, it was proposed, should come mainly from fuller utilisation of existing capacity. . . . In the last three or four years, unutilised capacity in some industries (e.g., cotton textiles) has been drawn upon, but there is still a considerable amount of unutilised capacity in various industries—in consumer as well as in producer goods industries." Planning Commission, "Installed Capacity and its Utilisation in Indian Industries," in *Second Plan Papers*, p. 174.

"The First Plan has emphasised as the first priority achievement of higher levels of production through the intensive utilisation of existing capacity. This objective has been broadly fulfilled; and in this category, production targets have been achieved in cotton textiles (mill sector), sugar, and vegetable oils. Increase in production from unutilised capacity as well as from significant additions to production capacity, have been secured more or less in accordance with the targets in cement, paper, soda ash, caustic soda and other chemicals, rayon, is the relatively large emphasis placed during the First Plan in increasing food production as against building up basic industrial capacity.

These factors (in addition to the shortness of the period and the roughness of the estimates) suggest caution in drawing conclusions for the future from First Plan experience. Despite the statistically favorable ratio of income growth to investment during the past few years, it remains to be seen whether the relationship in India over the next two or three decades will be much different from the customary 3 or 3 1/2 to 1. Meanwhile, as shown in Table 29, the framework for the Second Plan has been set up on the basis of a ratio slightly higher than that implied in the First Plan experience, but still quite low.

TABLE 29. RELATIONS BETWEEN DEVELOPMENTAL OUTLAYS
AND NATIONAL OUTPUT GROWTH ENVISAGED FOR
SECOND FIVE-YEAR PLAN

|  | Billions of Rupees (1952–1953 prices) | Ratio to Increase in National Income |
|---|---|---|
| National Income |  |  |
| 1955–1956 | 108.0 |  |
| 1960–1961 | 134.8 |  |
| Increase during Plan period | 26.8 |  |
| Net Investment, 1956–1957 through 1960–1961 |  |  |
| Total, incl. inventories and non-monetized | 69 | 2.58 |
| Monetized only, total | 61 | 2.28 |
| Monetized fixed investment only | 57 | 2.13 |
| Fixed investment, incl. non-monetized | 65 | 2.43 |
| Non-investment Public Developmental Outlay under the Plan, 1956–1961 | 10 |  |
| Total Developmental Outlay under the Plan, 1956–1961 | 79 | 2.95 |

Source: *Second Plan Outline*, pp. 24-26. This source provides the figures for total monetized investment and for non-investment public developmental outlay under the Plan, and also indicates an allowance of Rs. 4 billion for inventory accumulation included in the former. We have allowed Rs. 8 billion (roughly 1.5% of national income) for non-monetized investment.

bicycles, and certain other industries." Planning Commission, *The Second Five-Year Plan, Draft Memorandum*, 27 Dec., 1955 (mimeographed), Ch. VIII, p. 3.

It may be noted that the proposed Second Plan ratio for monetized investment, working out at 2.28 on a "synchronous" basis, would be equivalent to only 2.09 if we assume continuance of the projected 4.5 per cent per annum growth in national income and the same lag between investment and income as was assumed in the original long-range projections for the First Plan. It is thus about 30 per cent lower, on a comparable basis, than the ratio contemplated at the outset of the First Plan. A generally more sanguine outlook is also reflected in the fact that, while the formulators of the First Plan projected an average growth of national income at 3.9 per cent per annum for the next 27 years, the Second Plan projects a rate of 4.5 per cent per annum for the next five years.

We cannot attempt in this study to make any quantitative estimate of the capital/output ratio in India, either overall or by sectors. Experience suggests that even in countries where the data are much more complete and the prospective structural changes in the economy much less important, at best only an impressionistic answer can be reached. It will be possible and worthwhile, however, to explore some of the principal determinants of the prospective ratio, in the effort to form a judgment (1) as to whether in the near term this ratio will be relatively low, as the Indian planners expect, or relatively high; and (2) whether the ratio is likely to rise or fall in the longer run (the 1960's and 1970's).[4]

Of the many factors likely to influence the course of the ratio, we believe the following may be the most important, and shall consider each in turn:

1. Construction costs and standards.
2. The sources of improved technology.
3. Investment in housing and other welfare categories.
4. The relative importance of investment in agriculture.

[4] A useful discussion of factors influencing the capital/output ratio in various types of economy and stages of development is to be found in W. A. Lewis, *The Theory of Economic Growth*, Ch. V. A recent and noteworthy essay with particular reference to India, is Professor Colin Clark's series of four articles, "From Wealth to Capital Coefficients," in *The Eastern Economist*, January 20-February 24, 1956. Professor Clark here finds (1) that in general, coefficients are not quite so high as had been suggested by earlier estimates; (2) that India's coefficient will probably be rather low—say, 2.5—for some time, but will tend to rise; (3) that India's coefficient "may not have to ascend so long or so steeply as did those of other countries," before beginning to fall again, as he finds such coefficients tend to do in later stages of development.

5. The relative importance of investment in transport, communication, and other public services.
6. Efficiency in utilization of capital.
7. The choice of alternative capital-saving and labor-saving techniques in production.

*1. Construction costs and standards.*[5] It is a rule of thumb in more advanced industrial countries that about two-thirds of the net fixed investment outlays consist of construction and one-third of producers' equipment.

For producers' equipment in general, the unit cost in India (as measured by the ratio of the price of the equipment to the prices of goods and services in general) is probably not radically different from what it is in other major countries. For some specialized items not yet produced in India, there are the extra costs of importation; but these are items of high value in relation to bulk and the percentage addition to the cost is moderate.

For most types of construction, by contrast, it appears that costs in India (as measured in terms of other goods and services) may be a great deal lower than in the more advanced industrial countries of Europe and America. One reason is that the Indian climate makes simpler structures adequate. A further reason is that the processes of construction (aside from those involved in "engineering-type" construction) are themselves rather labor-intensive, not lending themselves to mechanization as well as, say, manufacturing. This tends to make the costs of construction relatively high in countries with high average labor-productivity and high wages, and relatively low in countries like India, where wages reflect a low overall productivity. Manpower is cheap in India, and construction everywhere uses a high proportion of manpower.

On this point, Colin Clark estimates that the rupee's worth in relation to the dollar when spent on ordinary construction is about five times what it is when spent on domestic goods and services in general. On a similar basis India appears to have a "comparative advantage" of about three to one over the United Kingdom in construction.[6] Since the products of construction do not enter into

---

[5] We shall confine the discussion here to monetized investment.

[6] "There is . . . one final consideration, which may in the end allow us to reckon for India a marginal capital coefficient considerably lower than that deduced from the experience of other countries . . . In respect of the main item, namely, building . . . you get far more real capital for your money than you

international trade, such wide differences between countries can persist for a long time. In other words, India is a country where construction is cheap, relative to other things, for the same reason that India is a country where personal services are relatively cheap.

This would suggest that the ratio between the cost of a structure and the value of its subsequent annual output of goods and services is likely to be, as a rule, much lower in India than would be the case with structures built for similar uses in say, Europe or the United States. For any given increment to national productive capacity, the necessary construction outlays would be less.[7] In view of the major importance of the construction component in investment as a whole, this would appear to be an important factor working for a low overall capital/output ratio in India.

*2. The sources of improved technology.* In the most economically advanced countries a very substantial amount of investment and related developmental outlay goes into the discovery of new technology and the experimentation necessary to make it commercially usable. This is by no means all reflected in the expenditures formally allocated to research and development facilities, laboratories, pilot plants, and the like, but also includes the extra sums unavoid-

---

do elsewhere . . . the purchasing power of the rupee over building as compared with its purchasing power over goods in general, is no less than five times as high in India as it is in the United States, three times as high as it is in present day Britain, or twice as high as it was in 19th century Britain. The reason for this paradox is that the operations of the building craftsman are much the same in all countries and times, and although the American bricklayer, with his mechanical hoist and other equipment, may work faster than the Indian bricklayer, his relative superiority in productivity is certainly very much less marked than is that of the American manufacturing operative over the Indian . . . Even if we assume that these relative advantages apply much less in the construction of commercial buildings and engineering structures, nevertheless the high purchasing power of the rupee in this field is so striking, and building represents such an important element in the total of national net investment, that it does seem that we can now safely conclude that the marginal capital coefficient to which Indian planners should work can safely be estimated at any rate well below the figure of 4 prevailing in 19th century Britain. To put the figure at 2 is probably too low, but it may well be as low as 2 1/2. Colin Clark, "From Wealth to Capital Co-efficients," *The Eastern Economist*, February 17, 1956, p. 252.

[7] It would be logical to try to substantiate this point indirectly by seeing whether construction outlays tend to account for a *smaller proportion of total monetized fixed investment in India* than the characteristic two-thirds. The available data are not adequate to determine this point conclusively; but according to one careful observer, Dr. Wilfred Malenbaum, construction in India in 1950-1951 was only about 45 per cent of total monetized fixed investment.

ably committed to techniques and products still not perfected and hence entailing high rates of capital obsolescence.

Precisely because India has lagged in the application of known technology, she can rely to a considerable extent on techniques, specialized equipment, and even specialized personnel from more advanced countries without having to go through the expensive and time-consuming process of evolving them all herself. For example, synthetic textiles and diesel locomotives are just being introduced in India—but the research and development work required to make this possible had already been done elsewhere. In countless other fields as well, India stands to gain by adopting the results of research and development work embodying investment already made in other countries.

There are of course limits to this economy. A substantial amount of Indian investment and other development outlay is indispensable in order to effect a successful transplant of techniques developed elsewhere (especially in view of the difference in cost and market conditions involved, which often call for important modifications). Moreover, successful international competition will increasingly require that in at least some branches of technology, India cannot long afford to remain behind but must participate in the pioneering work as well. In nuclear energy, for example, India is devoting a considerable allocation of resources to achieve and maintain an important position. For many decades, however, India should find it compatible with her development aims to spend a smaller proportion of national income on basic theoretical and industrial research than the more advanced industrial countries are spending. This being a form of investment with very long-delayed returns, the effect should be to favor a low overall capital/output ratio in India. Quantitatively, however, the effect is probably fairly small.

*3. Investment in housing and other welfare categories.* The field of general social welfare services provides a great deal of latitude for public policy. In general, outlays of this type, even when classed as "developmental," make a rather indirect contribution to national income—e.g., in terms of the health, morale, or skills of the coming generation of workers—or may give social satisfactions that escape national income accounting altogether. Security, cultural activities, and health all have important values of their own, largely outside the usual economic measurement of output. This class of expenditure, then, with some exceptions, may be classed as one with a high ratio of current outlay to near-term effect on national output.[8]

India's needs in this field are recognized as vast and pressing, and there is naturally a strong desire to try to meet them by organized public means.

> " '. . . most underdeveloped countries want the blessing of the welfare state today, complete with old age pensions, unemployment insurance, family allowances, health insurance, forty-hour week, and all the trimmings.'
> "Concerning the status of economic development most of the countries in question [in southern Asia] are, in many respects, comparable to the early stages of capitalism. But with respect to popular attitudes concerning the obligations of the state to the citizens and the limitations and responsibilities of private enterprise, these countries are in an advanced stage of welfare capitalism."[9]

On the other hand, recent revisions of the earlier proposals for the Second Five-Year Plan appear to reflect considerable caution about over-commitment of public resources in ways which might interfere with programs more directly or immediately increasing productivity. For example,

> "It is . . . necessary to exercise some restraint in the provision even of essential social services and opportunities in the interest of improving the productivity of the economy . . . It is hardly necessary to stress the fact that the effectiveness of 'investment' proper depends to a considerable extent upon the adequacy of what are called developmental social services. The question is one of keeping the right

[8] To say this is by no means to question the desirability or essentiality of such outlays. Moreover, it is clear that some special types (e.g., training of village workers, technicians, etc.) may produce high immediate returns in added productivity. A point to which we shall return later, however, is that the overall productivity effect of expenditures on social services depends to a very large extent on what proportion of these expenditures can be devoted to such direct assistance to, and improvement of, the labor force. If the proportion of dependents is high in the population (and in the *increments to* population), the necessary social service outlays for the population as a whole will be "diluted" in their application to the productivity of the current active labor force. In that case their contribution will be mainly in terms of the productivity of a *future* labor force; and so long as fertility remains high, the ratio of dependents to workers and the ratio of incremental to actual population will remain high, so that the dilution is no temporary phenomenon.

[9] Edward S. Mason, *Promoting Economic Development*, Claremont, California, 1955, p. 45. The first paragraph was in turn quoted from an unpublished manuscript by Benjamin Higgins.

189

balance, and it seems inevitable that in an economy seeking a rapid enlargement of the community's output, the first emphasis should be on the promotion of more directly productive forms of activity."[10]

The originally proposed rate of expansion of school facilities, for example, has been drastically cut back at least twice. One of the Directive Principles of the Constitution is that "the State shall endeavour to provide within a period of ten years [from 1950] free and compulsory primary education for all children until they complete the age of fourteen years."[11] The Second Plan Framework of 1955 recommended as a more modest 1961 target the provision of schools for 75 per cent of the children aged 6-11 and 30 per cent of those aged 11-14.[12] The *Draft Outline* of February, 1956, calls for only 60 and 19 per cent respectively.[13]

There is also an increased emphasis in later drafts of the Plan upon the possibilities of a greater share of responsibility for social welfare activities being assumed by local initiative, thus diminishing the load on the limited financial and administrative resources of the central and state governments.[14]

With these general considerations on welfare outlays as a background, we shall turn to a more specific and quantitative consideration of the investment implications in one principal welfare area: that of housing.

The requirements for investment in housing are one of the most important factors determining how effective a nation's savings can be in raising productivity. Housing is a "consumer" or "welfare" item essentially. Yet adequate housing may have an important bearing on the attitudes, health and efficiency of the labor force, and therefore its provision can in a sense be regarded as a form of investment in the human resources of the community. Consequently housing and similar investment occupy a hybrid or intermediate position in regard to economic development. If we choose to regard them as nondevelopmental, contributing directly only to consumer welfare, then they represent a diversion of part of the total investible

[10] *Second Five-Year Plan, Draft Memorandum*, Dec. 27, 1955 (mimeographed) Ch. I, pp. 13-14.

[11] *Second Plan Outline*, p. 183.

[12] "Draft Recommendations for the Formulation of the Second Five-Year Plan," pp. 56-57, and "The Second Five-Year Plan, A Tentative Framework," pp. 75-76, 98, in *Second Plan Papers*.

[13] *Second Plan Outline*, pp. 39, 184.    [14] *ibid.*, pp. 150, 157, 170.

resources at the expense of those available for investment in producers' goods, and the greater the claims of housing investment upon income the more difficult it is likely to be to mobilize sufficient funds for developmental outlays in the narrower sense. Alternatively, if we include housing investment and the like in a broader category of developmental outlays, we must recognize the fact that its direct effect in increasing output is very low per unit of investment, and must regard a relatively high rate of housing outlay as a factor contributing to a high overall capital/output ratio for the totality of investment. The implications are of course the same either way—housing investment competes with other forms of outlay which provide much more immediate and substantial returns in the form of increased productivity.

Investment in housing characteristically accounts for about a quarter of total fixed-investment outlays in those relatively advanced industrial countries for which data have been analyzed and which seem as a rule to have overall capital/output ratios of the order of 3 or 3 1/2 to 1.[15] This would suggest that an economy in which this proportion is notably greater would (ceteris paribus) tend to have a higher-than-usual capital/output ratio, while an economy in which a great deal less than a quarter of total investment goes into housing might be expected (ceteris paribus again) to have a relatively low overall ratio.

In India, it is easily apparent that housing is one of the most serious welfare needs. There is an enormous deficiency to be made up, in both qualitative and quantitative terms, not only in houses proper but also in related community facilities of various types, some of which require considerable capital investment. Not only is bad housing currently impairing standards of health, efficiency, and general welfare, but the pressure to improve it will certainly

---

[15] W. Arthur Lewis, *The Theory of Economic Growth*, pp. 210-211. The housing proportion varies with the rate of population growth and of urbanization. Professor Lewis' figures refer to *gross* investment. Houses depreciate more slowly than industrial plant and equipment combined, which would tend to raise the proportion of investment going to housing if we converted to a net investment basis; on the other hand, the expansion of the stock of houses is as a rule slower than the expansion in the stock of producers' capital, which tends to increase the proportion of depreciation to net investment and thus would have an effect in the direction opposite to that of the slow-depreciation factor. Further discussion of the proportion of housing to total investment in various development situations, and of the significance of alternative population growth rates in India in that connection, will be found in Chapter XVI, below.

become much stronger. From the standpoint of national planning, discontent about housing is an important objective factor to be weighed in assessing the relative urgency of various claims upon scarce investment resources, because not only actual welfare but also attitudes and efficiency are involved.

It is also unfortunately evident that the housing situation in India has been deteriorating for some time. There are estimated to be in India about 54 million rural and 11 million urban dwelling units, or approximately one to every six people. The felt needs have been increasing particularly rapidly in the past decade or so—in the rural areas because of recognition of the plight of specially disadvantaged groups, in the towns and cities because of the fairly rapid urbanization of population, and in both rural and urban areas because of the influx of refugees from Pakistan since Partition, and to some extent because of the increased aspirations aroused by national independence and the development effort. One evidence of the increasing shortage of urban housing is the fact that between 1941 and 1951, urban population increased by 16.3 million while only 1.7 additional occupied urban dwelling units were provided, thus raising the number of persons per unit from 5 to 6 in a single decade.[16] By now the ratio has risen further, to perhaps 6 1/2.

These grave housing deficiencies might seem to suggest that India might be under a very considerable handicap, relative to many other countries, in achieving a reasonably low overall investment/output ratio.

There are, however, some offsetting factors. First of all, there is the fact that housing investment is all construction, and construction of a highly labor-intensive type under Indian conditions of manpower supply, climate, and accepted housing standards. We have alluded earlier to India's "comparative advantage" in such types of construction. This means that far more people can be acceptably housed for a given outlay of investment resources in India than in any of the more economically advanced countries.

Secondly, there is the fact that more than four-fifths of India's population is rural. Even if urban population grows at a rate a little more than double the overall population-increase rate, as past trends suggest, the rural population still so predominates that for

[16] *Second Plan Outline*, p. 157; Planning Commission, "Level of Living," in *Second Plan Papers*, p. 642.

192

some time to come, only about one-third of the increments to population will be urban.

It would be going a little too far to dismiss the question of rural housing by saying that it will "take care of itself," but to a very large extent that is the case. The following statement by the Planning Commission is indicative of the way in which the rural housing problem is being approached:

> "In national extension and community project areas, 18,000 rural houses have been built and 95,000 houses have been reconditioned. Work in these areas has shown that, with a little guidance and some measure of assistance, village communities can provide themselves with better sanitation, drainage and lighting and introduce improvements in rural housing conditions in a relatively short period. Much can be done in rural areas through cooperative self-help, demonstration of improved housing and use of local materials and skills and of improved techniques."[17]

The important thing to note here is that improvement in rural housing and related community facilities is something that can be attained to a very large extent simply by the non-monetized investment activity of the villagers themselves. To the extent that they feel a need for such improvement they will not have any great difficulty in achieving it. The cash outlays involved, even in the cases where direct financial assistance is provided, appear to be quite small—of the order of a few hundred rupees per dwelling unit—and probably in the bulk of the cases there will be no direct outside assistance of this sort at all. Provision for rural housing in the Second Five-Year Plan involves only Rs. 50 million of public funds and about 120,000 units,[18] to be allocated on a highly selective basis to the most disadvantaged classes.

We may confine further attention here, then, to the problem of urban housing. The program envisaged for the next five years calls for construction of 2.1 million new urban units, or nearly 20 per cent as many as now exist. However, this will certainly not be entirely a net addition, as many houses will have to be scrapped. The necessary rate of scrapping was set at about 110,000 per annum during the 1950's originally;[19] but this was a figure used in arriving at total construction requirements which have proved to be far beyond what is attainable, so it seems not improbable that with

[17] *Second Plan Outline*, p. 157.   [18] *ibid.*, p. 160.   [19] *ibid.*, p. 159.

continuing severe shortage of houses the scrappage rate will be materially less than that, and the net addition to urban units implied by fulfillment of the program may be nearly 2 million in the next five years.

We have not been able to find any estimate of the total construction investment involved. There are no figures on private housing outlays past, current, or future, and only a minor part of the proposed public outlays are reported in the Plan documents. For that part ("Housing programmes to be carried out in the States and under the Ministry of Works, Housing, and Supply"), the proposed outlay is Rs. 1.13 billion and the number of units involved is 325,000. This implies an average outlay of Rs. 3,500 per unit. If we allow for the apparent fact that on the 142,000 units of "subsidized industrial housing" included, only about five-eighths of the cost is to be covered by public subsidy and loans, the apparent total outlay per unit would be Rs. 4,400.[20] But both figures probably include costs of land acquisition, which we should try to exclude as not representing any net investment. In the First Five-Year Plan, estimates of construction costs only for urban "tenements" were stated as Rs. 2,200 in towns and Rs. 3,300 in larger cities.[21] Costs may have risen since those estimates were formulated. In the light of all these indications, we can only hazard a guess that the average construction cost per unit under the proposed urban housing program might be of the order of Rs. 3,000 to 3,500.

It appears, then, that during the next five years something like Rs. 6 to 7 billion may be spent for urban housing construction. This figure represents only about 10 1/2 to 12 per cent of the total monetized fixed investment contemplated under the Plan (Rs. 57 billion). Even after making some additional allowance for the small monetized component of investment in rural housing, and taking into account the roughness of the estimates involved, it does not appear likely that the program involves devoting much more than 15 per cent of the monetized fixed investment to housing.

This is a low proportion in comparison with the 25 per cent cited

[20] *ibid.*, p. 160. We have omitted "rural" and "plantation" housing in making this calculation.

[21] *First Five-Year Plan*, p. 601. The estimates were prepared by the Central Public Works Department. Land-acquisition costs (here excluded) were estimated at Rs. 500 in towns and Rs. 700 to 1,000 in larger cities.

by Professor Lewis as typical in countries where an overall capital/output ratio of 3 or 3 1/2 to 1 has prevailed.[22]

We have, then, one more indication in favor of a rather low near-term capital/output ratio. But the qualification "near-term" is very important here. Even the most drastic curbs on "luxury housing" will not serve to improve or even maintain urban housing standards under a total program of the size envisaged for the next five years. It cannot be expected that either those who live in the houses or those who plan for housing will for long remain content with this degree of austerity in the face of visible improvements in other aspects of consumer welfare.

All this is abundantly recognized in India. No one regards the housing program as adequate. It is not so easy, however, to determine quantitatively just how far short of any standard of requirements this program falls, or what degree of further deterioration will result in the next five years.

As noted earlier, there are at present about 11 million urban housing units for nearly 70 million urban dwellers, representing a radically greater degree of overcrowding than was the case 10 or 15 years ago. Our projections indicate that India's total population will grow by 9 to 10 per cent in the next five years. If the historical pattern of an urban growth rate of a little more than double the overall rate is maintained, the urban population is likely to grow by at least 20 per cent in five years (as compared with the 33 per cent assumed for the *decade* 1951-1961 by the Planning Commission). This would mean that maintenance of present space standards would call for increasing the number of units by at least 20 per cent, or 2.2 million units. In addition, something would have to be added for unavoidable demolitions or abandonments of houses

[22] A strictly hypothetical calculation may serve to give an idea of the possible quantitative effect of this difference in ratios. If a country has an overall capital/output ratio of 3, and 25 per cent of its investment is in housing, with a capital/output ratio of (say) 10, the implied ratio for all other investments works out to 2.43. Applying these ratios of 10 and 2.43 to a country in which housing investment is only 15 per cent of total investment makes its overall capital/output ratio only 2.74. Thus the effect of the change in importance of housing, under these hypothetical assumptions, is to reduce the overall ratio from 3 to 2.74 in the absence of any change in the ratios for housing as such or for non-housing investment as such. Alternatively, if housing investment be assumed to have no effect at all in increasing national product (a capital/output ratio of infinity), the effect of reducing housing investment from 25 per cent to 15 per cent of the total would be to reduce the overall capital/output ratio from 3 to 2.64.

beyond all repair, so 2.5 million is a conservative gross figure. This is well in excess of what is actually planned, but would still make no provision for any alleviation of overcrowding; and with accumulating obsolescence the average condition of all urban houses would probably show deterioration even at this rate of construction.

Thus urban housing ranks as perhaps the most conspicuous austerity of the next phase of the development effort. To an indeterminable extent, this will interfere with current efforts to stimulate incentives and productivity. It will also build up increasing pressure for diversion of more investment to housing as the pressure becomes more and more serious. On this score alone, we should have to reckon with an increasing drain on investment resources after the next Plan, and a tendency toward an increasing capital/output ratio on that score. Finally, it is important to note that the magnitude of this diversion depends to a major extent on the *rate at which population increases*—it will be a far more serious problem in the event of a rapidly accelerated population growth than in the event of a continued moderate growth rate, because the bulk of the housing is to accommodate *increases* in population.

The same may be said, more broadly, of social services in general. They are essentially outlays for the benefit of people in their capacity as *consumers*, rather than outlays directly for the assistance of employed *workers* in making their work more productive. The degree of need envisaged, then, and the extent of the load imposed upon developmental resources by social welfare programs, is likely to depend on the size and felt needs of the *population* (and its increase), rather than on those of the *labor force*. In respect to education, of course, the number and rate of increase of *children* will be a decisive factor in determining the scale of outlays, since the goal is still to get all children up to age 14 into school as soon as possible.[23]

*4. Relative importance of investment in agriculture.* The required capital per unit of added capacity varies markedly between the different productive sectors of an economy. We have already alluded to the peculiarly high ratios applying in the welfare or social services sector, where the contribution to national output may be quite

[23] The effect of different trends of population upon requirements for housing, education and other social services will be analyzed in Chapter XVI.

indirect or unmeasured. But there are also large differences in ratios among such sectors as public utilities, heavy industry, light industry, agriculture and trade. Nonmechanized agriculture (which is the only type of farming we need to consider in India's case) is known to have a ratio much lower than manufacturing in general; in mining and heavy industry the ratio is very high; while in light industry, and probably in trade, it may be much closer to the agricultural ratio.

In India's case, the more capital-intensive categories will be required to expand faster than national income, while agriculture will not expand as fast as national income; and trade and personal and professional services probably no faster, if we are to judge by customary historical patterns of development. This may seem to portend a high overall capital/product ratio.

In a subsequent section we shall examine the utility and industry sectors more closely. But first it is important to note that, despite the prospect of agriculture's share in output diminishing, agricultural investment will continue to be of major importance. Agriculture is now much more important, relatively, in India than it is in more advanced countries or will be in the India of the distant future; so with even a moderate rate of growth, it will absorb a sizeable part of the total investment program. Thus, out of an expected increase of Rs. 26.8 billion in the national income during the Second Five-Year Plan, the growth of agricultural output is to account for Rs. 6.8 billion, or 27 per cent (as against 46 per cent during the First Plan). In the United States, by contrast, agriculture now accounts for only 7 or 8 per cent of the national income, and this ratio is decreasing; so the *expansion* of agriculture accounts for a quite insignificant part of the total expansion of the United States economy.

It is hardly possible to say with any accuracy what the prospective near-term capital/output ratio in Indian agriculture is likely to be. Actual output figures are inaccurate and highly variable, reflecting changing weather conditions; a revolution in attitudes and organization, and to some extent in methods, is taking place in Indian agriculture; and to a large but unknown extent, the increase in output will depend on factors other than investment per se. It may be worthwhile to note, however, that the net output of agriculture and the monetized outlays devoted to it under the first two Five-Year Plans show the following relation:[24]

|  | First Plan | Second Plan |
|---|---|---|
| Increase in net output (Rs. billions) | 7.8 | 9.4 |
| Monetized investment (Rs. billions) | 7.5 | 10.0 |
| Ratio of investment to output-increase | .96 | 1.06 |

The above figures suggest that the ratio for agriculture is of the order of 1 to 1. The margin of error is of course large, but it seems clear that the ratio must in any event be a relatively low one. Its lowness reflects to some extent the dependence of agricultural growth upon non-monetized investment and non-investment developmental outlays, both of which are excluded from the figures shown. In one important respect, however, the investment figures as shown may tend to overstate the ratio: a good part of the outlays for major irrigation projects affects output only after a lag of some years, and in a period when such outlays are increasing rapidly, the "carry-over" also increases, thus making the output growth understate the ultimate effects of the investment accomplished in the same period.

We may conclude that Indian agriculture has a much lower ratio of monetized investment to output-growth than the economy as a whole. It is also clear that Indian agriculture has a ratio that is low relative to that of agriculture in advanced industrial countries.[25] Since agriculture still accounts for 25 to 30 per cent of the total growth in output in India, the existence of a low incremental capital/output ratio on such an important segment of growth seems to furnish a weighty argument for a relatively low overall ratio in the near-term future.

[24] These are exceedingly rough estimates, based on figures given in "The Second Five-Year Plan, A Tentative Framework," in *Second Plan Papers*, p. 93, and *Second Plan Outline*, pp. 22, 24, 26, 35. The investment outlays represent monetized private and public investment for agriculture, community development, irrigation, and flood control. Both output and investment figures are expressed in billions of rupees at 1952-1953 prices.

[25] W. Arthur Lewis, *The Theory of Economic Growth*, pp. 205-206. Simon Kuznets, "Long-term Changes in the National Income of the United States of America Since 1870," Table 23, p. 122, in International Association for Research in Income and Wealth, *Income and Wealth*, Series II, Cambridge, England, 1952.

At the same time, it is reasonably clear that this source of a low overall ratio will diminish in the longer run, perhaps fairly rapidly. As development proceeds, the capital costs of further irrigation and land-improvement projects, and in general of programs for stepping up agricultural yields, will probably be larger in relation to results. The rural economy will become more monetized, so that a larger proportion of the agricultural investment will entail money outlay. And as agriculture continues to shrink in relative importance in the economy, the effect of low agricultural capital/output ratios will have a diminishing effect upon the overall ratio.

*5. Relative importance of investment in transport, communication and other public services.* It is often said that countries at an early stage of economic development must reckon with relatively high overall incremental capital/output ratios because of the necessity to devote a high proportion of investment to certain highly capital-intensive and long-term investments in "social overhead." This category of investment seems not to have been rigorously defined, but may be taken to include, in addition to some items of "social service" outlay already considered, such things as the development of transport, communications, and other public-utility systems.[26]

The ratio of invested capital to value of net output is relatively high in all these classes of investment, since their contribution to national output is in part an indirect one through the assistance they give to the production of goods and services by other industries. In some of these cases, in fact (e.g., roads, other than toll roads), the output does not appear on the market at all. And in view of the long time required in construction, and the economies of scale involved, public utility and public-service plant may in its early stages have a low utilization of capacity. Consequently a country which must devote an inordinately high proportion of its

[26] Professor W. Arthur Lewis estimates that in a "typical" program of investment for an advanced country, something like 35 per cent of the gross annual investment in fixed capital goes into "public works and utilities (roads, docks, transport, water, electricity, schools, hospitals, government buildings)." He goes on to say, "There is reason to believe that the proportion is particularly high in the first decades of development, and declines thereafter. This is because initial development calls for the establishment of a framework of utilities; and though it is also necessary to spend money on maintaining, improving and extending the framework, it is possible that these later expenditures are relatively not so heavy as those which have initially to be made." *op.cit.*, pp. 210-211.

resources to building up this sector must expect, as a rule, a rather high capital/output ratio during the period of rapid growth.

So runs the argument. We cannot, however, assume that it necessarily applies to India. India is a very large and densely-settled country which has had railroads, electric power systems, highways, a postal system, and other public utilities and services for a long time, on a scale presumably sufficient to have realized the principal economies of scale. The situation in India is quite unlike that prevailing in small, newly-settled, or sparsely-peopled countries in which such systems have to be erected from scratch. Essentially, what is needed in Indian public services is continuous expansion and modernization. The dilemma of whether to set up inefficiently small systems, or large ones far in advance of demand, seems less formidable in India than in most other low-income countries.

It is significant that the program for railroad expansion in India, for example, runs primarily in terms of improving the existing lines and rolling stock, with some double-tracking but no significant extension of lines into new territory.[27] Likewise in the case of other public utilities and services, the basic system is already there and needs essentially expansion and improvement. Thus, all urban places of any size already have road, telephone, telegraph and postal services. Over 95 per cent of the towns with populations of 10,000 or more, and about 80 per cent of the towns and villages with populations between 5,000 and 10,000 will have electricity by 1961 on the basis of the present schedule for expansion of the electric power system. There are nearly 50,000 post offices and over 8,000 telegraph offices.[28]

It is of course true that the expansion of all these services will have to proceed indefinitely at a considerably more rapid pace than the increase of national income; that present facilities are generally overtaxed; and that a large proportion of the *villages* lack electricity and roads. This does not imply, however, that it will be necessary for India to devote a larger proportion of *investment* to such purposes than is the case in the more advanced countries. The opposite

[27] Mileage has been increased about 1 per cent since Partition, largely involving the supplying of new all-Indian connections to replace former routes cut by the Indo-Pakistan border. The objective during the Second Plan is to build about 850 miles of new line (a 2 1/2 per cent addition), mainly "in connection with major industrial projects like steel plants, coal mines, etc." *Second Plan Outline*, p. 143.
[28] *ibid.*, pp. 104, 148-149.

might even be the case. In advanced countries too, the demand for public utility services increases faster than national income. As a result of the past working of this relationship, public utilities account for a much larger proportion of current national income in the more advanced countries than in India; so it is quite possible that in such countries their necessary continued expansion might call for a larger proportion of total investment than is the case in India. Thus far, then, we have no grounds for expecting that India's requirements for public utility expansion will contribute to making the overall capital/output ratio exceptionally high or low in comparison to the ratios prevailing in advanced industrial countries.

Nevertheless, in looking further we must recognize that the public utility sector as a whole is (1) characterized by a high capital-requirements ratio, (2) characteristically required to grow much faster than total national output in any developing and industrializing economy, and (3) presently overburdened in India. There is at least a possibility that the investment requirements of this sector may be unusually high in India's case, tending to raise the capital/output ratio for the economy as a whole. We shall therefore try to examine this sector a little more closely.

In the Second Five-Year Plan as presently outlined, public outlays are shown as follows, and may be considered to represent primarily actual investment.[29]

|  | *Billions of rupees* |
|---|---|
| Railways | 9.0 |
| Electric power | 4.4 |
| Roads and road transport schemes | 2.65 |
| Posts and telegraphs, civil aviation, broadcasting and other communications | 1.2 |
| Shipping, ports and harbors, and inland water transport | 1.0 |
| Total | 18.25 |

The total allocation of Rs. 18.25 billion amounts to 38 per cent of all public outlays under the Plan and nearly 3 per cent of the expected national income during the five years of the Plan. The

[29] Figures are as shown in *Second Plan Outline*, Annexure I, p. 35. Outlays for expansion of the Government locomotive and railway coach works are included under "Railways," and outlays for expansion of the Indian Telephone Industries are included under "Posts and telegraphs . . ."

corresponding ratios for the First Five-Year Plan allocations were 35 per cent and 1.6 per cent;[30] actual outlays were substantially smaller. It is clear that the Second Plan contemplates a considerable step-up in investment in this sector.

Proposed public and private *investment* in power, transport, and communications during the Second Plan period would come to a slightly smaller total figure, but still about Rs. 18 billion. The adjustments are roughly offsetting. About Rs. 1 billion of the public outlays under the Plan in this sector are non-investment, while the private investment outlays in "plantations, private transport, and electricity" are very roughly estimated at the same amount.[31]

To get some impression as to whether public-utilities investment during the next Plan period in India represents an exceptionally large proportion of total monetized fixed investment (as compared to experience in other countries), we may turn again to what Professor W. A. Lewis sets forth as the "typical" composition of the fixed investment outlay in advanced industrial countries where the overall capital/output ratio is 3 or 3 1/2 to 1. He gives "about 35 per cent" as the typical share of "public works and public utilities (roads, docks, transport, water, electricity, schools, hospitals, government buildings)."[32]

This is a somewhat broader category than we have under consideration, but a rough adjustment can be made. To approximate Professor Lewis' category, we must add "schools, hospitals, and government buildings" to our list. These investment outlays are presumably included in the "Social Services, Housing, and Rehabilitation" allocation of the Second Five-Year Plan, which amounts in all to Rs. 9.46 billion.[33] From an earlier draft proposal for the Plan we have the estimate that about one-third of the public outlays under these heads represent investment:[34] which would thus be about Rs. 3.15 billion. From this we should deduct the allocation for "housing" (Rs. 1.2 billion),[35] leaving a little less than Rs. 2 billion. Adding this to the Rs. 18 billion already estimated for public works investment, we have the round figure of Rs. 20 billion for investment

[30] *loc.cit.*
[31] *Second Plan Papers*, Table 4, p. 61; *Second Plan Outline*, p. 24.
[32] *The Theory of Economic Growth*, pp. 210-211.
[33] *Second Plan Outline*, Annexure I, p. 35.
[34] *Second Plan Papers*, Table 4, p. 61.
[35] *Second Plan Outline*, Annexure I, p. 35.

during the next Plan period in a category which we may hope is roughly comparable to Professor Lewis'.

This Rs. 20 billion amounts, by coincidence, to exactly 35 per cent of the proposed monetized fixed investment during the Second Plan period (Rs. 57 billion).[36] We have thus found no reason to characterize the Indian allocation of investment to this category in the next Plan period as either unusually high or unusually low—it appears to be about in line with the pattern in the more advanced industrial countries.

If we may draw any conclusion from this regrettably tenuous procedure, it is that the current degree of investment emphasis upon public utilities in India is not such as to imply an overall capital/output ratio higher than the characteristic 3 or 3 1/2 observed in advanced industrial countries. In other words, if one wants to argue for a substantially lower or higher ratio than that for India during the next five years, he must look elsewhere for support for the argument.

It is perhaps in order to examine some of the major components of the public-utilities sector to see whether there is anything exceptional or temporary about the indicated relations of investment to growth. Electric power and railways account for about 3/4 of the total public-utilities investment; we shall look briefly at each.

*(a) Electric power.* It seems that requirements for electrical energy in any country are almost invariably underestimated in the early stages of planning, both public and private. At the beginning of the First Five-Year Plan, India's total generating capacity was 2.3 million kw.[37] The rate of increase had been slow; and it was deemed sufficient, even taking into account large additional power requirements for irrigation pumping, to provide for 7 million kw. of additional capacity over the next 15 years (by 1966). During the First Plan, capacity rose from 2.3 million to 3.4 million kw. But in view of unexpectedly rapid growth in demand, and the shift to a more industrial emphasis in the Second Plan, the 1966 target has been raised from the original 9.3 million kw. to about 15 million, with the interim 1961 target now set at 6.8 million. This implies a doubling of capacity during the Second Plan period.

[36] *op.cit.*, p. 24.
[37] All figures in this paragraph are drawn from *Second Plan Outline*, pp. 103-104.

The longer-range trend of electric power expansion, as envisaged in 1955 by the Planning Commission, is as follows:[38]

| Plan period | Average annual percentage increase | Millions of kw. at end of period |
|---|---|---|
| 2nd (1956–1961) | 15 | 7 |
| 3rd (1961–1966) | 12 | 12 |
| 4th (1966–1971) | 9 | 18½ |
| 5th (1971–1976) | 7 | 25 |
| 6th (1976–1981) | 7 | 35 |
| 7th (1981–1986) | 7 | 50 |

According to the Planning Commission experts, the eventual growth rate of 7 per cent per annum (i.e., a doubling in 10 years) corresponds to the characteristic growth trend of electric generating capacity in "industrially advanced countries"; the much higher rates proposed during the next 15 years reflect estimated extra growth needed in the period of rapid industrialization and electrification of the country.[39]

Requirements and prospects for electric power expansion should of course be considered in the context of the overall energy needs of a developing economy. The available evidence from many countries in all stages of development suggests that *total use of inanimate energy* tends to remain roughly proportional to total national product. In 1951-1952, India's total inanimate-energy consumption was estimated at 6.15 metric tons coal equivalent per $1,000 of national income; the corresponding ratio in some more advanced industrial countries was:[40]

| | |
|---|---|
| Japan | 6.5 |
| Germany | 6.8 |
| France | 3.8 |
| U.K. | 6.4 |
| Canada | 5.9 |
| U.S. | 4.4 |

[38] H. J. Bhabha, *The Role of Atomic Power in India and its Immediate Possibilities,* International Conference on the Peaceful Uses of Atomic Energy, Geneva, 1955, para. 18. It may be noted that the February 1956 *Draft Outline* for the Second Plan, p. 104, puts the 1966 target at "about 15" million kw. rather than the 12 million shown here—entailing a maintenance of the 15 per cent annual growth rate through the Third Plan.

[39] *loc.cit.*

[40] Edward S. Mason, *Energy Requirements and Economic Growth* (National Planning Association, *Reports on Productive Uses of Nuclear Energy*), Washing-

It does not follow, however, that the sources of *commercial* energy (hydel power and mineral fuels) need to be expanded in India no faster than the growth of national income. At present, at least 3/4 of India's total inanimate energy consumption is supplied by *non-commercial* fuels (cowdung, straw, and wood),[41] and it is difficult to foresee any great expansion in those sources. Consequently the needed expansion in commercial energy supply will have to be, for some time, much faster than that of national income—perhaps three times as fast. The Second Five-Year Plan goals, calling for expansion of electric power capacity at 15 per cent per annum and coal output at 10.3 per cent per annum,[42] would seem not excessive in this light.

We may go on to inquire whether any such rates of expansion for coal and electric power would be required or feasible over the longer run. Our necessarily rather superficial examination of the question is by no means intended as a critique or competitor of the Planning Commission's detailed studies, but merely examines the overall results of the latter in the light of general growth relationships.

If we assume national income, and total energy requirements, to grow at 25 per cent per quinquennium and assume that the energy supplied from wood and dung will not increase at all, the energy supplied from commercial sources would have to increase during the 1960's at 9 per cent per annum, and during the 1970's at about 7 per cent per annum. It may be presumed that India's petroleum consumption will increase rapidly in any event, and particularly if additional oil is found in India; but at present that source furnishes only about 3 per cent of total energy.[43]

As to adequacy of coal resources, it has been estimated by the Planning Commission that if coal output in India were to increase at 7 per cent per annum over the next 30 years, the rate of mining attained by that time would still amount to only 1 per cent of

ton, 1955, Chart II, p. 11, and Table B, p. 42. Data for 42 countries are shown in the table and scatter-diagram cited. Of these, only Norway, U.K., Germany, South Africa, and Japan showed a ratio higher than India's.

[41] Bhabha, *op.cit.*, Table V.     [42] *Second Plan Outline*, p. 37.

[43] "Oil is found in Digboi in Assam, where the production amounts to 60 million gallons annually or about 7 percent of India's requirements [*i.e.*, 0.2 per cent of total Indian energy consumption]. There are indications that oil may be found in West Bengal in the east and near Cutch in the west. No reliable estimates of the oil reserves are available." Bhabha, *op.cit.*, para. 13.

presently known reserves per annum.[44] A substantial fraction of the expansion of electric generating capacity will be in thermal stations, but hydel power potential in India has been very roughly estimated at 35 to 40 million kw., or about as much as the *total* electric generating capacity (thermal and hydel) that would be reached by 1981 under the long-range expansion program envisaged by the Planning Commission. The long-run position in regard to *coking* coal is much less favorable.[45]

From all this, we may hazard the following conclusions:

1. Commercial energy resources in India are adequate to support any foreseeable growth in requirements for at least the period covered in our study.
2. The presently-planned near-term rate of expansion in electric power capacity is in keeping with the near-term growth of requirements.
3. During the 1960's and 1970's, substantially slower percentage rates of expansion in electric generating capacity and coal output will probably be sufficient.
4. The absolute amounts of new investment required for these expansions will continue to increase, but not markedly faster than national income, so that this category of investment need not claim a larger share of total available investment resources than has been assigned to it in the Second Five-Year Plan.

All the above assumes that still other commercial energy sources will continue to play a minor role. Actually, the use of oil will continue to increase. As possible "aces in the hole," India might develop more domestic oil production, might find natural gas (as Pakistan recently has done), and might find it economic, even before 1986, to supplement conventional energy sources with solar and/or nuclear energy, in both of which fields she has an unusually advantageous resource position.[46]

Our cursory examination of the electric power sector, then, seems to give no basis for amending, either for the short run or the longer run, our provisional conclusion; namely, that investment require-

[44] *ibid.*, para. 19. The author goes on to observe, "the coal reserves, therefore, appear to be sufficient in principle to enable the industrialization of the country at the maximum rate which can be considered feasible during the next few decades."

[45] *ibid.*, para. 2 (from *First Five Year Plan*, p. 340, with some later information supplied). At present about 2/3 of the generating capacity is thermal and 1/3 hydel (International Cooperation Administration, *Economic Aspects of Electric Power Production in Selected Countries*, Washington, July 1955).

[46] For a discussion of the last two potentialities, see Bhabha, *op.cit.*

ments in the public utilities sector are unlikely to contribute to making India's overall capital/output ratio exceptionally high or low relative to that in the more advanced industrial countries. The Second Five-Year Plan proposals led to that conclusion as applied to the next five years; it now appears that they are at least plausibly related to longer-range overall growth expectations, that the relative importance of power investment is not likely to be radically different in the subsequent two or three decades, and that development of adequate energy supplies during that period will not encounter basic resource deficiencies.

*(b) Railways.* We now turn to consider investment in railways, another area where a very high ratio of investment to added output is to be expected. In the Second Five-Year Plan, Government railways are allotted Rs. 9 billion, or about half the total investment in the public-utilities sector as we have defined it. (Private railways are relatively inconsequential in India.)

Here, as in the case of electric power, the rate of growth of requirements was underestimated at first, and targets have been radically stepped up in the formulation of the Second Plan.

At the outset of the First Five-Year Plan, it was optimistically expected that "passenger traffic has possibly reached the peak for the time being, but an increase of 10 per cent over the present levels of freight traffic is anticipated by the end of the period of the Plan."[47] The main emphasis of the program was on rehabilitation of run-down facilities rather than provision for any considerable expansion in carrying capacity.

During the First Plan period, however, both passenger and freight traffic demands increased more rapidly than had been anticipated, and shortage of railway capacity was an important bottleneck hindering overall achievement of the Plan's goals.

The Second Plan *Draft Outline* of February 1956 contains an estimate that in the next five years, with national income rising 25 per cent, rail freight tonnage will rise 51 per cent and passenger train services about 15 per cent.[48]

The freight traffic forecast has been worked out by the Planning Commission on the basis of the planned expansion in the various sectors of production and a number of specific industries such as

[47] *First Five-Year Plan*, p. 464.
[48] *Second Plan Outline*, p. 143.

steel and coal mining which have especially heavy transport requirements. Although we are in no position to duplicate or check those calculations, it is fairly easy to support their plausibility by a crude independent calculation.

The present composition of rail traffic is approximately as follows:[49]

|  | Per cent of total tonnage |
|---|---|
| Minerals[50] | 50–60 |
| Farm and forest products | 15–20 |
| Manufactures | 10–15 |
| All other | 10–15 |
| Total | 100 |

The expected rates of increase in various components of national product generally corresponding to the above are:[51]

|  | Percentage increase, 1956–1961 |
|---|---|
| Mining | 58 |
| Agriculture | 18 |
| Factory enterprises | 64 |
| All other | 25 |
| Total national output | 25 |

Now if we were to apply the first set of percentages as weights in averaging the second set, we should come out with an indicated overall freight tonnage increase of 40 to 50 per cent. This would probably be a slight underestimate, because within the respective sectors shown, rail transport requirements might well increase more than in proportion to net output. In the case of agriculture and small industries, this would occur because a larger proportion of the output will be moving out of local production areas to market as urbanization and exchange develop further. In the factory industry sector it would reflect the relatively faster growth of the heavy producers' goods industries with their large transport demands. Finally, imports requiring rail haul in India may well increase more than in proportion to domestic production.

[49] Calculated from data in Railway Board, *Report on Indian Railways*, 1953-1954, Vol. II.
[50] Includes coal hauled for railroad use, and also oil.
[51] *Second Plan Outline*, p. 26.

On the whole, then, the expectation of a 51 per cent increase in freight tonnage appears to be in keeping with the proposed rate and pattern of development for the next five years.

Unfortunately, however, it is not at present clear that provision for this increase in traffic can be made. Indeed, the Planning Commission states:[52]

". . . it is at present surmised that with the funds allotted to them [the railways] may not be in a position to carry all the additional traffic expected to be generated during the plan period and the facilities provided by them may fall short of requirements by about 10 percent in respect of rolling stock and by about 5 percent in respect of line capacity."

Elsewhere the estimate is made that the actual provision for increased freight tonnage will be only 35 per cent as against the 51 per cent growth in traffic demand.[53] The "uncovered gap" amounts to some 19 million tons in 1960-1961.

The expectation is that the 15 per cent increase in passenger traffic can be met, though at the cost of postponing any relief from the present acute overcrowding of trains.[54] The projected increase in demand is itself perhaps conservative, however. Total disposable consumer income is expected to increase somewhat more than 15 per cent and the income-elasticity of demand for passenger transportation is generally believed to exceed unity.

For rail transport we apparently have then a short-term situation resembling that of housing in one respect; namely, in that the maximum possible expansion for the present falls short of what is agreed to be adequate. Conceivably the effects on economic growth could be more serious in the case of the railway capacity deficiency, since freight carriage is very directly related to production.

It would be premature, however, to conclude either that transport deficiency will prevent fulfillment of the Plan's production targets or that railway investment will be a larger part of total investment than presently planned. The Indian railways are now under intensive expert study to discover ways of increasing the efficiency of their performance, and general experience elsewhere suggests that there is often an unsuspected degree of flexibility in railway capacity. At least one competent outside observer, in fact, has recently reported a belief that ways might be found for reducing the railway

[52] *Second Plan Outline*, p. 143.     [53] *ibid.*, p. 38.     [54] *ibid.*, p. 143.

investment allocation *below* the contemplated Rs. 9 billion without jeopardizing the success of the Plan.[55]

Among the possibilities mentioned are various measures to discourage growth of passenger train requirements (revision of schedules, fare increases, elimination of special bargain fares, etc.); changing some of the proposed electrifications to dieselizations; embargo of some types of freight in congested zones around major terminals; and modifying construction and maintenance-of-way standards in such a way as to reduce the immediate need for new investment, even at the cost of larger labor requirements or earlier replacements. The Planning Commission suggests also that:

> "Relief . . . may be expected in respect both of goods and passenger traffic by the retention of replaced overaged stock which is found in serviceable condition."[56]

A considerable diversion of added traffic from the railways to the roads may contribute importantly to the ultimate solution.[57] The highway construction program has been stepped up in the Second Plan as compared to the First, and the total mileage of surfaced roads is expected to increase 9 per cent as compared to 5 per cent in the First Plan.[58] The supply of trucks and busses could presumably be expanded fairly rapidly, and perhaps at a lower capital cost than equivalent additions to rail capacity would involve, and the existing road system could handle a larger volume of traffic. It is to be expected that if the railways do fail to handle all the traffic offered, provision will be made to ensure carriage of the traffic most essential to productive expansion and that most if not all of the "less essential" traffic might without too much difficulty be accommodated on the highways in that event.

In advance of the findings of the careful reexamination now in

[55] J. K. Galbraith, as reported in *The Hindu*, Madras, April 24, 1956.

[56] *ibid.*, p. 143. This suggestion would seem to have very considerable potentialities, in view of the fact that the Rs. 9 billion program seems to call for rolling-stock replacements considerably in excess of depreciation. The percentage of overage to total units would (if "replaced overage" units were actually withdrawn) be reduced from 32 in 1956 to 18 in 1961 in the case of locomotives, from 19 to 8.5 in the case of freight cars, and from 26 to 10.5 in the case of passenger coaches. (*ibid.*, p. 144).

[57] This has been recommended by more than one responsible observer in India. Cf. for example, B. V. Vagh, *Goods Transport and the Plan*, 1954, and *Road Transport in India*, 1955 (Eastern Economist Pamphlets).

[58] *Second Plan Outline*, p. 38.

progress, we cannot venture an opinion on the actual adequacy of the presently proposed investment allocation for the needs of the next five years. The numerous concrete suggestions for economy which have been forthcoming, however, and the fact that even some reduction in the present allocation has been seriously intimated, is reassuring.

On balance it appears likely that the share of railways in the investment program of the next five years will remain substantially as planned, and that there are good grounds for hoping that transport deficiency will not seriously interfere with overall development in that period. If the traffic demands of this period are met to a large extent by rationing of transport or by letting the transport plant deteriorate, there will be a backlog of necessary extra investment to be made up in subsequent Plan periods. On the other hand, if plant is maintained and it is found that a good part of the increased traffic can be diverted to the highways, railways investment may not have to claim so large a share in the budgets of later Plans.

It is worth noting again that one of the important factors usually cited as contributing to high overall capital/output ratios in under-developed countries is that "economies of scale" are not obtained till a later stage. Railways and other utilities have to be built years or even decades in advance of the time when they can be intensively enough utilized to pay their way, because the building-up of adequate traffic for such utilization must itself await the availability of rail service.

It seems evident that this situation does not apply in regard to Indian railways in the near future. Utilization of existing lines is high and increasing. The relatively small amount of new trackage proposed under the Second Five-Year Plan will be primarily to serve ready-made heavy industrial traffic, and may be presumed to be fairly adequately utilized from the outset. Over the longer run, to be sure, it has been proposed that a more ambitious program of railway extension be undertaken, to further the development of some areas not now served. If and when this type of program is undertaken, it might involve some sinking of capital far in advance of profitable utilization. Even that possibility, however, must be qualified by recognition of the very high density of settlement in nearly all parts of India, the growing possibility of using road development as an alternative where it will economize on capital, and

211

finally the fact that the whole proposal for large-scale railway extension is regarded not as a "must," but as something to be undertaken when and if the necessary resources can be spared.

Finally, a word in regard to highway development. The claim of road construction upon investment resources is lightened to a very considerable extent by the fact that this kind of investment can use mainly local labor and materials, and that the bulk of the work on village access roads is being undertaken by the villagers themselves under the rural development program, representing a form of investment (partly non-monetized) which uses resources that would otherwise go to waste.

In the case of the whole "public utilities and public works" sector, we found that its share of total monetized fixed investment in India, on the basis of Second Five-Year Plan proposals, was the same as has been characterized as representative for the investment programs of advanced industrial countries where the overall capital/output ratio is 3 or 3 1/2 to 1. We may now try a similar comparison in respect to the narrower field of investment in transport and communications. In India, investment in that field for the next five years is programmed at about Rs. 13 1/2 billions, or 23 to 24 per cent of total monetized fixed investment. Some roughly comparable percentages from more advanced countries are shown below.[59]

| | |
|---|---|
| Norway | 30 |
| Belgium | 24 |
| Netherlands | 23 |
| France | 19 |
| U.K. | 17 |

Here again we see no basis for arguing that the role of transport investment in Indian development, at least as contemplated for the

[59] Jan Tinbergen, *The Design of Development*, mimeographed, February 7, 1956, p. 59. These figures were taken from the United Nations, *Economic Survey of Europe Since the War*, with adjustments for comparability. They are averages, for four to five postwar years, of gross investment devoted to railways (including tramways), shipping, air transportation, motor traffic, and communications, as percentages of total gross fixed investment. It may be surmised that the very high Norwegian ratio reflects that country's prominence in world shipping. The same authority states (*op.cit.*, p. 19), that, ". . . as a rule of thumb, derived from past experience, *investments in transport facilities are a fairly constant proportion of total investment, amounting to about 20-25 percent.* This applies to countries of differing structure and to periods of different 'prime movers' of development; it applies to the era of railway construction as well as to the era of industrial development." (Italics supplied.)

212

near term, is likely to contribute to a markedly high or low overall capital/output ratio in relation to those applying in the more advanced industrial countries.

*6. Efficiency in utilization of capital.* A factor often cited as contributing to high capital/output ratios in the less advanced countries is poor utilization of capital. When operating and supervisory personnel are poorly trained, illiterate or semi-literate, and not accustomed to working with modern machinery, for example, maintenance tends to be poor, and the frequent interruptions and rapid deterioration of equipment increase capital costs. At the management level, traditionalism or lack of expertise may show up in poor production coordination or poor investment planning, with consequent underutilization of capacity. Finally, the lack of reliable information on a variety of technical and economic matters, and deficiencies in planning techniques or personnel, may make for wasteful allocations of investment resources at the central administrative level.[60]

This factor is undoubtedly operative in India, but one may question whether it will have any important effect in producing a high capital/output ratio. The fragmentary information available suggests that in the case of new plants in factory industries with techniques similar to those in advanced western countries (e.g., cement making), the fixed capital investment per unit of capacity in India is not materially different from that in the more advanced countries. This would suggest that such factors as higher depreciation may be offset by certain minor substitutions of labor for capital, which can generally be found where labor is cheap.

The utilization of capacity in many manufacturing industries in India was reported quite low as recently as 1953-1954.[61] But there

[60] "Next, the capital-income ratio is expected to be higher because of greater waste of capital. Of this there cannot be much doubt. . . . Workmen are less skilled, and handle their tools less carefully . . . roads, buildings, and other equipment are not so carefully maintained; hence depreciation rates are much higher in the less developed countries. There is also waste, it is thought, because there is more mal-investment, due to greater ignorance of what is possible. The resources of the less developed countries . . . are less well mapped, and less is known about potential markets. . . . Hence great blunders are made . . . for this very reason, capital tends to stick to the beaten tracks, with the result that there is over-investment in some activities and under-investment in others . . . it seems almost inevitable that we must expect waste to be relatively greater in the countries with least experience." Lewis, *op.cit.*, pp. 203-204.

[61] "Installed Capacity and its Utilisation in Indian Industries," in *Second Plan Papers*, pp. 174-197.

are indications that rising demand and fairly severe restrictions on capacity expansion are improving the utilization rate, and further efforts to economize on expansion-investment are to be taken for granted so long as capital remains scarce. For the period of the Second Five-Year Plan, it is expected that extremely little additional investment will be permitted in the large-scale production of consumer goods apart from the sugar-refining and paper industries.[62] To the extent that capacity utilization can be improved, there is of course a temporary factor working in favor of a low incremental capital-output ratio, though we are not disposed to assign very great effect to this consideration.[63]

It is also important to note that where improved methods are being introduced in India with labor unaccustomed to intricate machinery, the mechanization is generally being effected by easy stages, though mainly for a different reason: in order to minimize technological unemployment. This means that the operation and maintenance requirements cannot get far ahead of the mechanical aptitude and training of the workers. It is likely to be a long time, for instance, before the tractor and the truck make very extensive inroads on the primacy of the bullock in rural India.

It is also true that the allocation of investment in India is hampered by lack of adequate data about resources, costs, markets, and other economic variables. For example, the lack of a ground water survey makes it difficult to avoid the risk of costly errors in irrigation development. But on the whole India is in a far better condition than other countries with comparable levels of income, both in respect to basic data and in respect to planning personnel and organization. There does not seem to be any warrant for assuming an *increasing* degree of mal-investment, and in many respects it is clear that the Government and private industry will be able to use the improving

[62] *The Second Five-Year Plan, Draft Memorandum*, Dec. 27, 1955, Ch. I, p. 7. The proposed total public and private investment in large-scale consumer-goods industries other than paper and sugar is only Rs. 900 million, or about 1 1/2 per cent of total investment contemplated under the Plan. Of this 900 million, Rs. 540 million is in silk, cotton, wool, and rayon textiles.

[63] Capacity and production figures by industry in the organized manufacturing sector, 1955-1956, are set forth in *Second Plan Outline*, pp. 123-129. Sizeable margins of unused capacity appear in virtually every industry, though it is not possible to judge to what extent or under what conditions these margins might really be exploited. The capacity and output targets for 1960-1961 (*ibid.,*) are in most cases identical to one another, suggesting that possibilities for improving utilization have been, to say the least, optimistically viewed.

controls and information to better and better advantage in channelling capital into the desired fields. Under these circumstances, one is inclined also to doubt the applicability to India of Professor Lewis' point about capital sticking too tenaciously to the beaten track and in this way perpetuating mal-distributions of investment.[64] It is probable that the amenability of the investment pattern to central planning control will increase during the period under review.

Consequently, it does not seem reasonable to regard the "waste of capital" factor as likely to bring about a high overall capital/output ratio in India.

7. *The choice of alternative capital-saving and labor-saving techniques in production.* The final factor which we shall consider, bearing on the determination of the overall capital/output ratio in India, is an exceedingly broad and pervasive one. We believe it may be of great importance, though it is impossible to provide even a rough quantitative judgment of its effects. It will therefore be examined in some detail.

The essential point here is that the proportions of various production factors employed in any type of production are not rigid, and that there is a strong economic incentive to take advantage of such technical flexibility as may exist in these proportions by economizing on the use of the relatively more costly or scarce factors. Since the supply of labor is very large relative to the supply of capital in India, there are strong pressures favoring the use of production methods which require less capital per man than do the methods that are most efficient in countries with more capital per man. There seem to be very few kinds of production (and those mostly in certain large-scale continuous-process industries in the chemical and metallurgical fields) where there is not a substantial amount of flexibility to be exercised in the proportions of labor to fixed capital.

In an approximate way, we may presume that the relative plenty of labor and dearth of capital are already reflected in the production methods now used in India. In a few large-scale factory industries, about as much capital per unit of output seems to be used in India as in advanced western countries, though more men are used. We have already conjectured that in these cases the factor of inferior

[64] Cf. above, p. 213, note 60.

215

maintenance and production control may approximately offset the small economies in use of capital obtainable by virtue of more lavish use of manpower. But nearly everywhere else in the production system, there would seem to be opportunities for reducing the capital requirements per unit of output below western standards.

This is most clearly the case in agriculture, where the incremental capital/output ratio in India is probably of the order of 1 to 1.[65] In many manufacturing industries the flexibility of the ratio is much smaller. But it is a fair presumption that over a considerable field of production, the *potential* difference in optimum capital/output proportions as between India and advanced western countries may be considerably greater than the *present* difference.

The presumption for the existence of such a potential differential, which would allow further scope for capital economies in India, lies in a fact already alluded to, near the end of Chapter X; namely that the scientific study of production techniques has to date been confined almost entirely to countries where the main goal in view has been the reduction of labor costs rather than capital costs. As a result, Indian production techniques in small-scale industry can be presumed to be characteristically either (1) simply traditional and obsolete, without benefit of modern knowledge, or (2) based on the copying of western techniques which are really efficient only in a context of high wages and cheap capital. The latter course tends to be imposed by the fact that most equipment has been western-designed and industrial engineers largely western-trained, in default of any alternative doctrine.

If the scientific working-out of appropriate production methods for Indian conditions is, as suggested above, a largely unexploited field, it seems to follow that very considerable economies (in the form of capital saving) could result from even rather elementary research and extension work in this field. Acting upon this belief, the Indian Government is beginning to devote substantial effort to the development of sound "labor-intensive" or "capital-saving" methods. This is motivated in part by the objective of making the severely limited supply of capital go as far as possible in providing increased output; it is also motivated in part by the desire to provide increasing employment. Primarily the two aims go hand in hand,

[65] cf. discussion in section 4 above.

though they may diverge when there is a question of the desirability of providing fuller employment even where no additional output results.[66]

To some extent, the policy of encouraging capital-saving production methods extends over the whole economy, with the support of the Government, general public sentiment, and (in industries where labor organizations are active) organized labor. In this broad application, however, it involves primarily a retardation of any changes which threaten to produce technological unemployment, and at worst is subject to the abuses and dangers which a doctrinaire attitude on that subject involves. The important area of positive action at present is in the sector loosely termed "small enterprises," which is believed to have a potential for supplying a greatly increased output of certain products which otherwise (in view of the limited supplies of capital) would be forthcoming in smaller volume, and with far less employment, in the large-enterprise sector. In the Second Five-Year Plan, it is hoped that an invigorated and ex-

[66] In recent years there has been extensive controversy among economic theoreticians and development specialists on the appropriate criteria for allocating investment, and in particular on the question of whether it is more conducive to development, in a country with plentiful labor and little capital, to apply the available capital intensively to a small fraction of the labor force or extensively to a larger fraction. (1) The former approach implies use of the most advanced labor-saving techniques and maximizing productivity per man employed in that sector of the economy where the new development capital is invested. (2) The latter approach implies maximization of the output per unit of investment as the basic criterion; assumes that where wages are low and there is extensive unemployment and underemployment, the capital/manpower ratios most desirable from the standpoint of overall national output and welfare will, in a great many industries at least, be lower than they are in an advanced economy where labor is more costly and scarce relative to capital; and concludes, therefore, that the optimum allocation of investment will involve a somewhat more even spread of the available capital over the labor force than would be consistent with the criterion of maximum output per man employed in the organized industrial sector of the economy. Cf., for example, Walter Galenson and Harvey Leibenstein, "Investment Criteria, Productivity, and Economic Development," in *Quarterly Journal of Economics*, LXIX:3, August 1955, pp. 343-370, as representing the former viewpoint and also as citing some references to opposing views.

It is not a part of our task in this study to decide whether the Indian Government's development policy is the best that could be followed, either for its own economic and social objectives or for any others that we might suggest. We seek merely to foresee what the main lines of that policy will be, as a guide to a judgment on the effects of alternative trends of population growth. It will, however, be clear from our text that we believe that, on the whole, policy in India will follow the latter of the two alternative approaches set forth at the beginning of this note; and that in some types of production, this will help in coping with capital deficiencies.

panded small enterprise sector may supply a large part of the needed increase in consumer goods, so that investment in large-scale plants for such production can be kept minimal.

The "small enterprise" sector has not been surveyed in detail and no one knows just how much it produces or how many people are occupied in it on a full or part-time basis. The latest estimates, however, credit it with producing about 7.8 per cent of the national income and employing roughly the same percentage of the active labor force. Its overall relative importance has been declining for many decades on account of the destructive competition of larger-scale industry, and is estimated to have declined even a little further during the First Five-Year Plan, when efforts to resuscitate it were still mainly in a discussion stage. It is expected that by the end of the Second Plan, its percentage share in national income will have gone up to about 8.1 per cent, or the same share as in 1950-1951: in other words, the hope is to arrest the decline and begin a gradual increase in the importance of this sector.[67]

Many types of production are involved. The different types of problems involved are reflected in the administrative division of the field into six parts, viz.:

> Handloom weaving
> Khadi (hand spinning) and village industries
> Small-scale industries
> Handicrafts
> Sericulture
> Coir products (coconut fiber)

The most important single industry involved, and the one in which promotional activity is furthest advanced, is handloom weaving (primarily of cotton cloth). It gives some work to about 2 million persons, and supplies about one-seventh of the cotton cloth production of India plus a significant fraction of the wool and silk cloth output. Khadi is symbolically important out of all proportion to its quantitative output (something like 1 per cent of the yarn production of India).

The principal "village industries" on which programs have been proposed include hand-pounding of rice, village oil mills (ghanis),

[67] *Second Plan Outline*, p. 26.

village tanning and leather footwear, sugar (gur and khandsari) match making, soap, pottery, basketry, and paper, as practiced in the villages.

The "small-scale industries" tend to be a little less exclusively minimum-scale and rural than the above. Schemes have been, or are being, prepared for a considerable number of them, including carpentry, blacksmithing, sports goods manufacturing, tanning and leather goods, pottery, metal pressed wares, small hand tools, bicycles, and surgical and mathematical instruments.

The "handicraft" sector embraces too many separate products to enumerate. It is in this sector and the handloom sector that the bulk of the luxury items in the small-enterprise sector are produced.

The whole small-enterprise sector is very little mechanized, and because of past decline many of the industries involved (notably handlooms) possess large reserves of unutilized skilled labor and of the traditional forms of production equipment. A part of the case for public assistance to the sector is based on the argument that the incremental capital/output ratio there will be much lower than it would be in alternative larger-scale production establishments making equivalent products, and therefore that the growth of national output will be fostered by allocating some new capital to this sector in preference to its larger-scale competitors. It is also argued, however, that some additional capital can be generated in conjunction with revival of small industries, and finally that the broadening of employment opportunities involved in this labor-intensive type of production is necessary and desirable in the interests of national output and welfare.

Actually, no one really knows how much of an advantage this line of development offers in terms of a lower capital/output ratio. Several considerations suggest that the real net saving of capital is smaller than appears at first sight. In the first place, the existing old-style equipment needs improvement and some replacement, even when idle units are at hand: an important part of the program involves the designing, production, and distribution of improved handlooms, improved hand rice mills, improved ghanis, improved spinning wheels, and the like. Secondly, equipment is on the whole less fully used in small-scale enterprises than in factories, and this differential is likely to persist, although diminishing in the event of a brisk growth in demand. The working capital requirements per unit

219

of output are much higher, as a rule, in small-scale industry, on account of slower and more decentralized production and the far greater number of people employed in relation to output. Problems of materials supply, quality control, labor training, marketing, and finance all impose relative handicaps on the small-scale producer. However, these disadvantages can to some extent be either removed, or the burden shifted elsewhere, by programs of government assistance; and it has been concluded that substantial programs of such assistance are a good investment at this stage in India's development.

A substantial part of the program is viewed by most responsible planners as a useful and productive transitional step in development rather than the building of a permanent element of the economic structure. Technological change is not to be frozen, but is to be controlled in order to effect an orderly and more rapid transition to the ultimate objective, which is described by the Planning Commission as "a modern economy based on capital-intensive and roundabout processes of production."[68] In other words, it is recognized that as the build-up of capital proceeds, the value of human labor in India will rise relative to capital costs and it will become advantageous to adopt less labor-intensive techniques. A substantial small-industry sector will of course remain, as is the case in more advanced industrial countries (e.g., Japan), in integrative association with factory industry and also for supplying certain specialties and art goods where standardization is not wanted; but it is to be expected that the bulk of the "village industry" category and the handlooms will eventually give way to larger-scale methods.

For at least a good part of the period here under study, however, it would appear (1) that a determined effort will be made to expand the small-enterprise sector faster than the national income, and (2) that a successful program along these lines can result not merely in fuller employment but in a more rapid growth of output by virtue of greater returns on India's limited resources of developmental funds. The promotion of small-scale enterprise will involve a relatively high proportion of non-investment development outlay in relation to the actual investment involved.

Most of the basic issues of principle appear now to be decided. Thus, it is agreed that:

[68] *The Second Five-Year Plan. Draft Memorandum*, Dec. 27, 1955, Ch. IX, p. 6.

1. The program should make maximum use of the available labor force, considering its location, skills, and equipment. This implies decentralized production and avoidance of radical technical change in favor of step-by-step improvement.
2. The organization of producers should, to a major extent, be in the form of cooperatives.
3. Where the small-scale industry competes directly with a large-scale industry, a "common production programme" should be worked out, involving (a) estimation of the growth in demand for the product, (b) a decision, on broad public-policy lines, as to what part of the output can and should be allocated to the small-scale producers, and (c) decisions as to the types of product on which the small-scale and large-scale producers, respectively, are to specialize.
4. A wide variety of forms of protection and assistance to small-scale producers will be used, the emphasis depending on the situation in the particular industry involved. Out-and-out subsidies will be used to some extent, but regarded as temporary and transitional expedients.

The small-enterprise-assistance program has not as yet had large results in more than a few industries (e.g., handloom), since during the First Five-Year Plan the work was largely concerned with settling such basic issues as the above, making exploratory studies and experiments, and setting up organization and plans. Public developmental expenditures under this head totaled less than Rs. 160 million during the first four years of the First Plan, and a further Rs. 155 million was budgeted for the final year. For the Second Plan, a provisional allocation of Rs. 2 billion (4 per cent of the total public outlay under the Plan) has been made. This is considerably less than was recommended by the Karve Committee;[69] but the still evidently unsettled state of a great many decisions about implementation (e.g., power looms, the Ambar Charkha (multiple-spindle hand spinning wheel), and limitations on factory expansion) suggest that, unless such decisions are reached in the near future, there may be further delay in proceeding with even the reduced scale of expenditure.

The means of assistance contemplated (some of which are already in use) are so numerous that a mere list must suffice. They include:[70]

[69] *Report of the Village and Small Scale Industries Committee (Second Five-Year Plan)*, New Delhi, 1955, p. 66.

[70] Cf. report cited in previous note; also *Second Plan Papers*, pp. 326-334; *The Second Five Year Plan, Draft Memorandum*, Dec. 27, 1955, Ch. IX; *Second Plan Outline*, Ch. XI.

1.  Publicly-supported research and development work on new methods and equipment.
2.  Instruction in use of improved methods.
3.  Loans to producers (with the Reserve Bank of India charged with overall responsibility).
4.  Government aid in setting up improved organization for marketing (either to final consumers, as in the case of handicrafts and handloom cloth, or to factories in the case of small enterprises producing parts, sub-assemblies, or supplies).
5.  Preferential Government purchasing of small-industry products for departmental use.
6.  Government action to improve or assure the supply of materials for small producers (e.g., by requiring spinning mills to produce enough surplus yarn to supply handloom weavers, or "encouraging" large-scale tanneries to produce surplus findings for small shoemakers).
7.  Adjustment of rail and road transport rates to the advantage of small-scale receivers and shippers.
8.  Adjustment of electric power rates to the advantage of small-scale power users.
9.  Tax adjustment to ease the burden of successive sales taxes on the many stages of distribution often involved in marketing the output of small producers.
10. Goernment advertising and other sales promotion of small-scale products, at home and abroad (particularly in the case of handicrafts and handloom cloth).
11. Government assistance in establishment of grading facilities and quality control.
12. Government-subsidized provision of improved working facilities for small industries: workshop space, with mechanized "central facilities" such as power saws or heat-treating equipment for use by a number of enterprises; also, provision of more fully-serviced "industrial estate" facilities in larger towns.
13. Direct subsidies to producers (wherever possible, on a temporary basis).
14. Restraint of large-scale competition in order to protect small-scale enterprises, inolving:
    a. Excise taxes on large-scale output.
    b. "Reservations": i.e., the designation of certain items for small-scale production exclusively.
    c. Restrictions on further expansion of large-scale capacity, by agreement or by denial of licenses to expand.
15. Encouragement in the development of rural exchange systems for non-monetized production, along lines already pioneered in some areas in West Bengal.

In view of the firm policy commitment and the extensive armory of devices available for implementing it, there seems to be no doubt that the Second and probably subsequent Plans will see a major effort to expand the small enterprise sector. It cannot yet be foreseen just how far this will go or how successful the various measures will be; but even allowing for some failures and some waste of capital, the net effect is likely to be in the direction of reducing the overall capital/output ratio and broadening employment.

*8. Overall indications.* From the foregoing discussion of factors likely to affect the capital/output ratio, there appears no ground to expect an unusually high ratio, and a fair presumption for expecting the ratio to be rather on the low side in the near-term future, as compared with the ratios of 3 to 1 and higher which characteristically prevail in more advanced industrial countries.

It should also be noted, however, that many of the most important considerations making for a low ratio will have a diminishing effect in that direction as development proceeds. Thus, the backlog of unutilized trained manpower and equipment in some of the small industries will be progressively absorbed or will diminish in usability; the demand for housing and welfare services will become more insistent; further urbanization will contribute to this last effect and also add to the costs of satisfying even minimum standards in that field; continued growth of the organized industry sector will impose relatively larger claims on total monetized investment resources; the effort to increase agricultural output will almost certainly eventually run into increasing capital costs; and as India's level of technology rises, probably a larger relative outlay will be called for in order to maintain an adequate position in research and development.

The incremental capital/output ratio has been discussed in the present chapter primarily in terms of monetized fixed investment; it is presupposed that complementary non-investment development outlays and non-monetized investment will be forthcoming as well. We should assume that the latter will, at least over the longer run, play a diminishing role.

From the discussion in Chapter XII, it appeared safe to predict that the proportion of national income made available for development outlays, in either a broad or a narrow sense, will tend to rise substantially as per capita incomes rise, and at a rate which will depend to a very large extent on the rate of improvement in per capita incomes. In the present chapter we have concluded that the overall ratio of these outlays to the increments in total product that they induce will be fairly low in the immediate future but is likely to show a rising trend over the longer run.

These two trends—an increasing proportion of income devoted to development, and an increasing incremental ratio of development outlays to resultant incremental output—would of course have opposite effects on the rate of growth of output, tending to make it more nearly uniform over the whole period under consideration than it might otherwise be. This agrees with the outlook of the Planning Commission, which appears to envisage a growth (at a roughly constant rate) of about 25 per cent per Plan period for several quinquennia into the future.

This does not imply, however, that our findings up to this point necessarily support the feasibility of that or any other particular rate of growth. At almost every point in the discussion, we have found occasion to make any final judgment contingent to a very important extent upon the growth of per capita output; and (as an important determinant of per capita output, and also in its own right) the growth of population. We have thus far postponed any evaluation of the significance of the population-growth factor; but with the background provided by the discussion thus far, we can now try to take it into account. This will be the task of Part Four.

◇◇◇◇◇◇◇◇◇◇◇◇◇◇◇◇

# INFLUENCE OF POPULATION GROWTH
# ON INDIAN ECONOMIC DEVELOPMENT

# CHAPTER XIV

## DEMOGRAPHIC INFLUENCES ON INDIA'S PROSPECTIVE ECONOMIC GROWTH

### A. Introduction

HAVING in the previous chapters developed our views on the range of possibilities for India's population growth in the next three decades and on the principal factors affecting economic development, we now turn to the other major part of our study: the prospects for economic development in the light of these population trends.

We emphasize that it is not our purpose to develop a forecast of the rate of economic growth, under any population assumption. We are concerned instead with an attempt to weigh the influence of possible changes in human fertility in India in terms of the *relative* rates of economic progress attainable under alternative maximum and minimum fertility trends.

To approach this question of the differential effect realistically, it was necessary to begin with a fairly detailed examination of the structure of the Indian economy and the foreseeable broad outlines of its development during the next three decades. This had two purposes.

The first purpose was to identify factors and relationships through which different population trends would be most likely to influence in an important way the overall rate of progress.

The second purpose was to obtain a very rough idea of the plausible range of economic trends. This was necessary in order to validate our whole approach to the demographic-economic problem. For example, had it appeared in the light of this survey of the economy that India faced economic retrogression even with the most favorable assumptions we could make regarding population, our population projections would have been untenable. Our assumption of rapidly declining mortality would have been invalidated, and it would become necessary to use very different mortality

227

projections for high and low fertility. On the other hand, if an examination of the Indian economy had suggested that progress would be rapid and easy even with the most unfavorable assumptions we could make in regard to population growth, then India might have seemed a somewhat less urgent exemplar of the problem under study. Here also, basic assumptions underlying our population projections themselves would have been invalidated.

We have been concerned, then, not with making a positive economic forecast or projection but with validating the exclusion of two conceivable extreme possibilities, as well as with identifying the critical variables through which different courses of fertility would influence economic growth.

### B. How Population Changes may Influence Economic Growth in India: the Framework of Analysis

In Chapter III we set forth a brief catalog of the ways in which population change—size, growth rate, and age structure—might affect the development of any low-income economy. In Chapters IV to VI we described the changes in the population of India expected in the next thirty years under contrasting assumptions about the course of fertility. The abstract relations outlined in Chapter III now need to be applied in the specific context of these population projections, and in the light of the particular features of the Indian economy analyzed in Chapters VIII to XIII and summarized in Chapter VII.

When we examine the effect of different courses of fertility in this specific context, however, the separate consideration of population size, rate of growth, and age composition (as outlined in Chapter III) is not a convenient framework of analysis.

Since even our lowest projection—with an immediate, fairly rapid and extensive fertility decline—yields a large increase in population, the question of whether the size of India's population is "too large" is not directly relevant to our approach. Nevertheless, population size has an important if indirect influence on the economic analysis. For example, with a smaller initial population there would be a larger margin of uncultivated land, and more room for increased employment and output in agriculture.

So it is with the rate of population growth as a separate factor affecting economic development. The alternative projections we consider do not differ by having different growth rates for all population elements. Since fertility levels are the differentiating factor, only the younger age groups have different growth rates. In other words, the growth differences are so intimately connected with differences in age distribution that it is not profitable to attempt a separation of effects.

Consequently we shall consider each alternative population projection as a whole, and take up the effect of each whole pattern of population development upon three major economic factors:

1. The supply of labor.
2. The allocation of current national output to various uses.
3. The capacity and motivation for work and economic change.

The *supply of labor* is determined partly by the pattern of population growth. Other things being equal, a larger available input of labor would be expected to bring increased total output. In the next chapter, we shall examine the prospective development of manpower supply in India as affected by alternative fertility trends.

Several important categories may be distinguished in the *allocation of national income*. One is net capital formation or investment. Another is meeting ordinary immediate consumer wants, or what we might call "unproductive consumption." A third, hybrid category might be called "productive consumption" or "investment in human resources," since it does not take the form of the creation of capital goods as conventionally defined but does have an eventual effect in enhancing productivity.

The allocation of current output among these three categories will be influenced by the way population develops, whether the allocation is effected by free individual choice or administered. Specifically, in the Indian context, the programs for increased food production will depend on the nutritional needs and demands of an increasing number of *consumers*; basic and primary education programs will depend on the number of *children*; investment to equip production workers will be geared to an attempt to employ the available *labor force* more fully; and so on. We may expect, then, that our alternative projected population growth patterns would imply somewhat different allocations of output as development proceeds.

229

Finally, the *capacity and motivation* of various portions of the labor force will be affected directly and indirectly by different courses of fertility. Increases in levels of consumption—even that earlier labeled "unproductive consumption"—will tend, up to a point, to improve the physiological capacity and psychological outlook of Indian workers. Hence a higher level of consumption arising from a different pattern of population development is self-reinforcing, and will tend in turn to increase total national output. In addition, the *growth* of income per consumer will be significant in determining the extent to which various groups are imbued with hope or become discouraged and noncooperative.

It is clear that population trends affect the pace of expansion of output by helping to determine not merely how many hands there are to work, but also by the extent to which output can be plowed back into development, and the vigor, enterprise, and cooperation mustered in support of the development effort. After examination in Chapter XV of the effects of alternative population growth patterns via labor supply, we shall discuss in Chapter XVI effects via the amount and character of saving and investment, and effects via consumption levels. Finally, in Chapter XVII we shall show by illustrative calculations how these effects combine to produce cumulatively divergent trends in expected output and consumption (total and per capita) with different courses of fertility.

◇◇◇◇◇◇◇◇◇◇◇◇◇◇◇◇◇◇◇◇◇◇◇◇◇◇◇◇◇◇◇◇◇◇◇◇◇◇◇◇◇◇◇◇◇◇◇◇◇◇◇◇

# CHAPTER XV

# POPULATION GROWTH AND LABOR SUPPLY

◇◇◇◇◇◇◇◇◇◇◇◇◇◇◇◇◇◇◇◇◇◇◇◇◇◇◇◇◇◇◇◇◇◇◇◇◇◇◇◇◇◇◇◇◇◇◇◇◇◇◇◇

THE AMOUNT of manpower productively applied depends on the size of the population in conjunction with (1) the proportion of the population participating in the labor force, and (2) the extent to which the labor force participants are in fact utilized.

As we have already seen, our alternative population projections imply a much narrower range of alternatives in the rate of growth of the population of "working ages," which we may take to be represented by those of ages 15-64, than in rates of growth of total population.

Not all persons in that age bracket, of course, are in the labor force. It is usually reckoned that the labor force currently comprises about 40 per cent of the total Indian population, whereas more than 58 per cent of the population are of "working ages."[1] The bulk of the non-participants in this age bracket are of course women, who are in general performing essential home services but are not available for gainful employment outside the household.

The number of persons in the "working age" bracket shows a little faster growth, in the latter part of the period, in the "high" or sustained fertility population case than in the cases where fertility falls (see Table 30). The difference does not appear, of course, until 15 years after the difference in birth rate is established.

In relative terms, the difference is small. Between the extreme low and high projections, it is nil through 1966, less than 1 per cent

---

[1] At present, a significant proportion of India's children below age 15 are in the labor force, and on the other hand the customary retirement age in many occupations is lower than in Western countries and well below 65. It is likely that a progressively closer approximation of the actual labor-force age limits to the 15-64 limits here used will ensue in the course of development foreseeable in the next decade or two. A constitutional Directive Principle calls for getting the children up to age 14 into school as rapidly as possible. For purposes of the present discussion, use of the age bracket 15-64 to delimit the "population of working age" is sufficiently accurate. According to the 1951 Census, 142 million people, or 40 per cent of the population, were "self-supporting" or "earning dependents" and the other 60 per cent "non-earning dependents." In that year 58.6 per cent of the population were aged 15-64; the percentage in 1956 was 58.3 by our estimates.

TABLE 30. NUMBER OF PERSONS IN "LABOR FORCE
AGE GROUP" (15-64) UNDER ALTERNATIVE
POPULATION PROJECTIONS, 1956–1986
(millions)

|      | Projection | | | Difference, High–Low |
|------|------|--------|------|------|
|      | *Low* | *Medium* | *High* | |
| 1956 | 223 | 223 | 223 | 0 |
| 1961 | 242 | 242 | 242 | 0 |
| 1966 | 266 | 266 | 266 | 0 |
| 1971 | 295 | 295 | 295 | 0 |
| 1976 | 327 | 330 | 330 | 3 |
| 1981 | 358 | 371 | 371 | 13 |
| 1986 | 385 | 411 | 417 | 32 |

in 1976, and about 8 per cent in 1986. For the 30-year period as
a whole, the number of *man-years* of theoretically possible labor
force participation implied would be only 2.35 per cent larger under
the maximum population-growth projection than under the minimum. In view of the cumulative nature of development and the
importance of achieving gains earlier rather than later, it is worth
noting that even this small difference would be bunched in the last
part of the period under consideration.

In regard to the factor of labor-force participation by those of
"working ages," the important point is whether the rate of such
participation is likely to show significantly different behavior under
one of our projected population trends as against another. Here,
one likely effect can be noted. The two extreme population trends
differ greatly in relative number of children.

The number of children (under 15) per 100 persons of "working ages" (15-64) would follow strikingly divergent trends under
the alternative projections, as shown in Table 31.

The figures in Table 31 suggest the great differences in *family
size and composition* that would develop under the alternative
population hypotheses. If (as seems highly probable) the labor
force participation of women tends to be hampered by more frequent births and larger numbers of children in the family, it is clear
that the high-fertility population trend is relatively unfavorable to
female labor force participation, as compared with the lower-fer-

TABLE 31. NUMBER OF CHILDREN (UNDER 15) PER 100 PERSONS IN "LABOR FORCE AGE GROUP" (15-64) UNDER ALTERNATIVE POPULATION PROJECTIONS, 1956–1986

|  | Projection | | |
|---|---|---|---|
|  | *Low* | *Medium* | *High* |
| 1956 | 67 | 67 | 67 |
| 1961 | 68 | 69 | 69 |
| 1966 | 67 | 72 | 72 |
| 1971 | 62 | 72 | 74 |
| 1976 | 56 | 66 | 75 |
| 1981 | 50 | 56 | 77 |
| 1986 | 46 | 47 | 79 |

tility trends. Moreover, the difference in family size becomes more and more marked in the 1970's and 1980's, just when rising income levels, better employment opportunities, and higher standards of maternal and child care would combine to make women's decisions about labor force participation increasingly dependent on the number of children in the household and less dependent on other factors such as custom or stark necessity.

We may conclude, then, that the labor force as a whole will grow until at least the mid-1970's at a rate independent of the course of fertility; and that even after that, the more rapid growth of the number of "working-age" people under the high population projection would probably not yield a proportionately faster growth in labor force as compared to the low population projection.

It is only too obvious that at present, and for some time to come, the amount of useful manpower input is not measured nor effectively limited by the number of persons of labor force age. Both unemployment and underemployment are high. With increasing industrialization, urbanization and monetization of the economy, and the weakening of extended-family ties that will accompany these trends, it is to be expected that the non-utilization of manpower will become more and more manifest as unemployment rather than in the present semi-concealed form of underemployment. This will increase the urgency of efforts to promote fuller employment, which already is a policy objective of the same order of priority as the increase of overall output.

From the discussion in earlier chapters, it is clear that the creation of new employment opportunities is limited essentially by the supply of development funds, the availability of trained personnel, and the ability to organize and mobilize men and resources for production, which depends to a considerable extent on morale and incentives especially in the backward and low-productivity sectors of the economy. It would follow that if we are to assess the prospects for better utilization of manpower under the circumstances implied by the alternative population growth trends, we must take account of the impact of population growth rates upon such factors as savings, investment allocation, training programs, and incentives. It is these factors, rather than any possible alternatives in the rate of overall labor force growth, which will determine growth of output during the next 30 years.

The faster growth (after 1976) of labor force under the high population trend as compared with the lower will contribute to output only if the higher population trend also implies superior progress in supplying the development funds, training, and incentives needed to make manpower applicable and more productive. A rounded conclusion on that point must be deferred till after the discussion occupying the next two chapters; but a few observations may be appropriately made here in regard to the prospective quality and attitudes of the labor force.

The more rapid growth in number of dependents in the high-fertility case will in the first instance impose greater claims on the incomes produced by the working population than would be the case under more moderate population growth, as is shown by the figures in Table 32.[2] It is sometimes argued that this pressure could have a stimulating effect: i.e., that if burdened with a larger number of dependents, the employed Indian might work harder, or the unemployed Indian might look more industriously and successfully for something to do. To rely on this argument, however, is tantamount to saying that India's development is being retarded by *lack of sufficient privation*. All the evidence is to the contrary. Particularly in the rural sector, where development is furthest behind

[2] This gives a rough measure of the additional consumer pressure upon income imposed by higher fertility *even if productivity could be assumed to rise at a rate independent of fertility*, which we shall see is an unwarranted assumption. The actual difference in pressure of consumer needs would be (as shown later) much greater still.

and income levels lowest, the most recalcitrant obstacle to development is precisely the apathy and hopelessness that have resulted from centuries of repression and stagnation. Privation is clearly present to excess already. The key to added effort is recognition of the possibility of some substantial and lasting improvement. This story is being repeated over and over (and will ultimately be repeated some half-million times) in the individual villages of India as the community development program gradually makes headway against inertia.

TABLE 32. APPROXIMATE NUMBER OF NON-EARNING
DEPENDENTS PER EARNER UNDER ALTERNATIVE
POPULATION PROJECTIONS, 1956–1986
(assuming total number of full and part earners is 68.4
per cent of number of persons aged 15-64, as in 1951)

|  | Projection | | |
| --- | --- | --- | --- |
|  | Low | Medium | High |
| 1956 | 1.51 | 1.51 | 1.51 |
| 1961 | 1.53 | 1.55 | 1.55 |
| 1966 | 1.52 | 1.60 | 1.60 |
| 1971 | 1.46 | 1.60 | 1.63 |
| 1976 | 1.37 | 1.51 | 1.65 |
| 1981 | 1.29 | 1.37 | 1.69 |
| 1986 | 1.24 | 1.25 | 1.71 |

Both apathy and poverty contribute, of course, to limiting the effort of the peasant and other low-income producers. It it not a simple matter to devise worthwhile ways of putting in extra effort in a crowded rural economy where virtually the only assets a producer has are his bare hands, his fields and perhaps a bullock or two. Capital, improved methods, and hope are all needed to improve output in that situation, and the arrival of additional children furnishes none of these.

Perhaps the one type of activity that might respond favorably to a faster growth of population would be primitive, "non-monetized" rural investment, particularly in housing. Non-monetized investment uses the idle time of the peasant, plus generally free local materials, and depends on what he considers to be his needs and his ability and incentive to try to meet them. With a faster increase of population, the need for rural housing would be more keenly felt and might tend to increase the scale of non-monetized investment. On the other hand, the dispelling of hopelessness and apathy, and the encouragement of ambition and self-help, would be more difficult. Thus there are factors working in each direction, and the net effect cannot be predicted but seems likely to be small. Moreover, by the time when there appears any great difference between conditions under "high fertility" and conditions under "low fertility" trends (that is to say, the late 1970's), it is more than likely that non-monetized investment will be on the decline anyhow. Its relative importance will certainly be far less by then than it is now. Finally, this type of investment involves primarily farm housing; and though it directly affects current welfare, the effect upon productive efficiency is much less clear and direct than in the case of most forms of monetized investment.

All in all, then, we shall not go far wrong in assuming that the growth contribution from the non-monetized investment of labor will be about the same under either maximum or minimum population growth conditions.

The next point to examine is whether the faster population growth would be conducive to raising output in other ways than by supplying larger numbers. As we have seen earlier, the slightly faster growth of working-age population in the 1970's and 1980's under sustained fertility cannot in itself be counted on as contributing to additional output—the crucial questions are its quality and the extent to which it can be used. As to the quality and adaptability of the labor force, the principal factors will be acquired skills, acceptance of more regular and more organized work routines, greater literacy, and willingness to change methods, work place, and branch of production. These are all factors which, if affected at all by a faster rate of growth of dependents, would be affected adversely. We shall examine in the next chapter the added strain which a faster growth in number of children would impose upon educational facilities in general, which would certainly imply added difficulty in raising standards of literacy and training for both working adults and for children. The possible effect of larger families upon labor mobility (between jobs and between places) is more problematical, but seems on balance more likely to be adverse than favorable.

Finally, a word is in order about the implications of alternative fertility assumptions for labor supply and economic growth *after 1986*. Our analysis thus far might be accused of partially begging the question of the economic advantages of sustained fertility, in that it has considered only a period (1956-1986) in which high fertility means vastly more children and only a few more adult producers. Is it possible that when these additional children grow to productive ages, they might constitute an aid rather than a hindrance to economic development, so that in a longer time perspective the higher-fertility alternative would appear in a more favorable light than our analysis suggests?

We think not. But discussion of this important question is reserved for Chapter XXII.

# CHAPTER XVI

# POPULATION GROWTH AND THE
# DISPOSITION OF INCOME

◇◇◇◇◇◇◇◇◇◇◇◇◇◇◇◇◇◇◇◇◇◇◇◇◇◇◇◇◇◇◇◇◇◇◇◇◇◇◇◇◇◇◇◇◇◇◇◇◇◇◇◇◇◇◇

IN CHAPTER XV we examined the effect population growth might have on growth of output by virtue of its contributing additional members to the labor force. We found that, as between our maximum and minimum projections, the difference in population of labor force ages is relatively small and appears only near the end of the period under study. The really important question is how effectively available manpower can be used. This will depend largely on how incomes are used, and specifically on what proportion of income can be devoted to uses that enhance productivity and make it possible to broaden employment of the available labor force. In the present chapter, we turn to this crucial question of uses of national income.

The aspect of population from which we have to start here is accordingly that of *consumer* needs and wants. The ultimate purpose of the disposition of income is to meet those requirements more adequately over the short and long run. But individuals, business enterprises, and governments have to make a compromise between fuller satisfaction of current wants and provision for better satisfaction of later wants through increasing the flow of goods and services—"development" in the broadest sense.

Here as in the last chapter, we are concerned with the significance of the *differences* between our alternative projections of population. Table 33 presents these projections in a relevant aspect, showing levels and rates of growth for both the actual number of people and the number of "equivalent adult consumers,"[1] which is in general a better basis for gauging relative consumption needs.

The larger number of consumers at any given future date, under the high-fertility projection, imply a larger requirement for con-

---

[1] In calculating equivalent adult consumers, the number of males over ten is multiplied by 1, the number of females over ten is multiplied by .9 and the number of children under ten by .5.

sumer goods and services. Thus by 1971, the population would be 7 per cent larger under the high projection than under the low projection, and the number of equivalent adult consumers would be 5 per cent larger. By 1986, the difference in populations would be 32 per cent; in equivalent adult consumers, 24 per cent.

TABLE 33. PROJECTIONS OF TOTAL POPULATION AND OF EQUIVALENT ADULT CONSUMERS, AND GROWTH RATES BY FIVE-YEAR PERIODS, 1956–1986

| | Population | | | Equivalent Adult Consumers | | |
|---|---|---|---|---|---|---|
| | High | Medium | Low | High | Medium | Low |
| Number (millions) | | | | | | |
| 1956 | 384 | 384 | 384 | 317 | 317 | 317 |
| 1961 | 424 | 424 | 420 | 348 | 348 | 346 |
| 1966 | 473 | 473 | 458 | 387 | 387 | 379 |
| 1971 | 532 | 524 | 496 | 434 | 431 | 415 |
| 1976 | 601 | 569 | 531 | 490 | 474 | 449 |
| 1981 | 682 | 603 | 562 | 555 | 512 | 480 |
| 1986 | 775 | 634 | 589 | 629 | 545 | 507 |
| Average Annual Increase (millions) | | | | | | |
| 1956–1961 | 8.0 | 8.0 | 7.2 | 6.2 | 6.2 | 5.8 |
| 1961–1966 | 9.8 | 9.8 | 7.6 | 7.8 | 7.8 | 6.6 |
| 1966–1971 | 11.8 | 10.2 | 7.6 | 9.4 | 8.8 | 7.2 |
| 1971–1976 | 13.8 | 9.0 | 7.0 | 11.2 | 8.6 | 6.8 |
| 1976–1981 | 16.2 | 6.8 | 6.2 | 13.0 | 7.6 | 6.2 |
| 1981–1986 | 18.6 | 6.2 | 5.4 | 14.8 | 6.6 | 5.4 |
| Average Annual Increase (per cent) | | | | | | |
| 1956–1961 | 2.0 | 2.0 | 1.8 | 1.9 | 1.9 | 1.8 |
| 1961–1966 | 2.2 | 2.2 | 1.7 | 2.1 | 2.1 | 1.8 |
| 1966–1971 | 2.4 | 2.1 | 1.6 | 2.3 | 2.2 | 1.8 |
| 1971–1976 | 2.4 | 1.6 | 1.4 | 2.5 | 1.9 | 1.6 |
| 1976–1981 | 2.5 | 1.2 | 1.1 | 2.5 | 1.5 | 1.3 |
| 1981–1986 | 2.6 | 1.0 | 0.9 | 2.5 | 1.2 | 1.1 |

In addition to the difference in sizes of population at any given period, which is reflected in the level of demand for current consumption, there is an important and much larger difference in *rates of increase* of population. A substantial share of public and private outlays in the "social welfare" category, and particularly those involving construction and other *investment*, is required in order to make provision for the *expansion* of population. Here the difference between our alternative projections shows up even more dramatically. By 1971-1976, the annual increase of population will be 97 per cent larger in the high-fertility case than in the low-fertility case, and the annual increment of equivalent adult consumers will be 65 per cent larger. By 1981-1986, these differentials will have risen to 244 per cent and 174 per cent respectively.

We now address ourselves to the question of how these rather considerable differences in consumer population and growth rates (as between alternative projections) would be likely to affect the success of efforts to raise productivity, employment, and output. This question will be approached in terms of the effect of the size and growth of the consuming population upon the *use of income*.

### A. Alleged Stimulating Effects of Rapid Population Growth

First of all we may take note of two arguments that have been advanced to the effect that a larger or faster-growing consumer population may be a stimulus to more rapid growth of output. In essence these arguments involve (1) the economies of scale and (2) the reduction of unproductive "hoarding."

The former argument has been stated as follows by Colin Clark:[2]

". . . Most of the economic operations of a modern community are carried out in such a way that, if there were an increase in the population and the size of the market, organization would become more economical and productivity per head would increase, not decrease."

This argument fits the special case of an "under-populated" country, which is characteristically a country with large undeveloped resources and sparse population. As noted in a somewhat different connection in Chapter XIII, it cannot be generalized, and India is one of the countries where it seems most obviously inapplicable. The basic weakness of the argument is that it simply begs the question of the influence of population size on progress, by assuming that a larger population means a larger market (i.e., increased total income). If the economies of scale depended merely on the size or density of the population, then India (with a population second only to China's, and a density 36 per cent higher than in Europe exclusive of the U.S.S.R. and 5 1/2 times as high as in

[2] "Population Growth and Living Standards," *International Labour Review*, LXVIII:2, August 1953, p. 101.

the United States) would seemingly be already in a practically un-rivalled position of advantage. As we have already seen in Chapter XIII, the Indian market is large enough now to command very considerable economies of scale in the chief public service and heavy industries; a further expansion of that market cannot arise from additional population unless total income is thereby increased.

The second argument attributes a stimulating effect not to the size but to the rate of growth of the consuming population. It refers to a situation in which the additional wants implied by added popu-lation lead consumers to spend a larger proportion of their incomes and save less. This increased effective demand for consumer goods (including durable consumer goods such as houses) in turn makes investment more profitable, and thus investment, employment, and output all rise.

This argument is clearly applicable in some development situa-tions. In an advanced industrial economy in which decisions to save and decisions to invest are made to a large extent by different people, and not upon closely correlated criteria, progress may be inhibited by overall deficiency of demand, either cyclically or secu-larly, because the attempted saving (savers refraining from con-sumption out of income) exceeds the attempted investment (in-vestors creating capital). When this happens, there is underemploy-ment of all types of productive resources. A spurt in population may cure it by stimulating the savers to spend a larger part of their incomes on consumer goods and the investors to invest more on facilities needed to accommodate the new population and its wants. No new natural resources or technological improvements are re-quired. An increased willingness to spend out of existing incomes, either for consumer goods or for capital-formation, is all that is needed, and a population spurt is one of several possible changes that may bring this about.

This is not a type of situation, however, that can easily arise in a low-income country with scanty capital, and we believe it will not be applicable in India in the foreseeable future. The remarks of W. A. Lewis are worth quoting on this point:

"The possibility that the level of saving may be too high has to be taken into account by countries which are already so well stocked with capital that the incentive to invest is weak, and there is danger of a chronic shortage of investment opportunities . . . It is arguable

241

whether any such countries exist . . . In the less developed countries there is no such danger. Whatever may be the case in the more developed countries, the obstacle to greater investment in the less developed countries is that the current propensity to save is too low."[3]

The essential point here is that in India's case the controlling limits to increased output lie not in any reluctance to spend incomes, but in the availability of capital and development funds plus the skill, enterprise, cooperation, adaptability, and vigor of all segments of the labor force. The existence of an able and aggressively development-minded government, with strong controls over both saving and investment and a large direct role in both processes, is a further guarantee that development will not be held up by hoarding (withholding of incomes from both consumption and productive investment).

Before leaving this point, however, we shall allude briefly to two special forms of hoarding often mentioned as handicaps to economic development.

It is often said that through the centuries India and certain other countries have sunk vast quantities of wealth in totally unproductive hoards of precious metals and jewels. Though very little is known about the possible size of such accumulations, one source suggests that they may be of the order of a month's national income in India.[4] If so, and if their accumulation has required centuries, the rate of net accumulation must have been quite negligible in relation to the national income, and any conceivable effect of the future rate of population growth upon output via this means can be ignored.

It is also said that in some underdeveloped countries large sums flow unproductively into the purchase of land. Actually the buying of land per se is of course not a "dissipation of savings" as is often carelessly alleged. It all turns on what the seller of the land does with the proceeds. As we have seen in earlier chapters, there will be a considerable degree of restriction on land dispositions that might be considered wasteful or contrary to national development policy. Moreover the transfer of farm land (which is the category mainly in view in this connection) will be subjected to increasing

---

[3] *The Theory of Economic Growth*, London, 1955, p. 216.

[4] United Nations, *Measures for the Economic Development of Under-Developed Countries*, 1951, p. 35.

controls designed to prevent both undue concentration and excessive fragmentation of holdings, and to promote more effective utilization.

In short, we see no way in which the more rapid population growth trend could realistically be expected to assist development by providing a more rapid growth in effective demand.

ALLOCATION OF INCOME

With these minor points cleared away, we may now put the question of the effects of population growth upon Indian economic development in terms of the influence of population growth on the allocation of total income among various uses having different impacts upon economic growth.

In this respect there is a quasi-continuous gradation of uses. At one extreme, we have investment in the formation of capital directly and specifically used in the production of goods and services for sale or exchange. At the other extreme, we have consumer expenditures on current subsistence. In between there are many types of investment and other outlay which serve both immediate welfare and ultimate developmental ends.

Any categorization is necessarily both rough and arbitrary, but it may be helpful to think of all expenditures as being distributed among three types:

1. Investment in productive facilities.
2. Other investment and development outlays, serving both production and welfare purposes.
3. Outlays essentially for consumer welfare.

The allocation of the national income among these uses is of course accomplished partly by individuals and business firms and partly by governments. The individual takes what income he has after taxes and allocates some to food, clothing, housing and other consumer wants; some he may invest personally in improving his farm or other productive property; some perhaps may go into further training or education for some member of the family, which also could be called "investment" in a broad sense; and finally he may hold part of his income as idle savings. The Government takes what funds it can muster from revenues and borrowing, and allocates them to some directly productive investments in, say, a steel

243

works, to some nonproductive uses like the military establishment, and a host of uses with mixed productive and welfare effects and varying degrees of developmental implications. Private firms may invest retained earnings, capital raised through the sale of shares, or borrowed funds.

In considering the factors likely to determine the proportion of national income that can be tapped for public expenditure and private investment, we identified as especially important the level of per consumer income, the increased importance of large-scale organized industry, cooperatives and the monetized economy in general as compared to the "subsistence" sector, the development of a more effective system of financial organization (particularly to serve small producers and to mobilize small savings), the enhancement of the effectiveness of the tax system, and the relative expansion of the public sector.

We have already seen (Chapter XII) that the question of the proportion of income available for development is intimately tied up with the question of the Government's capacity and disposition to obtain revenue through taxation and other devices. This is true partly because the Government is assuming a primary role in the effort to increase total saving and investment, and will attempt to save and reinvest a large proportion of whatever funds it can secure, as well as trying to foster private investment. It is also true because both private saving and the payment of taxes by the individual are at the expense of his immediate consumption, and for this reason encounter a common limit or resistance.

An individual left to his own devices is likely to devote a very high proportion of his total income to immediate consumer wants if his income is low; with higher levels of income, more is devoted to forms of consumption which serve a long-range productive or developmental purpose (e.g., education) or is saved and hence available for investment. A government with concern for the welfare and the good will of its people will follow essentially the same policy, making the diversion of a larger share of income to non-consumption purposes contingent upon an absolute increase in the amount left to be devoted to consumption.

The extent to which increments of income will be tapped for investment and other developmental use will be largely a matter of Government policy, and cannot be predicted. It seems certain that with increased per capita incomes, an increased proportion will go to development; on the other hand, it seems also certain that much less than the whole increment will be diverted, since the maintenance of an upward trend in consumption levels is essential to any voluntary development program.

The factors determining availability of funds from various internal sources have been examined in some detail in Chapter XII, with some indication of the pervasive influence of per capita income levels. We may seek some light on the degree of austerity likely to be acceptable to India's planners by looking at some expectations formulated for the Second Five-Year Plan.

The expected increase in overall saving is stated as follows:[5]

"An investment programme of Rs. 6100 crores implies *a big effort on the part of the community*. If, as is expected, national income over the next five years increases by about 25 percent, this programme would mean raising the rate of investment in the economy from the present level of about 7 percent of national income to nearly 12 percent by the end of the second plan. *Allowing for a measure of external resources being available to supplement domestic savings, the latter will have to rise from the current level of about 7 percent of national income to more than 10 percent by the end of the plan.*"

The context implies that the investment figures cover monetized investment only, and we may therefore interpret the savings figures in the same way.

The expected increase in national income per equivalent adult consumer is from Rs. 342 to Rs. 403, or about Rs. 60.[6] Applying the percentages of saving in the passage quoted above, we find expected savings per consumer rising by Rs. 15-20 (from Rs. 24 to somewhat more than Rs. 40). It appears, then, that 1/4 to 1/3 of the increase in per consumer income is to be added to monetized saving. An increase in non-monetized saving is also expected, but no estimates of this are available.

It is quite likely that efforts may be made later to achieve a still higher marginal ratio of saving to income. Increasing monetization of the economy and improved financial organization might make

[5] *Second Plan Outline*, p. 25. (Italics supplied.)
[6] This is based on the Planning Commission's implied forecast of 1956-1961 population growth rather than our own projections, since we are here concerned with gauging official views.

this increasingly feasible. Purely for purposes of a rough illustrative calculation, we shall here take a marginal ratio of one-third.

On that assumption we can illustrate quantitatively the effects of alternative population levels in terms of the allocation of national income between consumption and saving. This is done in Table 34.

TABLE 34. RESULTS OF ILLUSTRATIVE CALCULATION SHOWING EFFECT OF CONSUMER POPULATION UPON PERCENTAGE OF NATIONAL INCOME SAVED

| Percentage ratio of monetized domestic saving to national income, if national income is: | Population Projection | | |
|---|---|---|---|
| | High | Medium | Low |
| In 1971 | | | |
| Rs. 175 billion | 11.1 | 11.2 | 12.0 |
| " 200 " | 13.8 | 14.0 | 14.7 |
| In 1986 | | | |
| Rs. 300 billion | 14.5 | 17.0 | 18.2 |
| " 350 " | 17.2 | 19.3 | 20.3 |
| " 400 " | 19.2 | 21.1 | 22.0 |

Note: These figures are based on the estimate that monetized domestic saving was 7 per cent of national income in 1956 and on the assumption that one-third of subsequent increases in income per equivalent adult consumer are added to saving.

The relevance of this illustration is not vitiated by two facts noted in Chapter XII; namely (1) that in other countries, historically rising per capita incomes have not always been accompanied by a rising percentage of income saved, and (2) that in India the rate of increase in availability of funds from domestic sources for investment and other developmental purposes will certainly depend on many factors in addition to the rate of growth of per capita income. These considerations were taken into account (in Chapter XII) in framing our ideas of the general level of future savings ratios in later decades as compared with the present. At the present stage of the discussion, we are interested not so much in that comparison as in the *comparison of possible saving ratios, at any given future time and aggregate income level, under alternative assumptions as to the size of the population.* To put it graphically, our illustrative Table 34 is designed to be read *across* rather than *up and down.* For this kind of comparison, which attempts to isolate the effect of different population sizes with other factors "held constant," there is considerably greater justification for using the type of formula employed here; though of course the value of the marginal coefficient cannot be predicted with any exactitude. The larger the coefficient, the greater the effect of alternative population assumptions upon the proportion of income saved.

## ALLOCATION OF INVESTMENT AND PUBLIC FUNDS

We next turn to the question of the effect of alternative population growth assumptions upon the pattern of allocation of those funds which are made available for investment and for public outlays in general.

Specifically, we seek to find out whether larger or more rapidly growing population tends to change the relative emphasis or distribution between those outlays which have relatively *large and immediate* growth effects (developmental outlays in a restricted sense) and those whose growth effects are relatively *small or remote* (e.g., primarily welfare, administrative, or defense expenditures).

If we choose to relate economic growth to a relatively *narrow* category of outlays, for example producers' investment alone, then the question is whether population affects the flow of funds to those uses and thereby affects (via a capital/output ratio) the growth of overall output. If we choose to attribute some growth effects to a very *broad* range of outlays, including say those on social welfare programs, then the question is whether population affects the capital/output ratio by shifting the balance between high-ratio and low-ratio outlays.

Either approach can be defended; and in the next chapter, when we address ourselves to some quantitative calculations, we shall have to make an arbitrary choice. For the present, we shall attempt merely to throw some light on the effects of alternative population assumptions by examining two important "borderline" or "high capital/output ratio" types of outlay in the social welfare field: (1) education, and (2) housing.

## EXPENDITURES ON EDUCATION

Education is one of several areas where Government expenditures would almost certainly rise in response to greater population growth. Moreover, the difference in educational expenditures resulting from different courses of fertility is particularly marked, because the differences between our projected populations consist mainly of children. For example, the difference of 120 millions between our high and low projections for 1981 comprises 106 million extra children (aged 0-14) and only 14 million extra persons over 15.

Expenditures on education can be viewed both as consumption outlays—enhancing the satisfactions of the individual receiving the education and adding to his qualifications as a citizen—and as social investment, ultimately enhancing the productivity of the labor force. In the latter aspect, the time lag is of course quite long so far as elementary education is concerned. The larger expenditure required to meet any given educational standard for a larger number of children entails diversion of funds which could otherwise be used in direct improvement of the productivity of the current labor force.

Current expenditure on education is the largest single non-defense current public expenditure in India.[7] In addition, during the First Five-Year Plan, education received nearly half of the developmental allocation to "Social Services," which in turn accounted for nearly one-sixth of total public developmental expenditure.

We have made rough calculations of the additional expenditures on education which might be associated with the higher trend of fertility over the next thirty years. The estimates apply solely to expenditures related to compulsory public education. A hypothetical program was drawn up for the achievement of 100 per cent coverage in an eight-year basic education system (applying to the 6-13 age group) by 1981. The 1955-1956 enrollment for these ages was only 50 per cent of the 6-11 age group and 20 per cent of the 11-13 age group. The program takes into account the recent scaling-down of the initial highly ambitious goals for education,[8] but is intended primarily as illustrative rather than as a forecast. Cost estimates for the various components of expenditure were based on figures in the Report of the Committee on the Ways and Means of Financing Educational Development, published in early

[7] In 1953-1954, 8.8 per cent of total current expenditure by all levels of government went into education. Taxation Enquiry Commission, *Report*, Vol. I, pp. 244-245.

[8] Cf. pp. 189-190 above.

1950. Allowances for increases in teachers' salaries, etc., were made in the Committee estimates.[9]

The results of the calculation are as follows. The difference in population (between the high-fertility and low-fertility projections) in the age group 6-13 jumps from 11 million in 1971 to 43 million in 1981 and 67 million in 1986. The average annual difference in expenditure on compulsory elementary education amounts to roughly Rs. 2 billion in 1981-1986. For the whole period 1956-1986, the extra costs of elementary education under high fertility amount to Rs. 20 to 25 billion.

An alternative response to the larger number of children under high fertility would be to increase outlays less than here suggested but to accept a lower standard of education. It must be recognized, however, that the expenditures per pupil allowed for in these calculations are already rather minimal.

The main impact of higher fertility is in the number and proportion of children, and the additional cost attendant on a larger increase in the number of children is particularly evident in the field of education. Other types of social service expenditure would likewise be larger if the same level of essential services had to be provided to a larger population. Health services are another area in which additional children probably increase total needs disproportionately, if account is taken of costs of prenatal and maternity services.

*Housing.* Housing is one of the largest categories of social welfare investments with high capital-output ratios. The proportion of total investment going into such investments will obviously exert a major influence on the level of the incremental capital-output ratio for the economy as a whole. An important feature of housing and certain other forms of "social overhead" investment is the possibility of their postponement for a period without adverse repercussions on the growth of total output. This feature becomes especially important in the case of transition-stage developmental programs, such as that for India. During this stage the lower the rate of housing

[9] The basic figures used for our calculations were the following: current expenditure per pupil-year, Rs. 31.5 (net of depreciation and interest); cost of teacher training, Rs. 30 per pupil (for an average two-year training program and 30 pupils per teacher); expenditure on construction, Rs. 32.5 per pupil.

construction—compatible with acceptable minimum welfare standards—the faster the growth of total output can be.

Some comparative figures from the experience of the United States and the U.S.S.R. may serve to illustrate the latter point and at the same time to indicate the orders of magnitude involved. Because of difficulties in obtaining comparable classifications for the two countries, it is not possible to compare directly the overall outlays on housing and urban facilities.[10] A measure of the ratios of investment in housing to investment in industry, however, should serve as a useful index of the differences in composition of total outlays for the two countries. Since 1890 in the U.S., except for unusual periods, industry and housing have each received about one-fourth of total investment. As noted in Chapter XIII, this proportion for housing is fairly typical in advanced economies. During the 1930's the U.S.S.R. allocated to industry roughly 40 per cent, and to housing only 10 per cent.[11] More recently, in the 1950's (i.e., after the reconstruction period) the indications are that housing has been getting about half as large a share as industry in the U.S.S.R.

The Soviet pattern of investment during the 1930's clearly reflected a decision to postpone, so far as possible, social overhead investment. The result was an unusually rapid short-period growth of total production. Recognition of a longer-run necessity to allocate investment to social overhead is perhaps suggested in the more recent rise in allocations to housing.

There may be considerable latitude in the timing of social overhead expenditure in India during the coming decades. But such expenditure will be considered essential up to some minimum level and it will constitute an important fraction of total outlays. Our intention is to attempt some measure of how the "essential" level of these outlays may be affected by the differences between alternative population growth trends.

[10] If one were to treat the expenditure under roughly similar groupings as significant, one can say that the fraction of total investment devoted to this category was roughly twice as high in the U.S. as in the U.S.S.R. For example, the fraction was about a quarter of total investment in the U.S.S.R. for the post-1928 period and about half of total investment in the U.S. for 1880-1912. See Norman M. Kaplan, "Capital Formation and Allocation," in Abram Bergson (ed.), *Soviet Economic Growth*, New York, 1953, Tables 2.7, 2.8, pp. 52, 54.

[11] *ibid.*, pp. 52, 54, 56, 58, 61. "Industry" includes mining, manufacturing, and electric power. Kaplan gives 8.9 per cent for *urban* housing in the U.S.S.R. during the 1930's.

Rural housing investment in India during the next few decades seems likely to remain mainly non-monetized, though this will depend to some extent on the nature of future government policies in the promotion of rural industries and on the pace of general monetization of the economy. We shall concern ourselves here primarily with urban housing needs.

We have noted at an earlier point (p. 137) a general tendency for the urban population of India to grow at a percentage rate a little more than double that of the total population. This relationship conforms fairly well to the experience of the last few decades and is implicit in the Planning Commission's expectations for the 1950's. We used it in Chapter X as a rough guide to the probable rate of urbanization under a "neutral" or intermediate assumption as to the overall rate of population growth.

We feel, however, that it would not be reasonable to apply the identical rule of thumb for urbanization to both our maximum and minimum population projections. Were we to do so, we should have the 1986 population 37 per cent urban under the maximum population growth assumption as against 28 per cent under the minimum. It seems more reasonable to suppose that the difference would be substantially less than that, if we could make allowance for the effects of higher fertility in (1) retarding the overall progress of developmental and industrialization with which urbanization is associated, (2) retarding the shift of consumption patterns from farm products to industrial products by retarding growth of per capita income, and (3) restricting mobility. At the same time, the much faster growth of population under high fertility might be expected to lead to a *somewhat* faster increase in the proportion of urban to total population, if only because more towns and villages will pass the threshold size to qualify as urban.

Consequently we shall adopt a rather arbitrary intermediate assumption in regard to rates of urbanization. We shall apply the 2-to-1 growth rate ratio not to total population but to population of "labor force ages" (15-64). This implies a much smaller difference in urban growth rates between our maximum and minimum cases.

The results of the calculation are set forth in Table 35. The urban population in ages 15 and over have been projected to 1981 and 1986 at *double the annual percentage rates of growth of the population of labor-force ages* in our projections.[12] We have then assumed that the proportion of people aged 15 and over is *the same in the urban population as in the country as a whole.*[13] By this

TABLE 35. RESULTS OF ILLUSTRATIVE CALCULATION OF URBAN POPULATION BY BROAD AGE GROUPS, 1981 and 1986

| | *Total Population* | | *Urban Population* | | | *Urban Population as Percentage of Total* |
|---|---|---|---|---|---|---|
| | *All ages* | *15–64* | *All ages* | *0–14* | *Over 14* | |
| | Number (millions) | | | | | |
| 1956 | 384.3 | 223.3 | 71.3 | 27.8 | 43.5 | 18.6 |
| 1981, high | 681.5 | 371.1 | 206.7 | 86.6 | 120.1 | 30.4 |
| " low | 561.6 | 357.6 | 163.8 | 52.2 | 111.6 | 29.2 |
| 1986, high | 775.1 | 417.5 | 264.5 | 112.4 | 152.1 | 34.1 |
| " low | 588.6 | 384.8 | 184.2 | 54.9 | 129.3 | 31.3 |
| | Absolute Increase (millions) | | | | | |
| 1956–1981, high | 297.2 | 147.8 | 135.4 | 58.8 | 76.6 | – |
| " low | 177.3 | 134.3 | 92.5 | 24.4 | 68.1 | – |
| 1956–1986, high | 390.8 | 194.2 | 193.2 | 84.6 | 108.6 | – |
| " low | 204.3 | 161.5 | 112.9 | 27.1 | 85.8 | – |
| | Percentage Increase | | | | | |
| 1956–1981, high | 77.4 | 66.2 | 189.9 | 211.5 | 176.1 | – |
| " low | 46.2 | 60.1 | 129.7 | 87.8 | 156.5 | – |
| 1956–1986, high | 101.6 | 87.0 | 271.0 | 304.3 | 249.7 | – |
| " low | 53.1 | 72.4 | 158.3 | 97.5 | 197.2 | – |
| | Absolute Difference between High and Low (millions) | | | | | |
| 1981 | 119.9 | 13.5 | 42.9 | 34.4 | 8.5 | – |
| 1986 | 186.5 | 32.7 | 80.3 | 57.5 | 22.8 | – |

means, we have projected the 1981 and 1986 urban populations of children (0-14) and adults (15 and over) for the high and low population-growth cases.

The figures in the last two rows of Table 35, showing differences between high and low urban populations, are the key to an estimate of the additional urban housing costs that would be entailed over

[12] Growth rates for population 15-64 and for all ages 15 and over are almost identical, since the proportion of population in ages of 65 and over is very small.
[13] This assumption is roughly in accord with the results of the 1951 Census, which showed a slightly higher proportion of children in rural than in urban areas.

the next 25 to 30 years under the high-fertility assumption. It will be seen that these differences consist predominantly of children.

We shall not attempt to estimate the extent to which this additional population might be housed in *additional* dwelling units as against *larger average* dwelling units, since this would involve highly conjectural predictions about the structure of family relationships and living arrangements. It may be surmised, however, that since the main difference between the "high" and "low" cases is in the number of children, the major difference in terms of dwelling units would be in terms of size rather than number. In order to get a rough evaluation of the necessary extra investment in housing facilities, we shall simply take Rs. 3,500 as representing the cost of providing dwelling space for an urban household of present average size and composition,[14] and pro-rate the cost to children and adults under the assumption that a child (under 15) requires half as much space as a person of 15 or older.

At present, there seem to be at least 6 1/2 persons per urban dwelling unit.[15] In view of the obvious overcrowding, however, and to allow for the institutional population and the fact that a substantial number of people in the cities now have no housing at all, we shall consider an average household of 5 1/2 persons. Since about 39 per cent of the population is now of ages 0-14, we can think of this average household as comprising 3.355 "adults" (15 and over) and 2.145 children. The average cost of Rs. 3,500 per dwelling unit thus breaks down to Rs. 790 per adult and Rs. 395 per child.

Using those figures, we find that housing of the extra urban population involved in the high-fertility case as compared to the low-fertility case would call for additional construction outlays of Rs. 20.3 billion between 1956 and 1981, or Rs. 40.7 billion between 1956 and 1986. In the period 1981-1986 the annual average additional outlay required under high fertility would be Rs. 4.1 billion.

If we took into account a possible requirement for monetized investment in *rural* housing over the same periods, the totals would be increased only slightly. If we assume that there is an average

[14] This figure is in line with the discussion on page 194 above. It is likewise suggested by Wilfred Malenbaum, *Economic Growth in India, 1955/56-1960/61* (processed), p. 6.

[15] Cf. page 192 above.

money outlay of Rs. 500 (for purchased materials) per unit, and apply the same procedure as in the case of urban housing, the difference between investment totals under high and low fertility would be increased to Rs. 24.9 billion for 1956-1981 and Rs. 47.2 billion for 1956-1986. The average annual difference in outlay between 1981 and 1986 would be increased to Rs. 4.5 billion; i.e., by about one-tenth.[16]

Our calculation on differential outlays for housing and education due to difference in the population projections illustrates one aspect of the costs of continued high fertility. Even with rather conservative assumptions, the differential outlays for these purposes amount to about Rs. 6 billion per annum in the five-year period 1981-1986. This would correspond to more than 2 per cent of a national income 2 1/2 times as great as that of 1956, and perhaps 15 to 20 per cent of total investment. The total difference in outlays on housing and compulsory education over the 30-year period 1956-1986 adds up to a figure of the order of Rs. 60 to 65 billion. A more comprehensive evaluation of differences in social overhead outlays would certainly yield a higher total.[17]

SOCIAL SERVICE OUTLAYS AND PRODUCTIVITY

It appears, then, that the costs of providing social services for a population growing on the basis of sustained high fertility would be very much greater than the costs of providing services on an equal standard for a population growing more slowly under declining fertility. The greater burden of such expenditures in the high-fertility case reflects basically, in fact, the difference in population structure between the two cases. Social service outlays are required to provide for the needs of the increasing *consumer* population.

[16] An interesting incidental result of the projections shown in Table 35 is that under low fertility the rural population would have virtually stabilized by 1981, at about 400 million. Under high fertility, it would be 475 million in that year and would be increasing at 1.5% per annum between 1981 and 1986.

[17] For example, our treatment of education covered only compulsory education over the first eight years of schooling. The Committee on the Ways and Means of Financing Educational Development expected that in addition to compulsory education, 20 per cent of the 14-16 age group would attend senior high schools. This alone would add another 10 to 15 per cent to our annual differential expenditure on education during the period 1981-1986. Also, if investment in urban facilities in general is proportional to urban housing investment, as suggested earlier, there should be a considerable additional difference in expenditure. Finally, it is to be noted that our allowance for urban housing costs provides for no significant improvement in present low housing standards.

The larger that population (and its increments) in relation to the size of the active labor force, the larger will be the proportion of such outlays absorbed by non-producers.

Since the active labor force, as shown in Chapter XV, is unlikely to be significantly larger in the higher-fertility case, it is evident that the additional social service expenditures necessitated by high fertility could not contribute anything toward a higher total output in that case as compared to the declining-fertility case during the period in question. It is worth emphasizing that this conclusion is in no way inconsistent with the fact that social service outlays are socially and economically essential to current welfare and development.

It remains to be noted once more that our cost calculations were not forecasts. It would indeed be unrealistic to assume that outlays for social services would really be as much greater under higher fertility as has been calculated above on the provisional hypothesis of equal standards of education, housing, health, and the like under both alternative population trends. As has already been intimated in the discussion on education, a more plausible assumption would be that the greater stringency of resources relative to demands under the high-fertility case would in fact lead to a lower and less adequate standard of services than would be adopted under the easier conditions of the low-fertility case. There would be slower progress toward such goals as universal literacy and decent urban housing. This would in turn mean a less favorable development of the quality and incentives of the labor force itself, and thus a retardation in the increase of productivity and in the growth of total national output.

Viewed realistically, then, the allocation of resources to social services under high fertility would involve both (1) diversion of a larger proportion of available funds, at the expense of development outlays to aid producers as such, and (2) a less rapid improvement in the skills and incentives of the labor force. Achievement of development aims would thus be impaired both in the short and the long run.

CONSUMPTION AND PRODUCTIVITY

Our survey of the implications of alternative population growth trends thus far shows that with reduced fertility there would be a somewhat more rapid growth of *total output* than with unchanged fertility. The combination of a somewhat larger output with a substantially smaller number of consumers means, of course, that *average* consumption levels would rise markedly faster if fertility were to decline than if fertility were maintained. The prospect of higher levels of consumption associated with lower fertility raises the question of a possible "feed-back" effect. Would higher consumption per capita in turn have some effect on productivity?

There are reasons for believing that rising consumption levels will contribute to increasing productivity, and that the faster rise associated with reduced fertility would enhance this effect. Two principal factors are involved here: physiological capacity for work, and psychological incentives to higher productivity.

The greater physiological capacity for work arises primarily from a higher level of food consumption.[18]

There are many reasons for expecting more effective work from a better nourished Indian population. As shown in Chapter VIII, the estimated average diet in India falls well short of the dietary standard recommended by the Nutrition Advisory Committee of the Indian Council of Medical Research. In every category except food grains, the implication is a major deficiency in the so-called protective foods, and possibly a slight deficiency in average caloric intake. It is certain that even if average caloric intake is approximately at an adequate level for normal activity, the poorer segments of the population must be well below adequate standards. There is ample evidence that motor performance and the capacity for work both deteriorate with an inadequate caloric intake and that the

---

[18] It seems clear that a major improvement in physiological capacity for work can be expected as a result of improvements in medical care and public health. We have assumed that these improvements will effect a drastic reduction in mortality, and the decreased incidence of debilitating diseases (for example, malaria or dysentery) should lead to a more vigorous and effective labor force. Thus, the virtual elimination of malaria can be expected to increase the effectiveness of agricultural work as well as to reduce absenteeism in non-agricultural employment. By a wry coincidence, seasonal malaria rates often reach their peaks at crucial periods in the crop cycle, such as planting and harvesting. (S. R. Bhombore, C. Brooke Worth, and K. S. Manjundiah, "A Survey of the Economic Status of Villagers in a Malarious Irrigated Tract in Mysore State, India, Before and After DDT Residual Insecticidal Spraying," *Indian Journal of Malariology*, Vol. 6, No. 4, Dec. 1952.) However, these improvements in productivity will be very nearly independent of the course of fertility.

deterioration is aggravated by other nutritional deficiencies.[19] However, we know of no sufficiently reliable basis for a quantitative estimate of the rise in output to be expected from a given improvement in per capita food supply. We shall merely point to the suggested qualitative implication of the significantly better diet possible for the population in the declining fertility case (where the number of mouths to be fed grows much less rapidly, and production possibilities more rapidly) than under high fertility. Aside from short-term effects on output, it is worth noting that one of the worst and most intractable food deficiencies is in dairy products and that the main impact of high fertility is on the number and proportion of children, whose needs in that food category are relatively high.

The notion that higher levels of consumption would also aid psychologically in raising output reflects the belief that an essential for the success of economic development in India is the acceptance of the idea that material improvement is possible. The steady trend of rising consumption should make the acceptance of the idea of progress much easier. On the other hand, if most of the rise in output is absorbed in maintaining constant levels of consumption for a rapidly expanding population, inertia becomes more difficult to overcome. Apathy is an obstacle to the highly important effort to improve skills and material equipment in the millions of individual producing units of rural India.

Thus the differential increase in per capita *consumption* per se will play an important role in increasing overall productivity. The effect is additional to the increased development potential deriving from the higher private savings and public revenues yielded by larger per capita incomes.

In this chapter we have examined a number of ways in which a difference in the rate of population growth over the next 25 to 30 years will affect the possibilities for increasing aggregate output: through its effect on the supply of funds for public outlays and investment as a whole, through the allocation of these funds to different types of use, and through the reactions of the individual to his current and prospective level of economic welfare. We have found impressively pervasive indications that lower fertility could

[19] Ancel Keys, et al., *The Biology of Human Starvation*, Minneapolis, The University of Minnesota Press, 1950, Vol. I, pp. 689-748.

lead not merely to a more rapid growth in *per capita* output, but also to a more rapid growth in *aggregate* output than would be attained if fertility is maintained.

We have, however, not yet done justice to the case by taking into account the cumulative interaction of the many relationships discussed, when they work in combination over an extended period. This we shall seek to do in the next chapter.

◇◇◇◇◇◇◇◇◇◇◇◇◇◇◇◇◇◇◇◇◇◇◇◇◇◇◇◇◇◇◇◇◇◇◇◇◇◇◇◇◇◇◇◇◇◇◇◇

# CHAPTER XVII

# PROJECTIONS OF THE EFFECT OF REDUCED FERTILITY ON INDIAN ECONOMIC GROWTH

◇◇◇◇◇◇◇◇◇◇◇◇◇◇◇◇◇◇◇◇◇◇◇◇◇◇◇◇◇◇◇◇◇◇◇◇◇◇◇◇◇◇◇◇◇◇◇◇

## 1. CONSTRUCTION OF MODEL

As we have explained at earlier points, a central purpose of the economic part of our analysis is to get a roughly quantitative measure of the economic significance of a reduction in fertility.

To arrive at this measure, we shall calculate projections of India's overall economic progress under both sustained (high) and progressively reduced (low) fertility, and examine the size of the differential and the way in which it arises. This comparison will be worked out not for just a single pair of economic projections with high and low fertility, but for a number of different pairs using different assumed economic coefficients. The purpose of these different comparisons is to test the degree to which the differential economic effect associated with lowered fertility persists in the face of widely varying assumptions about the absolute rate of progress and the non-demographic variables determining it.

This plurality of projections reflects the fact—previously reiterated—that we do not pretend nor attempt to forecast the rate of economic development in India, beyond the statement that we think it will fall somewhere within the extremely wide range of rates that is compatible with our assumptions regarding mortality and fertility trends. None of the projections in this chapter is to be taken as a forecast.

Our calculations in this chapter entail a "model" of the Indian economy, designed to take into account—as realistically as an extremely simplified model can—the main relevant features of that economy as explored in previous chapters.

Specifically, we assume that the rate at which output can be expanded will depend very largely on (1) the resources that can be devoted to investment in productive facilities and certain other developmental outlays, and (2) the incentives and energy of the labor force. These are of course not the only important growth determinants, but they seem to be the growth determinants *most clearly affected by the difference between our alternative rates of population growth.* Other important determinants such as the wisdom of government policies, the international situation, the availability of technical knowledge from outside India, and the progress of administrative organization, may be regarded as relatively little affected by the difference between the population growth alternatives, and are therefore left aside and not introduced explicitly as variables in this calculation. The *size* of the labor force is also left aside, not because the growth of output is considered independent of increases in the labor force, but because (as we have argued earlier) the size of the labor force is not much affected before 1986 by different courses of fertility.

It is clear from our earlier discussion that both the availability of funds for development and the quality and energy of the labor force will depend on the rate of improvement of levels of living in India, which may be roughly measured by increase in national income per equivalent adult consumer. But this improvement itself will of course reflect *previous* inputs of labor effort and development outlay in addition to the rate of population growth. Consequently, a more rapid initial improvement in levels of living is likely to provide the basis for a still more effective effort later; and on the other hand, a slackening or disappointingly low initial rate of progress may make further progress cumulatively more difficult. To appreciate the full significance of the cumulative effect, it is helpful to work out the implications of the relations between population and economic development on a time-sequence basis in the form of projections of the trend of development, even at the risk of seeming to attribute a fictitious accuracy to the numbers used.

So far as investment is concerned, we shall take explicitly into account *monetized* investment only, ignoring the not insignificant non-monetized component. This course is followed for several reasons. Firstly, very little is known about the magnitude of non-monetized investment, and by its very nature it will continue to elude quantitative evaluation. Secondly, we have concluded earlier that this is the type of investment that is perhaps least likely to differ significantly in trend under more rapid as against less rapid population increase; consequently it has less bearing on the central purpose of our inquiry. Thirdly, non-monetized investment involves largely rural housing, and to that extent is much less directly related to increases of productivity than most other types of investment. Finally, it seems probable that non-monetized investment will be playing a still smaller, and a rapidly decreasing, role in the national economy by the time really substantial divergences appear between our alternative population trends (that is to say, in the 1970's and after).

We do not believe that the omission of non-monetized investment from this calculation is likely to distort substantially the indicated differential effect of higher as against lower population growth, though allowance for it might if anything slightly enhance the indicated advantages of the lower population growth trends.

Committing perhaps a more serious sin of omission, we shall ignore also the overall effect of average *consumption* levels upon the vigor, efficiency, and adaptability of the labor force, independent of the level of investment and other developmental outlays. Allowance for this factor would certainly increase the indicated difference between the course of development under high and low population growth respectively; but any attempt to make such allowance would have to be based on pure guesswork.

Pursuant to the discussion in Chapters XII and XIII, we shall assume that a prime determinant of the rate of development is the allocation of national output to the combined category of public outlays plus private investment, which we shall hereafter call $F$; and that the amount of funds available for such outlays will depend upon both the national income $(Y)$ and the level of average income per equivalent adult consumer $(Y/C)$.[1] In symbolic terms, the equation determining $F$ is as follows:

$$(1) \qquad F = C \left[ \frac{F_0}{C_0} + a \left( \frac{Y}{C} - \frac{Y_0}{C_0} \right) \right]$$

$$\text{or,} \quad F = aY - \left( \frac{aY_0 - F_0}{C_0} \right) C$$

where $Y$ is national income (at 1952-1953 prices) and $C$ the number of equivalent adult consumers, and the subscript $(_0)$ denotes the base year 1956.[2]

[1] The concept of the "equivalent adult consumer" was defined on page 88.

[2] The various equations underlying the projections are assembled for convenient reference in the Note appended to this chapter.

During the Second Five-Year Plan, it is envisaged that total public outlays will be about Rs. 93.5 billion, while private investment totals Rs. 23 billion and national income totals Rs. 618 billion.[3] These figures would imply that during this period 116.5/618, or 18.9 per cent, of national income would be devoted to $F$ outlays. At present the corresponding ratio appears to be between 15 and 16 per cent.[4] We may presume that a rise in this ratio is (a) a necessary condition for accelerated growth of national output, and (b) increasingly feasible and likely as per-consumer income rises.

To quantify the relationship posited in Equation (1), we shall assume that 30 per cent of all post-1956 increments in income per equivalent adult consumer are added to the sums available for $F$ per consumer (i.e., in Equation (1), $a = .30$). This implies a slightly more conservative view of the possibilities of increasing investment and public revenues during the Second Plan period than would be suggested by the Planning Commission's target figures just cited, if our population estimates are assumed to apply. The Planning Commission, however, allows for substantially less population growth, which would mean a more rapid rise in per consumer income and hence enhanced saving and revenue potentialities.

If, as a rough estimate, we take the 1956 total of $F$ as 15 1/2 per cent of a national income of Rs. 108 billion—i.e., $F_0 = $ Rs. 16.8 billion—our formula for projecting $F$ outlays for future years is:

$$(1') \qquad F = .30\,Y - 49.27\,C$$

with $F$ and $Y$ in billions of rupees (at 1952-1953 prices) and $C$ in billions of equivalent adult consumers.

It may be noted that we have made no explicit mention of investment funds or assistance from abroad, though it is hoped to secure from external sources a substantial part of the funds needed for the Second Five-Year Plan. In view of the lack of any basis for a long-range forecast of the availability of external as against internal funds, it seems justifiable to assume that in general the

[3] cf. Table 25.

[4] Total monetized net investment is estimated at about 7 per cent of national income, and in 1953-1954 the non-investment outlays of the central and State governments combined were a little more than 8 per cent of national income (cf. Tables 23, 24 and text).

availability of external funds will vary proportionately to the success which India achieves in mobilizing internal resources, so that no radical change is envisaged in the relative importance of external to internal funds. The formula as given above is intended as inclusive of all funds, from both domestic and external sources.

Next we must take account of the fact that not all $F$ outlays contribute equally to development. This question has been discussed in Chapters XII, XIII, and XVI. It is impossible to draw a line with any precision, since most forms of outlay have some ultimate bearing on development. We shall try to find some simple way, however, to incorporate into our calculations a recognition of the difference between (1) those outlays which equip or assist *active producers* and thus raise aggregate output in a relatively direct and immediate way, and (2) those which serve primarily the welfare of the *population as a whole* and have characteristically a diluted, indirect, or delayed effect on output.

We shall accordingly make a semi-arbitrary division of total private investment and public outlays ($F$) into two categories— "direct growth" ($D$) and "welfare" ($W$)—in realization of the fact that these labels are only very roughly descriptive.

Thus, in symbolic terms,

(2) $$F = D + W$$

In the "welfare" category we shall put all public expenditures outside the five-year plans, plus the "social services, housing and rehabilitation" category of Plan outlays, plus a minor fraction of private investment which we may attribute to housing (chiefly urban, since most rural housing has already been excluded as non-monetized). The "direct growth" outlays will be the remainder, comprising the major part of private investment and also the major part of public Plan outlays.

If we take the proposals for the Second Five-Year Plan as a guide, we find that public outlays under the Plan, exclusive of the "social services, housing, and rehabilitation" category, come to Rs. 38.5 billion and total private investment to Rs. 23 billion.[5] From the latter, something like Rs. 6 billion should be deducted for housing and other welfare-type investments.[6] This makes the $D$ (direct growth) outlays about Rs. 55.5 billion for five years. As

[5] *Second Plan Outline*, pp. 24, 35.  [6] *ibid.*, p. 24.

263

stated earlier, the total expected $F$ outlays for the same period come to Rs. 116.5 billion and total national income to Rs. 618 billion. The Plan thus contemplates total $F$ outlays averaging about 18.9 per cent of national income, of which $D$ accounts for 9.0 per cent and $W$ for 9.9 per cent.

It is unfortunately not possible to be even this definite about the 1956 values of $D$ and $W$. Net fixed investment, however, is thought to be running at about 7 per cent of national income. On the public side, this category corresponds fairly closely in size to Plan outlays exclusive of the social services category, and the same is not too far from true on the private side also, if we add to fixed investment an allowance for normal inventory accumulation and subtract welfare-type construction. As a rather crude working approximation for 1956, then, we shall take $D$ as 7 per cent of national income (or Rs. 7.6 billion); which (by subtraction from our earlier estimate of $F$) would give $W$ as 8.5 per cent, or Rs. 9.2 billion.

It appears from the available estimates that an effort is being made to increase $D$ outlays faster than $W$. In view of general policy pronouncements and the actual revisions of targets in the course of formulating the Second Plan, it seems likely that the Government will continue to give the direct growth outlays ($D$) priority over the outlays for general government and social services and to private investment in areas other than those directly related to production.

Over the longer run, the demands for welfare ($W$) outlays will be based in part on the size and rate of increase of *population* to be provided for (the numerical relation being perhaps most obvious in the case of provision of elementary schools). These demands, and the extent to which they are met, will however also depend on what the people "can afford," which implies a dependency upon levels of *per capita income*. Evidently the size of the population, the rate of its growth, and the level of per capita income will all play some part in determining the allocation of funds for "welfare" purposes, though none of these can realistically be taken as the sole determinant.

It seems reasonable to approach this problem by first differentiating between two kinds of $W$ outlays which we may call $W_c$ and $W_i$. The former are those required for the *current needs of the existing population* and would be needed even in the absence of any population growth; the latter are those required to provide *facilities for additional people.* With high fertility, of course, additions to population by 1986 would be much larger than with low fertility (Chart 9).

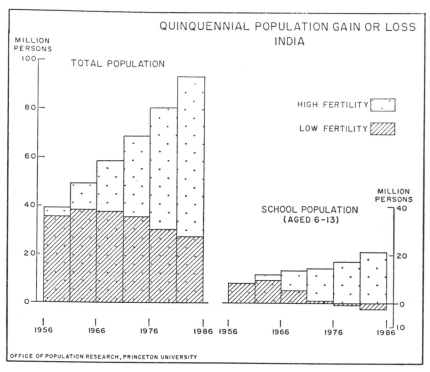

Chart 9. Quinquennial Increases in Total Population and in Population of Primary School Age, with High and Low Fertility, India, 1956-1986.

In symbolic terms,

$$(3) \qquad W = W_c + W_i.$$

We are in no position to make any genuine estimate of the relative magnitudes of $W_c$ and $W_i$ at any date, and shall have to be content with trying to choose a plausible assumption. It is clear that the assumption we make about the relative amounts of these two kinds of outlays in 1956 implies also something about their quantitative relation to population and its growth. Thus, in 1956, population was increasing at an estimated rate of 1.72 per cent per annum (see Table 6 above). If we were to say that 10 times as large a $W_i$ outlay is required for each added person as the annual recurrent, $W_c$ outlay per person, then the ratio of $W_i$ to $W_c$ outlays in 1958 would be 10 times 1.72 per cent, or 17.2 per cent.

On the basis of an impression that the "capital/output ratio" in welfare expenditures is unusually high, we shall arbitrarily assume for our illustrative calculations that 10 times as much $W_i$ is required to make initial provision for an added person as is thereafter required each year for $W_c$ by one person. This implies that the ratio of $W_i$ to $W_c$ is 10 times the annual ratio of population growth $(p)$.

In symbolic terms,

(4) $$\frac{W_i}{W_c} = 10p$$

For example in 1956, $W_i$ would be 17.2 per cent as large as $W_c$, and 17.2/117.2, or 14.7 per cent, of the total $W$ outlays of about Rs. 9.2 billion. Thus the assumed 1956 values $W_{i_0}$ and $W_{c_0}$ are Rs. 1.35 billion and 7.85 billion respectively. With an accelerated population growth, our assumptions make $W_i$ rise faster than $W_c$; with a slackening of population growth, $W_i$ rises slower than $W_c$.

We shall now assume, for projection purposes, that as living standards in India rise, the standard of "requirements" for $W_c$ outlays reflects this improvement. Characteristically higher per consumer income levels are associated with an increased fraction of income devoted to saving and investment and a diminished fraction to ordinary consumption. We shall assume, for lack of any better-grounded hypothesis, that $W_c$ outlays will tend to behave in an intermediate fashion and will absorb a *constant* percentage of income throughout the period: 7.25 per cent, as estimated for the base year 1956. In symbolic terms,

(5) $$W_c = \left[ \frac{(W_c)_0}{Y_0} \right] Y = .0725 \, Y$$

Next, we assume that the standards for outlays of the $W_i$ type will show a parallel response to a general rise in living standards—in other words, that $W_i$ outlays *per added person* will go up at the same rate as $W_c$ outlays *per capita*, maintaining the 10-to-1 ratio we have posited. In symbolic terms,

(4′) $$W_i = 10 \, p \, W_c = .725 \, p \, Y$$

and thus,

(3′) $$W = .0725 \, Y \, (1 + 10p)$$

Next we must make some assumptions about the degree and kind of productive effect to impute to $W$ outlays. First, we shall think of $W$ outlays as having a productive effect much less intensive and direct than that of "direct growth" ($D$) outlays (i.e., more outlay will be required relative to the growth thereby induced). We shall accordingly attach fractional *weights* ($e_c$ and $e_i$ respectively) to the $W_c$ and $W_i$ outlays before combining them with $D$.

We shall at the same time try to take account of the fact that these are essentially outlays for *consumers*, and that their effects on productivity are diluted or delayed to a greater extent if a greater proportion is earmarked for children or other dependents. We propose to allow for this by thinking of the $W$ outlays as pro-rated among the whole population, and attributing to the *labor force's pro-rata share* a productivity effect that is just as prompt as that of direct growth outlays; while the remainder of the $W$ outlays is assumed to affect output only after a 15-year lag. In the case of $W$ outlays occasioned by children (e.g., maternity and child care, and primary education) a long lag of this character is obviously involved; we believe that a great many of the benefits of other types of $W_c$ outlays going to nonmembers of the labor force can also reasonably be assumed to contribute to national productivity in such indirect and complex ways that the full effect is not felt within the decade.

We can now set forth all our assumptions about the productive effects of the various types of $F$ outlays in a formula for what we may call "equivalent growth outlays" and denote by the symbol $G$:

$$(6) \quad G = D + (e_c W_c + e_i W_i) L + (e_c W_c + e_i W_i)_{t-15} (1 - L)_{t-15}$$

where the subscript ($t-15$) refers to a date 15 years earlier than the current year, and where $L$ is the ratio of labor force to population (Table 36).

In our initial set of projections we shall take $e_c = .5$ and $e_i = 0$ (which implies giving a diluted and partly delayed growth effect to $W_c$ and no growth effect to $W_i$). In subsequent projections we shall also try some alternative assumptions about these weights.

For our initial projections (Projection 1), then, the formula for $G$ becomes:

$$(6') \quad G = F - W + .5 L W_c + .5 (1 - L)_{t-15}(W_c)_{t-15}$$

or

$$G = Y(.2275 - .725 p + .03625 L) + .03625 Y_{t-15}(1 - L)_{t-15} - 49.27C$$

267

The introduction of the 15-year lag in growth effects for part of the $W$ outlays poses a data problem. The $G$ outlays for 1956-1971 would depend in part on the $W$ outlays and labor force/population ratios of the period 1941-1956, and such data are not at hand. It has not seemed worth while to undertake the arduous job of estimating them, in view of the fact that (1) the quantitative effect of this component of $W$ outlays upon overall economic growth in our projections is relatively minor and (2) the figures based on 1941-1956 could not in any case have any bearing on the differential economic effects of future high versus low fertility which is our primary concern.

We shall therefore simply make an easy substitution, to fill in the $W_c(1-L)$ figures for 1941-1956 which are assumed to have their impact in 1956-1971. The procedure is as follows:

For the year 1956, $W_c(1-L)$ is 4.36 per cent of national income, or Rs. 4.70 billion. We shall assume an increase between 1951 and 1956 proportional to the estimated growth of real income (about 18 per cent); and for the decade 1941-1951, for which there are no comparable real-income estimates, we shall make the series move in proportion to population increase (about 1 1/4 per cent per annum).

This gives the following "substitute data" for $(W_c)_{t-15}(1-L)_{t-15}$:

| $t$ | Amount (Rs. billions) |
|---|---|
| 1956 | 3.50 |
| 1961 | 3.74 |
| 1966 | 3.96 |
| 1971 | 4.70 |

These figures apply, of course, to both our high-fertility and low-fertility projections as far as 1971, since they are presumed to represent the delayed effect of outlays prior to 1956.

If now we examine the implications of our assumptions in regard to (1) direct individual consumption, (2) welfare outlays, and (3) direct growth outlays, we find that a significantly rising trend of per-consumer income implies a markedly diminishing proportion of income devoted to direct consumption, a roughly constant proportion devoted to $W$,[7] and a markedly increasing proportion

[7] $W_c/Y$ has been assumed constant at 7.25 per cent; the smaller component $W_i/Y$ increases if the percentage rate of population growth is accelerating and decreases if it is slackening.

devoted to $D$. The rapidity with which the proportions diverge will depend primarily on the rate at which the level of living rises.

Next, we must assign some quantitative measure to the relation between equivalent growth outlays ($G$) and the ensuing increase in national income. Since our population projections are worked out and presented on a quinquennial basis, it is convenient to assume that the amount of $G$ outlay in any 2 1/2 year interval determines the rise in national income over the next interval, and to derive the necessary population projections by simple interpolation between our quinquennial estimates.

Our discussion in Chapter XIII led to the conclusion that the ratio between development outlays and consequent increases in Indian national output is currently rather low (i.e., favorable), and will remain fairly low for some time, but with a rising trend as development proceeds. In the present calculation we are semi-arbitrarily attributing all increases in national output to the $G$ category of outlays which start at a (1956) level of slightly over 10 per cent of national income. The national income now appears to be increasing at a rate of 3 to 4 per cent per annum, though the actual increases vary considerably from year to year on account of such changeable factors as crop yields. This would suggest that the ratio between $G$ outlays and increases in income in the recent past may have been about 3 to 1. For the Second Five-Year Plan, an increase of Rs. 26.8 billion is hoped for on the basis of private and public monetized *investment* totaling Rs. 61 billion, which would imply an incremental *investment*/output ratio of 2.28. However, $G$ runs now perhaps 40 to 50 per cent larger than investment, and the implied ratio for the Second Plan is stated on a no-lag basis. With adjustments for these conceptual differences, the Plan goals would support a ratio of about 3 between $G$ and the resulting increment in $Y$. We shall therefore adopt it for our initial projections. The symbol $R$ designates this ratio.

We should now provide for a subsequent gradual rise in $R$, in keeping with the findings of Chapter XIII. Some of the factors underlying a prospective rise appear to be related primarily to improvement in living standards, while others appear to be related primarily to the growth of population or of total income. We shall, in our initial projections, simply give $R$ a steadily rising trend over time, which would raise it gradually from 3.0 to 3.6 during the period 1956-1986 at the rate of 0.02 per annum.

In symbolic terms,

$$(7) \qquad Y_{t+2.5} = Y_t + \frac{2.5\,G}{R}$$

$$(8) \qquad R = m + nt$$

and, for our initial set of projections,

$$(8') \qquad R = 3.0 + .02t$$

## 2. CALCULATION OF PROJECTIONS

We now have at hand all the ingredients for constructing hypothetical projections of the trend of national output under our alternative fertility assumptions. Specifically, the initial data (for 1956) are as follows:

| | | |
|---|---|---|
| $(Y)$ | National income | Rs. 108 billion |
| | | (1952-1953 prices) |
| $(C)$ | Equivalent adult consuming population | .3168 billion |
| $(L)$ | Ratio of labor force to population | .398 |
| $(p)$ | Annual rate of population growth | 1.72 per cent |

and the subsequent values for $C$ and $L$ are as presented in Tables 33 and 36, with interpolation between the quinquennial items to provide a series by 2 1/2-year intervals. The values of $p$ (at 5-year intervals) can be read from Table 6 by subtracting the death rate from the corresponding birth rate. The increases in $Y$ over each 2 1/2-year interval are calculated from Equation (7).[8]

[8] It may be helpful in visualizing the structure of our projection model if we examine step by step the calculation for some specific time period as an illustration. Let us take, for example, the projected situation in 1976 and see how the projected growth over the subsequent 2 1/2-year interval is worked out. In this illustration, each figure is stated first for the low-fertility case, without parentheses, and then for the high-fertility case (in parentheses). Occasional apparent arithmetical discrepancies are due to rounding-off.

In 1976, the aggregate national income as projected from previous years is Rs. 219.6 (209.7) billion. With a population of 449.4 (490.1) million equivalent adult consumers, the average per consumer income is Rs. 488.7 (427.9). This exceeds the 1956 per consumer income by Rs. 147.7 (86.9). Of this excess, 30 per cent, or Rs. 44.3 (26.1) is added to the per consumer $F$ outlays of 1956,

TABLE 36. PROJECTIONS OF PERCENTAGE OF INDIAN
POPULATION IN THE LABOR FORCE, 1951–1986
(assuming that 40 per cent of the population was in the labor force in 1951
and that the ratio of labor force to population aged 15-64 remains constant)

|  | Low-fertility Projection | Medium-fertility Projection | High-fertility Projection |
|---|---|---|---|
| 1951 | 40.0 | 40.0 | 40.0 |
| 1956 | 39.8 | 39.8 | 39.8 |
| 1961 | 39.6 | 39.2 | 39.2 |
| 1966 | 39.7 | 38.5 | 38.5 |
| 1971 | 40.6 | 38.5 | 38.0 |
| 1976 | 42.2 | 39.8 | 37.7 |
| 1981 | 43.7 | 42.1 | 37.2 |
| 1986 | 44.7 | 44.4 | 36.9 |

The results of this set of projections, under the various fertility trends, are shown in Tables 37, 38, and 39, and Charts 10 and 11. As has already been emphasized, the significance of these figures

making the 1976 $F$ outlays Rs. 97.1 (78.9) per consumer or Rs. 43.8 (38.8) billions in the aggregate.

Now, the $W_c$ outlays, at 7.25 (7.25) per cent of national income, will amount in 1976 to Rs. 15.9 (15.2) billion, or Rs. 29.9 (25.3) per capita. The $W_i$ outlays will then have to be Rs. 299 (253) per annually added person in order to reflect parallel improvement in the standards for $W_c$ and $W_i$ alike. The number of people added to the population in 1976 is 6.2 (14.9) million, so the aggregate $W_i$ outlays in that year will be Rs. 2.0 (3.8) billion. This makes the total $W$ outlays Rs. $15.9 + 2.0 = 17.9$ billion ($15.2 + 3.8 = 19.0$ billion). The direct growth or $D$ outlays are accordingly Rs. $43.8 - 17.9 = 25.9$ billion ($38.8 - 19.0 = 19.8$ billion).

Of the total $W_c$ outlays of 15.9 (15.2) billion, we can allocate 42.2 (37.7) per cent, or Rs. 6.7 (5.7) billion, to members of the labor force on a pro-rata basis, since the labor force constitutes 42.2 (37.7) per cent of the total population. We assign a weight of one-half to the labor force's share, so that this type of outlays contributes the equivalent of Rs. 3.3 (2.8) billions to $G$.

The non-labor-force share of the $W_c$ outlays, Rs. 9.2 (9.5) billions, is assumed to have no growth effect till 1991. But in 1976 there will be a growth effect from the Rs. 9.2 (9.2) billion of $W_c$ outlays made in 1961. In 1961, 60.4 (60.8) per cent of the population was outside the labor force. That fraction of the $W_c$ outlays is assumed to have a growth effect deferred till 1976. So we have Rs. 5.6 (5.6) billion of those 1961 outlays to take into account in 1976. They are given half weight, and thus a further Rs. 2.8 (2.8) billions is added to $G$ on this account.

This makes the total of equivalent growth, or $G$, outlays for 1976 Rs. $25.9 + 3.3 + 2.8 = 32.0$ billion ($19.8 + 2.8 + 2.8 = 25.4$ billion).

The amount of $G$ outlays required to raise national income by Re. 1 is assumed to have risen to Rs. 3.4 by 1976. Dividing the $G$ outlays of 1976 by this $R$ ratio we have Rs. 9.4 (7.5) billion as the annual increment of growth. Over a 2 1/2-year period this amounts to Rs. 23.5 (18.7) billions; so the next projected figure for aggregate national income, dated "1978 1/2," is Rs. $219.6 + 23.5 = 243.1$ billion ($209.7 + 18.7 = 228.4$ billion).

271

lies not in the actual trends shown but in the indicated difference between the outcomes *under different fertility assumptions.*

To bring out the extent and character of this differential traceable to fertility, these three tables go into some detail of analysis of the initial projections. Table 37 and Chart 10 run entirely in terms

TABLE 37. SELECTED CATEGORIES OF INCOME AND
OUTLAYS PER CONSUMER (PROJECTION 1)
(indices, 1956 = 100)

|  | 1956 | 1961 | 1966 | 1971 | 1976 | 1981 | 1986 |
|---|---|---|---|---|---|---|---|
| **Income** | | | | | | | |
| High fertility | 100 | 107 | 114 | 120 | 126 | 132 | 138 |
| Medium fertility | 100 | 107 | 114 | 121 | 131 | 148 | 170 |
| Low fertility | 100 | 108 | 117 | 128 | 143 | 165 | 195 |
| *F* Outlays | | | | | | | |
| High fertility | 100 | 114 | 127 | 138 | 150 | 161 | 174 |
| Medium fertility | 100 | 114 | 127 | 140 | 161 | 192 | 237 |
| Low fertility | 100 | 116 | 133 | 154 | 184 | 228 | 284 |
| Income—*F* | | | | | | | |
| High fertility | 100 | 106 | 111 | 116 | 121 | 126 | 131 |
| Medium fertility | 100 | 106 | 111 | 117 | 126 | 139 | 158 |
| Low fertility | 100 | 106 | 114 | 123 | 136 | 154 | 179 |
| $W_c$ Outlays[a] | | | | | | | |
| High fertility | 100 | 107 | 114 | 120 | 126 | 132 | 138 |
| Medium fertility | 100 | 107 | 114 | 121 | 131 | 148 | 170 |
| Low fertility | 100 | 108 | 117 | 126 | 143 | 165 | 195 |
| "Consumption" = (income − $F$ + $W_c$) | | | | | | | |
| High fertility | 100 | 106 | 112 | 116 | 122 | 127 | 132 |
| Medium fertility | 100 | 106 | 112 | 118 | 126 | 140 | 159 |
| Low fertility | 100 | 107 | 114 | 124 | 136 | 155 | 180 |

[a] The indices for $W_c$ outlays are identical with those for income, since $W_c$ outlays are assumed to maintain a constant ratio to income throughout the period.

of income and outlays per equivalent adult consumer, compared to 1956 as a base year. For example, the projected per consumer income rises 38 per cent in the 30 years 1956-1986 under high-fertility assumptions, and 95 per cent under low-fertility assumptions. This is not the whole story, however, since the disposition of income is different in the two cases. With a more rapidly rising income, the "average consumer" supplies a more rapidly increasing flow of $F$ outlays under low fertility than under high fertility.

In order to get a better measure of rising living levels than the simple income-per-consumer ratio provides, we have shown in Table 37 two other measures. *Income less F* corresponds, very roughly, to disposable income less personal saving, or to what the

TABLE 38. ANNUAL RATES OF INCREASE IN NATIONAL INCOME, PER-CONSUMER INCOME, AND PER-CONSUMER "CONSUMPTION," BY FIVE-YEAR PERIODS (PROJECTION 1)

| | *Percentage Increase Per Annum* | | | | | |
|---|---|---|---|---|---|---|
| | 1956–1961 | 1961–1966 | 1966–1971 | 1971–1976 | 1976–1981 | 1981–1986 |
| **National Income** | | | | | | |
| High fertility | 3.3 | 3.3 | 3.4 | 3.4 | 3.4 | 3.5 |
| Medium fertility | 3.3 | 3.3 | 3.4 | 3.5 | 3.7 | 4.0 |
| Low fertility | 3.3 | 3.5 | 3.7 | 3.9 | 4.2 | 4.5 |
| **Income per Consumer** | | | | | | |
| High fertility | 1.4 | 1.2 | 1.0 | 1.0 | 0.9 | 0.9 |
| Medium fertility | 1.4 | 1.2 | 1.2 | 1.6 | 2.1 | 2.8 |
| Low fertility | 1.5 | 1.6 | 1.8 | 2.3 | 2.9 | 3.4 |
| **"Consumption" per Consumer** | | | | | | |
| High fertility | 1.2 | 1.0 | 0.9 | 0.8 | 0.8 | 0.8 |
| Medium fertility | 1.2 | 1.0 | 1.0 | 1.4 | 1.9 | 2.5 |
| Low fertility | 1.3 | 1.4 | 1.6 | 2.0 | 2.6 | 3.0 |

household spends for consumer goods and services. This measure of consumer wellbeing shows a little less rapid rise than does income alone, and a somewhat smaller differential between the low-fertility and high-fertility cases.

We have applied the label "consumption" to *income less F plus* $W_c$, though the term is very far from exact. For that reason we shall keep it in quotes. This measure includes the "welfare" outlays (both private and public) that are directed to the needs of the existing population, but not those ($W_i$) which are required for expanding services or facilities to population increments. This measure behaves almost exactly like *income less F*, since the $W_c$ outlays are themselves by assumption a constant fraction of income.

273

From the standpoint of adequacy to meet the developing economic aspirations of the people, it may well be that the absolute level of per-consumer income or "consumption," or its total rise during the 30-year period, is less relevant than the rate of current improvement at any time during the period. Results of the projection on this basis are presented in Table 38. Whether we take

TABLE 39. SELECTED CATEGORIES OF OUTLAYS RELATED TO GROWTH, AS PERCENTAGE RATIOS TO NATIONAL INCOME (PROJECTION 1)

|  | 1956 | 1961 | 1966 | 1971 | 1976 | 1981 | 1986 |
|---|---|---|---|---|---|---|---|
| **High fertility** | | | | | | | |
| $F$ | 15.5 | 16.5 | 17.3 | 17.9 | 18.5 | 19.0 | 19.5 |
| $D$ | 7.0 | 7.7 | 8.4 | 8.9 | 9.4 | 9.9 | 10.4 |
| $W$ | 8.5 | 8.8 | 8.9 | 9.0 | 9.0 | 9.1 | 9.1 |
| $W_i$[a] | 1.2 | 1.5 | 1.6 | 1.7 | 1.8 | 1.8 | 1.9 |
| $G$ | 10.1 | 10.6 | 11.1 | 11.7 | 12.1 | 12.6 | 13.1 |
| **Medium fertility** | | | | | | | |
| $F$ | 15.5 | 16.5 | 17.3 | 18.0 | 19.0 | 20.2 | 21.5 |
| $D$ | 7.0 | 7.7 | 8.4 | 9.6 | 10.7 | 12.2 | 13.5 |
| $W$ | 8.5 | 8.8 | 8.9 | 8.4 | 8.3 | 8.0 | 8.0 |
| $W_i$[a] | 1.2 | 1.5 | 1.6 | 1.2 | 1.0 | .8 | .7 |
| $G$ | 10.1 | 10.6 | 11.1 | 12.3 | 13.5 | 15.0 | 16.4 |
| **Low fertility** | | | | | | | |
| $F$ | 15.5 | 16.6 | 17.6 | 18.7 | 19.9 | 21.3 | 22.6 |
| $D$ | 7.0 | 8.1 | 9.1 | 10.4 | 11.8 | 13.3 | 14.7 |
| $W$ | 8.5 | 8.5 | 8.4 | 8.3 | 8.2 | 8.0 | 7.9 |
| $W_i$[a] | 1.2 | 1.3 | 1.2 | 1.1 | .9 | .7 | .7 |
| $G$ | 10.1 | 11.0 | 11.9 | 13.1 | 14.6 | 16.1 | 17.5 |

[a] By assumption, $W_c = 7.25$ per cent of national income throughout.

income per consumer or "consumption" per consumer, the high-fertility case shows an annual improvement rate that steadily decelerates, while the low-fertility case shows accelerating improvement, and the "medium"-fertility case shows progress beginning to accelerate in the 1970's after fertility has begun to decline.

Table 38 also shows the rate at which aggregate national income is growing in the three fertility cases. This makes it clear that our high-fertility projection does not imply cessation or slackening of overall growth—in fact there is a slight acceleration of growth

274

during the period. The inauspicious showing of the high-fertility case in terms of improvement in levels of living is traceable entirely to the accelerated growth in the number of consumers that high fertility produces.

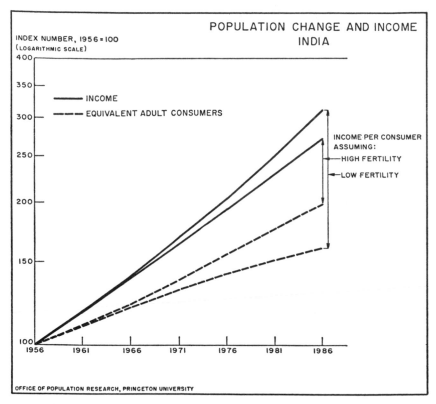

Chart 10. Total National Income, Consumers, and Income per Consumer, with High and Low Fertility, India, 1956-1986.

Table 38 also indicates that the projected growth of *aggregate as well as per-consumer* income is faster under low fertility than it is under high fertility.

Table 39 and Chart 11 bare some of the mechanism of the simplified model underlying these projections, by showing how the different levels of fertility affect the allocation of funds to different uses related to economic growth. In the low-fertility case, *F* outlays grow faster in relation to national income than in the high-fertility case, because the increases in income per consumer are larger and

275

we have assumed that the fraction of income which the people and the government are willing to set aside for $F$ outlays will depend on how fast the level of per consumer income rises.

Next we see from Table 39 and Chart 12 that the part of $F$ outlays devoted to the less immediately productive $W$ outlays is considerably larger under high fertility than under low fertility, because of the larger and more rapidly growing population to be

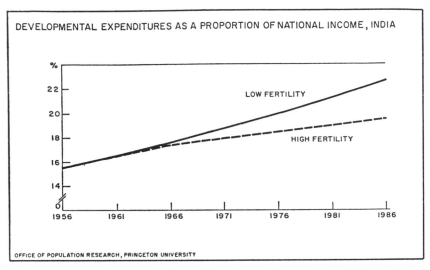

DEVELOPMENTAL EXPENDITURES AS A PROPORTION OF NATIONAL INCOME, INDIA

OFFICE OF POPULATION RESEARCH, PRINCETON UNIVERSITY

Chart 11. Developmental Expenditures as a Proportion of National Income, with High and Low Fertility, India, 1956-1986.

provided for. The difference is particularly marked in respect to the $W_i$ category of outlays, which reflect the increments in population. Consequently, the high-fertility case involves (in comparison with low fertility) a smaller fraction of income available for $F$, but a larger fraction of income diverted to "welfare" purposes. The high-fertility case, consequently, shows a much smaller ratio of "direct growth" $(D)$ outlays to income than the low-fertility case does, and also a much smaller ratio of $G$ outlays to income. It is that last ratio which, in our model, determines the rate of growth of aggregate national income.

As we have just seen, "welfare-type" outlays claim a larger part of the economy's output under high fertility. But at the same time (see Table 37 and Chart 12), the level of welfare-type outlays

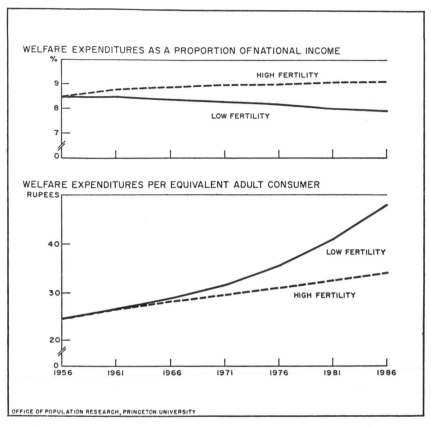

WELFARE EXPENDITURES AS A PROPORTION OF NATIONAL INCOME

HIGH FERTILITY

LOW FERTILITY

WELFARE EXPENDITURES PER EQUIVALENT ADULT CONSUMER

LOW FERTILITY

HIGH FERTILITY

OFFICE OF POPULATION RESEARCH, PRINCETON UNIVERSITY

Chart 12. Welfare Expenditures per Equivalent Adult Consumer, and Welfare Expenditures as a Proportion of National Income, with High and Low Fertility, India, 1956-1986.

*per consumer*, and consequently their *adequacy*, is much lower under high fertility than under low fertility. This illustrates numerically a point made in our earlier discussion regarding schools, hospitals, and other public services.[9]

[9] For convenient reference, the relevant passage from Chapter XVI is quoted here: ". . . the greater stringency of resources relative to demands under the high-fertility case would in fact lead to a lower and less adequate standard of services than would be adopted under the easier conditions of the low-fertility case. There would be slower progress toward such goals as universal literacy and decent urban housing. This would in turn mean a less favorable development of the quality and incentives of the labor force itself, and thus a retardation in the increase of productivity and in the growth of total national output. Viewed realistically, then, the allocation of resources to social services under high fertility would involve both (1) diversion of a larger proportion of available funds, at the expense

So far, we have been discussing the results of a single set of projections (Projection 1), calculated on the basis of some rather crude estimates and arbitrary assumptions. We have been at some pains to disclaim any significance for this set of projections as forecasts of the pace of development, but have emphasized the indications of the differential economic effect associated with lowered fertility. We now seek to determine whether some of these rough estimates and shaky assumptions can be altered without depriving the results of significance. Specifically, we want to see how the *differential between* low-fertility and high-fertility rates of economic growth behaves when we manipulate certain parameters in our formulas. The various experimental manipulations are described below.

*The (a) coefficient.* In projecting $F$ outlays, we assumed that 30 per cent of all increments of per consumer income after 1956 would be added to $F$. In what follows we shall try both a smaller and a larger alternative value for this proportion; namely, 25 and 35 per cent.

*The (e) coefficients.* In calculating the "equivalent growth outlays" $(G)$, we initially attributed to $W_c$ outlays half as great a growth effect per rupee as was attributed to "direct growth" $(D)$ outlays; and we attributed to $W_i$ outlays no growth effect whatever. In terms of our formula notation, we assigned to $W_c$ outlays a weight $e_c = .5$, and to $W_i$ outlays a weight $e_i = 0$. We propose now to try two different combinations of weights, namely:

$$e_c = e_i = .5$$
$$e_c = e_i = 0$$

*The (R) coefficient.* In calculating the effect of $G$ outlays in increasing the national income, we initially assumed that at the outset of the period, Rs. 3.0 of $G$ outlays were required in order to raise the level of the total national income by Re. 1; and that this proportion

of development outlays to aid producers as such, and (2) a less rapid improvement in the skills and incentives of the labor force. Achievement of development aims would thus be impaired both in the short and the long run."

In our projection model we have taken account of the dependence of national economic growth upon welfare-type outlays (in both the long and the short run) by assigning to these outlays a partly immediate and partly delayed contribution to the $G$ outlays that determine growth.

($R$) would rise at a uniform rate, reaching 3.6 in 1986.[10] Both the assumed initial 1956 value of $R$ and its subsequent rate of increase are conjectural, and the initial value was chosen primarily on the basis of getting a reasonable fit between the early part of our projection and the apparent present rate of growth so far as that can be judged.

We shall retain that criterion, and keep the rate of growth in the *first 2 1/2-year step from 1956* uniform in all our variant projections. Consequently we make two kinds of manipulation in our assumptions regarding $R$.

The first of these concerns the rate at which $R$ is assumed to rise during the period. We shall try the two following formulas for $R$, one of which involves no increase at all and the other of which involves an increase twice as fast as in the basic projection (Projection 1):

$$R = 3.0$$
$$R = 3.0 + .04t$$

Secondly, in the cases already discussed, in which we experiment with different $e_c$ and $e_i$ weights for the $W$ outlays, we must make compensating adjustments in $R$ in order to keep the initial 2 1/2-year national income growth uniform for all projections. For example, when we raise $e_i$ from zero to .5, this raises the calculated $G$ outlays for 1956 from Rs. 10.93 billion (in Projection 1) to Rs. 11.50 billion, or by about 5.2 per cent. Consequently, for the projection in which $e_i = .5$, we use an $R$ which is 5.2 per cent higher throughout than the $R$ of Projection 1. By the same token, the projection in which $e_c = e_i = 0$ calls for an $R$ that is *lower* than the $R$ of Projection 1.

In respect of $a$, $e$, and $R$, then, we propose to try out two new assumed values for each, in order to test the effect upon the projected differential consequences of low as against high fertility.

If we rang all the changes on these alternative assumptions in their various combinations, there would emerge an unwieldy array of twenty-seven projections for each fertility assumption. We shall therefore content ourselves with manipulating the parameters one

[10] Any comparison of our $R$ with the more familiar incremental investment/output or "capital/output" ratio should take account of the fact that the "equivalent growth outlays" ($G$) to which we apply our $R$'s are, as noted earlier, substantially more inclusive and larger in amount than investment outlays proper. The appropriate $R$ is accordingly larger in our model.

at a time. This yields a more manageable array of seven sets of projections.

The results of applying the seven different projection formulas to the high-fertility and low-fertility population trends are presented in Table 40.

TABLE 40. COMPARISON OF PROJECTED PER-CONSUMER INCOME UNDER LOW FERTILITY TO PER-CONSUMER INCOME UNDER HIGH FERTILITY, ACCORDING TO VARIOUS ALTERNATIVE PROJECTION FORMULAS, 1956–1986

| | Percentage Ratio of Low-Fertility to High-Fertility Per-Consumer Income | | | | | | | Projected 1986 Income per Consumer (1956 = 100) | |
|---|---|---|---|---|---|---|---|---|---|
| | 1956 | 1961 | 1966 | 1971 | 1976 | 1981 | 1986 | High Fertility | Low Fertility |
| Basic Projection 1 $(a = .30)$ $(e_i = 0)$ $(e_c = .5)$ $(R = 3.0 + .02t)$ | 100 | 101 | 103 | 107 | 114 | 126 | 141 | 138 | 195 |
| Alternative Projections Testing Effect of Different Marginal $F/Y$ Ratios: | | | | | | | | | |
| Projection 2 $(a = .25)$ | 100 | 101 | 103 | 107 | 113 | 124 | 138 | 129 | 177 |
| Projection 3 $(a = .35)$ | 100 | 101 | 103 | 107 | 115 | 127 | 145 | 150 | 217 |
| Alternative Projections Testing Effect of Different Imputations of Growth Effects to $D$, $W_c$, and $W_i$ Outlays: | | | | | | | | | |
| Projection 4 $(e_i = e_c = 0)$ | 100 | 101 | 103 | 108 | 116 | 130 | 148 | 157 | 233 |
| Projection 5 $(e_i = e_c = .5)$ | 100 | 101 | 103 | 107 | 113 | 124 | 138 | 138 | 191 |
| Alternative Projections Testing Effect of Different Trends in $R$: | | | | | | | | | |
| Projection 6 $(R = 3.0)$ | 100 | 101 | 103 | 107 | 115 | 126 | 143 | 155 | 221 |
| Projection 7 $(R = 3.0 + .04t)$ | 100 | 101 | 103 | 107 | 114 | 125 | 140 | 126 | 176 |

The last two columns of the table, showing the projected 1986 levels of income per consumer relative to 1956, are included merely to illustrate the wide degree of variation in results that arises from manipulation of the various coefficients in the way described. Thus under low fertility, projected 1986 per consumer income might, according to these figures, be anywhere from 76 to 133 per cent above the 1956 level. This array of results should suffice to show the inapplicability of any of these projections as a forecast of likely economic growth, since we have no real basis for defending any one of the seven combinations of underlying assumptions as the best.

The main body of the table, however, does give a positively significant result. It shows that through this whole gamut of projections, despite the wide variation in rates of progress that they imply, the *differential associated with reduced fertility* is remarkably persistent and stable. For the first 15 years of the period it is virtually identical for all seven projections; by 1981, it runs between 24 and 30 per cent; and in 1986 it still varies only between the fairly narrow limits of 38 and 48 per cent.

The largest variation is associated with the rather drastic redistribution of imputed growth effects among $D$, $W_c$, and $W_i$ outlays that is incorporated in Projections 4 and 5. Our procedure of making a compensatory adjustment in $R$ in those projections implies of course that when we impute an increased growth effect to $W_i$ (Projection 5 compared with Projection 1), this reduces the imputed growth effect of both $W_c$ and $D$. The differential advantage of lower fertility is largest in Projection 4, where growth is made to depend entirely on $D$ outlays, because under low fertility the ratio of $D$ to $W$ outlays will always be higher than under high fertility.

A higher assumed value for the $a$ coefficient (35 per cent, in Projection 3) slightly enhances the differential advantage of low fertility, as would be expected. To an even smaller extent, a constant $R$ (Projection 6) works in the same direction, by giving a greater growth effect to the relatively heavy $G$ outlays of the latter part of the period in the low-fertility case.

281

## NOTE

*Recapitulation of Equations Underlying Economic Projections in this Chapter*

(1)
$$F = C \left[ \frac{F_0}{C_0} + a \left( \frac{Y}{C} - \frac{Y_0}{C_0} \right) \right]$$

$$\text{or, } F = a Y - \left( \frac{a Y_0 - F_0}{C_0} \right) C$$

(2)
$$F = D + W$$

(3)
$$W = W_c + W_i$$

(4)
$$\frac{W_i}{W_c} = 10p$$

(5)
$$W_c = \left[ \frac{(W_c)_0}{Y_0} \right] Y = .0725 \, Y$$

(6)
$$G = D + (e_c W_c + e_i W_i) L + (e_c W_c + e_i W_i)_{t-15} (1 - L)_{t-15}$$

(7)
$$Y_{t+2.5} = Y_t + \frac{2.5 \, G}{R}$$

(8)
$$R = m + nt$$

### Key to Symbols

$Y =$ national income (in Rs. billions at 1952-1953 prices)

$C =$ number (in billions) of "equivalent adult consumers" (i.e., population adjusted by giving children of under 10 years a weight of 0.5, females 10 and older a weight of 0.9, and males 10 and older a weight of 1.0)

$F =$ public expenditures plus net monetized private investment (in Rs. billions at 1952-1953 prices)

$W =$ welfare-type $F$ outlays, assumed to contribute less directly or less strongly to raising $Y$ than other $F$ outlays (i.e., $D$) (in Rs. billions at 1952-1953 prices)

$W_c =$ that part of $W$ outlays attributed to the needs of the existing population

$W_i =$ that part of $W$ outlays attributed to the needs of the current increment of population

$D\ =$ direct-growth-type $F$ outlays (in Rs. billions at 1952-1953 prices)

$p\ =$ ratio of annual population increment to current population

$G\ =$ "equivalent growth outlays" defined as shown in Equation 6 (in Rs. billions at 1952-1953 prices)

$t\ =$ time, in years from 1956

$R\ =$ ratio of the $G$ outlays in any year to the amount by which the annual rate of $Y$ increases in the ensuing 2 1/2-year interval (as stated in Equation 7)

$a, e_c, e_i, m, n\ =$ parameters assigned various alternative values as detailed in Table 40

Subscript $(_0)$ refers to the base year 1956 (for some series, 1955-1956).

Subscript $(_t)$ (i.e., reference to any current year) is to be understood where no specific time subscript appears.

◇◇◇◇◇◇◇◇◇◇◇◇◇◇◇◇◇◇◇◇◇◇◇◇◇◇◇◇◇◇◇◇◇◇◇◇◇◇◇◇◇◇◇◇◇◇◇◇

# CHAPTER XVIII

# SUMMARY AND CONCLUSIONS
# OF PART FOUR

◇◇◇◇◇◇◇◇◇◇◇◇◇◇◇◇◇◇◇◇◇◇◇◇◇◇◇◇◇◇◇◇◇◇◇◇◇◇◇◇◇◇◇◇◇◇◇◇

THE PRINCIPAL RELATIONSHIPS between alternative courses of fertility and economic development are fairly simple. The essential points of the analysis may have been obscured, however, in our long descriptions of the Indian population and the Indian economy. A brief summary may be helpful.

After summarizing the principal conclusions, we shall indicate where the most questionable assumptions were made, and try to show how the conclusions should be qualified on that account.

## THE POPULATION PROJECTIONS

The future populations presented in Part One were calculated in all cases on the basis of a projected sharp decline in mortality, leveling off in the 1970's. We used three different hypotheses as to fertility, viz: (1) unchanged fertility, (2) a 50 per cent decline in fertility between 1956 and 1981, and (3) a 50 per cent decline concentrated in the fifteen years after 1966.

The highest of these three courses of fertility would yield a population of 775 million by 1986, growing at 2.6 per cent per annum at that time and with 42 per cent of the population under age 15. The lowest fertility course would produce about 590 million, growing at an annual rate of 1.0 per cent, and with only 30 per cent under age 15. If the decline in fertility were to begin in 1966 and reach 50 per cent by 1981, the result in 1986 would be a population of 634 million, with a 1986 growth rate and age distribution much like those of the lowest projected.

## EFFECTS ON ECONOMIC DEVELOPMENT OF
## ALTERNATIVE COURSES OF FERTILITY

High fertility produces larger populations because it means more births. Thus for many years the difference in numbers in our projected populations is concentrated in the childhood ages. As a consequence, the larger projected population has almost no advantage over the smaller in terms of potential working force until near the end of the thirty-year period we have analyzed, and even then the difference is small. The slightly greater number of persons of working age by 1986 under higher fertility would not necessarily provide a larger useful working force, for two reasons. First, the difficulties of finding useful employment for a rapidly growing labor force imply that a faster growth rate might simply add to the already large pool of unemployed and underemployed. Such an outcome is made more probable by the slower accumulation of capital when fertility is high. Second, the necessity for devoting much more time to child care would limit the participation of women in the labor force.

When other determinants of national output are examined, it becomes clear that total output would grow faster with reduced fertility than with continued high fertility. Since the number of "equivalent adult consumers" in the high-fertility projection comes to exceed the number in the lower-fertility projections by an ever wider margin, the difference in income on a per-consumer basis becomes very marked. With high fertility, a smaller total product must be divided among many more consumers than would be the case under low fertility.

A more rapid increase in the number of consumers (mostly children) is the ultimate cause of the slower rise in total output with the higher projected population trend. The more rapid increase in number of consumers restrains the rise of total output in several ways:

1. A larger number of consumers tends to increase the fraction of any given national output that is allocated to current consumption, and thus restricts the mobilization of resources for promoting economic growth. It tends to reduce private savings and the ability of the government to raise funds for development.
2. A larger number of consumers (especially children) forces the expenditure of savings and tax receipts for purposes that raise national output less, or less immediately, than other uses. More must be spent for primary education, housing, and "social overhead" purposes generally.
3. With smaller per capita consumption due to a larger number of consumers, the labor force would be less productive, partly because of more widespread malnutrition and partly because rising

consumption is needed to combat apathy and to provide better work incentives.

These effects have a cumulative impact. The higher total income, combined with a smaller number of consumers, in the low-fertility projected population makes it possible to have a much larger and more effective development program. The more effective program then leads to still more rapid growth of income. Illustrative calculations (cf. Table 40) show that per-consumer income would attain a level about 40 per cent higher by 1986 with reduced fertility than with continued high fertility. These calculations are based on what seem to us reasonable assumptions about savings rates, capital-output ratios, and the like.

When the assumed value of the numerical parameters are altered, the projected trend of economic growth is of course changed for *both* projected populations; but this does not markedly affect the *comparative* results under high as compared to low fertility. In all instances the low-fertility population has a calculated per-consumer income at least 38 per cent larger by 1986. Also, in all instances, the calculations show a much more rapid growth rate of total output *in 1986* with low fertility. A typical pair of values (Projection 1) is 4.5 per cent per annum growth in total output with reduced fertility and 3.5 per cent with unchanged fertility. These imply, respectively, *per-consumer* income growing at about 3.4 per cent per annum and less than 1 per cent per annum.

Our calculations of the cumulative effect make allowance for the greater level of mobilized funds with reduced fertility, and for the possibility of using funds in a more immediately productive manner. They do not take account of higher productivity arising from higher levels of consumption. On the other hand, no account is taken of possible additions to product that might result from the slightly larger labor force accompanying high fertility. But as was explained earlier, the possibility of realizing larger labor contributions is moot. We believe that the net effect of neglecting these two factors in our quantitative projections is in the direction of understating the economic advantages of low fertility.

An alternative way of appraising the gains from reducing fertility is to ask how much the economic progress resulting from fewer births would cost *without* a reduction in fertility. One way of calculating this cost is to determine what marginal rate of saving would be required with high fertility to match the trend in income per consumer achieved with low fertility. How much extra austerity would be needed to offset the effects of a continued high level of births?

A calculation based on the same simple model used in Projection 1, Chapter XVII, yields a needed marginal $F/Y$ rate of 46 per cent. In other words, 46 per cent rather than 30 per cent of increases in income per consumer would have to be channeled into private investment plus public outlays. The siphoning off of rising income would need to be half again as great to offset the effects of more rapid population increase.[1]

Two pertinent considerations are neglected in these calculations:

1. The possible national value of a larger population and the personal pleasure possibly derived from large families (both being implicitly ignored when we treat two situations as equivalent on the basis of equal incomes *per consumer*). On this score it should be noted that even with reduced fertility the population of India would grow by 50 per cent in the next 30 years; and because of reduced mortality, the average number of living children per family would remain quite large.

2. In considering the further prospects at the end of 30 years, with a large reduction of fertility, the outlook beyond 1986 would be more promising, even if higher savings rates had enabled a high fertility population to attain the same economic levels. The better outlook would result from a more favorable age distribution, a slower annual rate of population increase, and probably a more favorable relation to resources. These questions are more thoroughly examined in Chapter XXII.

Our *intermediate* population projection depends on an assumed decline in fertility that does not begin until 1966 but makes up for lost time, so to speak, by declining 50 per cent in 15 years rather than in 25. The income per consumer calculated for this projection lies nearly midway in 1986 between the income of the population with unchanging fertility and that of the lowest fertility projection. Thus in 1986 the economic gains from a reduction of fertility beginning ten years later but proceeding faster are about half as great

[1] If a 46 per cent marginal $F/Y$ ratio were assumed for the *low* fertility case as well, the income per consumer in 1986 would be about 50 per cent greater than under high fertility.

as the gains to be expected from a decline in fertility that begins immediately. This calculation illustrates the surprisingly large advantages attaching to an *early* reduction in fertility.[2]

Throughout the comparison of the economic effects of unchanged high fertility and of rapidly declining fertility, our criterion of economic progress has been real income per consumer. The use of this single criterion is not based on the belief that the only aim of Indian economic policy is to raise income per capita. But with respect to certain other objectives (such as the reduction of inequalities of income) the implications of different courses of fertility are not so immediate as with respect to the growth of total and per capita income.

One of the purposes of the Government of India in fostering economic development is to mitigate unemployment and underemployment. The rapid expansion in the number of persons of labor force age that will occur in the next few decades, regardless of whether fertility is reduced, increases the urgency of expanding employment as well as output. It is clear that the reduction of fertility promises a much higher level of achievement in assuring productive employment to those who seek it. Unemployment and underemployment in India are the result chiefly of an inadequate supply of capital and resources with which labor can work. Since it is precisely the faster expansion of these factors that accounts for the greater rise in output with reduced fertility, there seems no reason to doubt that job opportunities would also be greater.

## A BRIEF RE-EXAMINATION OF SOME ASSUMPTIONS

The assumptions about birth and death rates that form the basis for our population projections have been described at some length in Part One. One of the most important of these assumptions is that Indian death rates will be reduced from about 25 1/2 to about 15 per thousand in the twenty years from 1956 to 1976, by which time the decline in mortality is assumed to level off. It is further assumed

---

[2] The logical basis for the advantages of an early start is the cumulative character of both economic and demographic growth. Early growth lays the groundwork for more rapid later growth. Hence any measure, whether it is a reduction in fertility or a development program that enhances economic productivity, will have a much larger payoff thirty years hence if instituted quickly rather than with a delay.

that the same mortality risks by age and sex will apply whether fertility is reduced or not. In effect, mortality reduction has been assumed independent of economic development. The basis for this assumption of independence is primarily the notable success of low-cost public health measures in other low-income areas, where death rates have been reduced to an extent and at a rate often exceeding what we have assumed for India. These mortality improvements have frequently occurred without any visible evidence of rising per capita incomes. Moreover, health activities will no doubt be given a high priority. Thus, if population growth makes the attainment of some of the development objectives difficult, the health program would be one of the last to be sacrificed.

It must nevertheless be conceded that mortality reduction may never be *wholly* independent of the success of economic development, and can be considered as approximately so only if two important qualifying conditions are met. First, per capita income must not be *lowered* too far. If income (especially the food component of income) per equivalent adult consumer were to be reduced much below the current levels in India, it is doubtful that very much could be attained in the way of reduced mortality rates. In other words, the assumption that mortality reduction can be considered the same for both fertility patterns is even approximately valid only if national output, and especially the supply of food, at least keeps up with the growth of the consumer population. One reason so much emphasis was placed on the agricultural sector in our discussion of the Indian economy is that we were much interested in whether something of the order of a doubled food supply in the next twenty-five years was achievable. Our survey of the factors governing agricultural output led to a tentative affirmative conclusion. The illustrative calculations in Chapter XVII, in addition, lend some support to the belief that even with high fertility the growth of total output may keep up with the growth in the number of equivalent adult consumers.

However, all of these calculations are conjectural; and in fact any number of contingencies might make it impossible to raise total income as fast as population with continued high fertility. Among the contingencies that could intervene are a series of monsoon failures (there has lately been a quite unusual succession of good crop years); an unforeseen high capital/output ratio (both our estimates and the official Indian estimates of a low ratio are in large part conjectural); the failure of either the population generally or the necessary large number of recruited leaders at all levels to build up and sustain the needed enthusiasm; and the possibility of either internal political conflict or involvement in war. If for any of these reasons our assumptions of the possibilities of economic development prove grossly overoptimistic, then the growth of income might fail to keep pace with the growth of population. We believe that the tendency would still be for the differential in per-consumer income to be of the same order as our calculations show as long as the population projections can be assumed to hold. However, with a substantial reduction in per capita income in the high-fertility population, it would probably prove impossible to attain and hold the low death rates assumed in the population projections. Under these circumstances the difference in population size between the high and the low fertility cases might be less than our projections show, and the final result might be a smaller differential in per-consumer income. The differential would be smaller, however, only because official income statistics provide no measure (except perhaps via the patently inadequate use of figures on medical care and funerals) for the suffering and sorrow associated with disease and premature death.

The second qualifying condition that must be met before the independence of mortality reduction from the rate of economic development will hold even approximately is that the *upper* range of per capita income considered must not be extended too high. The mortality experience that we have projected for India shows a slackening rate of improvement, with the crude death rate leveling off at about 14 deaths per 1,000 population, and the expectation of life at birth getting no higher than about 52 years. Much better mortality experience than this has been attained in other low income areas. The reason that our projected mortality rates level off is that those reductions in mortality rates requiring intensive medical care, improvements in nutrition, and the like, will be more difficult to achieve and will come more slowly than the rapid and relatively easy payoff realizable from low-cost public health techniques. It may well be that our reasoning on this score is mistaken, and that mortality rates will in fact continue to decline for a longer period than we have estimated. In twenty-five or thirty more years, there will no doubt be further innovations in low-cost public health and additional experience in designing and administering health programs in low-income areas. If these improvements have a large effect, lower death rates than we have assumed will be achieved in the latter part of the 30-year period covered by the projections.

In the low fertility population, with a 40 per cent higher income per consumer in 1986, "welfare" expenditures per consumer would also be about 40 per cent again as great in 1986 as in the high fertility case according to our calculations (Table 37). With a smaller number of pregnancies and a smaller number of children born each year, the quality and extent of pre-natal and infant care that could be provided would be appreciably higher. In other words, if favorable or optimistic assumptions about economic development prove warranted, our provisional assumption that progress in reducing death rates is independent of economic progress would be an increasingly poor approximation by the end of the 30-year period we have analyzed. However, lower mortality rates associated with more rapid increases in per-consumer income could not have any important quantitative effect before the late 1970's. Our illustrative calculations show trends in per-consumer income which diverge only very gradually. As late as the quinquennium 1971-1976, the per-consumer income with low fertility would be only about 10 per cent greater than with high fertility. Moreover, *differences in death rates in the last ten or fifteen years of the interval for which we have projected populations would produce only slight differences in population size and composition by the end of the period.* This is so because differences in growth rates have a cumulative effect, which is not much apparent in the first few years after their appearance. In other words, the most important effect of allowing for greater prospective improvements in mortality associated with low fertility would be to narrow the difference in growth rates in 1986 between our projected populations. This narrowed difference in growth rates might possibly diminish slightly the very much greater rate of improvement associated with low fertility in 1986. On the other hand, any greater improvement in health would tend to have a positive effect on productivity. Moreover, as we mentioned earlier, better health is itself an achievement at least on a par with increases in income as recorded by conventional statistics.

291

WIDER APPLICABILITY OF THE ANALYSIS

◇◇◇◇◇◇◇◇◇◇◇◇◇◇◇◇◇◇◇◇◇◇◇◇◇◇◇◇◇◇◇◇◇◇◇◇◇◇◇◇◇◇◇◇◇◇◇◇◇◇◇◇◇

# CHAPTER XIX

# INTRODUCTION TO PART FIVE

◇◇◇◇◇◇◇◇◇◇◇◇◇◇◇◇◇◇◇◇◇◇◇◇◇◇◇◇◇◇◇◇◇◇◇◇◇◇◇◇◇◇◇◇◇◇◇◇◇◇◇◇◇

THE ECONOMIC IMPLICATIONS of different courses of population growth in India during the next two or three decades are significant enough in their own right. However, there are many areas in the world with low average incomes and high average fertility; and it is natural to ask to what degree the conclusions we reach in our study of India apply in other contexts.

It is also natural to inquire whether the advantages for economic development inherent in a decline from high levels of fertility are limited to the first two or three decades. In this section we shall attempt to deal with these two questions.

We shall first inquire what demographic, economic, and social conditions warrant conclusions similar to those reached about India. Which conclusions are peculiar to India, and which have a wider bearing? In Chapter XX we shall discuss whether somewhat different demographic conditions affect our conclusions, while in Chapter XXI we shall raise the question of the applicability of our conclusions in somewhat different *economic* contexts. Finally, in Chapter XXII, the relations between different patterns of population growth and economic development are explored during the period after 1986. The alternative projections of the Indian population involved only slight differences for 30 years in the size of the labor force—differences slight enough to be considered negligible in the economic analysis. It might appear that by stopping at the end of two or three decades we have totally neglected the period during which *favorable* effects of high fertility—namely, a more rapidly increasing labor force—would begin to appear. It is precisely this point to which Chapter XXII is addressed.

In exploring the extension of our analysis to other areas, we shall refer frequently to economic and demographic data from Mexico. We have made a brief analysis of demographic and economic prospects in Mexico that, in its major components, parallels our study of India. It involves projections for thirty years of the Mexican population, based on an estimate of the course of mortality and alternative assumptions about fertility. A summary of the salient features of demographic prospects in Mexico, including population projections, is contained in Appendices B and C.

◇◇◇◇◇◇◇◇◇◇◇◇◇◇◇◇◇◇◇◇◇◇◇◇◇◇◇◇◇◇◇◇◇◇◇◇◇◇◇◇◇◇◇◇◇◇◇◇◇◇◇◇

# CHAPTER XX

# POPULATION CHANGE AND ECONOMIC DEVELOPMENT IN LOW-INCOME AREAS WITH DIFFERENT DEMOGRAPHIC CONDITIONS

◇◇◇◇◇◇◇◇◇◇◇◇◇◇◇◇◇◇◇◇◇◇◇◇◇◇◇◇◇◇◇◇◇◇◇◇◇◇◇◇◇◇◇◇◇◇◇◇◇◇◇◇

THERE ARE many areas other than India that can be accurately characterized as having low incomes and high fertility. Because quantitative comparisons of income in different areas cannot be precise, it is difficult to define the term "areas with low incomes" with precision. Included by this designation would be all of the countries of Asia, excepting Japan and the Asian portions of the Soviet Union; Indonesia; the Near Eastern countries, except Israel; most of Africa with the exception of areas of European settlement; Central America; most of the Caribbean area; South America, except Argentina and Uruguay. It is easier to be quantitative in specifying what is meant by high fertility: namely, a gross reproduction rate of about 3.0 or higher and a crude birth rate of about 40 or higher. Very nearly all of the areas just listed are characterized by such levels of fertility.

However, these areas are not nearly so uniform with respect to demographic characteristics other than fertility, nor with respect to their detailed social and economic characteristics. Their populations range in size from the 80 thousand or so in British Honduras to about 600 million in China. Some have already achieved very impressive reductions in mortality (for example Ceylon, and many of the countries in Latin America), and have a current and prospective rate of growth substantially more rapid than in India.

Do these differences in population size and in the probable levels of mortality and growth during the next thirty years imply a different kind of relationship between fertility and the likely success of economic development?[1]

[1] It must be conceded at the outset that few other areas have the same range of possible fertility changes as in India. At least there are few other areas where

The size of a population in an area could influence our conclusions in several ways. With a smaller population than India's the possibility of achieving economies of scale through population growth might be greater, and a much larger proportionate dependence on international trade might be possible. We shall return to the latter question in the next chapter. As to the relation of population to resources, and as to the possible advantages to be gained by larger-scale economic operations, it is clear that these questions are associated primarily with alternative patterns of growth *in the labor force*. In restricting our analysis to a thirty-year period and to contrasts in fertility trends, we have ruled out substantial differences in the population of working ages.[2] A smaller population than India's in the sense of a more favorable endowment of resources relative to population would be beneficial under either sustained or reduced fertility; but the *differential* advantage of reduced fertility would not be greatly affected. Thus, in Mexico, the fact that the rural population has not so fully saturated the arable land as in India means that acreage under cultivation may be expanded by some 50 per cent in the next thirty years, as compared to perhaps 10 per cent in India. This possibility no doubt enhances the likelihood of increasing national output in Mexico; but since the projected growth in population at labor force ages is about the same for both high and lowered fertility, the advantage of additional availability of land would be much the same.

We turn now to low-income areas with high fertility that are distinguished from India by having different current and expected levels of mortality, and hence of growth. Would a 50 per cent linear drop in fertility in 25 years in these areas—without regard to its feasibility—have an effect on economic growth similar to that we have found for India? Provided only that the likely course of mortality can legitimately be assumed as largely independent of fertility, the answer to this question is yes. If, however, the possibilities for expanding output were less hopeful than those in India, an assump-

---

the possibility of a government program supporting the spread of family limitation is as clear and immediate. When we speak of extending the Indian conclusions to other areas, then, it must be noted that we refer to a choice between unchanging and rapidly declining fertility that is, in many of those areas, much more hypothetical than in India.

[2] This topic will, however, be discussed in Chapter XXII.

tion of a single and favorable course of mortality development might become quite unrealistic. Under these circumstances, it is not realistic to analyze the difference between high and low fertility population projections solely in terms of the different prospective development of income. If one posited a large decline in income associated with sustained fertility, it might become necessary to express this increasing poverty partly by an arrested or reversed mortality decline. In areas where this qualification does not apply, however, the existence of mortality rates—present and likely to develop—markedly different from those in India would not in themselves produce a different relation between fertility decline and economic growth—not, at any rate, during the first two or three decades.

Favorable mortality prospects—caused, for example, by the early formation of an effective public health organization—would certainly have an influence on economic development. Better health would usually accompany lower mortality rates. Population growth would be more rapid with (typically) a greater acceleration in the growth of the number of children and a somewhat larger fraction of the population in dependent ages.

However, the high and low fertility populations would be affected alike, and the difference in their economic prospects would remain very much the same. Both populations would benefit from a healthier and more vigorous labor force, both would grow more rapidly at all ages, and both would have a somewhat higher dependency burden than with higher mortality rates.

For example, a still more favorable course of mortality than we have projected for India might produce a population over 15 years of age that was 10 per cent larger in 1986 than in our high fertility projection. With the expected greater improvement in survivorship in childhood, the population under 15 might be 11 per cent larger. But the *low* fertility population over 15 and under 15 would also be increased by about 10 per cent and 11 per cent respectively, and the contrast between the high and low fertility projections would be essentially unaltered.

By an exactly analogous argument, a less sanguine view of the future course of mortality in India might alter the expected course of economic development, but not the expected negative association between the growth of income per consumer and the level of fertility. This relative independence of our principal conclusions from the precise course of projected mortality is doubly reassuring. In the first place, we have assumed a more rapid drop in India's death rates than other observers and it is reassuring to find that this drop, while of greatest importance to India, is not crucial to our argument. Secondly, it is reassuring to find that the wide differences in mortality among low-income areas do not in themselves restrict the general applicability of our conclusions.

The similarity of the relations between sustained and reduced fertility projections under different mortality assumptions is illustrated concretely by the projections we have prepared for Mexico, 1955 to 1985. Salient figures from these projections are shown in Tables 41 and 42, and in Chart 13. The basis for these projections and the techniques employed are set forth in Appendices B and C. The expectation of life at birth (for both sexes) in Mexico in 1955 is estimated at 52.9 years—somewhat higher than the projected figure for India in 1986. The projected Mexican expectation of life rises to 69.6 years in 1985. This much better level of mortality (in conjunction with an initial level of fertility somewhat higher than in India) implies much higher rates of growth in Mexico than in India during the next 30 years. The initial annual growth rate is 30.3 per mill compared to 17.2, and the rate after 30 years is (with sustained fertility) 36.4 compared to 25.7. The projected population after 30 years is 2.76 and 2.05 times the initial population with high and low fertility respectively, while the corresponding figures for India are 2.02 and 1.53. But the ratio of the projected high fertility population to that with low fertility is very nearly identical—1.34 in Mexico and 1.32 in India. The population aged 15-64 in the two projections after 30 years has a ratio of 1.09 in Mexico and 1.08 in India, while the ratio of the high fertility to the low fertility population at ages under 15 is 1.87 in both instances.

The essential points in this chapter can be stated in a few words:

1. Populations differing from India's in size and density relative to resources, or in current and likely future mortality levels, will on this account tend to have different economic prospects.
2. If a population is characterized by low income and high fertility, the influence on economic development *of different courses of fertility* will be generally *the same* as in India, despite differences in size, density, and mortality levels.

TABLE 41. PROJECTED POPULATION OF MEXICO, 1955–1985,
BY BROAD AGE GROUPS
(in '000's)

| Age | 1955 | 1960 | 1965 | 1970 | 1975 | 1980 | 1985 |
|---|---|---|---|---|---|---|---|
| rtility Assumed Unchanged | | | | | | | |
| 0–14 | 13,357.0 | 15,929.4 | 18,963.9 | 22,509.3 | 26,779.0 | 32,152.8 | 38,829.2 |
| 15–64 | 16,459.0 | 19,070.4 | 22,121.4 | 25,925.5 | 30,663.8 | 36,247.4 | 43,299.1 |
| 65+ | 982.0 | 1,060.2 | 1,314.9 | 1,664.7 | 2,011.5 | 2,495.1 | 2,769.1 |
| Total | 30,798.0 | 36,060.0 | 42,400.2 | 50,099.5 | 59,454.3 | 70,895.3 | 84,897.4 |
| Per Cent Distribution | | | | | | | |
| 0–14 | 43.37 | 44.17 | 44.73 | 44.93 | 45.04 | 45.35 | 45.74 |
| 15–64 | 53.44 | 52.89 | 52.17 | 51.75 | 51.58 | 51.13 | 51.00 |
| 65+ | 3.19 | 2.94 | 3.10 | 3.32 | 3.38 | 3.52 | 3.26 |
| rtility Assumed to Decline 50%, 1955–1980 | | | | | | | |
| 0–14 | 13,357.0 | 15,588.8 | 17,476.3 | 18,782.4 | 19,618.2 | 20,173.9 | 20,832.4 |
| 15–64 | 16,459.0 | 19,070.4 | 22,121.4 | 25,925.5 | 30,336.9 | 34,802.4 | 39,651.2 |
| 65+ | 982.0 | 1,060.2 | 1,314.9 | 1,664.7 | 2,011.5 | 2,495.1 | 2,769.1 |
| Total | 30,798.0 | 35,719.4 | 40,912.6 | 46,372.6 | 51,966.6 | 57,471.4 | 63,252.7 |
| Per Cent Distribution | | | | | | | |
| 0–14 | 43.37 | 43.64 | 42.72 | 40.50 | 37.75 | 35.10 | 32.94 |
| 15–64 | 53.44 | 53.39 | 54.07 | 55.91 | 58.38 | 60.56 | 62.69 |
| 65+ | 3.19 | 2.97 | 3.21 | 3.59 | 3.87 | 4.34 | 4.38 |
| ertility Assumed to Decline 50%, 1965–1980 | | | | | | | |
| 0–14 | 13,357.0 | 15,929.4 | 18,963.9 | 21,707.9 | 23,248.0 | 23,204.0 | 22,885.1 |
| 15–64 | 16,459.0 | 19,070.4 | 22,121.4 | 25,925.5 | 30,663.8 | 36,247.4 | 42,517.1 |
| 65+ | 982.0 | 1,060.2 | 1,314.9 | 1,664.7 | 2,011.5 | 2,495.1 | 2,769.1 |
| Total | 30,798.0 | 36,060.0 | 42,400.2 | 49,298.1 | 55,923.3 | 61,946.5 | 68,171.3 |
| Per Cent Distribution | | | | | | | |
| 0–14 | 43.37 | 44.17 | 44.73 | 44.03 | 41.57 | 37.46 | 33.57 |
| 15–64 | 53.44 | 52.89 | 52.17 | 52.59 | 54.83 | 58.51 | 62.37 |
| 65+ | 3.19 | 2.94 | 3.10 | 3.38 | 3.60 | 4.03 | 4.06 |

3. An exception must be noted where very low incomes with sustained fertility are expected, so that mortality improvements may be prevented or reversed. Under such circumstances, the analysis would require modification, although qualitatively its flavor would be somewhat the same.

These statements pertain only to extending our conclusions about India to areas with certain different demographic characteristics.

301

TABLE 42. VARIOUS MEASURES OF VITAL RATES FOR
PROJECTED POPULATION OF MEXICO, 1955–1985

| Expectation of life, years: | 1955 | 1960 | 1965 | 1970 | 1975 | 1980 | 1985 |
|---|---|---|---|---|---|---|---|
| Males | | | | | | | |
| At birth | 51.0 | 55.1 | 58.4 | 61.4 | 63.6 | 65.9 | 67.8 |
| At age 10 | 52.9 | 55.1 | 56.9 | 58.4 | 59.4 | 60.4 | 61.2 |
| At age 50 | 21.1 | 22.1 | 22.8 | 23.4 | 23.8 | 24.2 | 24.5 |
| Females | | | | | | | |
| At birth | 54.8 | 58.9 | 62.3 | 65.2 | 67.8 | 69.7 | 71.4 |
| At age 10 | 55.4 | 57.7 | 59.6 | 61.1 | 62.4 | 63.2 | 63.9 |
| At age 50 | 23.1 | 24.1 | 24.9 | 25.4 | 26.0 | 26.3 | 26.6 |
| Birth Rate (per 1,000 population) | | | | | | | |
| Fertility unchanged | 44.2 | 42.4 | 41.8 | 41.3 | 41.3 | 41.3 | 41.3 |
| Fertility decline from 1955–1980 | 44.2 | 38.5 | 34.7 | 31.3 | 28.1 | 24.5 | 25.2 |
| Fertility decline from 1965–1980 | 44.2 | 42.4 | 41.8 | 35.0 | 29.3 | 23.6 | 25.4 |
| Death Rate (per 1,000 population) | | | | | | | |
| Fertility unchanged | 13.9 | 10.4 | 8.9 | 7.5 | 6.6 | 5.7 | 4.9 |
| Fertility decline from 1955–1980 | 13.9 | 10.1 | 8.7 | 7.4 | 6.6 | 4.8 | 5.8 |
| Fertility decline from 1965–1980 | 13.9 | 10.4 | 8.9 | 7.3 | 6.5 | 3.8 | 5.6 |
| Natural Increase (per 1,000 population) | | | | | | | |
| Fertility unchanged | 30.3 | 32.0 | 32.9 | 33.8 | 34.7 | 35.6 | 36.4 |
| Fertility decline from 1955–1980 | 30.3 | 28.4 | 26.0 | 23.9 | 21.5 | 19.7 | 19.4 |
| Fertility decline from 1965–1980 | 30.3 | 32.0 | 32.9 | 27.7 | 22.8 | 19.8 | 19.8 |

The possibility of extending them to areas where the social and
economic contexts are significantly different from India's will be
discussed in the next chapter.

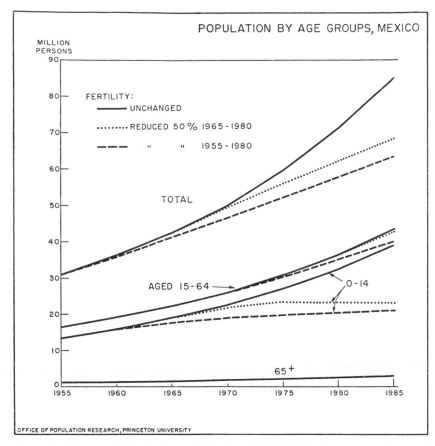

Chart 13. Projected Population of Mexico, 1955-1985. Total population and population by broad age groups, with various fertility assumptions.

# CHAPTER XXI

◇◇◇◇◇◇◇◇◇◇◇◇◇◇◇◇◇◇◇◇◇◇◇◇◇◇◇◇◇◇◇◇◇◇◇◇◇◇◇◇◇◇◇◇◇◇◇◇◇◇

## POPULATION CHANGE AND ECONOMIC DEVELOPMENT WITH DIFFERENT INITIAL ECONOMIC CONDITIONS

◇◇◇◇◇◇◇◇◇◇◇◇◇◇◇◇◇◇◇◇◇◇◇◇◇◇◇◇◇◇◇◇◇◇◇◇◇◇◇◇◇◇◇◇◇◇◇◇◇◇

THE BASIC REASON for expecting higher levels of living with reduced as compared to sustained fertility in India is that lower fertility tends simultaneously to produce a faster growth in total product and to produce a slower growth in the number of consumers. In Chapter XX it was found that demographic differences among low-income, high-fertility areas do not alter the nature of these effects. In this chapter we shall see whether differences among these areas in economic and social characteristics would produce a fundamentally different relationship.

Reduced fertility will always reduce growth in the number of consumers; the question is whether in areas with somewhat different economic circumstances a lower course of fertility tends to increase (to approximately the same degree as in India) the growth of total output. The faster expected growth of output in India resulted from a labor force of about the same size (but of greater productivity because of higher consumption levels) combined with larger and more productive developmental outlays.

If in any country the basic determinants of growth in output and the factors governing the allocation of income are the same as in India, in all likelihood the relation between fertility and growth in output will be much the same. We shall consider four sets of conditions under which the allocation of income or the stimulation of growth in output might operate differently, and hence might yield a different relation of fertility to economic development:

1. The principal obstacle to a larger and faster growing national output is in some instances an inadequate stimulus to investment rather than a deficient supply of investible resources. If sustained fertility would stimulate investment, the economic advantage of reduced fertility might be much smaller, or even negative. We have discussed this point twice before (pp. 20 to 22 and 240 to 242, above) and will dismiss it here with only two brief additional com-

304

ments. First, in low-income areas where inflation is chronic—and such areas are many—the higher consumption function potentially associated with a higher level of fertility seems unlikely to serve as a useful stimulus. Second, the expected population growth rate during the next 2 or 3 decades in countries now in the early stages of development is high, even if fertility should be linearly reduced by 50 per cent. For India the low fertility annual growth rate averages 14.3 per thousand, and for Mexico 24.0 per thousand. Thus even if the "stagnation thesis" were accepted as applicable to low-income areas, it does not follow that the lower of our assumed courses of fertility would be an inadequate stimulus to demand. In short, the importance of deficient aggregate demand as a barrier to the growth of low-income areas is moot, and even if it *is* a barrier, the lower path of fertility provides a population growing by 50 to 100 per cent in 30 years, a growth that might well supply any stimulus needed from this source.

2. International transactions could conceivably change the nature of the relation between alternative courses of fertility and economic development. If a country relies heavily on its earnings in foreign trade to finance purchases of capital equipment, or if much of its investment originates in loans from abroad, the question arises as to whether success of development is responsive to demographic variables. Perhaps the relation between growth of income and the course of fertility would diverge widely from what we found in India. We shall discuss this question in a later portion of this chapter, using the Mexican economy as an example.

3. Perhaps the special character of India's plans for economic development partly accounts for our finding a negative association between prospective fertility levels and national output during the next 30 years. The Indian government is emphasizing improvements in the current welfare of the whole population, especially its most impoverished segments; it is paying special attention to agriculture; and it expects to promote the growth of output in a mixed economy, where the public sector will assume ever rising importance. Other countries are pursuing development with different emphasis and by different strategies. In the last part of this chapter, we shall inquire whether these differences in aims and methods would imply a basically different relation between population growth and the growth of output.

4. The relation between the course of fertility and the pace of economic development might be different for low-income areas that have made a more substantial start than India on industrialization, in reducing dependence on subsistence agriculture, and in enlarging national income. If the general determinants of growth are the same as in India, the *direction* of the relation of fertility to increases in total

income, and especially in income per consumer, should be no different. Indeed, the calculations in Chapter XVII showed that variations in the estimated size of various coefficients and parameters resulted in a 1986 ratio of low-fertility income per consumer to high-fertility income ranging only from 1.38 to 1.48. This relative constancy suggests that if the determinants of growth are of the same general character, the quantitative relation between low- and high-fertility growth of income will be similar. Nevertheless, the question remains whether different initial conditions in the same general framework of growth determinants lead to similar or dissimilar results.

We have tested this question by making a numerical estimate for Mexico deliberately patterned after the calculations for India in Chapter XVII. It was assumed that welfare expenditures would rise to the level relative to national income estimated for India, that public outlays plus private investment would rise in proportion to changes in income per consumer—in short, equations of the same form as (1) to (8) recapitulated on page 282 were assumed to apply to the Mexican economy during 1955-1985. The values used for economic parameters, however, were drawn from Mexican sources; and the demographic data were taken from our projections of the Mexican population.

Mexico's population is about twice as highly urbanized as India's; 58 per cent of the labor force (in 1950) was engaged in agriculture (compared to 70 per cent in India); per capita income in Mexico is estimated as some 2 or 3 times that in India (though such international comparisons are of course of dubious value); gross investment constitutes some 14 per cent of national income, compared to less than 10 per cent in India; and the growth of national product has averaged some 7 per cent per annum since 1939, compared to about 3 per cent per annum since 1951 in India (and probably slower growth prior to 1951).

The outcome of the calculation is a ratio of low-fertility to high-fertility income per consumer in 1985 of 1.41. The similarity of this figure to those calculated for India shows that the initial economic position, while it affects the prospective pace of development for both high and low fertility, does not materially influence the relative economic advantages of fertility reduction.

## Is the Effect of Fertility on Economic Development Materially Altered by International Transactions?

Transactions with other countries impinge on the growth of income in low-income areas in ways too numerous and complex for us to list satisfactorily, much less to analyze adequately. Fortunately, it is *not* part of our purpose to weigh the advantages and disadvantages of foreign trade, foreign loans, or foreign gifts in the economic development of these areas. We are concerned only with whether such transactions lead to a different kind of relationship between fertility and the growth of national income from that which we have discerned for India in an analysis where international transactions were only incidentally mentioned.

Mexico will serve as a specific example of a low-income country in which international transactions are a larger fraction of national income than in India.

The importance of international transactions (other than gifts) to economic development ultimately rests on the traditional advantages of trade—the gains obtained by exporting commodities that the country is relatively well-equipped to produce, and importing the commodities that it can produce only at relatively high cost. These gains are often particularly important to a country that is attempting to change from an agrarian to an industrialized economy, because it needs industrial capital equipment that is much more efficiently obtained abroad than from domestic sources—if indeed such equipment is available at all domestically. The growth of national income requires a high level of investment. A balanced program of efficient investment often calls for large-scale importation of capital goods. The growth of national output then depends on: (1) obtaining a large volume of foreign exchange; and (2) the use of this foreign exchange to purchase capital goods. We shall show that the reduction of fertility from high levels makes it easier to achieve both of these ends.

There is a preliminary question to be disposed of. When a country has built a large export trade, variations in the demand for exports have important direct effects on the national income and hence on the pace of development. A reduced international demand for exported goods reduces incomes in the exporting industries, the demand for materials purchased by those industries, and the demand for consumers' goods purchased by persons whose incomes depend on those industries. The resultant shrinkage of income tends to reduce the volume of private developmental expenditures, and may thus retard the pace of long-run growth as well as producing a temporary setback in activity.

The vulnerability of an exporting economy to fluctuations in international demand is particularly acute when exports consist predominantly of one or two items. The list of items composing the major portion of Mexico's exports has in recent years been lengthened so that the effect of fluctuations in the demand for individual commodities has been somewhat mitigated. However, Mexican prosperity and the pace of Mexican development remain sensitive to international fluctuations. The recession in Mexico in 1953-1954 is attributed to the termination of the high levels of demand associated with the war in Korea, and to the economic recession in the United States.

The question of a high and stable international demand for the exports of a low-income country, while often of crucial importance, is extraneous here. Fluctuations in such demand are almost wholly outside the control of the exporting country, and are certainly not affected to a perceptible degree by different courses of fertility. We can only consider the possibility of variations in foreign demand as a random element making economic projections—under either high or low fertility—even more uncertain.

Taking the level of foreign demand for exports as given, then, we turn to the question of the effect of different courses of fertility on the ability of a developing economy to utilize international transactions as an aid to more rapid development. This ability turns on two principal factors: the volume of foreign exchange that the country can acquire, and the capacity to spend foreign exchange for purchases that best contribute to the growth of output. In most instances, the use of foreign exchange to purchase capital goods can be considered a measure of its effective allocation for the promotion of growth. *We shall show that the reduction of fertility tends both to increase the supply of foreign exchange and to make it easier to use this supply for purchases of capital goods.*

DIFFERENCES IN FERTILITY AND THE SUPPLY OF
FOREIGN EXCHANGE

A low-income country can obtain foreign currency and claims through a variety of transactions, the principal means being commodity exports, tourist expenditures by foreign nationals, and loans from abroad. Table 43 shows the sources of Mexico's receipts in three recent years. Tourist expenditures, plus remittances and other miscellaneous sources of exchange, have only a remote connection with different courses of fertility,[1] and we shall not discuss them further.

TABLE 43. MEXICO'S AVERAGE RECEIPTS FROM
INTERNATIONAL TRANSACTIONS, 1953–1955

|  | Average in U.S. Dollars (millions) | Per Cent of Total |
|---|---|---|
| Exports, including precious metals | 696 | 62.1 |
| Expenditures by foreign tourists | 330 | 29.5 |
| Remittances from Mexican workers abroad | 29 | 2.6 |
| Long term credits | 58 | 5.2 |
| Other | 7 | .6 |
| Total Receipts | 1,120 | 100.0 |

Source: *Comercio Exterior de México*, February 1955, and March 1956.

Receipts from *exports* will be significantly affected by the trend of fertility. The effect arises for two reasons: first, because the output of exportable commodities would be different if fertility trends differed; and second, because of different tendencies for the domestic consumption of exportable commodities. For both reasons, the sale of exports would tend to be *less* in the event of sustained high fertility.

The output of exportable commodities would be enlarged by reduced fertility both because the *total supply* of developmental capital would be larger, and because the *share* that could be devoted to export industries would be greater. The total supply would be greater for reasons already stated—more savings and tax receipts available, and a higher fraction of such funds used productively. The larger share of capital available for export industries would eventuate because certain commodities—especially food—may have a low elasticity of demand with respect to price and income, but a demand that is relatively responsive to the number of consumers. These commodities tend to be locally produced and consumed, especially in low-income areas. With lowered fertility and a reduced number of consumers, the capital that would otherwise be channeled into expanding the production of such goods for additional

[1] To the degree that tourist expenditures are increased by investment in hotels, transportation equipment, and other facilities, it might be argued that the greater availability of capital with reduced fertility could increase tourism.

309

persons could be used to increase the output of exported commodities. The agricultural sector of Mexico provides a specific example. In recent years the output of the chief exportable agricultural commodities has increased very rapidly,[2] permitting the enlargement of the fraction of total export value contributed by agricultural commodities. However, the faster growth of population accompanying sustained fertility would eventually create a need to divert funds— and perhaps land—to local foods and other domestically consumed crops.

Loans from abroad are more remotely influenced—if at all—by the course of fertility. If foreign loans and investment are attracted by rising national income, the more rapid growth associated with reduced fertility would attract a large volume of funds from abroad.

As was noted earlier, factors outside our frame of reference are powerful determinants of foreign earnings. Chief among these are commercial policies and the level of business activity in the rest of the world. For Mexico the policies and prosperity of the United States are crucial. A prosperous United States will provide a large demand for Mexican exports, mounting tourist expenditures in Mexico, employment for Mexican workers who will send back remittances, and will enlarge the supply of loans and investment funds. However, the prosperity of the United States can scarcely be considered dependent on the course of fertility in Mexico, and it enters our analysis only as a source of increased uncertainty in the future pace of Mexican development.

### DIFFERENCES IN FERTILITY AND THE USE OF
### FOREIGN EXCHANGE

Many low-income countries in the early stages of economic development find it necessary to import much of their capital equipment. To limit their investment to goods that could be produced internally would either be nearly impossible or at least grossly inefficient. In Mexico imported capital equipment has constituted 35 to 40 per cent of gross investment in recent years;[3] her balanced development will require for many additional years equipment that

[2] Cotton, coffee, henequén, tomatoes, and pineapple. According to the Nacional Financiera, the output index for those commodities shows a 91% rise in 1955 over 1950, compared to a 42% rise for domestically consumed agricultural products. Nacional Financiera, *Informe Anual*, 1956, p. 171.

[3] *Comercio Exterior de México*, February and March, 1956.

can only be obtained abroad; and even in the remote future investment in Mexico will no doubt be more fruitful and efficient if equipment can be purchased on world rather than exclusively on domestic markets.

In order to acquire foreign-made capital equipment, a developing country must in addition to acquiring command of foreign exchange be able to allocate a sufficient portion of these funds to capital goods purchases. Any tendency for larger expenditures on imported consumers' goods could make it difficult to finance a continued large volume of imported producers' goods. The greater growth in the number of consumers with sustained fertility implies a higher level of consumption out of a given national income—or a higher average propensity to consume. Part of this higher propensity will be reflected in a higher propensity to import consumers' goods. As was stated earlier, there are commodities—especially food—for which the demand responds sharply to changes in numbers. With sustained fertility, the rise in the demand for such commodities may at first divert resources from export industries (reducing the supply of foreign exchange); if the supply proves inelastic, the rising demand may also result in large-scale imports. A limited availability of land and ground water would ultimately make the supply of food products inelastic as population continues to grow. Under these circumstances rapid population growth would generate a larger demand for food and other "necessities" without generating a correspondingly enlarged domestic supply, and the consequent imports of consumers' goods would limit the capacity to import needed capital goods.

The circumstances just described are approximately those in the Mexican economy. In recent years as part of the program of economic development, Mexican authorities have sought to limit the importation of consumers' goods. The allocation of Mexico's total international expenditures in recent years is shown in Table 44. Of the expenditures on imports, about 40 per cent have been for durable producers' goods, and an additional 30 per cent have been for producers' materials.[4] Because of large increases in agricultural output, Mexico has been more or less self-sufficient in food in recent years. But it will be much more difficult to maintain self-sufficiency

[4] *Comercio Exterior de México*, January 1956 (Supplement), and March 1956.

at reasonable cost with a growth in population of 175 per cent instead of 105 per cent in the next 30 years.

TABLE 44. MEXICO'S AVERAGE EXPENDITURES IN
INTERNATIONAL TRANSACTIONS, 1953–1955

|  | Average in U.S. Dollars (millions) | Per Cent of Total |
|---|---|---|
| Imports | 828 | 78.2 |
| Tourist expenditures and border trade | 154 | 14.6 |
| Amortization of debt and credit | 46 | 4.3 |
| Other payments | 31 | 2.9 |
| Total Expenditures | 1,059 | 100.0 |

Source: Same as Table 43.

The generally higher level of consumption with a given national product and high fertility tends to curtail exports and to promote the import of consumption goods at the expense of capital goods. The slower growth of national income associated with high fertility also tends (with less certainty) to discourage international loans and investment. Thus the effects of different fertility on income growth via international transactions are in the same direction as the effects within the domestic economy. In fact the effects arise for fundamentally similar reasons. The pressure of a larger number of persons increases the consumption of currently available product— at the expense of using either domestic resources or foreign exchange to give the maximum impetus to future output. Higher consumption means that less is available to invest—or to export. Larger current needs mean that domestic funds—and foreign exchange—must be used in less productive ways.

## Is the Effect of Fertility on Economic Development Different under Different Developmental Policies?

There are many routes that have been or are now being tried in making the transition from a low-income agrarian economy to a more specialized and prosperous economic organization. The possibilities range from the use of the coercive powers of the state to foster a centrally planned industrial reorganization (as in the Soviet

312

Union and presumably in Communist China) to the direction and financing of industrial growth by individuals and private corporations (as was characteristic of the development of the economy of the United States). The development of India is following a strategy and stressing aims not precisely duplicated elsewhere. Among the prominent goals of Indian development are: aid to agriculture and the rural economy, the reduction of disparities in income, the promotion of fuller employment, the extension of the public sector of the economy, and the wider spread of "welfare" benefits. It is possible that these special features of economic development in India have led us to analytical results that would not apply elsewhere.

Which among the alternative paths of development is superior—on political grounds, on economic grounds, or both—is a matter of major interest and importance. The same may be said of the question as to whether in a low-income economy a strong emphasis on immediate welfare helps or impedes ultimate increases in well-being. These are issues we do not have to face here. However, the extension of our analysis to other areas *does* depend on whether different aims and strategies of economic development imply that the course of fertility has a different influence on the success of development. We shall not ask, then, whether one route or another is a better way to economic development, but only whether—regardless of the route—reduced fertility always tends to enlarge national product over a period of two or three decades. If so, the short-run advantages of fertility would always be more or less similar to those in India, 1956-1986.

The extension of our conclusions to other modes of economic development can be tested by asking whether the principal causal elements at work in India also hold elsewhere. As we saw in the preceding chapter, alternative courses of fertility have similar differential *demographic* effects in all areas where fertility is currently high. Whether the differential *economic* effects are similar (with different strategies of development) depends on the following:

(a) Would sustained fertility and reduced fertility yield about the same numbers in the labor force for two or three decades? Would a much smaller number of children under 15, in conjunction with only slightly fewer persons 15 and over, imply no important reduction in the supply of productive workers?

313

(b) Would a larger number of children increase the fraction of the national product consumed?

(c) Would high fertility increase the allocation of resources to relatively unproductive "welfare" purposes?

These questions will now be examined one by one.

(a) *Would the size of the labor force for 20 or 30 years in all cases be little affected by the course of fertility?* Whatever the route to industrial development, the course of fertility would affect the age distribution as in our projections of the Indian population. Differences between high and low fertility populations would inevitably be concentrated in the childhood ages, and for two or three decades the number of persons over 15 could differ only slightly.

A labor force of larger effective size during this period could arise with sustained fertility only if children under 15 made important labor contributions, and if women were not withdrawn from production because of larger families.

In spite of the prevalence of child labor in India (as in other low-income areas), we have assumed that extra children would make a negligible contribution to output. This assumption rests on the expectation that a growing educational program will curtail labor-force participation by children, on the recognition that with "concealed" and overt unemployment child labor may relieve adult labor without adding substantially to the total of useful work done, and on the belief that work by children is often of low average productivity.

If we are mistaken about the prospective contributions of child labor in India, or if we consider a strategy of development that attempts to make maximum use of child labor, our conclusions would be somewhat modified. However, the modifications would be slight. While in low-income areas children may not wait until age 15 to begin working, they cannot enter the labor force at birth. The existence of child labor does not remove the greater burden of dependency associated with sustained fertility.

In the next chapter we shall discuss the implications of the larger labor force ultimately associated with sustained fertility. It is perhaps arbitrary to assume that the difference in labor force size between sustained and declining fertility is unimportant for 25 or

30 years. If labor force participation were to begin at age 10 rather than age 15, the time when high fertility brings a faster growth in the number of workers would be somewhat advanced. Reduced participation of children is almost inevitable with economic development, it should be noted, if only because literacy and training become more essential. We reserve discussion of the effects of a more rapidly growing labor force until the next chapter, noting here only that in the absence of extra capital to be used with a larger number of workers, the contribution to total product—if positive at all—will be much less than proportionate to the additional numbers.

(b) *With a given national product, would more consumers mean higher consumption?* Reduced fertility promotes a faster growth of output primarily because a larger fraction of the national product can be used for development. This relationship will fail only if the extra demands for consumption generated by additional children are denied. National savings and investment would almost certainly be smaller with high fertility if a program for maximum economic growth were operated by a government with a very tight control over the economy. It might appear that such a government could ruthlessly hold down consumption and divert resources to investment even if the number of children was very large. However, if the number of children were smaller, the same degree of ruthlessness would produce *more* investment. Where coercion and tight control are in force, lower fertility would produce faster growth unless the government woodenly ignored the popular level of well being and deprivation in establishing its investment levels.

We shall now try deliberately to picture a strategy of economic development where savings and investment are just as large with high fertility as with low. Assume that public savings are negligible, that private savings are concentrated at the upper end of a very unequal income distribution, and that the small sector of the population responsible for all of the saving has low fertility at the outset, and hence is not subject to the alternative assumptions of fertility that apply to the population as a whole. Finally, assume that the division of national income—and of increases in income—between the saving and non-saving sectors of the population is not affected by variations in the course of fertility. In other words, the savers themselves have constant fertility, and their income is not affected by the fertility of the remainder of the population. Under these circumstances, the funds available for development would be independent of the course of fertility.

A number of questions must be raised before this picture is accepted as a realistic possibility. Consider first the assumption that savings remain at zero among the numerically preponderant low-income part of the population no matter what the course of fertility. This part of the population shares the same fraction of national income whether its fertility is high or low. Hence income per consumer in this sector would be much higher with reduced than with sustained fertility. We may imagine as a specific instance a constant level of real earnings for wage-earners and subsistence farmers. If fertility were unchanged each wage earner would on the average have a slightly larger number of dependents to provide for than before, while with reduced fertility the average number of dependents would become much smaller. For an invariant zero level of savings to hold, all of the gains from reduced dependency would have to be taken up by higher levels of consumption. While this possibility cannot be dismissed out of hand, it seems to us an unlikely one. An actual income distribution is continuous, and at the point on the continuum just below the "savers," there will probably be many families that would have positive savings if the family became smaller. It would be even more difficult to accept the possibility of continued zero savings as fertility is reduced if real wages were to rise rather than remain constant.

We next suppose that real wages *decline* so that income per consumer with reduced fertility remains approximately constant. Then there would be no occasion for savings to be generated by reduced fertility, and in the absence of available credit not much possibility of dissaving with sustained fertility. Thus the perverse possibility of falling real earnings among a majority of the population—including substantial reductions in consumption if fertility is sustained—*can* be taken to imply that savings would be genuinely independent of fertility. These falling earnings must be assumed to occur while national income as a whole rapidly rises.

In fact, of course, the progressive impoverishment of the lowest income groups while upper incomes rose would generate increasing pressure for remedy. With any effective popular voice in affairs, earnings would surely be maintained at least high enough to meet some minimum standards of income per consumer. But as soon as the possibility of maintaining minimum standards of consumption is entertained, the division of income among savers and non-savers can no longer be considered independent of the level of fertility. To maintain a given standard of consumption, more income must accrue to non-savers with sustained than with reduced fertility. With sustained fertility national savings would be reduced because the share of the national income flowing through the hands of savers would be smaller.

In other words, if the lower income range is assumed to have constant or rising *earnings*, it seems probable that reduced fertility would result in some positive level of savings among former non-savers, while if low-income *consumption* per head is merely kept from deterioration, redistribution of income would insure higher savings as a consequence of reduced fertility.

It is doubtless possible that the relation of fertility to the growth of total national income might be *weaker* where the major source of developmental funds is a high-income segment whose fertility is already low. Low fertility would almost always produce higher incomes per consumer (as in India), but the difference might in some circumstances be less.

(c) *Would high fertility always mean more resources used for relatively unproductive "welfare" purposes?* In India a large part of public revenues and of private savings will be used for housing, schools, maternal and infant care and other welfare purposes. These expenditures—both current and on capital account—would of course be larger with high fertility. Under another strategy of development that placed little or no emphasis on short-run welfare, these expenditures might be less, and the diversion of resources (with high fertility) from the most productive uses might be less pronounced.

To resist the pressure of the educational, housing and welfare needs of the extra children would add long-run difficulties, however—of an illiterate labor force, of low morale, and of generally low productivity. The growth of national income would thus tend to be somewhat slowed by the needs associated with sustained fertility under *any* strategy of development; although with differing emphasis on welfare expenditures, the difference in growth might occur at a different time and have a different magnitude.

317

The effect of a different institutional setting on the relation of fertility to economic growth can be illustrated by a brief examination of a specific example. The setting for economic development in Mexico differs from that in India in aims and strategy as well as in ways discussed earlier. Even though the government in Mexico is the product of a revolution, and operates under a revolutionary constitution, and although it has played an increasing role in encouraging the growth of the economy, economic development seems to be more under the leadership of private entrepreneurs, and less subject to government management and direction than in India. While there has been perhaps more emphasis in Mexico than in India on reforms in the ownership of land,[5] there is so far *less* emphasis on government action to relieve other causes of rural backwardness and poverty. It might be also said that welfare expenditures do not occupy as prominent a place in Mexico as in India. For example, expenditures on education have not kept pace with the rise in real national income over the past 15 years, even though school facilities remain wholly inadequate.

In Mexico there is no equivalent of the Planning Commission and the Five-Year Plan that are so prominent in India, and no federal agency performing a function equivalent to the Community Development Administration. Encouragement of economic development by the government has taken the form of making credit more readily available, the construction of a network of highways, the extension of irrigation and hydroelectric installations and other public works. Much of the benefit from these measures has accrued to rapidly expanding urban manufacturing and commercial enterprises on the one hand, and to the advanced commercialized sector of agriculture on the other.

In short, Mexico's development in recent years seems to have been concentrated in certain segments of the economy, while a segment where a large fraction of the labor force is employed has undergone relatively little change. The sector that has been bypassed by development, so to speak, is the corn-raising agrarian sector that still preserves many preconquest customs, including techniques of production. This sector is characterized by small land holdings, low crop yields, dependence on a single crop, illiteracy, a high

[5] There has also, of course, been much more time since the Mexican revolution than since Indian independence to put land reforms into effect.

proportion of persons speaking indigenous dialects, low rates of school attendance among the children, and, of course, low average incomes.

Do these features of Mexico's economic development imply that reduced fertility would not raise total national product? We saw earlier that if a high income sector with initially low birth rates were responsible for most of the national savings, if income distribution were unaffected by fertility, and if welfare expenditures were low, national product might grow at about the same pace under either course of fertility.[6] The closest we can come to matching these conditions in Mexico is to conjecture that the bulk of Mexican savings are derived from upper income urban groups and the most prosperous commercial farmers, and to assume that expenditures for welfare will remain relatively small, and that the share of national income going to the non-saving lowest income agricultural sector will be independent of fertility levels.

But in the first place urban fertility is not nearly as low as it would be if there were a major nationwide decline. Such a national decline would be shared by groups whose savings would be increased if they had smaller families. Secondly, an important fraction of Mexico's development is financed out of government revenues, and it would be easier to increase these at higher levels of per capita income—easier, in other words, if a given product were divided among fewer people. Thirdly, there is a growing awareness of the need in a more prosperous Mexico to spend more on education, housing, and health. Finally, while the poorer agrarian portion of the population has not gained proportionately from recent economic advances, real per capita income has apparently not declined; and even with further rapid population growth, at least enough developmental effort will no doubt be diverted to low-income agrarians to arrest any decline in income. But more effort will be required with sustained than with reduced fertility.

Thus even when we deliberately search for differences between the Mexican setting and that of India, we still come to the conclusion that a reduction in fertility would add substantially to total output.

The last two chapters can be summarized in a simple proposition:

[6] Income per consumer would still be about 20-25 per cent higher at the end of 30 years of fertility decline, because of the smaller number of consumers.

*If a country now has low incomes, a high birth rate (say, 40 per thousand or higher) and is in the process of reorganizing its economy to a more productive form, it will achieve a higher total product during the next 20 or 30 years if it reduces its fertility. This greater product is in addition to the per capita gains resulting from a division of the product among a smaller number of consumers.* The differential advantage to be gained by reduced fertility is in the same general range whether the country is large or small, has just begun to reduce its mortality or has already made major advances in health, is relatively self-sufficient or rather heavily engaged in trade, and whether development is following a socialist or capitalist pattern.

◇◇◇◇◇◇◇◇◇◇◇◇◇◇◇◇◇◇◇◇◇◇◇◇◇◇◇◇◇◇◇◇◇◇◇◇◇◇◇◇◇◇◇◇◇◇◇◇◇◇◇◇

# CHAPTER XXII

# THE ECONOMIC EFFECTS OF DIFFERENT COURSES
# OF FERTILITY AFTER 30 YEARS

◇◇◇◇◇◇◇◇◇◇◇◇◇◇◇◇◇◇◇◇◇◇◇◇◇◇◇◇◇◇◇◇◇◇◇◇◇◇◇◇◇◇◇◇◇◇◇◇◇◇◇◇

THE CONCLUSION that a decline in fertility in low-income countries would have substantial economic benefits in contrast with sustained fertility has to this point been based entirely on—and applied only to—a period of twenty-five or thirty years. During this interval two of the three major determinants of income growth—the availability of resources and the size of the labor force—would be more or less independent of the course of fertility, while the third major determinant—the size and nature of developmental effort—would be more favorable with reduced fertility. After twenty-five or thirty years, however, the greater growth of the labor force resulting from sustained fertility can no longer be ignored. Additional hands would surely begin to contribute additional output. Perhaps by concentrating on the interval during which sustained fertility produces merely additional dependents, we have concealed the ultimate advantages of more births. We shall now address this question directly.

To examine the question in a specific context, the two limiting population projections for India have been extended an additional 25 years—from 1986 to 2011. We have not attempted to project further changes in fertility and mortality after 1986. Thus the projection of the faster growing population involves fertility rates unchanged at estimated 1951 levels, and mortality risks unchanged at projected 1986 levels. The projection of more slowly growing population is based on an assumed continuation after 1986 of fertility rates at one-half the estimated 1951 levels. The projections are presented in Table 45, and in Chart 14. They continue to show contrasting growth rates and age distributions. By 2011 the sustained fertility population is somewhat more than twice as large as the population with low fertility. The larger population has about twice as many "equivalent adult consumers," about 1.7 times as many persons in the labor force ages, and more than three times as many persons in the dependent ages.

TABLE 45. PROJECTED POPULATION OF INDIA, 1986–2011,
BY BROAD AGE GROUPS
Population (millions)

| Age (Years) | 1986 | 1991 | 1996 | 2001 | 2006 | 2011 |
|---|---|---|---|---|---|---|
| | | Sustained Fertility | | | | |
| 0–14 | 329 | 378 | 432 | 494 | 567 | 650 |
| 15–64 | 417 | 472 | 536 | 612 | 699 | 800 |
| 65+ | 29 | 32 | 36 | 40 | 44 | 48 |
| Total | 775 | 882 | 1,005 | 1,146 | 1,310 | 1,498 |
| Equivalent Adult Consumers | 629 | 715 | 815 | 929 | 1,061 | 1,213 |
| | | Fertility Reduced by 50%, 1956–1981 | | | | |
| 0–14 | 175 | 175 | 179 | 182 | 183 | 182 |
| 15–64 | 385 | 408 | 426 | 441 | 455 | 467 |
| 65+ | 29 | 32 | 36 | 40 | 44 | 48 |
| Total | 589 | 616 | 641 | 663 | 682 | 697 |
| Equivalent Adult Consumers | 507 | 531 | 554 | 574 | 592 | 607 |

We shall compare economic progress with different courses of fertility in two ways: first, by a more or less qualitative comparison of the various forces affecting output per worker and income per consumer, and second, by extending the economic projections of Chapter XVII for another 25 years in a slightly altered form that takes explicit account of differences in the size of the labor force.

While greater numbers in the labor force add to the total product, faster growth of the labor force implies a lower output per worker than slower growth. The reason for this result is that with a faster growing labor force more capital must be diverted to provide tools and equipment for the extra workers so that they will be as productive as the existing labor force, and thus less will be available, *ceteris paribus*, for increasing output per worker. Consider specifically the projected Indian population 50 years from now (in 2006). The labor force with sustained fertility would be growing at about

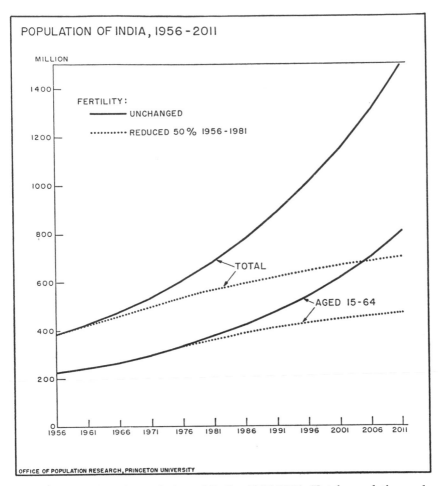

Chart 14. Projected Population of India, 1956-2011. Total population and population at ages 15-64, with high and low fertility.

2.5 per cent per year, while with reduced fertility, the growth would be at a rate of only 0.5 per cent per annum. Suppose that in both instances investment added 5 per cent to the capital stock. With the slower growing labor force, 90 per cent of this new investment could be used for raising output per worker, whereas with the more rapid growth only 50 per cent could be so used. Thus output per worker would be subject to less growth with sustained fertility— if the growth in capital were the same in both instances. But as of 1986 annual investment will be much *smaller* with high than with

323

low fertility. Thus, at the outset, the combination of a faster growth of the labor force with a lower level of investment doubly assures that output per worker with sustained fertility will fall progressively farther behind output per worker with reduced fertility. Moreover, with lower incomes per consumer in 1986 and a continued high burden of dependency, the slower growth of output per worker will result in a widening gap in per consumer income, in per capita savings, and in the ability to use development funds productively.

Against these forces tending to retard output per worker with high fertility relative to low, the single element favorable to faster growth of total output is a larger and more rapidly growing number of workers. The existence of this element makes it uncertain that total national output with reduced fertility would continue to exceed total output with sustained fertility. In fact our model projections show that, when a generous allowance is made for the productivity of additional labor, total output with sustained fertility would overtake total output with reduced fertility within 25 years after 1986. These projections are based on the favorable assumption that resource bottlenecks will not cause sharply rising costs.

A firm conclusion emerges from this discussion: The combined effect of the need for more duplication of facilities with faster growth, the greater burden of dependency, and the lower initial level of incomes is an ever-widening gap in output per worker and in income per consumer between the two projected populations.

We shall now try to show more quantitatively the cumulative interaction of the various forces at work during the period 1986-2011. Our method is to extend the principal series of economic projections outlined in Chapter XVII. It is essential in this extension to make explicit allowance for an increasing labor force. No such allowance was made in Chapter XVII because only inconsequential differences (if any) in the number of effective labor force participants would occur by 1986.

The basis for the extended projections is a version of the Cobb-Douglas production function relating output to the size of the labor force and the stock of capital. The version we employ assumes constant returns to scale, so that if the labor force and the stock of capital are each increased by 3 per cent, output also rises by precisely 3 per cent. We shall examine this assumption critically at a later stage. Specifically the following equation has been used:

(1)
$$\frac{Y_t}{Y_0} = \left(\frac{L_t}{L_0}\right)^m \left(\frac{K_t}{K_0}\right)^{1-m}$$

where $Y_t$ is national income, $L_t$ is the size of the labor force, and $K_t$ is the cumulated stock of capital at time $t$. $Y_0$, $L_0$, and $K_0$ are the magnitudes at the base period 0 (in our calculations, the base year is 1986). In logarithmic form, (1) becomes

(2)
$$\log\left(\frac{Y_t}{Y_0}\right) = m \log\left(\frac{L_t}{L_0}\right) + \left(1 - m\right) \log\left(\frac{K_t}{K_0}\right)$$

For small changes, this equation implies that the proportionate increase in national income is the weighted average of the proportionate increase in the labor force and the proportionate increase in the stock of capital. The weights are an expression of the relative effectiveness of labor and capital in increasing output. The function assures that for any value of the weights a given net investment would have a greater proportionate effect when the capital stock is small than when it is large. The coefficients $m$ and $1 - m$ express the relative effectiveness of the two factors with a given stock of capital and supply of labor. If $m$ is large, labor is relatively effective. By fitting time series and cross-sectional data in the United States, values for $m$ of .7 or higher have been obtained. We think it more realistic, in view of the level of education, training, and economic organization in India, to use a lower coefficient for the labor force. The coefficient employed in the principal series of calculations is 0.5[1]—implying that a given per cent increase in the stock of capital or in the size of the labor force would be equally effective in raising output.

To calculate the output for a date after 1986 the following data are required: the proportionate rise in the labor force between 1986 and the date in question, the cumulative investment during this interval, and the stock of capital in 1986. The proportionate rise in the labor force was estimated from the population projections under the assumption that the rise was in the same proportion as the increase in the number of persons 15-64.[2] The cumulative

---

[1] A second series of calculations was made with $m = 0.7$. The results (tempering but not basically altering the main conclusions) are given below. See Table 46 and Chart 15.

[2] It was contended earlier that labor force participation by women would be reduced by high fertility. We assume that this reduction would approximately

investment was determined by summing investment levels at 2 1/2-year intervals, calculated as in Chapter XVII. The effective addition to capital was considered equal to the developmental component of mobilized funds—the $D$ outlays defined in equation (2) in Chapter XVII. $D$ was calculated in each interval beginning in 1986. Finally the stock of capital in 1986 was estimated by substituting the rise in income, the increase in labor force, and the cumulated amount of net investment calculated in Chapter XVII for 1956-1986 in a Cobb-Douglas equation with $m = .5$. This substitution yields an estimate for the capital stock in 1956 as well as in 1986. The high fertility calculations led to an estimated capital stock in 1956 of Rs. 165 billion, while the low fertility calculations yield an estimate of Rs. 187 billion.[3] The arithmetic mean of these estimates was accepted as the best single figure. Adding the cumulated investment 1956-1986 led to a total stock in 1986 of Rs. 942 billion with low fertility and Rs. 801 billion with high.[4]

The outcome of the calculations is shown in Table 46, and Charts 15 and 16. Note that income per consumer with reduced

---

offset the slightly larger numbers in 1986 at ages 15-64. No significant further barrier to women's participation arises after 1986 on account of relative family size, however. In effect, then, we assume that the number of available labor force participants in 1986 is about the same for the high and low fertility populations, and that thereafter increases are in proportion to increases in the number of persons 15-64.

[3] The calculation was based on the following equation:

$$\log \frac{Y\ 1986}{Y\ 1956} = .5 \log \frac{L\ 1986}{L\ 1956} + .5 \frac{K\ 1986}{K\ 1956}$$

and data from economic Projection 1 in Chapter XVII. For the high-fertility and low-fertility cases of this projection in Chapter XVII, we find a ratio $\dfrac{Y\ 1986}{Y\ 1956}$. We assume that the ratio of the population 15-64 in 1986 to that in 1956 for the low-fertility projection establishes the ratio $\dfrac{L\ 1986.}{L\ 1956.}$ The equation then determines $\dfrac{K\ 1986}{K\ 1956}$. The sum of developmental outlays 1956-1986 was then set equal to $K\ 1986 - K\ 1956$. The quite different figures for the high- and low-fertility projections led to relatively slight differences in the estimates of $K\ 1956$.

[4] When $m = .7$, the *proportionate* increase in capital must be larger to be consistent with our Chapter XVII calculations of the rise in total output. With this coefficient, the capital stock in 1956 is estimated as only Rs. 70 billion, and the 1986 estimates become Rs. 695 billion and Rs. 836 billion.

fertility continues to gain, reaching very nearly double the income per consumer with sustained fertility by 2011 when $m = .5$. The economic advantages of reduced fertility are distinctly *not* limited to a transition period before labor force growth is affected.

Little significance can be attached to the absolute magnitudes of income per consumer obtained in these calculations. We emphatically disclaim any intention to *predict* the income levels that can be reached 30 years from now, much less 50. The value of these computations is that they show the *relative* rise in incomes under different courses of fertility, with identical assumptions about how the growth of output is determined.

One of the reasons for uncertainty in projecting levels of attainable income so far in the future is our inability to foresee future technological advances. Will there not be more or less unlimited abundance based on atomic energy (the fission of heavy elements and the fusion of abundant light elements), on the production of food from unicellular green plants or from harvesting crops grown in the sea, on automation, and on discoveries not yet visualized? There may indeed be developments that will speed the growth of India's income, and alleviate some of the impending shortages of resources by providing substitutes. But it is the nature of technical change to require capital if it is to be effective. The *fuel* costs of atomic energy may turn out to be very low, but the installations for releasing the energy in useful form will be elaborate, and will require large investments. Ponds for growing algae

TABLE 46. PROJECTED OUTPUT PER CONSUMER IN INDIA, 1956–2011, WITH SUSTAINED AND REDUCED FERTILITY

(Output per consumer 1956 = 100.)

| Assumptions | 1956 | 1986 | 1991 | 1996 | 2001 | 2006 | 2011 |
|---|---|---|---|---|---|---|---|
| $m = .5$ | | | | | | | |
| Sustained Fertility | 100 | 138 | 144 | 152 | 158 | 165 | 172 |
| Fertility Reduced | | | | | | | |
| 50%, 1956–1981 | 100 | 195 | 221 | 248 | 276 | 306 | 338 |
| $m = .7$ | | | | | | | |
| Sustained Fertility | 100 | 138 | 143 | 148 | 152 | 156 | 160 |
| Fertility Reduced | | | | | | | |
| 50%, 1956–1981 | 100 | 195 | 213 | 229 | 243 | 258 | 272 |

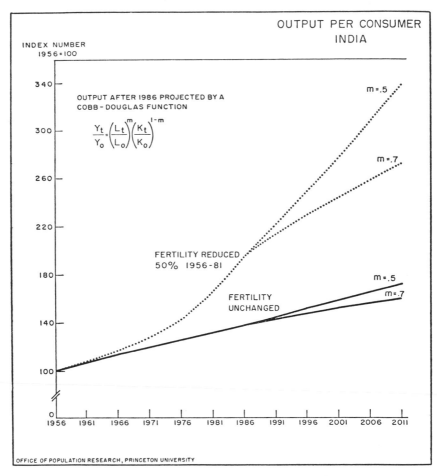

OUTPUT PER CONSUMER
INDIA

INDEX NUMBER
1956=100

OUTPUT AFTER 1986 PROJECTED BY A
COBB-DOUGLAS FUNCTION

$$\frac{Y_t}{Y_0} = \left(\frac{L_t}{L_0}\right)^m \left(\frac{K_t}{K_0}\right)^{1-m}$$

FERTILITY REDUCED
50% 1956-81

FERTILITY
UNCHANGED

m=.5
m=.7

OFFICE OF POPULATION RESEARCH, PRINCETON UNIVERSITY

Chart 15. Projected Output per Consumer, with High and
Low Fertility, India, 1956-2011.

and equipment for processing these plants into edible form will be
costly. It is precisely in having more resources available for fruitful
investment that we have found the principal economic advantage of
reduced fertility. Technological possibilities may ultimately prove
our projections conservative under *both* fertility assumptions; but
in that event the superior capacity to exploit technical possibilities
with reduced fertility could only widen the gap in projected income
per consumer.

Another source of uncertainty in projecting income levels is the

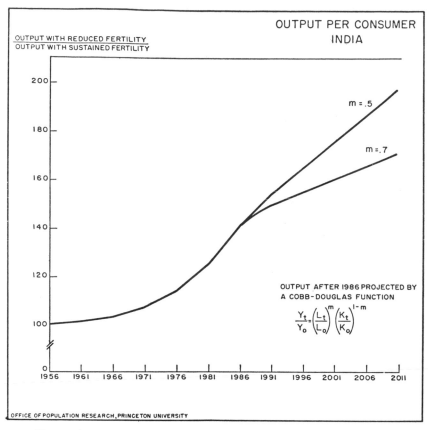

Chart 16. Ratio of Output per Consumer with Reduced Fertility to Output with Fertility Unchanged, India, 1956-2011.

question of whether growth will be restrained by a lack of space and resources. If it should be, the continued use of a Cobb-Douglas function with exponents totaling to unity would be misleading. To describe the case in which rising real costs (diminishing returns) accompany simultaneous expansion of labor and capital, the coefficients should sum to less than unity. The increase of output would be less than shown by our version of the Cobb-Douglas function. We briefly examined the availability of resources in analyzing the period before 1986, and concluded that the range of output growth contemplated would not encounter rigid ceilings because of limited resources. It is not nearly so reasonable to assume the absence of serious limitations in the period 1986-2011. Total output is calcu-

329

lated to grow to a multiple of some five to seven times its present level by 2011. Resource bottlenecks—particularly in agricultural land—could well become acute. There are three reasons for expecting resource limitations to be a more serious handicap with sustained than with reduced fertility. The first is that in 50 years (at most) our projections show total output with sustained fertility overtaking output with reduced fertility, even though output per worker and per consumer continues to fall behind. Thus to the degree that diminishing returns and rising costs are associated with a large value of output at constant prices, the faster growing population eventually encounters the more difficult problems. However (in the second place), it is not merely the growing value of output that accounts for pressure on resources, but the *composition* of output. The composition of the output associated with a larger population would press more insistently on land, both because a much larger fraction of consumption would be agricultural products, and because living space would compete more sharply with other land uses. (Recall that sustained fertility implies an Indian population by 2011 four times as large as the 1956 population and about 60 per cent as large as the present population of the entire world.) Finally, technical advances—such as harvesting food from the sea or special ponds—that would relieve pressure on resources are for reasons already expounded more likely to occur with an easier supply of capital.

Everything considered, the relatively rapid rise in income per consumer accompanying reduced fertility is more plausible than the continued moderate rise projected as accompanying sustained fertility (see Chart 15).

## Long-run implications of fertility differences

In the long run, the lack of adequate space and resources is logically certain—unless fertility is reduced—to impose a ceiling on rising consumption, then to lower the availability of food per consumer, and ultimately to cause a rise in death rates. These conclusions all follow from the mathematics of geometric increase. The growth accompanying high fertility and reduced mortality would raise India's population to 1.5 billion persons in the next 55 years, and in the following century to something like 20 to 25 billion persons. These numbers imply a population density for all India comparable to the density of the metropolitan area of New York. It seems unlikely that any technical change will make it possible to support such an enormously dense population. In 1200 years a continuation of 1951 fertility levels and projected 1986 mortality risks would produce an Indian population heavier than the entire mass of the earth—a patent impossibility. Either fertility must fall, or mortality must rise.

In fact, a gap between birth and death rates cannot be indefinitely sustained in any area no matter how high its current income. At current growth rates, the population of the United States would outweigh the earth in 2500 years. Before then, clearly, either American fertility must fall or American mortality rise. In the long run, high fertility is incompatible with low mortality. In the long run the *size* generated by indefinite growth becomes the dominant factor in the economics of population.

High fertility is a necessity for human survival when mortality risks are great. When mortality risks are reduced, high fertility becomes a burden—by increasing the dependency ratio, by diverting capital from uses that would raise per capita output, and in the long run by overwhelming any finite resources. If better health and longer life are valued, high fertility must be considered an extravagance. A population with high incomes and ample resources may be able to afford it for a period, perhaps for many decades. But a low-income area with high fertility that chooses the luxury of sustained births inevitably chooses to forego a much more rapid expansion of per capita incomes. Reduced fertility permits higher per capita income in the short run and in the intermediate future; in the distant future it can avert the otherwise inevitable return of poverty and high death rates.

<<<<<<<<<<<<<<<<<<<<<<<<<<<<<<<<<<<<<<<<<<<<<<<<<<<<<<

# CHAPTER XXIII

# POPULATION GROWTH AND ECONOMIC
# DEVELOPMENT IN LOW INCOME
# AREAS: SUMMARY

<<<<<<<<<<<<<<<<<<<<<<<<<<<<<<<<<<<<<<<<<<<<<<<<<<<<<<

WHERE AVERAGE INCOME, levels of education, and the prevalence of literacy are low, and where self-sufficient, small-scale agriculture is the usual occupation, birth rates are high—40 or more births per thousand population. Death rates range from very low—below 10—to rates approaching the birth rate. The widening tendency in areas of this sort during recent years is a precipitous drop in mortality risks. The result is current or imminent growth rates of 2 or 3 per cent per annum, rates without large-scale precedent in the history of settled areas.

Rapid improvements in mortality in these areas occur in response to increasingly effective low-cost public health measures. These measures can be introduced without profound social or economic changes; it is likely, on the other hand, that when effective economic development occurs, so will a modern health program. Such a program is nearly inevitable with industrialization because modernization of the economy means the importation of new ideas and customs; and effective public health techniques are more easily imported from the same sources.

High fertility means many children per adult, whether or not the population is growing rapidly. Reductions in mortality do not affect this general rule; in fact, the usual pronounced drop in mortality among the very young typically *increases* the fraction of children when death rates fall and fertility continues high.

The typical demographic pattern in low income areas thus has two salient features: (1) a young population, with a high ratio of dependents to earners; and (2) an actual or incipient high rate of growth. In the long run, the rapid growth of population must stop. Within a few centuries a constant geometric increase at 2 or 3 per cent per year would produce absurdly high numbers—for example, more than one person per square foot. Clearly fertility must eventually be reduced, or mortality rates must resume a high level.

Much discussion of population growth and economic development has stressed the ultimate impossibility of continued population growth in terms implying that the upper level of tolerable population size is near at hand in low income areas. This implication may indeed be correct in many instances. Often, however, an attempt to state the ceiling that population must not exceed—for example, by estimating the limits of food output—diverts attention from the relative merits of feasible alternative patterns of population development. If it turns out that output can be expanded more than pessimistic estimates imply, there is a natural tendency to minimize the problems of population growth. If the pessimists are wrong in saying that the food supply cannot be increased, it is natural to conclude that their fears about population growth are wholly mistaken. Without regard to the question of how many people can be fed with given agricultural resources, it is clear that a reduction of fertility from high levels has immediate economic advantages. The pace of economic development depends on the diversion of resources from consumption to uses that raise future output. A population with a high ratio of dependents to producers consumes more of a given output and devotes less to investment. Thus high fertility, which produces a high level of dependency, promotes consumption at the expense of investment.

During an interim of 2 or 3 decades either sustained or reduced fertility would result in approximately the same number of available workers. With fewer dependents, the population with reduced fertility could invest more and hence gradually produce more. With progressively fewer consumers dividing a progressively larger total product, reduced fertility would result in markedly higher economic welfare. Higher levels of consumption would in turn strengthen the forces leading to higher output through better incentives and improved physiological capacity.

The advantages of reduced fertility continue after this interim period ends. When sustained fertility produces a faster growing labor force, it would be necessary to invest a higher proportion of the national income than with reduced fertility, to produce comparable increases in output per worker. But the higher burden of dependency with sustained fertility means a tendency to invest *less* of the national income. Thus the gap in output per consumer continues to widen. These effects would hold even if there were adequate agricultural resources to feed a large population.

There is a possible advantage of a growing population neglected in the above argument: the possibility of economies of scale that could be achieved only with larger numbers. In raising the possibility of economies of scale, it is important not to attribute a large volume of sales (that makes large scale production possible) to the existence of a large population, when the volume actually originates in high average incomes. One must also avoid attributing large-scale, low-cost operation to the large size of the labor force, when the real sources of economy are technological advance, abundant capital, and skillful organization. Thus mass production of automobiles is possible in the United States primarily because of the large stock of capital and the large national income in the United States rather than primarily because Americans are especially numerous. (They are, in fact, less than half as numerous as Indians.)

Even in those instances where economies of scale could be more readily achieved with a larger labor force, the accompanying necessity for investment means that a gradual shift to larger numbers would be better than an abrupt one. In fact from the point of view of economic efficiency the ideal way for a sparsely settled low-income area to realize the economies of large-scale production would be through immigration of adult rather than through natural increase. If adult immigration could be combined with a sharp reduction in fertility, the advantages of a larger labor force could be achieved without the burden of supporting large numbers of nonproducers.

The economic advantages of reduced fertility thus begin immediately and cumulate for an indefinite period into the future. The immediate advantages are substantial: a 50 per cent linear reduction in fertility in twenty-five years provides in 3 decades an income per consumer some 38-50 per cent higher than would occur with sustained fertility. In 25 more years, reduced fertility would yield an income per consumer about twice as high as with continued high fertility. If one takes account of the favorable effects of technological change and of the stimulus provided by higher consumption on the one hand, and of limits imposed by pressure on land and other resources on the other, these estimates of the gains obtained from reduced fertility appear conservative.

If reduced fertility produces such impressive economic benefits from the outset, and is essential in the long run to prevent the return of extreme poverty and high mortality rates, how can the recent startling rises in per capita income in Mexico, and the slower but still real progress in India be explained? The answer is that apparently there are economic parallels to the opportunities for quickly reducing mortality in areas with high death rates. Where primitive agriculture is the dominant occupation, there are frequently ways of achieving rapid increases in output at low cost through industrialization and improvements in agricultural methods. However, these possibilities in no way reduce the gains to be derived from lower fertility. With a lower birth rate a *still faster* rise in output could be obtained. The possibility of rapid increases in output in some low-income areas does mean that the eventual calamitous effects of high fertility will not prove overwhelming *in the near future*. An interval is thus available in these countries during which forces promoting reduced fertility can be developed. However, to postpone the reduction of fertility is to forego the opportunity for a more rapid rise in immediate wellbeing, and to shrink the potential growth in incomes per capita for the indefinite future.

Mexico may be able to achieve rising economic welfare for 30 years or even for a half-century without major declines in fertility. It seems implausible that she could afford high fertility for a full century, when the population of Mexico would approach 900 million persons. Even in the near future, Mexican prospects would rise faster and more surely with a lower birth rate. In India the period during which sustained fertility can be tolerated without a resumption of high mortality is shorter. The advantages of a reduced birth rate are comparable, but in India the existence of a breathing spell before high fertility endangers rising incomes (and even endangers the achievement of lower death rates) is less certain, and the length of any such breathing spell is surely much less.

At any stage in the foreseeable future of the low-income countries with high fertility, a reduction in fertility would produce important economic advantages. Since these advantages are cumulative, the ultimate benefits of fertility reduction are greater, the sooner it occurs.

# APPENDIX A

◇◇◇◇◇◇◇◇◇◇◇◇◇◇◇◇◇◇◇◇◇◇◇◇◇◇◇◇◇◇◇◇◇◇◇◇◇◇◇◇◇◇◇◇◇◇◇◇◇◇◇

## METHODS EMPLOYED IN ADJUSTING INDIAN POPULATION DATA AND PREPARING PROJECTIONS OF THE INDIAN POPULATION, 1956–1986

◇◇◇◇◇◇◇◇◇◇◇◇◇◇◇◇◇◇◇◇◇◇◇◇◇◇◇◇◇◇◇◇◇◇◇◇◇◇◇◇◇◇◇◇◇◇◇◇◇◇◇

ALTERNATIVE estimates of possible population changes during the next 30 years are a key factor in our analysis of Indian population growth and economic development. The construction of these estimates involved adjusting the 1951 census age and sex distribution, making estimates of recent levels of mortality and fertility by age, and projecting mortality and fertility rates 30 years into the future. The procedures employed and the assumptions made are discussed briefly and non-technically in Chapters IV-VI. This Appendix is a fuller and more technical explanation.

### COMPONENT PROJECTION

The technique of projection employed yields data on future populations distributed by sex and five-year age groups. (See Tables 3, 4, and 5.) This technique, known as component projection, requires knowledge (or estimates) of the number of persons in each five-year age group for each sex at some initial date (usually the date when a census is taken); knowledge (or estimates) of the fraction of each group surviving each five-year interval (during which, of course, the survivors become five years older); knowledge (or estimates) of the number of children born per 1,000 women in each age group; and knowledge (or estimates) of the number in each group leaving or entering the country. Knowing the 1951 female population by age, one can estimate the number at ages 5-9 in 1956 by applying estimated survivorship rates to the number 0-4 in 1951, and the number 10-14 in 1956 as survivors of those 5-9 in 1951, etc. Surviving net migrants (known or estimated) during 1951-1956 can be added in. The group 0-4 in 1956 can be estimated in two steps: first by estimating the number of births in the interval through a combination of estimated fertility rates for each age group and the size of the group; and second by estimating the fraction of those born who survive. Experience shows that the sex ratio at birth can be considered constant without introducing important errors. In India it can be assumed that international migration will be negligible.

The basic elements needed to project the Indian population to 1986 by this technique are:

337

1. The best available data with regard to the 1951 population distributed by age and sex.

2. The best available life table for 1951 and the best available data with regard to fertility rates by age of woman in 1951.

3. Estimates of how mortality risks and fertility rates have changed since 1951.

4. A method for projecting mortality and fertility rates by age from 1956 to 1986.

If age reporting were highly accurate and enumeration complete in Indian censuses, the age and sex distribution in 1951 could have been taken directly from the census itself. Likewise, were births and deaths completely registered and accurate ages reported on certificates of registration, birth and death statistics through 1956 could be taken from official statistics. As might be expected when more than 80 per cent of the population is illiterate, the ages reported in the census are clearly quite unreliable, while birth and death registration are so incomplete as to be nearly useless. Consequently we resorted to an analysis of the sequence of decennial Indian censuses (extending back to 1881) in an attempt to construct estimates of birth rates, death rates by age, and the age and sex distribution of the Indian population as of 1951. Separate estimates of these figures had been made in various publications of the 1951 Census of India, but these estimates had the defect (for our purposes) of inconsistencies. For example, the smoothed as well as the raw age distribution published by the Census is inconsistent in some respects with the birth rates and life table for the 1941-1951 decade estimated by the Census.

*The use of Lotka's stable-population concepts to determine the state of the population in 1951*

An inspection of Indian censuses shows that changes in age distribution since 1891 appear to have been relatively minor. The fact, in addition, that the growth rate per decade apparently fluctuated only slightly between 1921 and 1951 suggests that the theory of stable populations developed mostly by Lotka might be useful in estimating death rates by age, birth rates, and in correcting the 1951 census for erroneous age reporting.[1] A slight extension of the theory to fit it to these purposes is needed.[2] The final result of applying stable-population concepts is an estimated 1951 age distribution and a set of vital rates for 1951 that are consistent with one another and with past censuses,

[1] A. J. Lotka, *Théorie analytique des associations biologiques*, Part 2, *Analyse démographique avec application particulière à l'espèce humaine*, Paris, Hermann et cie., 1939.

[2] For an application to Egyptian data of this extension of Lotka's theory, see M. A. El-Badry, "Some Demographic Measurements for Egypt Based on the Stability of Census Age Distributions," *Milbank Memorial Fund Quarterly*, Vol. XXXIII, No. 3, pp. 268-305, July 1955.

which are by a wide margin the most reliable series of Indian population statistics.

Lotka's theory shows that when there is a constant schedule of fertility rates by age of mother, of mortality rates by age, and no migration, an unchanging age distribution and a constant annual rate of growth will eventually be established.

Two equations summarize the relations among variables in the stable population (of the female sex):

(1)
$$\frac{n(a)}{N} = b\, e^{-ra}\, p(a)$$

(2)
$$\int_0^\omega e^{-ra}\, p(a) m(a) = 1$$

The first equation states that the fraction of the population at each age $(\frac{n(a)}{N})$ is proportional to the product of a growth factor $(e^{-ra}$, where $r$ is the annual rate of growth) and the probability of surviving from birth to age $a$ $(p(a))$. The factor of proportionality is the birth rate $(b)$ of female infants in the stable female population. The birth rate equals the fraction of the population at age zero (at birth). When $a$ is zero, $e^{-ra}$ and $p(a)$ are each equal to unity.

The second equation is a consequence of the fact that the product of the number of women at each age times the probability of bearing a female child at that age $(m(a))$ summed for all ages to the highest attained, $\omega$, equals the number of births. Equation (2) shows the dependence of $r$ (the constant growth rate of the stable population) on fertility rates $(m(a))$ and mortality rates or their converse, survival rates $(p(a))$. The higher the fertility rates and the higher the probability of surviving to the childbearing ages, the greater the rate of growth.

If a closed population has a nearly unchanging rate of growth and a nearly unchanging age distribution for many decades, it may be assumed with only a slight chance of error that its age distribution is the stable one of equation (1), with a life table $(p(a))$ representing the average mortality risks of the period, and a birth rate $(b)$ reflecting the average maternity rates. Mortality risks and fertility rates may fluctuate during the period, producing corresponding slight aberrations in age distributions, but neither mortality nor fertility could very well be subject to a pronounced trend, because such trends would show up in noticeable changes in the age distribution, the growth rate, or both.

It has been shown elsewhere that a change in fertility levels (with mortality risks constant) has a pronounced effect on age distributions.[3]

[3] A. J. Coale, "The Effects of Changes in Mortality and Fertility on Age Composition," *Milbank Memorial Fund Quarterly*, Vol. XXXIV, No. 1, pp. 79-114, January 1956.

The effect of changes in mortality rates on age distributions *can* be marked (for example, excess mortality in wartime can strongly affect the age distribution of males). However, the *observed peacetime* mortality changes in countries of various regions and with varying general levels of mortality have effects on age distributions that are restricted in pattern and limited in extent.[4]

A decline in fertility, by reducing numbers at the outset of life, erodes the base of the age pyramid and increases the fraction of the population at older ages. In the long run, a lower level of fertility with mortality risks constant produces a flatter, less steeply tapering age distribution. Mortality improvements (from the high levels prevailing in India) typically produce the greatest proportionate improvement in the probability of surviving in the infant and young childhood ages. Sometimes (though not always) above-average improvements in survivorship also occur at ages above 50. Mortality improvements shared equally by *all* ages have *no* effect on the age distribution, but merely increase the growth rate. Above-average improvements in survivorship under age 5 have effects very much like a slight rise in fertility. Above-average improvements at ages over 50 increase the fraction at the older ages.

These effects of changes in vital rates have been summarized as a background for the following statements:

(1) A decline in fertility alone would produce a marked effect on the Indian age distribution and would reduce the intercensal rate of growth.

(2) A decline in mortality alone would have one certain effect (to increase the growth rates) and another probable effect, if the age pattern of improvement took the typical form. The probable effect would be a slight increase in the fraction at the younger ages (and perhaps in ages over 50) on account of the usual above-average improvements in survivorship at infant and young child ages (and the frequent above-average increases in survivorship above 50).

(3) A simultaneous decline in mortality and fertility would:

(a) Raise the growth rate if the decline in the crude death rate were greater, and reduce the growth rate if the crude birth rate fell more.

(b) Increase, decrease, or leave constant the fraction at the younger ages depending (roughly speaking) on whether the per cent improvement (in excess of the average) in the probability of surviving to age 4 or 5 exceeded, equalled, or fell short of the percent decline in fertility.

[4] A. J. Coale, *op.cit.*, and "The Effects of Declines in Mortality on Age Distribution," Papers presented at the 1955 Annual Conference of the Milbank Memorial Fund. *Trends and Differentials in Mortality*, New York, Milbank Memorial Fund, 1956.

These propositions, in turn, provide a basis for interpreting the stability of the age distributions in the Indian censuses since 1931, together with the relatively constant growth rate since 1921. The age distributions for 1931, 1941, and 1951 are shown in Chart A-1. The

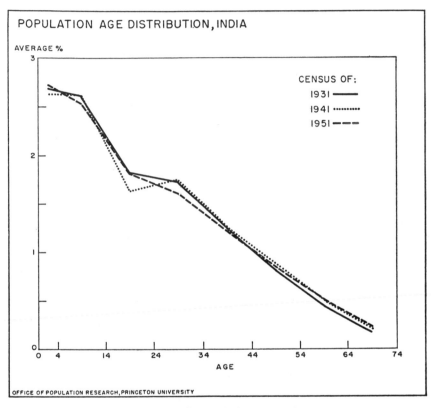

Chart A-1. Average Per Cent of Population at Each Age, by Age Groups 0-3, 4-13, 14-23, . . . 64-73, India, Censuses of 1931, 1941, and 1951.

The data for this figure were calculated at the Office of Population Research from census statistics. None of the censuses published a single-year age distribution for all India. The 1951 Census published single-year distributions by province; we obtained an all-India single-year distribution by addition. A 1941 age distribution was available for only 7 provinces (Assam, Bihar, Bombay, Madhya Pradesh, Orissa, Uttar Pradesh, and West Bengal). The 1931 and 1941 distributions were published only in smoothed form. In smoothing, the original figures had first been combined in these groups: 0-3, 4-6, 7-13, 14-16, 17-23, etc. Then smoothed five-year groups were estimated as follows: The number 0-4 was estimated as those 0-3 plus one-half those 4-6, the number 5-9 as one-half those 4-6 plus one-half those 7-13, etc. By simple algebra it is possible to reconstruct an unsmoothed distribution with the peculiar groupings 0-3, 4-6, 7-13, 14-16, etc. The single-year distribution for 1951 was put on a comparable basis.

341

differences are remarkably small. The average annual rate of growth during each of the three decades was 10.1, 14.0, and 12.5 per thousand, respectively. Since the rate of growth is the difference between a birth rate averaging above 40 per thousand and a death rate averaging about 30 per thousand, the variation is surprisingly slight. There are two plausible explanations for the near stability of the age distribution and the near constancy of the growth rate:

(1) Either the level of fertility *and* the mortality risks were essentially unchanging, *or*

(2) Mortality risks above age 5 were essentially constant and there was a slight decline in fertility offset by a decrease in infant and child mortality.

In *either* case, the age distribution in 1951 would be closely approximated (at least at ages above 5) by

$$\frac{n(a)}{N} = be^{-ra} p(a),$$

where $r$ is the *observed* average annual rate of growth, and $p(a)$ is a function (precisely equivalent to the $l_x$ life-table function with a radix of unity) expressing the average probability of surviving to each age during the years before 1951. $b$ is the birth rate for years just preceding 1951. It necessarily equals $1/\int_0^\omega e^{-ra} p(a) da$.[5]

There may be doubt as to whether thirty years (1921-1951) is a long enough period of unchanging growth rates to support the assumption of an age distribution stable in the Lotka sense. We are reassured on this point by the fact that the age distributions from 1891 to 1921 were also remarkably stable. Because of somewhat different errors in age reporting, the censuses through 1921 differ in detail from later censuses, but not in general form.[6] However, the average rate of growth prior to 1921 was much lower, as is clear from an inspection of Table 1 and Chart 2. It seems most likely, then, that after 1921 the average mortality experience in India was improved in comparison to the three earlier decades. However, mortality improvement has only secondary effects on the age distribution, and only a relatively short period is needed for the age distribution to approximate a slightly altered stable form after a decline in average death rates.

Lotka's stable population concepts, an analysis of how changes in vital rates affect age distributions, the observed stability of Indian age

---

[5] See Lotka, *op.cit.*

[6] Actually the awkward fact that only smoothed five-year age distributions were published in 1931 and 1941 makes it impossible to make a direct comparison between these distributions and those for earlier censuses.

distributions, and the constancy of growth rates taken together suggest the following possibilities:

(1) If there were an accurate life table for the period before 1951, it would provide a close approximation of the actual age distribution in 1951, free of age misreporting. (Since $\dfrac{n(a)}{N} = \dfrac{e^{-ra} \, p(a)}{\int_0^\omega e^{-ra} \, p(a) da}$,

with $r$ known). The age distribution would also make it possible to estimate the birth rate in the years before 1951.

(2) Conversely, if the age distribution in the Census of 1951 were accurate, multiplying the fraction at each age ($= be^{-ra} \, p(a)$) by $e^{ra}$ would yield a life table with a radix of $b$.

Unfortunately, age reporting even in recent Indian censuses, while patently improved over the reporting in the censuses of thirty or forty years ago, is extremely unreliable. Chart A-2 shows the number of males reported in 1951 by single years of age and by five-year age groups. Even with grouping, there are features that can scarcely reflect actuality, such as the gap in the adolescent and young adult ages, and the large number 5-9 relative to those 0-4. These features are found (in exaggerated form) in earlier censuses back to 1881.

The unreliability of age reporting means that reliable life tables cannot be constructed directly by multiplying the age distribution by $e^{ra}$ —and also means that life tables constructed by comparing consecutive censuses will not have reliable values by age. The official Indian life tables are based on apparent survivorship rates from one census to the next, and in order to avoid absurdities such as negative mortality rates, the reported census age distributions must be adjusted (smoothed) before survival rates are calculated. Mechanical smoothing processes work well only when deficits and excesses in persons reporting each age are balanced over fairly short intervals. When, as in the present instance, there are large displacements of reported age, or disproportionate omissions or improper inclusions of persons in broad age groups, mechanical smoothing will yield an age distribution still strongly affected by the original errors.

To escape this dilemma, we made use of two facts:

(1) While age misreporting makes it difficult to estimate probabilities of surviving accurately age by age, errors of estimation tend to cancel, so that an overall average measure of mortality risk (such as an expectation of life) can be estimated with adequate accuracy. Specifically, if one avoids the treacherous childhood years (when infant mortality plays such a large role in determining the expectation of life, and where age reporting and completeness of enumeration are especially questionable),

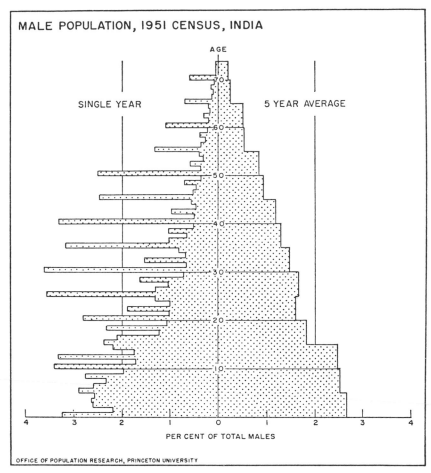

Chart A-2. Per Cent Distribution of Male Population by Single Years and Five-Year Averages, India, Census of 1951.

it is possible to make a reasonably reliable estimate of the expectation of life at age 10.

(2) There is a close relationship observable between the probability of surviving particular age intervals above age 10, and the expectation of life at age 10. This relationship can be observed in a large number (114) of life tables from areas with high mortality rates but more reliable vital statistics than India's.

From these facts a procedure was evolved that led to the construction of a plausible life table—plausible at least for ages above 5, and especially above age 10. The procedure was (in summary terms) to estimate the expectation of life at age 10 on the basis of the reported age distribution in 1951 and the recorded growth rate prior to 1951; and then to estimate life table values by age on the assumption that the *pattern* of mortality in India is typical of the general *level* of mortality. Estimates of mortality under age 5 were obtained by another (and less satisfactory) method.

With an estimated life table, a calculated average growth rate, an estimate of the sex ratio at birth, and the assumption that the age distribution approximates the Lotka stable form, we were able to calculate an age-sex distribution for 1951 that was consistent with:

(a) The stability of the reported age distribution from 1931 on, and the relative constancy of the growth rate after 1921.

(b) The general level of mortality risks above age 10, inferred either from the general pattern of age distribution above age 10 and the growth rate, or from differencing consecutive censuses.

(c) Evidence with respect to the birth rate in special areas with superior registration.

(d) A plausible sex ratio at birth (equal to the ratio for registered births).

As Chart 5 shows, the age distribution differs only slightly from the smoothed distribution in the Indian census, with the notable exception of the number of children under age 5. The smoothed figures, however, are not consonant with the level of infant mortality that even by conservative estimates exists in India, and it is nearly certain that in this respect our data are nearer to actuality.

In summary, we used the observed stability of the Indian census age distributions in conjunction with population theory to estimate a life table, an age-sex distribution, and the general level of fertility in India as of 1951. We turn to the technical details involved. The estimation of the growth rate, the construction of a life table, and the combination of these (through equation (1) above) to form an age distribution will be discussed in sequence.

## ESTIMATING THE GROWTH RATE, 1921-1951

We might have employed the growth rate for the decade 1941-1951, which is 13.2 per thousand when based on the estimated population within present Indian boundaries (Table 1) and is 12.5 when taken as the difference between census estimates of intercensal birth and death rates (Table 8). However, this would have put too much reliance on the least reliable decade for estimating intercensal population increase. The growth figure is unreliable because of the boundary changes that took place between 1941 and 1951, and because of the "displacement" of a large number of persons arising out of the partition of former India into present India and Pakistan. The 1951 census growth figure of 12.5 per thousand per annum is based on an attempt to estimate natural increase within the present boundaries of India. We chose to use instead an average growth rate from 1921 to 1951. Compounding the percent increases for 1921-1931 and 1931-1941 for all India with the estimated growth for 1941-1951 for present India turned out to give the same answer as the estimated increase since 1921 within the present boundaries. The average rate was 12.2 per thousand—insignificantly different in any case from the official figure for 1941-1951.

CONSTRUCTING A LIFE TABLE FOR THE PERIOD UP TO 1951

Life-table construction was the most complicated part of establishing the Indian demographic situation as of 1951. One possibility open to us was to use the official Indian life table for the decade 1941-1951 or some kind of average life table assembled from the official 1941-1951 table, the official 1921-1931 table, and Kingsley Davis' life table for the 1931-1941 decade. All of these life tables were prepared by comparing one census population with the preceding census population. Since the Indian population has, except for partition, been substantially a closed population, one could compute survivorship by age through a comparison of censuses a decade apart. However, because of the extremely inaccurate age reporting in the Indian censuses, the life-table constructors were forced to smooth the age distributions in some fashion before they calculated the various life-table functions. In other words, the detailed shape of the survivorship function really depends on how the life-table constructor chose to smooth the raw age distributions that he dealt with. One result is that a comparison of successive Indian life tables reveals a very erratic behavior in mortality by age. In short, the death rates at particular ages in the Indian life tables are as much determined by the way in which the original data were processed as by the real underlying mortality pattern in India.

There is a better chance, however, of obtaining a reliable estimate of the general level of mortality, especially above age 10, from census data. A conventional summary measure of mortality risks above age 10 is the expectation of life at age 10. We could have taken the value given in the official life tables for 1941-1950, based on apparent survivorship from the 1941 to the 1951 census. This value (average for both sexes) is 39.2 years. In the end we made our own estimate of $e^o_{10}$—41.3 years, about 5 per cent higher than the official figure. The difference between 39.2 and 41.3 years indicates the uncertainty in estimating overall mortality levels (even with young childhood years omitted) from the Indian census data.[7]

Our estimate of the expectation of life at age 10 was made from a crude life table based on stable-age distribution concepts. Since

$$\frac{n(a)}{N} = be^{-ra}\ p(a)$$

in a stable population, the product of the age distribution and $e^{ra}$ is $b \cdot p(a)$ — or a life table with a radix of $b$. If the age distribution

[7] The differences between these estimates are small compared to the changes in mortality we anticipate in the next two or three decades.

above age 10 is multiplied by $e^{ra}$, the result (except for a factor of proportionality) is a life table from age 10 on. The three most recent censuses appear to have essentially the same age distribution (see Chart A-1), and this distribution in conjunction with the average value of $r$ already described should suffice to make a life table above age 10. The similarity of the 1931 and 1951 distributions is particularly strong. What differences there are seem to be in a direction of less distorted age reporting in 1951. Thus the 1951 age distribution was used rather than some average. There was one gross adjustment made before the crude life table was constructed—filling in the conspicuous gap in the adolescent and young adult ages. The gap was filled by drawing a straight line between the midpoints of two 10-year age groups—at age 9 and 29. A similar adjustment was made in calculating the official Indian life tables.[8]

If the 1951 census age distribution is multiplied by $e^{ra}$, the result may be called a "reported life table." If the age distribution were accurate, the reported life table would closely approximate actual mortality risks; but the reported life table deviates from actual risks in a manner and to a degree similar to the deviation of the census age distribution from the actual. The expectation of life at age 10 is equal to the area under the $l_x$ (survivorship) function above age 10 divided by the height of the ordinate at 10 ($l_{10}$). The area under the "reported life table" above age 10 should not be excessively affected by errors in age reporting, since those missing at one age show up as excess at another. The ordinate at age 10 can be estimated (with a greater chance of error than in estimating the area, unfortunately) by averaging age-groups on either side of 10. The final outcome of this use of the age distribution and the stable-population concepts was an estimate for the expectation of life at age 10 of 41.36 years for males and 41.16 for females (as compared to 38.97 and 39.45 in the census life tables for 1941-1951).

The construction of the final life table we used at ages above 10 depended on the existence of a typical age pattern of mortality risks associated with a given overall level of mortality above age 10. To show that a typical pattern exists, linear correlation coefficients were calculated between the probabilities of dying within the fifteen years beginning at age 10, at age 25, at age 40, and at age 55 on the one hand, and the expectation of life at age 10 on the other. The coefficients were gratifyingly high. In order of advancing age they were —0.73, —0.96, —0.96, and —0.90 for males, and —0.83, —0.94, —0.94, and —0.86 for females. These correlations were based on life tables selected by two rules from a large collection of life tables assembled by George Stolnitz at the Office of Population Research. One rule was that the life table should be based, as far as we could tell, on registered mortality rather than on differencing censuses. The second rule was that the

[8] Census of India, Paper No. 2, 1954, *Life Tables—1951 Census*, pp. 15-17.

expectation of life at age 10 should be no higher than 52 for females.

The high correlation coefficients indicate that mortality risks *do* show similar patterns by age for similar overall mortality levels. The remaining problem is, given the existence of a pattern, to construct a detailed life table from an expectation of life at age 10. The straight-forward method that suggests itself (in view of the high linear correlations involved) is to estimate $_{15}q_{10}$, $_{15}q_{25}$, $_{15}q_{40}$, and $_{15}q_{55}$ by linear regression of these variables on $e^o_{10}$. The difficulty with this method is that $e^o_{10}$ is itself defined by the probabilities of dying above age 10. If a life table is constructed from $q_x$ values estimated by least squares linear regression on $e^o_{10}$, it will tend to have an expectation of life at 10 nearer the mean of the 114 original tables than the $e^o_{10}$ that one started with. Suppose $q_x$'s were estimated from a very low expectation of life—say, 32 years. Suppose a complete life table above 10 were constructed from these $q$'s. This life table would have an expectation at 10 of something like 34 or 35 years. As is well known, least-square regression lines yield estimates that always tend toward the mean value. While each separate $q_x$ estimated by regression techniques might be the best estimate for that particular age, the set of $q_x$'s so estimated turn out to be incompatible with the original expectation of life.

This difficulty was surmounted in two steps. To avoid the "regression toward the mean" involved in least squares analysis, the line used to represent the relation between each $_{15}q_x$ and $e^o_{10}$ had a slope intermediate to the two regression lines. "Intermediate" is the geometric mean, and the two lines in question are the regression of $_{15}q_x$ on $e^o_{10}$, and the regression of $e^o_{10}$ on $_{15}q_x$.[9] Even the intermediate line, however, will not give $q_x$ values exactly compatible with the original value of $e^o_{10}$ except by good luck.

To *ensure* compatibility, a second step was taken. A series of complete life tables was calculated using various initial values of $e^o_{10}$, and reading $_{15}q_{10}$, $_{15}q_{25}$, $_{15}q_{40}$, and $_{15}q_{55}$ from the "intermediate" lines of regression.[10] The resulting $e^o_{10}$'s were calculated. Then a graph was constructed with the resultant $e^o_{10}$ plotted against the $e^o_{10}$ from which the $_{15}q_x$'s were calculated. This graph makes it possible to select an "ingoing" value of $e^o_{10}$ whose sole function is to serve as the basis for estimating a set of $_{15}q_x$'s that imply precisely the desired $e^o_{10}$. The net result of these two steps is the creation of a life table[10] above age 10 with two properties:

(a) The pattern of mortality by age is a pattern typical of other life tables with the same mortality level.

---

[9] The intermediate line, it turns out, is the line that minimizes the sum of the squares of perpendicular deviations from the observations, provided each variable is expressed in standard deviation units.

[10] The calculation of $l_x$ values at five-year intervals, and at ages above 70 in these tables, is described below.

(b) The expectation of life at age 10 in the life table is precisely the one estimated from the age distribution and stable population theory.

Once the $_{15}q_x$ values had been estimated, it was a more or less mechanical matter to prepare a complete life table beginning at age 10. Using a provisional radix of 1,000 at age 10, the $_{15}q_x$'s were used to determine $l_{25}$, $l_{40}$, $l_{55}$, and $l_{70}$. A more or less arbitrary value of 10 for females and 8 for males was assigned to $l_{85}$. The $l_x$ values for intermediate ages were obtained by fitting a fifth degree parabola to these six points.

There remained the determination of mortality risks below age 10. Unfortunately for the reliability of our estimates, the correlation between these risks and the expectation of life at age 10 are much lower than correlations involving mortality risks above age 10. The correlations are particularly low with respect to infant mortality and mortality under age 5. For lack of a better procedure, $_5q_5$ was finally estimated from a regression of $_5q_5$ on $e^0{}_{10}$, even though the Pearsonian correlation was only —.40 for females and —.29 for males.

Infant mortality levels were so uncertain that two separate estimates were used in constructing 1951 life tables. The lower estimate is 200 per thousand (190 for females and 210 for males) and the upper is 250 (239 for females and 261 for males). Mortality risks up to age 5 were estimated by the relation $_5q_0 = 1.59\,_1q_0$. This figure (1.59) is an average obtained from 67 life tables in which the proportion surviving to age 10 was 70 per cent or less.

The evidence on which are based estimates of infant mortality above 200 per thousand is summarized in Chapter V.

Table A-1 shows the life tables associated with high and low infant mortality respectively.

1951 AGE-SEX DISTRIBUTIONS

According to the stable-age distribution theory that we have utilized at several points as the basis for our estimates, the age distribution in 1951 should be the product of the survivorship function in our life table and $e^{-ra}$. Just as we have assumed that the typical age pattern of mortality observed in a large collection of life tables gives a better means of estimating the specific mortality rates above age 10 than can be derived from the Indian census age distributions with their faulty age reporting, we also believe that the age distribution one obtains from the product of $e^{-ra}$ and our life table will be closer to reality than an age distribution derived by mechanical smoothing of the raw census data. Chart 5 shows the age distribution as estimated by the Indian census through a technique of mechanical smoothing, and as estimated by averaging our two limiting assumptions about infant mortality.

By applying the procedures just outlined, a stable age distribution is

## TABLE A-1. ABRIDGED LIFE TABLES FOR INDIA, 1951
### Infant mortality estimated at 200 deaths per 1,000 live births

| Age | Males $_5q_x$ | Males $l_x$ | Males $e_x^0$ | Females $_5q_x$ | Females $l_x$ | Females $e_x^0$ |
|---|---|---|---|---|---|---|
| 0 | .334 | 1,000 | 33.5 | .302 | 1,000 | 34.7 |
| 5 | .040 | 666 | 44.6 | .046 | 698 | 44.1 |
| 10 | .025 | 639 | 41.4 | .027 | 666 | 41.2 |
| 15 | .040 | 623 | 37.4 | .050 | 648 | 37.2 |
| 20 | .050 | 598 | 33.8 | .063 | 616 | 34.1 |
| 25 | .061 | 568 | 30.5 | .070 | 577 | 31.2 |
| 30 | .072 | 534 | 27.3 | .075 | 536 | 28.3 |
| 35 | .086 | 495 | 24.2 | .082 | 496 | 25.4 |
| 40 | .103 | 453 | 21.2 | .092 | 456 | 22.5 |
| 45 | .126 | 406 | 18.4 | .108 | 414 | 19.5 |
| 50 | .157 | 355 | 15.7 | .135 | 369 | 16.6 |
| 55 | .197 | 299 | 13.1 | .175 | 319 | 13.8 |
| 60 | .253 | 240 | 10.8 | .230 | 263 | 11.1 |
| 65 | .331 | 180 | 8.6 | .316 | 203 | 8.7 |
| 70 | .447 | 120 | 6.5 | .438 | 139 | 6.6 |
| 75 | .615 | 66 | 4.8 | .624 | 78 | 4.8 |
| 80 | .800 | 26 | 3.5 | .773 | 29 | 3.6 |
| 85 | 1.000 | 5 | 2.5 | 1.000 | 7 | 2.5 |
| 90 | | 0 | | | 0 | |

### Infant mortality estimated at 250 deaths per 1,000 live births

| Age | Males $_5q_x$ | Males $l_x$ | Males $e_x^0$ | Females $_5q_x$ | Females $l_x$ | Females $e_x^0$ |
|---|---|---|---|---|---|---|
| 0 | .415 | 1,000 | 29.6 | .380 | 1,000 | 31.0 |
| 5 | .040 | 585 | 44.6 | .046 | 620 | 44.1 |
| 10 | .025 | 562 | 41.4 | .027 | 592 | 41.2 |
| 15 | .040 | 548 | 37.4 | .050 | 576 | 37.2 |
| 20 | .050 | 526 | 33.8 | .063 | 547 | 34.1 |
| 25 | .061 | 499 | 30.5 | .070 | 512 | 31.2 |
| 30 | .072 | 469 | 27.3 | .075 | 476 | 28.3 |
| 35 | .086 | 435 | 24.2 | .082 | 441 | 25.4 |
| 40 | .103 | 398 | 21.2 | .092 | 405 | 22.5 |
| 45 | .126 | 357 | 18.4 | .108 | 367 | 19.5 |
| 50 | .157 | 312 | 15.7 | .135 | 328 | 16.6 |
| 55 | .197 | 263 | 13.1 | .175 | 283 | 13.8 |
| 60 | .253 | 211 | 10.8 | .230 | 234 | 11.1 |
| 65 | .331 | 158 | 8.6 | .316 | 180 | 8.7 |
| 70 | .447 | 106 | 6.5 | .438 | 123 | 6.6 |
| 75 | .615 | 58 | 4.8 | .624 | 69 | 4.8 |
| 80 | .800 | 22 | 3.5 | .773 | 26 | 3.6 |
| 85 | 1.000 | 4 | 2.5 | 1.000 | 6 | 2.5 |
| 90 | | 0 | | | 0 | |

obtained for the male population in India in 1951 and a stable age distribution for the female population; in fact, we get alternative distributions for each sex, one going with each assumed level of infant mortality. The simplest use one might make of these age distributions for each sex is to use them to distribute the reported number of males and the reported number of females in the 1951 census. However, an age distribution implies a certain number of births, and we find that the number of male births implied by the reported number of males in the 1951 census distributed according to our calculations exceeds the number of implied female births by some 12-15 per cent. The sex ratio at birth where data are complete and reliable rarely exceeds 105-106 males per 100 females anywhere in the world. In short, the reported figures in the Indian census are inconsistent with a plausible sex ratio at birth. We have met this anomalous situation by assuming that the sex ratio at birth in India is 105, and by increasing slightly the reported number of females and decreasing slightly the reported number of males in the 1951 census. If our adjustment is even approximately correct, the inference one can draw is that females in India were relatively underenumerated in the 1951 census. The status of women in the Indian culture gives at least a surface plausibility to this inference.

There is another hypothesis by which the apparent excess of males in the Indian population can be explained. There may be an especially high risk of mortality for young female children. It is asserted that ". . . there is a traditional fondness for male issues in most parts of the country and a corresponding dislike for female children. All the affection and care is bestowed on male children but female children are not much cared for. In the circumstances, it is to be expected that the slight advantage of female infants shown in a lower infant mortality rate shall soon wear itself out and that female mortality in the very young ages should be heavier than the male mortality."[11]

Thus there is a choice between explaining the recorded masculinity of the Indian population by assuming that the subordinate position of women caused their omission from the census, or by assuming that it caused their death in childhood. We have chosen the former explanation; the official census population data and life tables in effect accept the latter. Quite probably the truth lies somewhere in between; females are doubtless undercounted somewhat more than males, and their risks of death exceed the male in childhood somewhat more than our life table shows.

BIRTH RATES AND FERTILITY RATES FOR 1951

Our use of stable population theory yields a 1951 birth rate as well as giving a stable-age distribution (the 1951 age distribution) and age-specific mortality rates. The birth rate implied by the age distribution

---

[11] Census of India, Paper No. 2, 1954, *Life Tables—1951 Census*, p. 26.

when infant mortality is assumed to be 200 is 40.6, and when infant mortality is assumed to be 250 is 45.7. We must turn elsewhere, however, for estimation of the age-specific fertility rates in 1951 that gave rise to the estimated crude birth rates. Our procedure here was to make use of the results for Poona District (excluding Poona City) from a survey made by the Gokhale Institute,[12] and the age-specific fertility rates for 1950-1951 recorded in the Ramanagaram Health District. We first took the average of these two sets of age-specific fertility rates. We accepted this average as giving the pattern of age-specific fertility and adjusted the overall level so as to yield the number of births appropriate to our stable age distributions. In Table A-2 are shown three sets of fertility rates. The lowest are the fertility rates which yield the birth rate that goes with our low estimate of infant mortality, the intermediate set of rates are the average of those for Poona District and the Ramanagaram Health District; and the highest are the fertility rates adjusted to yield the birth rate associated with our high estimate of infant mortality. It is interesting and reassuring to note that the observed fertility rates for Poona and Ramanagaram, when applied to the age distribution that we have contrived for India in 1951, yield a birth rate intermediate between that associated with our low and our high estimate of infant mortality.

### TABLE A-2. LIVE BIRTHS PER 1,000 WOMEN IN INDIA BY FIVE-YEAR AGE GROUPS, AGES 15–44, 1951

| Age | Average Birth Rates in Ramanagaram and Rural Districts Near Poona | Rates Used with 1951 IMR of 200 | Rates Used with 1951 IMR of 250 |
|---|---|---|---|
| 15–19 | 193 | 178 | 201 |
| 20–24 | 270 | 250 | 282 |
| 25–29 | 252 | 233 | 263 |
| 30–34 | 190 | 175 | 198 |
| 35–39 | 140 | 130 | 146 |
| 40–44 | 54 | 50 | 56 |

### Indian Age Distribution and Birth and Death Rates, 1951

We shall recapitulate at this point the methods by which we estimated the 1951 age distribution and the 1951 birth and death rates for India. Our procedures depended heavily on the observed fact that the growth rates for the decades from 1921 to 1951 were very nearly constant and on the further fact that the age distribution for 1931, 1941, and 1951 were, when put on a comparable basis, nearly identical. These facts led

[12] Dandekar and Dandekar, *Survey of Fertility and Mortality in Poona District, 1953.*

us to infer that the age distribution was stable, in the Lotka sense, and consequently that the age distribution could be taken as the product of an essentially unchanging life table and a factor representing the essentially unchanging growth rate. We first used the reported age distribution and the average growth rate to estimate the general level of mortality above age 10. This estimate differed only slightly from the estimate obtained by Indian actuaries from a comparison of consecutive censuses. Next a life table was constructed for ages above 5 by assuming that the Indian life table would have a pattern of mortality by age which bore a typical relationship to the general level of mortality for ages above 10. We then assigned upper and lower limits to the 1951 infant mortality rate of 250 and 200 respectively, on the basis of a survey of all the evidence concerning infant mortality in India that we could assemble. A typical relationship between mortality under 5 and infant mortality was assumed. The life table thus derived, in conjunction with the average growth rate, provided a proportionate age distribution for each sex in India in 1951.

Thus the stable age distribution theory of Lotka was employed to give a corrected age distribution for 1951, and also used as an aid in estimating the age-specific mortality rates for 1951. The ordinate at age 0 in a stable age distribution is proportional to the birth rate, and our estimated birth rate for 1951 was so derived. The pattern of age-specific fertility for India in 1951 was estimated from birth data by age of mother in Ramanagaram Health District and from age-specific fertility rates based on a survey of the rural sections of Poona District. The crude birth and death rates that we finally obtained for 1951 depend, of course, on which of these two levels of infant mortality are assumed. When infant mortality is assumed to be 250 per thousand live births, the birth rate is 46 and the death rate is 33; when the infant mortality rate is assumed to 200, the birth rate is 41 and the death rate is 29.

SIZE OF THE 1951 POPULATION

The official data on the population of India in 1951 are somewhat ambiguous. The state of Jammu and Kashmir was not enumerated, nor were certain tribal areas in Assam. The population in 1951 of these two areas together was estimated at about 5 million (4.41 for Jammu and Kashmir, and .56 for the tribal areas of Assam).[13] Thus the census population is usually given as some 357 million for 1951—excluding the nonenumerated areas—while the official estimates of midyear populations supplied to the U.N. Population Division *include* these areas and imply a figure of about 362 million for 1951. As far as we can detect, the census figure of 357 has more often than not been employed in constructing national economic data such as national income. Since we

[13] Census of India, Paper No. 1, 1952, *Final Population Totals—1951 Census,* pp. ii-iii.

are primarily concerned with alternative patterns of population change, our basic analysis is little affected by whether a 1951 population of 357 or 362 million is used. The selection of 357 million as the point of departure of the projected populations was based on the belief that our projections would then be more consistent with the economic data we employed.

It is quite likely, in fact, that there was net underenumeration in 1951. In most population censuses there are undercounts of some groups and overcounts of others. The 1951 census in the United States, for example, involved a net undercount of some 1.4 per cent according to a special Post Enumeration Survey and of some 3 1/2 per cent according to an independent estimate.[14] A sample check of the 1951 enumeration in Indian households yielded an estimate that there was a net underenumeration slightly in excess of 1 per cent.[15] Our analysis of the age and sex distribution in 1951 indicates that there was a substantial undercount of children under 5 in the Indian census and also indicates—less persuasively—an undercount of females. A rough estimate of the two deficiencies in the census count is 20 to 25 million, indicating that if the deficiencies are the result of omissions, the total population should be given as some 380 million rather than the 357 million of the census.

To obtain a projection of the population of India including Jammu and Kashmir and the tribal areas of Assam, every population figure given in our projections should be multiplied by 1.014; and to make an adjustment for a very crudely estimated net undercount, the projected figures should be increased by 5 or 6 per cent.

ESTIMATED FERTILITY AND MORTALITY RATES, 1951-1986

Component projection five years at a time requires estimated age-specific survival and fertility rates for five-year age groups at five-year intervals. The remainder of the Appendix is a description of the technical details of how these rates were estimated. The considerations determining the direction and magnitude of estimated changes in vital rates were summarized in Chapter VI.

AGE-SPECIFIC SURVIVAL RATES, 1951-1986

To estimate the fractions surviving each five-year interval, life tables were constructed for the midpoints of the intervals—at 1953.5, 1958.5, . . . , 1983.5. Then the fraction surviving from birth to 0-4 years during a given interval was taken as $\dfrac{_5L_0}{5(l_0)}$ , from 0-4 to 5-9 as $\dfrac{_5L_5}{_5L_0}$ , etc.[16]

---

[14] A. J. Coale, "The Population of the United States in 1951 Classified by Age, Sex, and Color—A Revision of Census Figures," *Journal of the American Statistical Association*, Vol. 50, pp. 15-64, March 1955.

[15] Census of India, Paper No. 1 of 1953, "Sample Verification of the 1951 Census Count."

[16] This technique of computing survivors understates slightly the numbers (in

The life tables for these periods were constructed by the same mechanical steps employed in constructing the 1951 life table. These steps were:

1. To estimate $e^o{}_{10}$ and $_1q_0$ for each life-table date.
2. To select $_{15}q_x$'s for $x = 10, 25, 40$ and $55$ showing a typical age pattern of mortality, and consistent with the estimated $e^o{}_{10}$.
3. To estimate $_{15}q_{70}$ consistent with the improvement in mortality at other ages.
4. To estimate $_5q_5$ from $e^o{}_{10}$, and $_5q_0$ from $_1q_0$.
5. To construct a complete life table, including the interpolation of $l_x$ at five-year intervals for $x > 10$.

Each of these steps will be discussed in turn.

(1) The estimation of $e^o{}_{10}$ and $_1q_0$.

The increase in expectation of life at age 10 was estimated by combining two estimated rates of increase: (a) the estimated difference in $e^o{}_{10}$ between malarious and nonmalarious regions of Ceylon prior to the DDT campaign was added linearly over the ten years 1951-1961; and (b) the average annual increase in $e^o{}_{10}$ in eight low-income areas in recent years (with the exception of Taiwan, since 1920) was assumed to extend until 1971 at which time improvement was assumed to cease.

The raw material for estimating the increase in expectation of life at age 10 because of the malaria campaign is the differential in Ceylon in crude death rates and in infant mortality rates between malarious and nonmalarious districts. (Both differentials disappeared after DDT was introduced.)

This raw material is converted into an estimate of change in $e^o{}_{10}$ by the use of the following approximate and exact relations:

(1) $$CDR = DR(0\text{-}5)C(0\text{-}5) + DR(5+)C(5+)$$

(2) $$_5q_0 \cong 1.59 \, _1q_0$$

(3) $$DR(0\text{-}5) \cong \frac{_5q_0}{_5L_0}$$

---

a growing population) resulting from a given schedule of mortality risks. The principal source of understatement is the implicit assumption that the age distribution within each five-year age group is the same as the age distribution in the life table. In a growing population, the *actual* age distribution tapers more sharply than the life table. Throughout most of the life table the mortality rates at the later end of each five-year age interval are higher than at the beginning. Consequently, the mortality rates experienced by a five-year group distributed as in the life table will be somewhat higher than in the actual population. Hence the projection based on life-table survival rates will very slightly understate the number of survivors. A rough estimate indicates that older groups in 1986 may be understated by about 1 per cent on this account.

APPENDIX A

$$(4) \qquad {}_5L_0 \cong \frac{1}{4} l_0 + \frac{3}{4} l_1 + 2(l_1 + l_5)$$

$$(5) \qquad \triangle e^o{}_{10} \cong .721 + 691 \, \triangle \, DR(5+)$$

where $CDR$ is the crude death rate, $DR(0\text{-}5)$ and $DR(5+)$ are death rates under and over age 5; $C(0\text{-}5)$ and $C(5+)$ are the proportions of the population over and under age 5; ${}_nq_x$, ${}_nL_x$, and $l_x$ have the usual life-table meanings; and $\triangle$ means "change in."

From equations (1) through (4) the change in the death rate over age 5 can be derived as:

$$(6) \qquad \triangle DR(5+) =$$

$$\frac{\triangle CDR}{C(5+)} - \frac{C(0\text{-}5)}{C(5+)} \frac{.318 \, \triangle \, {}_1q_0}{\{1 - 1.19({}_1q_0 + {}_1q_0') + 1.42({}_1q_0 \cdot {}_1q_0')\}}$$

Then the change in expectation of life at age 10 can be estimated from (5). Equation (5) is a least squares regression line based on data from 16 countries where fertility is high, and with a pair of life tables showing a substantial change in $e^o{}_{10}$. In these countries, using the registered data for infant mortality and crude death rate, we estimated $\triangle DR(5+)$ by using equation (6), and then derived the least squares line expressed in (5). The correlation was .85.

Equation (6) was used to estimate the change in the death rate over age 5 that might be expected in India as a result of the antimalarial program. From equation (6) and Ceylonese data, it appeared that the difference in $DR(5+)$ between malarious and nonmalarious regions prior to spraying was about 6.8 deaths per thousand persons. Since about 5/9 of the Indian population lived in malarious districts, the drop in the all-India death rate above age 5 is estimated as (5/9) (6.8) or about 3.8 deaths per thousand persons. From equation (5), this change is estimated to be equivalent to about 3 1/3 additional years of life expectancy at age 10. Since the malarial program will almost certainly be complete by 1961, it was estimated that for each of the first ten years after 1951 the program would add 1/3 of a year to $e^o{}_{10}$ for each sex.

The next problem was to assess the probable rate of increase in the expectation of life at age 10 due to other factors than the anti-malarial campaign. A set of countries was selected, each having a life table at the beginning and at the end of an interval during which substantial public-health programs were applied. All of these countries were characterized by low incomes and, during the interval spanned by the pair of life tables, none of them benefited from a large-scale modern anti-malarial campaign.[17] The average annual increase in the expectation of

[17] The countries and intervals were: Portugal, 1941-1951; British Guiana, 1921-1946; Chile, 1920-1940; Costa Rica, 1927-1950; Jamaica, 1921-1946; Trinidad and Tobago, 1921-1946; Ceylon, 1921-1946; and Taiwan, 1906-1938.

life at age 10 was separately determined for males and females. For males the figure was .377 years per annum added to the expectation of life at age 10, and for females the corresponding figure was .395. These average annual improvements in expectation of life at age 10 were applied to the Indian expectation of life at age 10 starting in 1951 and continuing through 1971. The result when combined with the anti-malarial campaign was an expectation of life at age 10 of 48.46 for males and 48.36 for females in 1961, and of 52.23 and 52.31 respectively for males and females in 1971. The improvement in the expectation of life at age 10 was assumed to cease in 1971. This assumption is based on an impression that once the relatively easy public health measures have been exploited, further improvements in mortality will be more difficult to gain.

Next, we must give an account of the way infant mortality was projected. We first thought that infant mortality would be handled in a way precisely parallel to the projection of the expectation of life at age 10. In other words, we thought we would estimate the improvement in infant mortality which could be expected on the basis of Ceylonese experience with malaria control, and that we would further assume that infant mortality would decline at a rate characteristic of other low-income areas' experience. A change in infant mortality was assumed to occur among 5/9 of the Indian population equal to the difference in infant mortality between malarious and nonmalarious regions of Ceylon (about 80 deaths per 1,000 live births). However, the infant mortality rate which this technique yielded for 1971 seemed to be too high for an assumption that further improvements could not occur. We therefore decided that we would select an infant mortality rate that seemed to be attainable by 1981 on the basis of experience in low-mortality regions of India and of low-income areas outside India. This rate was a little under 90 per 1,000 births. It is about equal to the rate attained in Ceylon by 1948 and is approximately the same as the rate in 1951 in Bangalore City. The figures assumed for 1981 were 95 for males and 80 for females. The linear improvement was calculated that would carry the infant mortality rate from the estimated level in 1951 down to the levels just cited for 1981, when allowance is made for the additional improvement during the first ten years due to the anti-malarial campaign, affecting 5/9 of the population. When the 1951 infant mortality is estimated as 200, the projected decline carries it down to about 133 by 1961, about 110 by 1971, and about 88 by 1981. When the initial estimate of the infant mortality is 250, the decline is (as projected) somewhat more rapid, bringing the rate down again to 88 by 1981.

(2) The selection of $_{15}q_{10}$, $_{15}q_{25}$, $_{15}q_{40}$, and $_{15}q_{55}$.

These values were estimated from the "intermediate regression lines" of $_{15}q_x$ on $e^o_{10}$ in such a way as to yield the value of $e^o_{10}$ expected for 1961 and 1971. (No further change in $e^o_{10}$ is assumed after 1971.) The process of estimation was just the same as that used in making the 1951 life tables.

(3) The estimation of $_{15}q_{70}$.

It was assumed that the proportionate improvement in the probability of surviving from age 70 to age 85 will be the same as the proportionate improvement in $_{15}p_{55}$.

(4) The estimation of $_5q_5$ and $_5q_0$.

$_5q_5$ in 1961 and 1971 was estimated from the regression of $_5q_5$ on $e^0{}_{10}$. $_5q_0$ for 1961, 1971, and 1981 were estimated as equal to 1.59 $(_1q_0)$.

(5) The construction of complete life tables.

In 1961 and 1971 $l_x$ values at five-year intervals were calculated by fitting a fifth-degree parabola to points at ages 10, 25, 40, 55, 70, and 85, which were computed from the estimated $_{15}q_x$'s. Since $_5q_0$ and $_5q_5$ were already calculated, life-table values from birth to age 85 were readily constructed. $l_{90}$ was assumed to be zero, to avoid cumbersome formulae for "closing out" the life tables. The combination of $_5q_0$ for 1981 with the assumed unchanged mortality rates of 1971 above age 5 provides a life table for 1981.

The life tables for 1953.5, 1958.5, 1963.5 etc., were obtained from values of $q_x$ linearly interpolated from the tables of 1951, 1961, and 1971.

Since there are two separate courses of infant and child mortality, one with each estimated 1951 level, there are two sets of life tables converging on the same values in 1981. The life tables for 1961, 1971, and 1981 are shown in Tables A-3 and A-4.

ESTIMATED FERTILITY RATES, 1951-1986

It was assumed that fertility rates remained constant from 1951 to 1956. After 1956 the three courses described in Chapter VI were computed—unchanged fertility, 1956-1986; a linear decline by 50 per cent, 1956-1981, and constant thereafter; constant to 1966, a linear decline by 50 per cent, 1966-1981, and constant thereafter. In every instance any change in fertility rates was assumed to apply in equal proportion at all maternal ages. Any actual decline in fertility will of course *not* have this characteristic. However, more realistic-appearing assumptions about postponed marriages, especially sharp declines at the older ages, etc., would be important (in this context) only for their effect on births. Proportional fertility reductions have the virtue of simplicity, and produce just as plausible a time path of *births* as would other, more complicated, assumptions involving changing age patterns as well as changing levels of fertility.

Tables A-5 through A-10 and Chart A-3 show the projections resulting from an assumed level of infant mortality of 250 and of 200 in 1951. Since the high estimate of infant mortality connotes a high estimate of fertility, the projections associated with this estimate have a more rapid growth rate.

# TABLE A-3. ABRIDGED LIFE TABLES FOR INDIA, 1961, 1971 AND 1981

(Infant mortality in 1951 estimated at 200 deaths per 1,000 live births)

| Age | 1961 | | | 1971 | | | 1981 | | |
|---|---|---|---|---|---|---|---|---|---|
| | $_5q_x$ | $l_x$ | $e_x^0$ | $_5q_x$ | $l_x$ | $e_x^0$ | $_5q_x$ | $l_x$ | $e_x^0$ |
| **Males** | | | | | | | | | |
| 0 | .226 | 1,000 | 44.2 | .189 | 1,000 | 49.3 | .151 | 1,000 | 51.5 |
| 5 | .034 | 774 | 51.7 | .032 | 811 | 55.4 | .032 | 849 | 55.4 |
| 10 | .017 | 748 | 48.4 | .013 | 785 | 52.2 | .013 | 822 | 52.2 |
| 15 | .028 | 735 | 44.2 | .023 | 775 | 47.9 | .023 | 811 | 47.9 |
| 20 | .035 | 714 | 40.4 | .028 | 757 | 43.9 | .028 | 792 | 43.9 |
| 25 | .039 | 689 | 36.8 | .030 | 736 | 40.1 | .030 | 770 | 40.1 |
| 30 | .044 | 662 | 33.2 | .031 | 714 | 36.2 | .031 | 747 | 36.3 |
| 35 | .050 | 633 | 29.6 | .035 | 692 | 32.4 | .035 | 724 | 32.4 |
| 40 | .060 | 602 | 26.0 | .042 | 667 | 28.4 | .042 | 699 | 28.4 |
| 45 | .077 | 566 | 22.5 | .055 | 639 | 24.6 | .055 | 669 | 24.6 |
| 50 | .099 | 522 | 19.2 | .075 | 604 | 20.9 | .075 | 632 | 20.9 |
| 55 | .132 | 470 | 16.0 | .104 | 559 | 17.3 | .104 | 585 | 17.3 |
| 60 | .176 | 408 | 13.1 | .146 | 501 | 14.1 | .146 | 524 | 14.1 |
| 65 | .242 | 336 | 10.3 | .206 | 428 | 11.0 | .206 | 448 | 11.0 |
| 70 | .336 | 255 | 7.8 | .296 | 340 | 8.3 | .296 | 356 | 8.3 |
| 75 | .489 | 169 | 5.5 | .454 | 239 | 5.7 | .454 | 250 | 5.7 |
| 80 | .828 | 86 | 3.4 | .831 | 130 | 3.3 | .831 | 137 | 3.3 |
| 85 | | 15 | 2.5 | | 22 | 2.5 | | 23 | 2.5 |
| **Females** | | | | | | | | | |
| 0 | .197 | 1,000 | 45.7 | .162 | 1,000 | 51.0 | .127 | 1,000 | 53.1 |
| 5 | .036 | 803 | 51.6 | .031 | 838 | 55.7 | .031 | 873 | 55.7 |
| 10 | .014 | 774 | 48.4 | .009 | 812 | 52.4 | .009 | 846 | 52.4 |
| 15 | .032 | 763 | 44.1 | .024 | 805 | 47.8 | .024 | 838 | 47.8 |
| 20 | .043 | 739 | 40.4 | .033 | 785 | 43.9 | .033 | 818 | 43.9 |
| 25 | .047 | 707 | 37.1 | .036 | 760 | 40.4 | .036 | 791 | 40.4 |
| 30 | .049 | 674 | 33.9 | .037 | 732 | 36.8 | .037 | 763 | 36.8 |
| 35 | .051 | 641 | 30.5 | .038 | 705 | 33.1 | .038 | 734 | 33.1 |
| 40 | .057 | 608 | 27.0 | .042 | 678 | 29.3 | .042 | 707 | 29.3 |
| 45 | .068 | 574 | 23.5 | .051 | 650 | 25.5 | .051 | 677 | 25.5 |
| 50 | .088 | 534 | 20.0 | .067 | 617 | 21.7 | .067 | 642 | 21.7 |
| 55 | .118 | 487 | 16.7 | .092 | 575 | 18.1 | .092 | 599 | 18.1 |
| 60 | .160 | 430 | 13.6 | .129 | 522 | 14.7 | .129 | 544 | 14.7 |
| 65 | .223 | 361 | 10.7 | .188 | 455 | 11.5 | .188 | 474 | 11.5 |
| 70 | .318 | 281 | 8.0 | .275 | 370 | 8.5 | .275 | 385 | 8.5 |
| 75 | .474 | 191 | 5.6 | .433 | 268 | 5.8 | .433 | 279 | 5.8 |
| 80 | .823 | 101 | 3.4 | .829 | 152 | 3.4 | .829 | 158 | 3.4 |
| 85 | | 18 | 2.5 | | 26 | 2.5 | | 27 | 2.5 |

## TABLE A-4. ABRIDGED LIFE TABLES FOR INDIA, 1961, 1971 AND 1981
(Infant mortality in 1951 estimated at 250 deaths per 1,000 live births)

| Age | 1961 | | | 1971 | | | 1981 | | |
|---|---|---|---|---|---|---|---|---|---|
| | $_5q_x$ | $l_x$ | $e_x^0$ | $_5q_x$ | $l_x$ | $e_x^0$ | $_5q_x$ | $l_x$ | $e_x^0$ |
| **Males** | | | | | | | | | |
| 0 | .281 | 1,000 | 41.1 | .216 | 1,000 | 47.7 | .151 | 1,000 | 51.5 |
| 5 | .034 | 719 | 51.7 | .032 | 784 | 55.4 | .032 | 849 | 55.4 |
| 10 | .017 | 695 | 48.4 | .013 | 759 | 52.2 | .013 | 822 | 52.2 |
| 15 | .028 | 683 | 44.2 | .023 | 749 | 47.9 | .023 | 811 | 47.9 |
| 20 | .035 | 664 | 40.4 | .028 | 732 | 43.9 | .028 | 792 | 43.9 |
| 25 | .039 | 640 | 36.8 | .030 | 711 | 40.1 | .030 | 770 | 40.1 |
| 30 | .044 | 615 | 33.2 | .031 | 690 | 36.3 | .031 | 747 | 36.3 |
| 35 | .050 | 588 | 29.6 | .035 | 669 | 32.4 | .035 | 724 | 32.4 |
| 40 | .060 | 559 | 26.0 | .042 | 645 | 28.4 | .042 | 699 | 28.4 |
| 45 | .077 | 525 | 22.5 | .055 | 618 | 24.6 | .055 | 669 | 24.6 |
| 50 | .099 | 485 | 19.2 | .075 | 584 | 20.9 | .075 | 632 | 20.9 |
| 55 | .132 | 437 | 16.0 | .104 | 540 | 17.3 | .104 | 585 | 17.3 |
| 60 | .176 | 379 | 13.1 | .146 | 484 | 14.1 | .146 | 524 | 14.1 |
| 65 | .242 | 312 | 10.3 | .206 | 413 | 11.0 | .206 | 448 | 11.0 |
| 70 | .336 | 237 | 7.8 | .296 | 328 | 8.3 | .296 | 356 | 8.3 |
| 75 | .489 | 157 | 5.5 | .454 | 231 | 5.7 | .454 | 250 | 5.7 |
| 80 | .828 | 80 | 3.4 | .831 | 126 | 3.3 | .831 | 137 | 3.3 |
| 85 | | 14 | 2.5 | | 21 | 2.5 | | 23 | 2.5 |
| **Females** | | | | | | | | | |
| 0 | .249 | 1,000 | 42.8 | .188 | 1,000 | 49.5 | .127 | 1,000 | 53.1 |
| 5 | .036 | 751 | 51.6 | .031 | 812 | 55.7 | .031 | 873 | 55.7 |
| 10 | .014 | 724 | 48.4 | .009 | 787 | 52.4 | .009 | 846 | 52.4 |
| 15 | .032 | 714 | 44.1 | .024 | 780 | 47.8 | .024 | 838 | 47.8 |
| 20 | .043 | 691 | 40.4 | .033 | 761 | 43.9 | .033 | 818 | 43.9 |
| 25 | .047 | 661 | 37.1 | .036 | 736 | 40.4 | .036 | 791 | 40.4 |
| 30 | .049 | 630 | 33.9 | .037 | 709 | 36.8 | .037 | 763 | 36.8 |
| 35 | .051 | 599 | 30.5 | .038 | 683 | 33.1 | .038 | 734 | 33.1 |
| 40 | .057 | 569 | 27.0 | .042 | 657 | 29.3 | .042 | 707 | 29.3 |
| 45 | .068 | 536 | 23.5 | .051 | 630 | 25.5 | .051 | 677 | 25.5 |
| 50 | .088 | 500 | 20.0 | .067 | 598 | 21.7 | .067 | 642 | 21.7 |
| 55 | .118 | 456 | 16.7 | .092 | 558 | 18.1 | .092 | 599 | 18.1 |
| 60 | .160 | 402 | 13.6 | .129 | 506 | 14.7 | .129 | 544 | 14.7 |
| 65 | .223 | 338 | 10.7 | .188 | 441 | 11.5 | .188 | 474 | 11.5 |
| 70 | .318 | 262 | 8.0 | .275 | 358 | 8.5 | .275 | 385 | 8.5 |
| 75 | .474 | 179 | 5.6 | .433 | 260 | 5.8 | .433 | 279 | 5.8 |
| 80 | .823 | 94 | 3.4 | .829 | 147 | 3.4 | .829 | 158 | 3.4 |
| 85 | | 17 | 2.5 | | 25 | 2.5 | | 27 | 2.5 |

TABLE A-5. ESTIMATED POPULATION OF INDIA, 1951 AND 1956 AND
PROJECTED POPULATION, 1961–1986, BY SEX AND
FIVE-YEAR AGE GROUPS
(millions)
(Fertility assumed constant. Infant mortality in 1951 estimated at 200 deaths
per 1,000 live births)

| Age | 1951 | 1956 | 1961 | 1966 | 1971 | 1976 | 1981 | 1986 |
|---|---|---|---|---|---|---|---|---|
| Males | | | | | | | | |
| 0–4 | 27.0 | 29.6 | 33.5 | 37.5 | 41.7 | 47.1 | 53.7 | 60.9 |
| 5–9 | 22.1 | 23.8 | 26.8 | 30.7 | 34.7 | 38.9 | 44.2 | 50.5 |
| 10–14 | 20.1 | 21.4 | 23.2 | 26.1 | 30.0 | 33.9 | 38.0 | 43.2 |
| 15–19 | 18.3 | 19.5 | 20.9 | 22.7 | 25.6 | 29.5 | 33.3 | 37.3 |
| 20–24 | 16.5 | 17.6 | 18.8 | 20.3 | 22.1 | 25.0 | 28.7 | 32.5 |
| 25–29 | 14.6 | 15.6 | 16.8 | 18.2 | 19.6 | 21.4 | 24.2 | 27.9 |
| 30–34 | 12.8 | 13.7 | 14.9 | 16.2 | 17.6 | 19.0 | 20.8 | 23.5 |
| 35–39 | 11.1 | 11.9 | 13.0 | 14.2 | 15.6 | 17.0 | 18.4 | 20.1 |
| 40–44 | 9.49 | 10.2 | 11.2 | 12.3 | 13.6 | 15.0 | 16.3 | 17.7 |
| 45–49 | 7.91 | 8.52 | 9.39 | 10.5 | 11.7 | 13.0 | 14.3 | 15.6 |
| 50–54 | 6.40 | 6.91 | 7.66 | 8.61 | 9.72 | 10.9 | 12.1 | 13.3 |
| 55–59 | 4.96 | 5.38 | 6.01 | 6.83 | 7.79 | 8.86 | 9.95 | 11.1 |
| 60–64 | 3.64 | 3.95 | 4.46 | 5.14 | 5.93 | 6.83 | 7.76 | 8.72 |
| 65–69 | 2.44 | 2.67 | 3.06 | 3.58 | 4.20 | 4.90 | 5.64 | 6.41 |
| 70–74 | 1.43 | 1.58 | 1.85 | 2.22 | 2.67 | 3.17 | 3.70 | 4.26 |
| 75–79 | .664 | .744 | .907 | 1.13 | 1.40 | 1.70 | 2.03 | 2.36 |
| 80–84 | .208 | .233 | .284 | .363 | .463 | .577 | .703 | .836 |
| 85+ | .033 | .034 | .035 | .041 | .053 | .067 | .083 | .102 |
| Total | 180. | 193. | 213. | 237. | 264. | 297. | 334. | 376. |
| Females | | | | | | | | |
| 0–5 | 26.6 | 29.0 | 32.7 | 36.6 | 40.7 | 45.8 | 52.2 | 59.2 |
| 5–9 | 22.0 | 23.7 | 26.6 | 30.4 | 34.2 | 38.3 | 43.4 | 49.5 |
| 10–14 | 19.9 | 21.2 | 23.0 | 25.9 | 29.7 | 33.5 | 37.5 | 42.5 |
| 15–19 | 18.0 | 19.2 | 20.7 | 22.5 | 25.4 | 29.3 | 33.0 | 36.9 |
| 20–24 | 16.0 | 17.1 | 18.4 | 20.0 | 21.8 | 24.7 | 28.4 | 32.1 |
| 25–29 | 14.1 | 15.0 | 16.2 | 17.7 | 19.2 | 21.1 | 23.9 | 27.4 |
| 30–34 | 12.3 | 13.1 | 14.2 | 15.5 | 17.0 | 18.5 | 20.3 | 23.0 |
| 35–39 | 10.6 | 11.4 | 12.4 | 13.6 | 14.9 | 16.3 | 17.8 | 19.6 |
| 40–44 | 9.15 | 9.81 | 10.7 | 11.8 | 13.0 | 14.3 | 15.7 | 17.1 |
| 45–49 | 7.75 | 8.32 | 9.11 | 10.1 | 11.2 | 12.4 | 13.6 | 15.0 |
| 50–54 | 6.41 | 6.90 | 7.58 | 8.44 | 9.43 | 10.5 | 11.6 | 12.8 |
| 55–59 | 5.10 | 5.51 | 6.10 | 6.85 | 7.73 | 8.69 | 9.68 | 10.7 |
| 60–64 | 3.84 | 4.16 | 4.66 | 5.30 | 6.05 | 6.88 | 7.73 | 8.62 |
| 65–69 | 2.65 | 2.89 | 3.29 | 3.82 | 4.43 | 5.11 | 5.80 | 6.52 |
| 70–74 | 1.58 | 1.75 | 2.05 | 2.46 | 2.92 | 3.42 | 3.95 | 4.49 |
| 75–79 | .736 | .831 | 1.03 | 1.29 | 1.59 | 1.92 | 2.25 | 2.60 |
| 80–84 | .232 | .261 | .325 | .421 | .541 | .675 | .814 | .955 |
| 85+ | .040 | .041 | .042 | .049 | .062 | .079 | .098 | .119 |
| Total | 177. | 190. | 209. | 233. | 260. | 292. | 328. | 369. |
| Grand Total Both Sexes | 357. | 384. | 422. | 469. | 524. | 588. | 662. | 745. |

## TABLE A-6. PROJECTED POPULATION OF INDIA, 1971–1986 BY SEX AND FIVE-YEAR AGE GROUPS
(millions)

(Fertility assumed to decline linearly by 50 per cent, 1966–1981. Infant mortality in 1951 estimated at 200 deaths per 1,000 live births. Figures omitted are identical with those shown in Table A-5)

| Age | 1971 | 1976 | 1981 | 1986 |
|---|---|---|---|---|
| Males | | | | |
| 0–4 | 38.1 | 35.1 | 31.0 | 30.1 |
| 5–9 | | 35.5 | 32.9 | 29.2 |
| 10–14 | | | 34.7 | 32.2 |
| 15–19 | | | | 34.1 |
| Total | 261. | 281. | 297. | 310. |
| Females | | | | |
| 0–5 | 37.1 | 34.2 | 30.2 | 29.3 |
| 5–9 | | 35.0 | 32.3 | 28.7 |
| 10–14 | | | 34.2 | 31.7 |
| 15–19 | | | | 33.7 |
| Total | 256. | 276. | 291. | 304. |
| Grand Total, Both Sexes | 517. | 558. | 588. | 614. |

APPENDIX A

## TABLE A-7. PROJECTED POPULATION OF INDIA, 1961–1986 BY SEX AND FIVE-YEAR AGE GROUPS

(millions)

(Fertility assumed to decline linearly by 50 per cent, 1956–1981. Infant mortality in 1951 estimated at 200 deaths per 1,000 live births. Figures omitted are identical with those shown in Table A-5)

| Age | 1961 | 1966 | 1971 | 1976 | 1981 | 1986 |
|---|---|---|---|---|---|---|
| Males | | | | | | |
| 0–4 | 31.7 | 31.8 | 31.2 | 30.3 | 28.5 | 27.9 |
| 5–9 | | 29.1 | 29.4 | 29.1 | 28.4 | 26.8 |
| 10–14 | | | 28.5 | 28.8 | 28.4 | 27.8 |
| 15–19 | | | | 28.0 | 28.2 | 27.9 |
| 20–24 | | | | | 27.2 | 27.5 |
| 25–29 | | | | | | 26.5 |
| Total | 211. | 229. | 247. | 264. | 277. | 288. |
| Females | | | | | | |
| 0–4 | 31.0 | 31.0 | 30.4 | 29.5 | 27.7 | 27.1 |
| 5–9 | | 28.8 | 29.0 | 28.6 | 27.9 | 26.3 |
| 10–14 | | | 28.2 | 28.4 | 28.0 | 27.3 |
| 15–19 | | | | 27.7 | 28.0 | 27.6 |
| 20–24 | | | | | 26.9 | 27.2 |
| 25–29 | | | | | | 26.0 |
| Total | 207. | 225. | 243. | 259. | 272. | 283. |
| Grand Total Both Sexes | 418. | 455. | 490. | 522. | 549. | 571. |

363

TABLE A-8. ESTIMATED POPULATION OF INDIA, 1951 AND 1956, AND
PROJECTED POPULATION, 1961–1986, BY SEX AND
FIVE-YEAR AGE GROUPS

(millions)

(Fertility assumed constant. Infant mortality in 1951 estimated at 250 deaths
per 1,000 live births)

| Age | 1951 | 1956 | 1961 | 1966 | 1971 | 1976 | 1981 | 1986 |
|---|---|---|---|---|---|---|---|---|
| Males | | | | | | | | |
| 0–4 | 28.0 | 30.9 | 35.5 | 40.4 | 45.7 | 52.7 | 61.7 | 71.7 |
| 5–9 | 21.8 | 23.7 | 27.2 | 32.0 | 36.9 | 42.3 | 49.4 | 58.1 |
| 10–14 | 19.9 | 21.2 | 23.0 | 26.5 | 31.2 | 36.1 | 41.4 | 48.2 |
| 15–19 | 18.1 | 19.3 | 20.6 | 22.5 | 26.0 | 30.7 | 35.4 | 40.6 |
| 20–24 | 16.3 | 17.3 | 18.6 | 20.0 | 21.9 | 25.3 | 29.9 | 34.5 |
| 25–29 | 14.5 | 15.4 | 16.6 | 18.0 | 19.4 | 21.3 | 24.6 | 29.0 |
| 30–34 | 12.7 | 13.6 | 14.7 | 16.0 | 17.4 | 18.8 | 20.7 | 23.8 |
| 35–39 | 11.0 | 11.8 | 12.8 | 14.1 | 15.4 | 16.8 | 18.2 | 20.0 |
| 40–44 | 9.38 | 10.1 | 11.0 | 12.2 | 13.5 | 14.8 | 16.1 | 17.5 |
| 45–49 | 7.82 | 8.42 | 9.28 | 10.3 | 11.5 | 12.8 | 14.1 | 15.4 |
| 50–54 | 6.32 | 6.82 | 7.57 | 8.52 | 9.60 | 10.8 | 12.0 | 13.2 |
| 55–59 | 4.91 | 5.31 | 5.94 | 6.75 | 7.70 | 8.75 | 9.83 | 10.9 |
| 60–64 | 3.59 | 3.90 | 4.41 | 5.08 | 5.86 | 6.75 | 7.67 | 8.61 |
| 65–69 | 2.41 | 2.63 | 3.02 | 3.54 | 4.15 | 4.84 | 5.58 | 6.34 |
| 70–74 | 1.41 | 1.56 | 1.83 | 2.19 | 2.64 | 3.13 | 3.65 | 4.21 |
| 75–79 | .655 | .734 | .896 | 1.12 | 1.38 | 1.68 | 2.00 | 2.33 |
| 80–84 | .206 | .230 | .281 | .359 | .458 | .570 | .696 | .826 |
| 85+ | .033 | .033 | .035 | .041 | .052 | .066 | .083 | .101 |
| Total | 179. | 193. | 213. | 240. | 271. | 308. | 353. | 405. |
| Females | | | | | | | | |
| 0–4 | 27.6 | 30.5 | 34.9 | 39.6 | 44.7 | 51.4 | 60.0 | 69.7 |
| 5–9 | 22.0 | 23.8 | 27.2 | 31.8 | 36.6 | 41.8 | 48.6 | 57.0 |
| 10–14 | 19.9 | 21.2 | 23.2 | 26.5 | 31.1 | 35.8 | 40.9 | 47.6 |
| 15–19 | 18.0 | 19.2 | 20.7 | 22.7 | 26.1 | 30.6 | 35.2 | 40.3 |
| 20–24 | 16.0 | 17.1 | 18.4 | 19.9 | 22.0 | 25.3 | 29.7 | 34.2 |
| 25–29 | 14.1 | 15.0 | 16.2 | 17.6 | 19.2 | 21.2 | 24.4 | 28.7 |
| 30–34 | 12.3 | 13.1 | 14.2 | 15.5 | 16.9 | 18.5 | 20.4 | 23.5 |
| 35–39 | 10.6 | 11.4 | 12.4 | 13.5 | 14.9 | 16.3 | 17.8 | 19.7 |
| 40–44 | 9.14 | 9.80 | 10.7 | 11.7 | 13.0 | 14.3 | 15.7 | 17.1 |
| 45–49 | 7.74 | 8.31 | 9.10 | 10.1 | 11.2 | 12.3 | 13.6 | 14.9 |
| 50–54 | 6.40 | 6.89 | 7.58 | 8.43 | 9.42 | 10.5 | 11.6 | 12.8 |
| 55–59 | 5.10 | 5.50 | 6.10 | 6.84 | 7.72 | 8.68 | 9.67 | 10.7 |
| 60–64 | 3.84 | 4.16 | 4.66 | 5.30 | 6.05 | 6.87 | 7.73 | 8.61 |
| 65–69 | 2.65 | 2.89 | 3.29 | 3.82 | 4.42 | 5.10 | 5.80 | 6.52 |
| 70–74 | 1.58 | 1.75 | 2.05 | 2.45 | 2.91 | 3.42 | 3.94 | 4.48 |
| 75–79 | .736 | .831 | 1.02 | 1.29 | 1.59 | 1.92 | 2.25 | 2.60 |
| 80–84 | .232 | .262 | .325 | .420 | .541 | .674 | .813 | .955 |
| 85+ | .040 | .041 | .042 | .048 | .062 | .079 | .098 | .119 |
| Total | 178. | 192. | 212. | 238. | 268. | 305. | 348. | 400. |
| Grand Total Both Sexes | 357. | 385. | 425. | 477. | 539. | 613. | 701. | 805. |

## TABLE A-9. PROJECTED POPULATION OF INDIA, 1971–1986 BY SEX AND FIVE-YEAR AGE GROUPS

(millions)

(Fertility assumed to decline linearly by 50 per cent, 1966–1981. Infant mortality in 1951 estimated at 250 deaths per 1,000 live births. Figures omitted are identical with those shown in Table A-8)

| Age | 1971 | 1976 | 1981 | 1986 |
|---|---|---|---|---|
| **Males** | | | | |
| 0–4 | 41.7 | 39.3 | 35.7 | 35.5 |
| 5–9 | | 38.6 | 36.8 | 33.6 |
| 10–14 | | | 37.7 | 35.9 |
| 15–19 | | | | 37.1 |
| Total | 267. | 291. | 311. | 329. |
| **Females** | | | | |
| 0–4 | 40.8 | 38.3 | 34.7 | 34.5 |
| 5–9 | | 38.1 | 36.2 | 32.9 |
| 10–14 | | | 37.4 | 35.4 |
| 15–19 | | | | 36.7 |
| Total | 264. | 288. | 307. | 325. |
| Grand Total, Both Sexes | 531. | 579. | 618. | 653. |

APPENDIX A

## TABLE A-10. PROJECTED POPULATION OF INDIA, 1961–1986
### BY SEX AND FIVE-YEAR AGE GROUPS
(millions)

(Fertility assumed to decline linearly by 50 per cent, 1956–1981. Infant mortality in 1951 estimated at 250 deaths per 1,000 live births. Figures omitted are identical with those shown in Table A-8)

| Age | 1961 | 1966 | 1971 | 1976 | 1981 | 1986 |
|---|---|---|---|---|---|---|
| Males | | | | | | |
| 0–4 | 33.7 | 34.2 | 34.2 | 33.9 | 32.7 | 32.8 |
| 5–9 | | 30.3 | 31.3 | 31.6 | 31.7 | 30.8 |
| 10–14 | | | 29.6 | 30.6 | 30.9 | 31.0 |
| 15–19 | | | | 29.1 | 30.0 | 30.4 |
| 20–24 | | | | | 28.3 | 29.3 |
| 25–29 | | | | | | 27.5 |
| Total | 212. | 232. | 252. | 272. | 289. | 305. |
| Females | | | | | | |
| 0–4 | 33.1 | 33.5 | 33.4 | 33.0 | 31.8 | 31.9 |
| 5–9 | | 30.2 | 31.0 | 31.2 | 31.2 | 30.2 |
| 10–14 | | | 29.5 | 30.4 | 30.6 | 30.6 |
| 15–19 | | | | 29.0 | 29.9 | 30.1 |
| 20–24 | | | | | 28.2 | 29.0 |
| 25–29 | | | | | | 27.2 |
| Total | 210. | 230. | 250. | 269. | 286. | 301. |
| Grand Total Both Sexes | 422. | 462. | 502. | 541. | 574. | 606. |

366

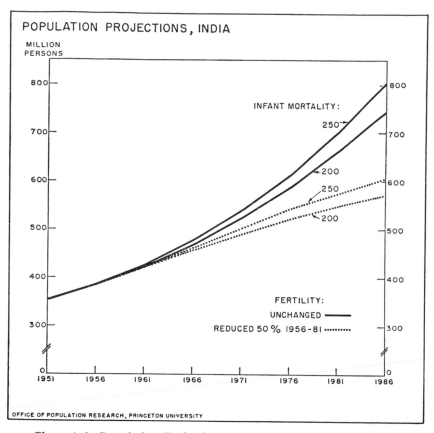

Chart A-3. Population Projections Assuming Various Changes in Fertility and Infant Mortality, India, 1951-1986.

# APPENDIX B

## METHODS EMPLOYED IN ADJUSTING MEXICAN POPULATION DATA IN PREPARING PROJECTIONS OF THE MEXICAN POPULATION, 1955–1985

THE basic method used in projecting the Mexican population was the same used for India—component projection. The ingredients required for making such a projection were the same: a base population for a recent year given by sex and five-year age groups; current mortality rates by age and sex; current fertility rates by age of mother; and projected mortality and fertility rates. However, the techniques employed in assembling these necessary ingredients were considerably less elaborate than those used for India.

The methods used were simpler because of the greater completeness of Mexican population data, particularly vital statistics; because an especially useful set of model life tables was published by the United Nations since the Indian projections were completed; and because of a recognition that some of the refined adjustments applied to Indian population data were unnecessary in that they made little difference to the economic analysis.

The principal steps prior to the purely mechanical process of the component projection itself were three (1) adjusting the Mexican census of 1950 to obtain data from which a 1955 base population by sex and five-year age groups could be estimated; (2) constructing life tables for estimating survivors during the interval covered by the projection; (3) estimating age-specific fertility rates. These steps will be discussed in order.

### ADJUSTING THE MEXICAN CENSUS OF 1950

Although a cursory examination is enough to show that the Mexican census of 1950 does not provide an accurate distribution of the population by age and sex, it was decided that only two adjustments would be made. The first was an adjustment to compensate for the patent underenumeration of children under 5 years of age. The second was to adjust for the apparent underenumeration of males between the ages of 10 and 35. Underenumeration of these groups is very common and appears to be sufficiently pronounced in the Mexican census to warrant adjustment.

The number of children under 5 in 1950 was estimated by applying a life table survival rate to the number of births recorded between June

30, 1945 and June 30, 1950.[1] The number of children estimated from the birth registration figures exceeded the number recorded as under 5 in the census by 14 per cent. The deficient enumeration of males between the ages of 15 and 34 is indicated by the following ratios of males to females in each age group:

| Age | Males enumerated per female |
|-----|------------------------------|
| 10-14 | 1.06 |
| 15-19 | .91 |
| 20-24 | .87 |
| 25-29 | .94 |
| 30-34 | .93 |

For the age group 5-9, the census ratio of the sexes is 1.04 and for 35-39 the ratio is .94. The number of males at age 10-14 relative to the number of females is a little higher than is plausible, and for ages 15 through 34 the ratio of males to females is too low to be accepted as valid. A simple adjustment was made. It was assumed that the number of females in the age groups between 10 and 35 was correctly enumerated and that the ratio of males to females in these age groups proceeded in the following linear fashion: 1.04 for age group 10-14, and 1.02, 1.00, .98 and .96 for successive five-year age groups. The net effect of this adjustment was to increase the male population between the ages of 10 and 34 by some 6 per cent. The two adjustments together added about 3 1/2 per cent to the enumerated population in 1950.

THE CONSTRUCTION OF MEXICAN LIFE TABLES

The most recent official life table for Mexico centered on the census of 1940. We needed to estimate survivorship values for the period 1950 to 1955 in order to establish a base population in that year and additional survivorship values for the six quinquennia between 1955 and 1985 in order to prepare our projections. In addition we needed an estimate of the fraction born between 1945 and 1950 who survived to the 1950 census date. The mortality risks by age in all of the life tables we used were derived from a set of model life tables published by the United Nations.[2] These model life tables represent the typical association between mortality rates by age observed in 158 national life tables at all levels of mortality. If one has a figure for the expectation of life at birth among the males in a given population, the model life table with the same expectation of life will exhibit a pattern of mortality by age

[1] The construction of the life table by which the survival rate was estimated is described below.

[2] United Nations, Department of Social Affairs, Population Branch. Population Studies No. 22, *Age and Sex Patterns of Mortality—Model Life Tables for Underdeveloped Countries*, New York, 1955.

representative of a large number of life tables with about the same general level of mortality.[3]

The use of the model life tables means of course that mortality by age is completely specified by the expectation of life at birth and mortality projection is reduced to making estimates of life expectancy. There were three different bases employed in estimating the expectation of life at birth for different life tables that we used in the projection. One method was employed for constructing a life table centered on the census of 1950; another method was used in estimating expectation of life for the periods 1945-1950 and 1950-1955; a third method was used for estimating expectation of life during the thirty-year interval covered by the projection (from 1955 to 1985).

The expectation of life at birth in 1950 was estimated by constructing an abridged life table from Mexican mortality data in 1950. The $m_x$ values published in the U N *Demographic Yearbook* were taken at face value for ages above 5. However, the substantial underenumeration of children under 5 leads to an overstatement of mortality rates at the younger ages, at least if death registration is more nearly complete than enumeration of children. We assumed that the infant mortality rate for 1950—based on infant deaths and registered births rather than enumerated infants—provided a better basis for estimating $_1q_0$. The separate infant mortality rate for each sex is not published. The $_1q_0$ values for males and females were obtained by assuming that the *ratio* of male to female mortality rates under one year of age listed in the *Demographic Yearbook* for 1955 was correct.

[3] There is a minor technical objection to our use of these model life tables. The basis for their construction was correlations between the life table death rate ($q_x$ values) at each age and at a lower age. Each model life table was constructed by starting with an infant mortality rate; reading a $_4q_1$ value from a regression equation of $_4q_1$ on $_1q_0$; then reading a $_5q_5$ value from a regression of $_5q_5$ on $_4q_1$, etc. The life table resulting from continuing this process up to advanced ages may be presumed to have in some sense a typical age pattern of mortality. It will of course have a well-defined expectation of life at birth, and the life table can be considered to exhibit the typical pattern of mortality by age associated with this expectation. However, it is not the best possible estimate of a typical pattern for a given life expectancy. If one were to plot the $q_x$ values from one of the U N tables as deviations from the mean expressed in units of the standard deviation, the $\dfrac{q_x - q'_x}{\sigma q_x}$ values would be seen to converge slightly toward zero, as one proceeded from age 0 to ages above 80. This convergence is an automatic consequence of the nature of regression lines. (See Appendix A, pp. 348 and 367.) In other words, the range of values of old-age mortality in the model life tables is more constricted relative to the set of observed values than the range of infant mortalities; hence, for a low expectation of life the value of infant mortality is somewhat higher and the value of old-age mortality somewhat lower than would be obtained by a different and perhaps better technique of estimating the typical pattern of mortality. These tables would be more appropriate for forming an estimated life table when the infant mortality rate is accurately known. However, in view of the crudity of the whole estimation procedure and of the relatively small difference that a more refined technique might make, we decided to employ the U N model life tables as they stand.

The published value for $_4m_1$ in 1950 was also adjusted for underenumeration of young children. For ages above 5 the age-specific mortality rates were converted to $_5q_x$ values by the Reed-Merrell method. As suggested by Greville,[4] the simple formula $_4q_1 = \dfrac{8 \cdot _4m_1}{2 + 4 \cdot _4m_1}$ was substituted for the Reed-Merrell formula for the age group 1-5. The expectation of life in the resulting abridged life table is 49.3 years at birth for males and 52.6 years for females. The $_5q_x$ values in the abbreviated life table differ little from the $_5q_x$ values of the U N model life table with the same expectation of life, meaning that it would make little difference which of the two life tables—the U N model life table or the abridged Mexican—were used in estimating survivors over a five-year period.

To estimate the expectation of life for the five-year interval prior to the 1950 census and for the five-year interval after the 1950 census, a relationship between ratios of expectation of life at birth and ratios of crude death rates in areas of high fertility was established. For 36 pairs of life tables in areas of high fertility (British Guiana, Chile, Costa Rica, Jamaica, Mexico, Trinidad and Tobago, Puerto Rico, Ceylon, Formosa, and Mauritius) the ratio of life-table death rates (the reciprocal of the expectation of life at birth) was compared with the ratio of crude death rates. For males the ratio of life table death rates can be estimated as .357 + .643 times the ratio of crude death rates, while for females the ratio of life table death rates can be estimated as .342 + .658 times the ratio of crude death rates. In both instances the scatter about the straight line represented by these equations is very small. Nearly two-thirds of the ratios of life table death rates lie within .025 of the value predicted by this relationship.

The average crude death rate for the interval June 30, 1945 to June 30, 1950, the crude death rate for the calendar year 1950, and the relationship described in the preceding paragraph were used to estimate the life expectancy at birth for males and females for the interval 1945 to 1950. The life expectancies for males and females respectively were 46.9 and 50.0 years. The recorded crude death rates from June 30, 1950 until June 30, 1955 were employed to estimate life expectancies for this five-year interval. The resulting estimates were 51.1 years for males and 54.6 years for females.

These expectations of life at birth for the five years preceding the 1950 census and the five years after the 1950 census were used by interpolation to select model life tables from the U N collection. The model life tables in turn provided survivorship values for estimating the number of children under 5 in 1950 and to estimate a population in 1955.

[4] T. N. E. Greville, "Short Methods of Constructing Abridged Life Tables," *The Record of the American Institute of Actuaries*, Vol. 32, No. 65, June 1943.

APPENDIX B

The number of persons over 5 in 1955 was estimated by applying survivorship factors to the adjusted 1950 census population. The number
of children under 5 in 1955 was estimated from births registered between
June 30, 1950 and June 30, 1955.

There remains the question of estimating the increasing expectation
of life in Mexico from 1955 until 1985. The device that was employed
here was a typical time pattern of increasing life expectancy. This
typical time pattern is a composite of recent mortality experience in
areas of both high and low death rates based on 26 observations of
increases of expectation of life in 20 different countries. The observations included life expectancies ranging from 40 to 74 years for females
and from 37 to 71 years for males. The curve of typical improvement
was based on an observed high correlation between the annual increase
of life expectancy and the level of life expectancy. The 26 observations
of improvements on which the correlation is based excluded life tables
based on intercensal differences (such as the life tables in India and
Egypt). Also it excluded life tables for years in which the country in
question was an active belligerent, or had recently been devastated in
war. Also excluded were life tables where the midpoint of the mortality
experience covered was earlier than 1937. The 26 pairs of life tables
qualifying on the basis of these rules yielded a correlation between
*average annual increase* in life expectancy and the *level* of life expectancy
of —.91 for males and —.85 for females. In other words, in recent years
there has been a strong and consistent tendency for countries with low
expectations of life to have a more rapid increase in life expectancy than
those with a high expectation of life. Thus when the expectation at birth
is 40 years, the typical rate of increase is about 1.27 additional years
of life expectancy per annum; and when the expectation is 60, the
typical annual increase is about .57 years added to the life expectancy.
A linear relationship between the annual change in expectation of life
and the level of expectation of life is equivalent to a differential equation

(1) $$\frac{dy}{dt} = a + by$$

The solution of this differential equation is an exponential function in
which the expectation of life at birth increases at a diminishing pace
as its level becomes greater. The actual function is as follows:

(2) $$y = (-\frac{a}{b}) - (-\frac{a}{b} - y_0) e^{b(t - t_0)}$$

The upper asymptote that the expectation of life approaches as a limit is

$$(-\frac{a}{b})$$

This turns out to be 84.2 years for females and 76.2 years for males.

372

Equation (2), then, describes the composite experience of a variety of countries in the last decade and a half. It can be used as a means of projecting future increases in life expectancy on the assumption that a country currently at any given level of mortality risks will experience future gains in mortality at a pace characteristic of recent experience. In estimating the expectation of life at birth in Mexico for the quinquennia 1955-1960, 1960-1965, . . . , 1980-1985, it was assumed that Mexico's experience would follow the composite curve. The resulting estimates of expectation of life at birth are shown in Table 42. The estimates for 1985 are about 68 years for males and 71 for females. These values are approximately the same as those reached in the late 1940's in the Scandinavian countries, the Netherlands, Australia, New Zealand, and among the white population in the United States.

The improvement in mortality in Mexico from 1940 to 1950 was very nearly as rapid as would be expected from the composite curve, while the recorded decline in mortality from 1950 to 1955 has been slightly more rapid than that postulated from average experience. The life tables employed for projection were obtained by interpolation from the model life tables published by the U N.

THE ESTIMATION OF BIRTHS

The number of births each year after 1955 was estimated by applying age-specific fertility rates to the projected female population. It was assumed that through 1955 fertility by age of mother in Mexico had not changed for many years. These essentially constant age-specific fertility rates were estimated from the recorded births by age of mother in Mexico in 1952 and the enumerated female population in 1950. The age-specific fertility rates resulting from dividing these births by this female population were adjusted to yield a birth rate equal to the average during the period 1946 through 1954. The alternative assumptions about the course of future fertility were designedly made parallel to the assumptions used in the Indian projections. The first assumption was of unchanged fertility from 1955 to 1985; the second, that age-specific rates fall linearly by 50 per cent between 1955 and 1980; and the third, that the rates fall linearly by 50 per cent between 1965 and 1980.

These projections are quite similar to a set constructed by the Population Division of the United Nations.[5] The U N projections were made before the 1950 census age distribution was available; they predicted a more gradual improvement in mortality; and their alternative fertility assumptions were slightly different from ours. The general range, however, is much the same. Thus, when fertility is assumed to remain

[5] United Nations, Department of Social Affairs, Population Division. Population Studies No. 16, *The Population of Central America (Including Mexico), 1950 to 1980*, New York, 1954.

unchanged our projected population for 1980 is $2.30 \times 1955$ population, while the corresponding U N estimate for a 1980 population is $2.19 \times 1955$ population. The principal reason for constructing our own estimates rather than using the U N estimate was to prepare alternative projections on assumptions more nearly parallel to those employed in preparing the projections for India.

# APPENDIX C

## NOTES ON THE POPULATION OF MEXICO

THE density of population in Mexico was no more than 35 persons per square mile in 1950, a density about one-eighth as great as that in India. However, the meaningfulness of the comparison is much reduced by the large proportion of Mexico's area that is arid, mountainous, or both. The area harvested per capita in 1950 was perhaps only some 10 to 20 per cent greater than in India. Here, again, comparison is difficult because of the much greater area in Mexico used solely for pasture, and because of differences in soils, rainfall, etc.

### RECENT GROWTH OF THE MEXICAN POPULATION

According to the Mexican population censuses, the population doubled between 1895 and 1950. The reported increase in population through 1921 was fluctuating, with growth rates per decade of about 8 per cent, 11 per cent, and —5 per cent. It is quite likely that at least some of the apparent decrease between 1910 and 1921 was due to the effects of the disturbed condition of the country on the quality of the 1921 census. Between the 1921 census and the 1930 census the reported increase was over 15 per cent, for the decade 1930 to 1940 the increase was some 19 per cent, and from 1940 to 1950 the increase was 31 per cent. The acceleration in population increase has been remarkable. The per cent increase in the decade 1940-1950 was very nearly as great as the per cent increase in the 35 years from 1895 until 1930.

### RECENT TRENDS IN MEXICAN FERTILITY AND MORTALITY

The rapid growth in the Mexican population since 1930 is obviously the result of an acceleration in the rate of natural increase rather than changes in the course of international migration. The registration of vital events in Mexico prior to 1930 was notably incomplete but the registered births and deaths since 1930 provide an adequate explanation for the accelerated growth of the population revealed by successive censuses. The recorded average natural rate of increase between 1930 and 1940 was 19.4 per thousand, while the average annual rate of growth calculated from census figures is 18.0 per thousand. In the decade 1940 to 1950 the average difference between birth and death rates is 25.5 per thousand, while the average intercensal growth rate is 27.2. The fact that registered events give a reasonably close account of recorded intercensal growth in population, considered in conjunction

375

with the sustained level of the registered birth rate, leads to the presumption that since 1930 registration of vital events has at least not deteriorated. While both birth and death rates may be somewhat deficient, the difference between the two is apparently of the proper general magnitude and there is reason for believing the trend to be generally correct.[1]

The registered birth rate has remained at very nearly a constant average in the face of substantial mortality declines, especially infant mortality. Actually, constant fertility rates under a regime of improving mortality with special improvements in the infant and childhood years cause changes in the age composition of the population that produce a slight drop in the crude birth rate. Thus, the assumption of constant fertility in our projections of the Mexican population produces a decline in the crude birth rate from 44.2 per thousand to 41.3 by 1985. It is quite possible that a decline of this general magnitude is concealed in the registered figures for recent years by improvements in the completeness of birth registration. On the other hand, it is possible that improvements in health have led to a slight increase in fertility rates because of fewer stillbirths and miscarriages.

PROSPECTIVE CHANGES IN MEXICAN MORTALITY AND FERTILITY

As is explained in Appendix B, the projections that we have prepared for the Mexican population during the period 1955 to 1985 are based on assumptions which by design parallel those underlying the projections of the Indian population. To be specific, the projections are derived from the best estimates we can make of the likely course of mortality rates, by age and sex, during the next 30 years and on two limiting and one intermediate assumption about the course of fertility. As in our Indian projections, we have constructed an estimate of the future course of mortality in Mexico by an analysis of the recent course of mortality in other countries. However, the progress in Mexico in reducing mortality rates has already been so substantial that a guide to the future cannot be sought in the experience of low-income areas alone. Mortality risks in Mexico are already at the lower end of the range of low-income experience. We have assumed that the course of improving chances of survival until 1985 in Mexico will follow a typical time pattern. The chance of

[1] There are various indications that the registration of Mexican vital events is less than wholly complete. One indication of defective registration is that States with median incomes well below the national average, with high levels of illiteracy, and other indications of extreme poverty, report infant mortality rates at, or in some cases well below, the national average. Among those with relatively low recorded infant mortality rates are Chiapas, Durango, Guerrero, Michoacán, Querétaro, Tlaxcala, and Yucatán, all of which are in the lower range in literacy and income. The reported infant mortality rate for these areas in 1951-1953 averages less than 80 per cent of the national figure. It is quite likely that the low registered rates for these areas is a reflection of incompleteness of registration rather than rates really below the national average.

376

survival is summarized in the expectation of life at birth. If the experience in the last two decades of a variety of countries is examined, there is a typical association between the level of life expectancy and the annual increments to life expectancy. This association is such that on the average when the expectation of life is low, the annual increase in life expectancy is large; and when the expectation of life is high, the annual increase on the average is low. When a straight line is fitted to the relation between annual increase in life expectancy and level of life expectancy, it turns out that when the expectation of life at birth is 40 years, the typical annual increase is about 1.27 added years of life expectancy per annum; and when the expectation is 60 the typical annual increase is about .57 years added to life expectancy. The correlation between average annual increase in life expectancy and its level is —.91 for males and —.85 for females. This relationship is derived from pairs of observations during the last 20 years in some 20 different countries. A linear association between level of expectation of life and annual increase in expectation of life implies a typical time pattern of mortality improvement. We have used this typical time pattern to estimate the course of improving chances of survival in Mexico until 1985. It is reassuring to note that estimates of improving survival chances from 1940 to 1955 in Mexico based on recorded mortality data fit the composite curve of mortality experience quite closely. Actually, the choice of a projected course of further mortality improvement in Mexico makes much less difference to the projected development of population than in India, provided that a reversal of the mortality decline is not contemplated as one of the possibilities. With merely a continuation of the recently recorded rate of natural increase in Mexico, the population would grow to about two and a half times its size by 1985, whereas our projected substantial further decline in mortality produces a population 2.75 times as large in 1985 as in 1955. The differences in size and age composition between the high and low fertility projected populations would be very much the same under any single projected course of mortality.

We have not attempted a detailed justification of unchanged fertility as an approximate upper limit during the next 30 years and of a linear decline of 50 per cent in 25 years as a lower limit. These limiting assumptions about the course of fertility were chosen rather to permit an analysis of Mexican prospects as parallel as possible to our study of India. Actually, there are important differences in the forces likely to affect fertility in Mexico as compared to India. Perhaps the most important feature of the likely course of Mexican fertility is the unlikelihood of any government program promoting family limitation. In other words, our fertility projection and the economic calculations based on it can be considered as illustrative of what would happen under a course of fertility which is in fact quite improbable. On the other hand, the

377

possibility of a fertility decline without an organized promotional campaign is perhaps somewhat stronger in Mexico than in India. In the first place, Mexico is somewhat further advanced toward such goals as higher per capita income, high levels of literacy, a reduced dependence on agriculture, and a more urbanized society.

A further reason for expecting a possible decline in Mexican fertility in the absence of an active campaign promoting family limitation is the rapid increase in the fraction of the population living in urban centers— an increase that may be expected to continue.

The per cent increase in the population living in places of less than 5 thousand population during the last three intercensal periods was 12.3, 11.6, and 11.8, respectively. In the same three periods the per cent increase in the population living in places with a population of more than 5 thousand was 25.7, 27.8, and 63.3. As a consequence the urban population (urban being defined as a place of more than 5 thousand persons) has increased from 25.6 per cent in 1930 to 35 per cent in 1950. The growth in population in urban places of the largest size class has been most spectacular. There were 95 per cent more residents of places with 100,000 or more inhabitants in 1950 than in 1940.

The continuance of this trend toward rapid urbanization could be expected to bring a reduction in fertility on two grounds. First, the generation and spread of the custom of family limitation is more likely and feasible in an urban than in a rural environment. And, secondly, there is a body of widely cited evidence indicating a substantial rural-urban differential in fertility already existing in Mexico.[2] The evidence most often cited is the higher ratio of children 0-4 to women 15-49 in areas having a higher proportion of their population rural. Other indices of fertility—birth rates or average number of children ever born, both of which are available for the States of Mexico—are also positively related to the per cent of the population residing in places of less than 5 thousand population.

Though there is little doubt of some sort of fertility differential (with higher rural than urban rates), the data available are not adequate for estimating how large the differential is, or even for being certain that the risks of childbearing for an urban resident are intrinsically lower than for a rural resident. There are several fragmentary bits of evidence indicating that a portion of the apparent differences, possibly a large portion, in rural and urban fertility may be due to selective migration rather than to basically different risks of childbearing. There is little doubt that a single woman is more likely to migrate from a rural to an urban place than a married woman; and that among the married mi-

[2] Robert G. Burnight, Nathan L. Whetten, Bruce D. Waxman, "Differential Rural-Urban Fertility in Mexico," *American Sociological Review*, Vol. XXI, pp. 3-8, 1956; and Nathan L. Whetten, *Rural Mexico*, Chicago, The University of Chicago Press, 1948, pp. 389-393.

grants at a given age, those with the smaller number of children would be more likely to migrate. Thus there is some tendency, at least, for the countryside to be depleted of low-fertility persons (single persons and persons with low marital fertility) and of course for the city to recruit such persons. The effect of such migration is to add to some degree to the female population of childbearing age (the denominator of the child-woman ratio) without adding proportionately to the numerator. Even if the intrinsic risks of becoming married and childbearing were the same in city and country, the effect of the migratory pattern described above would be to depress the urban fertility index and raise the rural index. The correlation between the fertility ratio and the per cent of the total population living in places of over 5 thousand in the States of Mexico in 1950 is —.55. However, when the estimated number of single women in each State is subtracted from the women in the denominator of the fertility index, the correlation is reduced to about —.21. Also the correlation between a fertility index and an index of net gains or losses by migration of women based on State-of-birth data is higher than the correlation between a fertility index and per cent urban. All of this reasoning is very tenuous and it can be used to support only a very tentative conclusion: namely, that it remains uncertain what part of rural-urban differences in Mexican fertility are due to basically different risks of childbearing in the urban environment, and what part are transitory effects due to the selective migration of less fertile persons. If the second cause accounts for most of the differences between rural and urban fertility the implication is that further increases in urbanization could not be expected to have much effect on the all-Mexico level of births. On the other hand if the difference between rural and urban fertility is large, and it reflects a fundamental difference in the risks of childbearing in the rural and urban environments, then the expected continuation of increasing urbanism could be expected on its own to effect a measurable reduction in the Mexican birth rate.

The likely course of mortality and fertility in Mexico during the next 30 years can be stated with considerable brevity, if not confidence or precision. Death rates, having fallen very extensively during the last 25 years, will continue to drop. Fertility will probably continue at least for a few years at the apparently unchanging level characteristic of its recent history. There is some possibility of a decline beginning in a few years as a consequence of the social and economic changes accompanying continued industrialization and urbanization. The basis for believing that such a decline will occur cannot be established without a better understanding than now available of the existence, extent, and circumstances of rural-urban and other differences in Mexican fertility levels. There is little doubt that an acceleration in the spread of education as well as a continuation of urbanization and industrialization would provide a more receptive environment for the spread of the small-family custom.

The actual level of both fertility rates and mortality risks at present and over the near future may be somewhat higher than the figures used in our projection. Complete registration of vital events under the circumstances prevailing in rural Mexico would be surprising. The birth and death of a child that survives for only a few days is particularly likely to go unrecorded. If birth and death rates are somewhat higher than we have supposed, our projections would not be affected in a way important to our economic analysis. The somewhat higher fertility rate would, if it remained unchanged, yield a higher ultimate rate of growth— assuming that mortality fell by the amount projected. But of course the projected decline in mortality can be well off the mark in either direction. As is shown by the projections of the Indian population in Appendix A, the use of a somewhat higher or somewhat lower initial estimate of fertility and mortality has only a slight effect on the proportionate differences between high and low fertility projections.

The projected population of Mexico by five-year age groups is shown in Tables C-1 to C-3.

TABLE C-1. PROJECTED POPULATION OF MEXICO, 1950–1985,
BY FIVE-YEAR AGE GROUPS FOR EACH SEX
(Fertility assumed unchanged)
(thousands)

| Age | 1950 | 1955 | 1960 | 1965 | 1970 | 1975 | 1980 | 1985 |
|---|---|---|---|---|---|---|---|---|
| **Males** | | | | | | | | |
| 0–4 | 2,294.8 | 2,752.3 | 3,274.9 | 3,832.2 | 4,554.0 | 5,443.0 | 6,575.8 | 7,965.5 |
| 5–9 | 1,865.1 | 2,181.7 | 2,646.6 | 3,177.3 | 3,745.2 | 4,471.6 | 5,370.1 | 6,514.6 |
| 10–14 | 1,570.5 | 1,838.1 | 2,157.0 | 2,622.8 | 3,154.7 | 3,722.4 | 4,449.7 | 5,349.7 |
| 15–19 | 1,411.2 | 1,546.5 | 1,815.7 | 2,135.6 | 2,601.6 | 3,133.2 | 3,701.2 | 4,429.2 |
| 20–24 | 1,232.6 | 1,378.7 | 1,517.9 | 1,788.5 | 2,110.0 | 2,574.8 | 3,106.9 | 3,676.0 |
| 25–29 | 1,017.3 | 1,198.5 | 1,348.1 | 1,490.7 | 1,762.9 | 2,084.5 | 2,549.6 | 3,082.4 |
| 30–34 | 703.6 | 987.8 | 1,170.9 | 1,323.0 | 1,468.2 | 1,740.3 | 2,062.8 | 2,527.4 |
| 35–39 | 748.4 | 681.4 | 962.9 | 1,146.8 | 1,300.6 | 1,446.9 | 1,718.9 | 2,041.1 |
| 40–44 | 587.2 | 720.4 | 660.8 | 938.8 | 1,122.6 | 1,276.5 | 1,423.6 | 1,694.3 |
| 45–49 | 534.7 | 559.0 | 691.7 | 638.5 | 911.3 | 1,093.0 | 1,246.4 | 1,392.9 |
| 50–54 | 405.3 | 500.2 | 528.3 | 658.5 | 611.1 | 875.2 | 1,053.3 | 1,204.1 |
| 55–59 | 261.4 | 369.5 | 461.7 | 491.8 | 617.1 | 575.0 | 826.9 | 998.3 |
| 60–64 | 265.2 | 229.1 | 328.7 | 415.1 | 445.9 | 562.1 | 526.5 | 760.2 |
| 65–69 | 164.8 | 218.5 | 192.4 | 279.7 | 356.9 | 385.8 | 489.8 | 461.1 |
| 70–74 | 113.6 | 123.3 | 167.5 | 150.1 | 221.3 | 284.8 | 310.7 | 397.2 |
| 75–79 | 62.7 | 73.4 | 82.3 | 114.3 | 104.4 | 155.6 | 202.7 | 223.2 |
| 80–84 | 41.1 | 32.5 | 39.7 | 45.9 | 65.3 | 60.5 | 91.7 | 120.9 |
| 85+ | 30.5 | 12.2 | 10.0 | 12.6 | 14.9 | 21.5 | 20.2 | 30.9 |
| Total Males | 13,310.0 | 15,403.1 | 18,057.1 | 21,262.2 | 25,168.0 | 29,906.7 | 35,726.8 | 42,869.0 |
| **Females** | | | | | | | | |
| 0–4 | 2,231.5 | 2,669.3 | 3,163.9 | 3,691.9 | 4,373.0 | 5,225.7 | 6,286.7 | 7,595.9 |
| 5–9 | 1,809.5 | 2,131.3 | 2,578.3 | 3,082.0 | 3,619.5 | 4,312.7 | 5,172.9 | 6,244.0 |
| 10–14 | 1,510.1 | 1,784.3 | 2,108.7 | 2,557.7 | 3,062.9 | 3,603.6 | 4,297.6 | 5,159.5 |
| 15–19 | 1,383.6 | 1,487.6 | 1,764.0 | 2,090.1 | 2,540.1 | 3,047.3 | 3,588.8 | 4,283.4 |
| 20–24 | 1,232.6 | 1,354.7 | 1,463.5 | 1,741.8 | 2,069.4 | 2,521.3 | 3,029.3 | 3,571.9 |
| 25–29 | 1,038.0 | 1,201.7 | 1,328.3 | 1,441.3 | 1,721.2 | 2,050.6 | 2,502.9 | 3,011.4 |
| 30–34 | 732.9 | 1,010.2 | 1,176.6 | 1,306.6 | 1,422.7 | 1,703.5 | 2,033.2 | 2,485.4 |
| 35–39 | 798.4 | 712.0 | 987.6 | 1,155.5 | 1,287.5 | 1,405.6 | 1,686.1 | 2,015.7 |
| 40–44 | 622.5 | 773.3 | 694.1 | 967.2 | 1,135.5 | 1,268.6 | 1,387.6 | 1,667.0 |
| 45–49 | 538.9 | 599.1 | 749.3 | 675.8 | 945.1 | 1,112.9 | 1,245.9 | 1,364.8 |
| 50–54 | 422.9 | 512.7 | 574.4 | 722.5 | 654.3 | 918.2 | 1,083.7 | 1,215.5 |
| 55–59 | 266.7 | 395.0 | 483.6 | 545.6 | 689.8 | 627.5 | 883.1 | 1,044.5 |
| 60–64 | 288.9 | 241.6 | 362.3 | 447.7 | 508.6 | 646.8 | 590.7 | 833.6 |
| 65–69 | 169.4 | 248.3 | 211.2 | 320.7 | 399.9 | 457.9 | 585.4 | 536.7 |
| 70–74 | 127.2 | 133.4 | 200.0 | 173.1 | 266.1 | 335.4 | 386.8 | 497.2 |
| 75–79 | 66.0 | 87.2 | 94.3 | 144.7 | 127.5 | 198.9 | 253.2 | 294.2 |
| 80–84 | 51.5 | 36.8 | 50.7 | 56.6 | 88.9 | 79.9 | 126.3 | 162.5 |
| 85+ | 38.9 | 16.4 | 12.1 | 17.2 | 19.5 | 31.2 | 28.3 | 45.2 |
| Total Females | 13,329.5 | 15,394.9 | 18,002.9 | 21,138.0 | 24,931.5 | 29,547.6 | 35,168.5 | 42,028.4 |
| Grand Total | 26,639.5 | 30,798.0 | 36,060.0 | 42,400.2 | 50,099.5 | 59,454.3 | 70,895.3 | 84,897.4 |

TABLE C-2. PROJECTED POPULATION OF MEXICO, 1960–1985,
BY FIVE-YEAR AGE GROUPS FOR EACH SEX[a]
(Fertility assumed to decline linearly by a total of 50 per cent
between 1955 and 1980)
(thousands)

| Age | 1960 | 1965 | 1970 | 1975 | 1980 | 1985 |
|---|---|---|---|---|---|---|
| Males | | | | | | |
| 0–4 | 3,101.7 | 3,243.2 | 3,398.0 | 3,501.8 | 3,509.3 | 3,717.5 |
| 5–9 | – | 3,009.3 | 3,169.6 | 3,336.5 | 3,454.9 | 3,476.7 |
| 10–14 | – | – | 2,987.9 | 3,150.3 | 3,320.2 | 3,441.8 |
| 15–19 | – | – | – | 2,967.6 | 3,132.3 | 3,304.9 |
| 20–24 | – | – | – | – | 2,942.7 | 3,111.0 |
| 25–29 | – | – | – | – | – | 2,919.5 |
| Total Males | 17,883.9 | 20,505.2 | 23,269.6 | 26,092.7 | 28,882.5 | 31,823.0 |
| Females | | | | | | |
| 0–4 | 2,996.5 | 3,124.4 | 3,262.9 | 3,362.0 | 3,354.9 | 3,545.0 |
| 5–9 | – | 2,918.9 | 3,063.2 | 3,217.9 | 3,328.0 | 3,332.1 |
| 10–14 | – | – | 2,900.8 | 3,049.7 | 3,206.6 | 3,319.3 |
| 15–19 | – | – | – | 2,886.0 | 3,037.2 | 3,196.0 |
| 20–24 | – | – | – | – | 2,869.0 | 3,022.9 |
| 25–29 | – | – | – | – | – | 2,852.1 |
| Total Females | 17,835.5 | 20,407.4 | 23,103.0 | 25,873.9 | 28,588.9 | 31,429.7 |
| Grand Total | 35,719.4 | 40,912.6 | 46,372.6 | 51,966.6 | 57,471.4 | 63,252.7 |

[a] Numbers not shown are identical with those in Table C-1.

## TABLE C-3. PROJECTED POPULATION OF MEXICO, 1970–1985, BY FIVE-YEAR AGE GROUPS FOR EACH SEX[a]

(Fertility assumed to decline linearly by a total of 50 per cent
Between 1965 and 1980)
(thousands)

| Age | 1970 | 1975 | 1980 | 1985 |
|---|---|---|---|---|
| Males | | | | |
| 0–4 | 4,145.2 | 4,043.9 | 3,787.8 | 3,955.9 |
| 5–9 | – | 4,070.2 | 3,989.7 | 3,752.6 |
| 10–14 | – | – | 4,050.3 | 3,974.5 |
| 15–19 | – | – | – | 4,031.7 |
| Total Males | 24,759.2 | 28,106.2 | 31,159.0 | 34,324.7 |
| Females | | | | |
| 0–4 | 3,980.4 | 3,882.4 | 3,621.2 | 3,772.3 |
| 5–9 | – | 3,925.5 | 3,843.2 | 3,596.6 |
| 10–14 | – | – | 3,911.8 | 3,833.2 |
| 15–19 | – | – | – | 3,898.9 |
| Total Females | 24,538.9 | 27,817.1 | 30,787.5 | 33,846.6 |
| Grand Total | 49,298.1 | 55,923.3 | 61,946.5 | 68,171.3 |

[a] Numbers not shown are identical with those in Table C-1.

387

government, 155, 161-166, 177-178
government policy regarding, in India, 155-156, 161-166, 168-175
individuals and small enterprises, 166-169, 178
large businesses, 155-159, 177
non-monetized saving and investment, 156, 175-176, 178
non-savers, 316
relation to income and other factors, 82, 153-155, 241-246, 316
sources, in India, 156, 177-178
scale economies with increased population, 18-19, 211-212, 240-241, 298, 333-335
schools in India, 190, 248-249
seeds, improved, in India, 101-102, 108-109
self-sufficiency, of India, 80, 123
sex ratio at birth in India, 351
small enterprise sector in India, 166-169, 178, 217-223
"social overhead" outlays in India, 199-200, 249-250, 254-255
Sovani, N. V., 61
stable population theory, 45, 338-339, 341-345
stagnation thesis, applicability in low-income areas, 241-242, 305
survival rates, age-specific, India, estimates, 354-356

Taeuber, Irene B., 58, 62
Taxation Enquiry Commission (India), Report, 77-78, 151, 156, 159, 161, 164
taxation in India, 77-78, 154-156, 158, 161-164, 166, 168, 177-178
Thirumalai, S., 112
Timbergen, Jan, 212

tourist expenditures in Mexico, 308-309

underemployment in India, 78-79, 116-117, 145-146, 223, 233, 288
underenumeration, Census,
India, 354
Mexico, 368-369
"underpopulated country," defined, 240
unemployment in India, 78-79, 145, 223, 233, 240, 288
United States economic conditions, influence on Mexico, 310
urban-rural income differentials in India, 85, 131-136
urbanization,
India, 137-138, 251-253
Mexico, 306, 378

Vagh, B. V., 210
village industries in India, 218-219 (see also small enterprises)
Viswanathan, D. J., 67

Waxman, Bruce D., 378
welfare expenditures (see also housing; education),
in India, projected, 273-277
in Mexico, 318
relation to fertility, 317-318
welfare state concept in India, 79
Whetten, Nathan L., 378
working ages, defined, 231 (see also labor force participation rates)
World Health Organization, Conference on Malaria, 67
Worth, C. Brooke, 256

Yield of crops in Indian agriculture, 99-104